TAKING SIDES

Clashing Views on Controversial

Social Issues

TWELFTH EDITION

Clashing Views on Controversial

Social Issues

TWELFTH EDITION

Selected, Edited, and with Introductions by

Kurt Finsterbusch
University of Maryland

McGraw-Hill/Dushkin
A Division of The McGraw-Hill Companies

To my wife, Meredith Ramsay, who richly shares with me a life of the mind and much, much more.

Photo Acknowledgment
Cover image: © 2003 by PhotoDisc, Inc.

Cover Art Acknowledgment
Charles Vitelli

Library of Congress Cataloging-in-Publication Data
Main entry under title:
Taking sides: clashing views on controversial social issues/selected, edited, and with introductions by Kurt Finsterbusch.—12th ed.
Includes bibliographical references and index.
1. Social behavior. 2. Social problems. I. Finsterbusch, Kurt, *comp.*
302
0-07-282278-3
95-83865

Printed on Recycled Paper

Preface

The English word *fanatic* is derived from the Latin *fanum,* meaning temple. It refers to the kind of madmen often seen in the precincts of temples in ancient times, the kind presumed to be possessed by deities or demons. The term first came into English usage during the seventeenth century, when it was used to describe religious zealots. Soon after, its meaning was broadened to include a political and social context. We have come to associate the term *fanatic* with a person who acts as if his or her views were inspired, a person utterly incapable of appreciating opposing points of view. The nineteenth-century English novelist George Eliot put it precisely: "I call a man fanatical when ... he ... becomes unjust and unsympathetic to men who are out of his own track." A fanatic may hear but is unable to listen. Confronted with those who disagree, a fanatic immediately vilifies opponents.

Most of us would avoid the company of fanatics, but who among us is not tempted to caricature opponents instead of listening to them? Who does not put certain topics off limits for discussion? Who does not grasp at euphemisms to avoid facing inconvenient facts? Who has not, in George Eliot's language, sometimes been "unjust and unsympathetic" to those on a different track? Who is not, at least in certain very sensitive areas, a *little* fanatical? The counterweight to fanaticism is open discussion. The difficult issues that trouble us as a society have at least two sides, and we lose as a society if we hear only one side. At the individual level, the answer to fanaticism is listening. And that is the underlying purpose of this book: to encourage its readers to listen to opposing points of view.

This book contains 40 selections presented in a pro and con format. A total of 20 different controversial social issues are debated. The sociologists, political scientists, economists, and social critics whose views are debated here make their cases vigorously. In order to effectively read each selection, analyze the points raised, and debate the basic assumptions and values of each position, or, in other words, in order to think critically about what you are reading, you will first have to give each side a sympathetic hearing. John Stuart Mill, the nineteenth-century British philosopher, noted that the majority is not doing the minority a favor by listening to its views; it is doing *itself* a favor. By listening to contrasting points of view, we strengthen our own. In some cases we change our viewpoints completely. But in most cases, we either incorporate some elements of the opposing view—thus making our own richer—or else learn how to answer the objections to our viewpoints. Either way, we gain from the experience.

Organization of the book Each issue has an issue *introduction,* which sets the stage for the debate as it is argued in the YES and NO selections. Each issue concludes with a *postscript* that makes some final observations and points the way to other questions related to the issue. In reading the issue and forming your own opinions you should not feel confined to adopt one or the other of the positions presented. There are positions in between the given views or totally outside them, and the *suggestions for further reading* that appear in each issue postscript should help you find resources to continue your study of the subject. At the back of the book is a listing of all the *contributors to this volume*, which will give you information on the social scientists whose views are debated here. Also, on the *On the Internet* page that accompanies each part opener, you will find Internet site addresses (URLs) that are relevant to the issues in that part.

Changes to this edition This new edition has been significantly updated. There are four completely new issues: *Does Television Violence Make Children Significantly More Violent?* (Issue 2); *Is Competition the Solution to the Ills of Public Education?* (Issue 14); *Is Mankind Dangerously Harming the Environment?* (Issue 19); and *Is Globalization Good for Mankind?* (Issue 20). In addition, for the issues on immigration (Issue 3), family (Issue 7), economic inequality (Issue 8), welfare reform (Issue 13), and drugs (Issue 17), one or both of the selections were replaced to bring a fresh perspective to the debates. In all, there are 15 new selections. Today the world is changing rapidly in many ways so that new issues arise, old ones fade, and some old issues become recast by events.

A word to the instructor An *Instructor's Manual With Test Questions* (multiple-choice and essay) is available through the publisher for the instructor using *Taking Sides* in the classroom. A general guidebook, *Using Taking Sides in the Classroom*, which discusses methods and techniques for integrating the pro-con approach into any classroom setting, is also available. An online version of *Using Taking Sides in the Classroom* and a correspondence service for *Taking Sides* adopters can be found at http://www.dushkin.com/usingts/.

Taking Sides: Clashing Views on Controversial Social Issues is only one title in the Taking Sides series. If you are interested in seeing the table of contents for any of the other titles, please visit the Taking Sides Web site at http://www.dushkin.com/takingsides/.

Acknowledgments I wish to acknowledge the encouragement and support given to this project over the years by Mimi Egan and Theodore Knight, former and present list managers for the Taking Sides series, and Juliana Gribbins, developmental editor.

I want to thank my wife, Meredith Ramsay, for her example and support.

I also want to thank George McKenna for many years as a close colleague and coeditor through many early editions of this book.

Kurt Finsterbusch
University of Maryland

Contents In Brief

Contents

American Enterprise Institute, argues that the United States needs a constant flow of immigrants to avoid population decline and also to avoid the diminishment of power and influence.

Editor and author Jeff Grabmeier presents evidence showing that women experience more stress than men and then analyzes why. Author Susan Faludi argues that men have been socialized into a sex role that cannot be successfully fulfilled due to current conditions.

Author Philip Yancey argues that men and women have strikingly different communication styles because they grow up in different cultures. A man is usually concerned about enhancing or maintaining status as he communicates, while a woman will usually communicate in ways that gain or maintain closeness. Professor of psychology Mary Crawford contends that the thesis that men and women have radically different communication styles is greatly exaggerated in the media and is based on simplistic stereotypes.

Editor and author Andrew Sullivan argues that the secular liberal state must grant the right of same-sex partners to marry. To not do so would be blatant discrimination. Professor of management and public policy James Q. Wilson presents arguments against legally recognizing same-sex marriages.

Professor of economics Walter E. Williams asserts that "the civil rights struggle for blacks is over and won," so affirmative action policies are unjust and adversely affect society. History professor Wilbert Jenkins dismisses the arguments against affirmative action as founded on the false logic that since the promised land has been reached, continuing affirmative action would be reverse discrimination. Jenkins maintains that an honest look at the facts reveals that affirmative action is still needed.

PART 4   POLITICAL ECONOMY AND INSTITUTIONS 187

Issue 11.   Is Government Dominated by Big Business?   188

Political sociologist G. William Domhoff argues that the "owners and top-level managers in large income-producing properties are far and away the dominant power figures in the United States" and that they have inordinate influence in the federal government. Jeffrey M. Berry, a professor of political science, contends that public interest pressure groups that have entered the political arena since the end of the 1960s have effectively challenged the political power of big business.

Issue 12.   Should Government Intervene in a Capitalist Economy?   206

Author Ernest Erber argues that capitalism creates serious social problems that require government intervention to correct. Economists Milton and Rose Friedman maintain that the market operates effectively and protects citizens better when permitted to work without the interference of government regulations.

Issue 13.   Has Welfare Reform Benefited the Poor?   226

John J. DiIulio, Jr., a professor of politics and public affairs, analyzes the enormous harm done—especially to the urban poor and, by extension, to all of society—by street criminals and their activities. Professor of philosophy Jeffrey Reiman argues that the dangers posed by negligent corporations and white-collar criminals are a greater menace to society than are the activities of typical street criminals.

Ethan A. Nadelmann, director of the Lindesmith Center, a drug policy research institute, argues that history shows that drug prohibition is costly and futile. Examining the drug policies in other countries, he finds that decriminalization plus sane and humane drug policies and treatment programs can greatly reduce the harms from drugs. Eric A. Voth, chairman of the International Drug Strategy Institute, contends that drugs are very harmful and that our drug policies have succeeded in substantially reducing drug use.

Editor and author Robert W. Lee argues that capital punishment is needed to deter people from committing murder and other heinous crimes, but more importantly, it is the punishment that is the most appropriate for these crimes. Legal scholar Eric M. Freedman counters that the death penalty does not deter crime and has unacceptable negative consequences, including the potential of killing innocent people, reducing public safety, and imposing considerable costs on society.

Research associate Chris Bright demonstrates how human actions are inadvertently altering and degrading the environment in ways that are harmful to humans. Bjorn Lomborg, a statistician at the University of Aarhus, Denmark, presents evidence that population growth is slowing down, natural resources are not running out, species are disappearing very slowly, the environment is improving in some ways, and assertions about environmental decline are exaggerated.

Murray Weidenbaum, chairman of the Weidenbaum Center at Washington University in St. Louis, argues that economic globalization benefits all countries that participate in world markets. Globalization produces more jobs than it eliminates, he contends, both for the world and for the United States. Herman E. Daly, professor at the School of Public Affairs at the University of Maryland, does not object to international trade and relations, but he does object to globalization that erases national boundaries and hurts workers and the environment.

Introduction

Debating Social Issues

Kurt Finsterbusch

What Is Sociology?

"I have become a problem to myself," St. Augustine said. Put into a social and secular framework, St. Augustine's concern marks the starting point of sociology. We have become a problem to ourselves, and it is sociology that seeks to understand the problem and, perhaps, to find some solutions. The subject matter of sociology, then, is ourselves—people interacting with one another in groups and organizations.

Although the subject matter of sociology is very familiar, it is often useful to look at it in an unfamiliar light, one that involves a variety of theories and perceptual frameworks. In fact, to properly understand social phenomena, it *should* be looked at from several different points of view. In practice, however, this may lead to more friction than light, especially when each view proponent says, "I am right and you are wrong," rather than, "My view adds considerably to what your view has shown."

Sociology, as a science of society, was developed in the nineteenth century. Auguste Comte (1798–1857), the French mathematician and philosopher who is considered to be the father of sociology, had a vision of a well-run society based on social science knowledge. Sociologists (Comte coined the term) would discover the laws of social life and then determine how society should be structured and run. Society would not become perfect, because some problems are intractable, but he believed that a society guided by scientists and other experts was the best possible society.

Unfortunately, Comte's vision was extremely naive. For most matters of state there is no one best way of structuring or doing things that sociologists can discover and recommend. Instead, sociologists debate more social issues than they resolve.

The purpose of sociology is to throw light on social issues and their relationship to the complex, confusing, and dynamic social world around us. It seeks to describe how society is organized and how individuals fit into it. But neither the organization of society nor the fit of individuals is perfect. Social disorganization is a fact of life—at least in modern, complex societies such as the one we live in. Here, perfect harmony continues to elude us, and "social problems" are endemic. The very institutions, laws, and policies that produce benefits also produce what sociologists call "unintended effects"—unintended and undesirable. The changes that please one sector of the society may displease another, or the changes that seem so indisputably healthy at first turn out to have a dark underside to them. The examples are endless. Modern urban life gives people privacy and freedom from snooping neighbors that the small town never afforded; yet that very privacy seems to breed an uneasy sense of anonymity and loneliness. Take another example: Hierarchy is necessary for organizations to function efficiently, but hierarchy leads to the creation of a ruling elite. Flatten out the hierarchy and you may achieve social equality—but at the price of confusion, incompetence, and low productivity.

This is not to say that all efforts to effect social change are ultimately futile and that the only sound view is the tragic one that concludes "nothing works." We can be realistic without falling into despair. In many respects, the human condition has improved over the centuries and has improved as a result of conscious social policies. But improvements are purchased at a price—not only a monetary price but one involving human discomfort and discontent. The job of policymakers is to balance the anticipated benefits against the probable costs.

It can never hurt policymakers to know more about the society in which they work or the social issues they confront. That, broadly speaking, is the purpose of sociology. It is what this book is about. This volume examines issues that are central to the study of sociology.

Culture and Values

A common value system is the major mechanism for integrating a society, but modern societies contain so many different groups with differing ideas and values that integration must be built as much on tolerance of differences as on common values. Furthermore, technology and social conditions change, so values must adjust to new situations, often weakening old values. Some people (often called conservatives) will defend the old values. Others (often called liberals) will make concessions to allow for change. For example, the protection of human life is a sacred value to most people, but some would compromise that value when the life involved is a 90-year-old comatose man on life-support machines who had signed a document indicating that he did not want to be kept alive under those conditions. The conservative would counter that once we make the value of human life relative, we become dangerously open to greater evils—that perhaps society will come to think it acceptable to terminate all sick, elderly people undergoing expensive treatments. This is only one example of how values are hotly debated today.

Three debates on values are presented in Part 1. In Issue 1, David Whitman challenges the common perception that morals have declined in America, while Gertrude Himmelfarb provides empirical support for the declining morality thesis. Issue 2 examines a major institution that can be seen as responsible for instilling values and culture in people—the media. This issue focuses in particular on media violence. W. James Potter criticizes the media for being filled with violence and for contributing to the violence and aggression of Americans, especially children. In response, Jib Fowles states that the research evidence on which Potter's thesis rests is weak, and he argues that it is based on misguided assumptions. The final culture/values debate, Issue 3, concerns the cultural impact of immigration. Patrick Buchanan argues that current levels of immigration are too high and that immigrant cultures are too different from American culture to be assimilated. Thus, immigration is threatening America's cultural unity. Ben Wattenberg counters that the cultural impacts of immigration will be minor because annual immigration amounts to only a third of a percent of the United States population. Furthermore, he maintains that immigration contributes to America's power and influence.

Sex Roles, Gender, and the Family

An area that has experienced tremendous value change in the last several decades is sex roles and the family. Women in large numbers have rejected major aspects of their traditional gender roles and family roles while remaining strongly committed to much of the mother role and to many feminine characteristics. Men have changed much less but their situation has changed considerably. Issue 4 considers whether current sex roles are more stressful for women or for men. Jeff Grabmeier contends that women suffer more stress than men because current practices still favor men and that women are not able to cope as well as men with current sex role expectations. Susan Faludi argues the opposite. Men's sex roles are incongruent with the current conditions and men do not know how to deal with the situation. Issue 5 focuses on the causes of communication problems between men and women. It has recently been advanced that such problems are largely the result of radically different conversation styles between the genders. Philip Yancey champions this view, contending that men's concerns about maintaining status and women's concerns about maintaining connections and closeness affects their interpretations of what they hear and say to each other. Mary Crawford asserts that this view has become popularized and exaggerated by the media and that the basis of the thesis is demeaning to women. Issue 6 debates whether same-sex marriages should be legal. Andrew Sullivan argues that "marriage is . . . the highest public recognition of a private commitment. . . . Denying it to homosexuals is the most public affront possible to their public equality." The opposing selection is a critical review and rebuttal of Sullivan's assertions by James Q. Wilson. Issue 7, which has been much debated by feminists and their critics, asks, Is the decline of the traditional family a national crisis? David Popenoe is deeply concerned about the decline of the traditional family, while Stephanie Coontz thinks that such concern amounts to little more than nostalgia for a bygone era.

Stratification and Inequality

Issue 8 centers around a sociological debate about whether or not increasing economic inequality is a serious problem. Christopher Jencks asserts that it is, while Christopher C. DeMuth argues that consumption patterns indicate that inequality has actually decreased in recent decades. Many commentators on American life decry the pathologies of the underclass as the shame of America.

Charles Murray is a leading proponent of this view and his article is republished in Issue 9. Barry Schwartz critiques Murray's view and argues that the current advanced stage of capitalism is largely responsible for eroding American ideals and producing the underclass.

Today one of the most controversial issues regarding inequalities is affirmative action. Is equality promoted or undermined by such policies? Walter E. Williams and Wilbert Jenkins take opposing sides on this question in Issue 10.

Political Economy and Institutions

Sociologists study not only the poor, the workers, and the victims of discrimination but also those at the top of society—those who occupy what the late sociologist C. Wright Mills used to call "the command posts." The question is whether the "pluralist" model or the "power elite" model is the one that best fits the facts in America. Does a single power elite rule the United States, or do many groups contend for power and influence so that the political process is accessible to all? In Issue 11, G. William Domhoff argues that the business elite have a dominating influence in government decisions and that no other group has nearly as much power. Jeffrey M. Berry counters that liberal citizen groups have successfully opened the policy-making process and made it more participatory. Currently, grassroots groups of all kinds have some power and influence. The question is, how much?

The United States is a capitalist welfare state, and the role of the state in capitalism (more precisely, the market) and in welfare is examined in the next two issues. Issue 12 considers whether or not the government should step in and attempt to correct for the failures of the market through regulations, policies, and programs. Ernest Erber argues that an active government is needed to protect consumers, workers, and the environment; to bring about greater equality; and to guide economic and social change. Milton and Rose Friedman argue that even well-intended state interventions in the market usually only make matters worse and that governments cannot serve the public good as effectively as competitive markets can. One way in which the government intervenes in the economy is by providing welfare to people who cannot provide for their own needs in the labor market. Issue 13 debates the wisdom of the Work Opportunity Reconciliation Act of 1996, which ended Aid to Families of Dependent Children (which was what most people equated with welfare). The editors of the *Economist* call this act "America's great achievement" because it greatly reduced welfare rolls and dramatically increased the employment of welfare mothers. Randy Albelda states that the reality is more depressing. The old welfare system helped women who were on welfare to prepare for and obtain good jobs while the new law practically forces women on welfare to take bad jobs at poverty-level wages.

Education is one of the biggest jobs of government as well as the key to individual prosperity and the success of the economy. For decades the American system of education has been severely criticized. Such an important institution is destined to be closely scrutinized, and for decades the American system of education has been severely criticized and many reforms have been attempted.

Two proposals for school reform are given in Issue 14. Chester E. Finn, Jr., Bruno V. Manno, and Gregg Vanourek argue that charter schools will open up choices for parents and that the competition will dramatically improve public school systems. James P. Comer maintains that charter schools can only modestly improve public schools. This is because the only reform that will produce dramatic improvements is one that will "base everything we do on what is known about how children and youths develop and learn."

The final issue in this section—doctor-assisted suicide—is truly one of life and death. The actions of Dr. Jack Kevorkian, who has assisted in over 100 patient suicides, have brought this issue into the public light. In Issue 15, Marcia Angell presents medical and ethical reasons why she believes that doctor-assisted suicide is merciful and right. Paul R. McHugh maintains that suicidal patients suffer from depression and that they can and should be treated therapeutically, not murdered.

Crime and Social Control

Crime is interesting to sociologists because crimes are those activities that society makes illegal and will use force to stop. Why are some acts made illegal and others (even those that may be more harmful) not made illegal? Surveys indicate that concern about crime is extremely high in America. Is the fear of crime, however, rightly placed? Americans fear mainly street crime, but Jeffrey Reiman argues in Issue 16 that corporate crime—also known as "white-collar crime"—causes far more death, harm, and financial loss to Americans than street crime. In contrast, John J. DiIulio, Jr., points out the great harm done by street criminals, even to the point of social disintegration in some poor neighborhoods. Much of the harm that DiIulio describes is related to the illegal drug trade, which brings about such bad consequences that some people are seriously talking about legalizing drugs in order to kill the illegal drug business. Ethan A. Nadelmann argues this view in Issue 17, while Eric A. Voth argues that legalization would greatly harm society. Drug use would mushroom and damage many lives, whereas the current war on drugs has considerably reduced drug use. Finally, Issue 18 asks whether capital punishment is justified. Robert W. Lee insists that some crimes are so heinous that only execution is an appropriate form of punishment. Furthermore, the death penalty is needed to deter murder. Eric M. Freedman asserts that the death penalty does not reduce crime, is extraordinarily expensive, and diverts scarce funds from more helpful purposes. Capital punishment also leads to the execution of many innocent people.

The Future: Population/Environment/Society

Many social commentators speculate on "the fate of the earth." The environmentalists have their own vision of apocalypse. They see the possibility that the human race could degrade the environment to the point that population growth and increasing economic production could overshoot the carrying capacity of the globe. The resulting collapse could lead to the extinction of much of the human race and the end of free societies. Other analysts believe that these fears are groundless. In Issue 19, Chris Bright shows how human actions can inadvertently degrade the environment in ways that adversely affect humans. In contrast, Bjorn Lomborg argues that the environment is improving in many ways and that environmental problems are manageable or will have mild adverse effects.

The last issue in this book assesses the benefits and costs of globalization. Murray Weidenbaum argues that economic globalization has been a demonstration of the basic economic theory that global markets and relatively free trade economically benefit all nations that participate. Even workers in the United States have benefited in spite of their complaints. Herman E. Daly counters that globalization, which dissolves national boundaries, hurts both workers and the environment.

The Social Construction of Reality

An important idea in sociology is that people construct social reality in the course of interaction by attaching social meanings to the reality they are experiencing and then responding to those meanings. Two people can walk down a city street and derive very different meanings from what they see around them. Both, for example, may see homeless people—but they may see them in different contexts. One fits them into a picture of once-vibrant cities dragged into decay and ruin because of permissive policies that have encouraged pathological types to harass citizens; the other observer fits them into a picture of an America that can no longer hide the wretchedness of its poor. Both feel that they are seeing something deplorable, but their views of what makes it deplorable are radically opposed. Their differing views of what they have seen will lead to very different prescriptions for what should be done about the problem.

The social construction of reality is an important idea for this book because each author is socially constructing reality and working hard to persuade you to see his or her point of view; that is, to see the definition of the situation and the set of meanings he or she has assigned to the situation. In doing this, each author presents a carefully selected set of facts, arguments, and values. The arguments contain assumptions or theories, some of which are spelled out and some of which are unspoken. The critical reader has to judge the evidence for the facts, the logic and soundness of the arguments, the importance of the values, and whether or not omitted facts, theories, and values invalidate the thesis. This book facilitates this critical thinking process by placing authors in opposition. This puts the reader in the position of critically evaluating two constructions of reality for each issue instead of one.

Conclusion

Writing in the 1950s, a period that was in some ways like our own, the sociologist C. Wright Mills said that Americans know a lot about their "troubles" but they cannot make the connections between seemingly personal concerns and the concerns of others in the world. If they could only learn to make those connections, they could turn their concerns into *issues*. An issue transcends the realm of the personal. According to Mills, "An issue is a public matter: some value cherished by publics is felt to be threatened. Often there is a debate about what the value really is and what it is that really threatens it."

It is not primarily personal troubles but social issues that I have tried to present in this book. The variety of topics in it can be taken as an invitation to discover what Mills called "the sociological imagination." This imagination, said Mills, "is the capacity to shift from one perspective to another—from the political to the psychological; from examination of a single family to comparative assessment of the national budgets of the world.... It is the capacity to range from the most impersonal and remote transformations to the most intimate features of the human self—and to see the relations between the two." This book, with a range of issues well suited to the sociological imagination, is intended to enlarge that capacity.

Internet Philosophical Resources on Moral Relativism

This Web site for *Ethics Updates* offers discussion questions, a bibliographical guide, and a list of Internet resources concerning moral relativism.

http://ethics.acusd.edu/relativism.html

The National Institute on Media and the Family

The National Institute on Media and the Family Web site is a national resource for teachers, parents, community leaders, and others who are interested in the influence of electronic media on early childhood education, child development, academic performance, culture, and violence.

http://www.mediaandthefamily.com

The International Center for Migration, Ethnicity, and Citizenship

The International Center for Migration, Ethnicity, and Citizenship is engaged in scholarly research and public policy analysis bearing on international migration, refugees, and the incorporation of newcomers in host countries.

http://www.newschool.edu/icmec/

National Immigrant Forum

The National Immigrant Forum is a pro-immigrant organization that examines the effects of immigration on U.S. society. Click on the links for discussion of underground economies, immigrant economies, race and ethnic relations, and other topics.

http://www.immigrationforum.org

The National Network for Immigrant and Refugee Rights (NNIRR)

The National Network for Immigrant and Refugee Rights (NNIRR) serves as a forum to share information and analysis, to educate communities and the general public, and to develop and coordinate plans of action on important immigrant and refugee issues.

http://www.nnirr.org

PART 1

Culture and Values

*S*ociologists *recognize that a fairly strong consensus on the basic values of a society contributes greatly to the smooth functioning of that society. The functioning of modern, complex urban societies, however, often depends on the tolerance of cultural differences and equal rights and protections for all cultural groups. In fact, such societies can be enriched by the contributions of different cultures. But at some point the cultural differences may result in a pulling apart that exceeds the pulling together. One cultural problem is the perceived moral decline, which may involve a conflict between old and new values. Another cultural problem in America is the failure of the normative system to keep violence in check to the degree that it used to. This raises the question of whether television is partly to blame and whether television should be regulated or its autonomy protected as a free speech issue. The final problem is whether current immigrants to the United States bring appropriate values and skills.*

- Is America in Moral Decline?

- Does Television Violence Make Children Significantly More Violent?

- Is Third World Immigration a Threat to America's Way of Life?

ISSUE 1

Is America in Moral Decline?

YES: Gertrude Himmelfarb, from *The De-Moralization of Society: From Victorian Virtues to Modern Values* (Alfred A. Knopf, 1995)

NO: David Whitman, from *The Optimism Gap: The I'm OK— They're Not Syndrome and the Myth of American Decline* (Walker & Company, 1998)

ISSUE SUMMARY

YES: Gertrude Himmelfarb, a professor emeritus of history, details some of the increasing moral problems in America and interprets them as being part of a larger pattern, which she calls "the de-moralization of society."

NO: Writer David Whitman empirically tests the moral decline thesis and finds that, according to the indicators that he employs, it is a myth.

Morality is the glue that holds society together. It enables people to deal with each other in relative tranquility and generally to their mutual benefit. Morality influences us both from the outside and from the inside. The morality of others affects us from outside as social pressure. Our conscience is morality affecting us from inside, even though others, especially parents, influence the formation of our conscience. Because parents, churches, schools, and peers teach us their beliefs and values (their morals) and the rules of society, most of us grow up wanting to do what is right. We also want to do things that are pleasurable. In a well-functioning society the right and the pleasurable are not too far apart, and most people lead morally respectable lives. On the other hand, no one lives up to moral standards perfectly. In fact, deviance from some moral standards is common, and when it becomes very common the standard changes. Some people interpret this as moral decline, while others interpret it as simply a change in moral standards or even as progress.

The degree of commitment to various moral precepts varies from person to person. Some people even act as moral guardians and take responsibility for encouraging others to live up to the moral standards. One of their major tactics is to cry out against the decline of morals. There are a number of such voices speaking out in public today. In fact, many politicians seem to try to outdo each other in speaking out against crime, teenage pregnancy, divorce, violence in the media, latchkey children, irresponsible parenting, etc.

Cries of moral decline have been ringing out for centuries. In earlier times the cries were against sin, debauchery, and godlessness. Today the cries are often against various aspects of individualism. Parents are condemned for sacrificing their children for their own needs, including their careers. Divorced people are condemned for discarding spouses instead of working hard to save their marriages. Children of elderly parents are condemned for putting their parents into nursing homes to avoid the inconvenience of caring for them. The general public is condemned for investing so little time in others and their communities while pursuing their own interests. These criticisms against individualism may have some validity. On the other hand, individualism has some more positive aspects, including enterprise and inventiveness, which contribute to economic growth; individual responsibility; advocacy of human rights; reduced clannishness and prejudice toward other groups; and an emphasis on self-development, which includes successful relations with others.

The morality debate is important because moral decline not only increases human suffering but also weakens society and hinders the performance of its institutions. The following selections require some deep reflection on the moral underpinnings of American society as well as other societies, and they invite the reader to strengthen those underpinnings.

Many have decried the high levels of crime, violence, divorce, and opportunism, but few argue the thesis of the moral decline of America as thoroughly and as passionately as Gertrude Himmelfarb, the author of the following selection. But is she reading the facts correctly? According to David Whitman in the second selection, the common viewpoint that a serious moral decline is in progress is a myth. He argues that numerous morality indicators do not show the decline that the decline thesis expects. Therefore, even in the face of the statistics on crime and divorce, Whitman concludes that there has not been a deterioration of moral conduct.

Gertrude Himmelfarb

 **YES**

A De-Moralized Society

The current statistics are not only more troubling than those a century ago; they constitute a trend that bodes even worse for the future than for the present. Where the Victorians had the satisfaction of witnessing a significant improvement in their condition, we are confronting a considerable deterioration in ours....

In the United States, the figures are no less dramatic. Starting at 3 percent in 1920 (the first year for which there are national statistics), the illegitimacy ratio rose gradually to slightly over 5 percent by 1960, after which it grew rapidly: to almost 11 percent in 1970, over 18 percent in 1980, and 30 percent by 1991—a tenfold increase from 1920, and a sixfold increase from 1960....

In teenage illegitimacy the United States has earned the dubious distinction of ranking first among all industrialized nations. The rate tripled between 1960 and 1991: for whites it increased almost fivefold; for blacks the increase was less spectacular, but the final rate was almost four times that of the whites. In 1990, one in ten teenage girls got pregnant, half of them giving birth and the other half having abortions.... In 1970, 5 percent of fifteen-year-old girls in the United States had had sexual intercourse; in 1988, 25 percent had....

⚜

There are no national crime statistics for the United States for the nineteenth century and only partial ones (for homicides) for the early twentieth century. Local statistics, however, suggest that as in England the decrease in crime started in the latter part of the nineteenth century (except for a few years following the Civil War) and continued into the early twentieth century. There was even a decline of homicides in the larger cities, where they were most common; in Philadelphia, for example, the rate fell from 3.3 per 100,000 population in midcentury to 2.1 by the end of the century.

National crime statistics became available in 1960, when the rate was under 1,900 per 100,000 population. That figure doubled within the decade and tripled by 1980. A decline in the early 1980s, from almost 6,000 to 5,200, was followed by an increase to 5,800 in 1990; the latest figure, for 1992, is somewhat under 5,700. The rate of violent crime (murder, rape, robbery, and aggravated assault) followed a similar pattern, except that the increase after 1985 was more precipitous and continued until 1992, making for an almost fivefold rise from 1960. In 1987, the Department of Justice estimated that eight of every ten Americans would be a victim of violent crime at least once in their lives. The incidence of nonviolent crime is obviously greater; in 1992 alone, one in four households experienced such a crime.

Homicide statistics go back to the beginning of the century, when the national rate was 1.2 per 100,000 population. That figure skyrocketed during Prohibition, reaching as high as 9.7 by one account (6.5 by another) in 1933, when Prohibition was repealed. The rate dropped to between 5 and 6 during the 1940s and to under 5 in the fifties and early sixties. In the mid-sixties, it started to climb rapidly, more than doubling between 1965 and 1980. A decline in the early eighties was followed by another rise; in 1991 it was just short of its 1980 peak....

There are brave souls, inveterate optimists, who try to put the best gloss on the statistics. But it is not much consolation to be told that the overall crime rate in the United States has declined slightly from its peak in the early 1980s, if the violent crime rate has risen in the same period—and increased still more among juveniles and girls (an ominous trend, since the teenage population is also growing). Nor that the divorce rate has fallen somewhat in the past decade, if it doubled in the previous two decades; if more people, including parents, are cohabiting without benefit of marriage (the rate in the United States has increased sixfold since 1970); and if more children are born out of wedlock and living with single parents. (In 1970, one out of ten families was headed by a single parent; in 1990, three out of ten were.) Nor that the white illegitimacy ratio is considerably lower than the black illegitimacy ratio, if the white ratio is rapidly approaching the black ratio of a few decades ago, when Daniel Patrick Moynihan wrote his percipient report about the breakdown of the black family. (The black ratio in 1964, when that report was issued, was 24.5 percent; the white ratio now is 22 percent. In 1964, 50 percent of black teenage mothers were single; in 1991, 55 percent of white teenage mothers were single.)

Nor is it reassuring to be told that two-thirds of new welfare recipients are off the rolls within two years, if half of those soon return, and a quarter of all recipients remain on for more than eight years. Nor that divorced mothers leave the welfare rolls after an average of five years, if never-married mothers remain for more than nine years, and unmarried mothers who bore their children as teenagers stay on for ten or more years. (Forty-three percent of the longest-term welfare recipients started their families as unwed teenagers.)

Nor is the cause of racial equality promoted by the news of an emerging "white underclass," smaller and less conspicuous than the black (partly because it is more dispersed) but rapidly increasing. If, as has been conclusively demonstrated, the single-parent family is the most important factor associated with the "pathology of poverty"—welfare dependency, crime, drugs, illiteracy, homelessness—a white illegitimacy rate of 22 percent, and twice that for white women below the poverty line, signifies a new and dangerous trend. This has already reached a "tipping point" in some working-class communities, creating a white underclass with all the characteristics of such a class. (Charles Murray finds a similar underclass developing in England, with twice the illegitimacy rate of the rest of the population; there it is a purely class rather than racial phenomenon.)

Nor can one be sanguine about statistics suggesting that drug use in the United States has fallen among casual users, if it has risen among habitual users; or that heroin addiction is decreasing, if crack-cocaine addiction is increasing (or, as more recent statistics show, both are on the rise); or that drug addiction among juveniles is lagging behind alcoholism. Nor can one take much satisfaction in the knowledge that the infant mortality rate has fallen, if it is disproportionately high in some groups, not because prenatal care is unavailable, but because single parents often do not avail themselves of it or because their drug or alcohol addiction has affected their infants....

In his essay "Defining Deviancy Down," Senator Moynihan has taken the idea of deviancy a step further by describing the downward curve of the *concept* of deviancy. What was once regarded as deviant behavior is no longer so regarded; what was once deemed abnormal has been normalized. As deviancy is defined downward, so the threshold of deviancy rises: behavior once stigmatized as deviant is now tolerated and even sanctioned. Mental patients can rarely be institutionalized or even medicated against their will; free to live on the street, they are now treated, and appear in the statistics, not as mentally incapacitated but as "homeless." Divorce and illegitimacy, once seen as betokening the breakdown of the family, are now viewed benignly as "alternative life styles"; illegitimacy has been officially rebaptized as "nonmarital childbearing"; and divorced and unmarried mothers are lumped together in the category of "single parent families." And violent crime has become so endemic that we have practically become inured to it. The St. Valentine's Day Massacre in Chicago in 1929, when four gangsters killed seven other gangsters, shocked the nation and became legendary, immortalized in encyclopedias and history books; in Los Angeles today as many people are killed every weekend.

It is ironic to recall that only a short while ago criminologists were accounting for the rise of the crime rates in terms of our "sensitization to violence." As a result of the century-long decline of violence, they reasoned, we had become more sensitive to "residual violence"; thus more crimes were being reported and apprehended. This "residual violence" has by now become so overwhelming that, as Moynihan points out, we are being desensitized to it.

Charles Krauthammer has proposed a complementary concept: "Defining Deviancy Up." As deviancy is normalized, so the normal becomes deviant. The kind of family that has been regarded for centuries as natural and moral— the "bourgeois" family, as it is invidiously called—is now seen as pathological, concealing behind the facade of respectability the new "original sin," child abuse. While crime is underreported because we have become desensitized to it, child abuse is grossly overreported, including fantasies imagined (often inspired by therapists and social workers) long after the supposed events. Similarly, rape has been "defined up" as "date rape," to include sexual relations that the participants themselves may not have perceived as rape at the time.

The combined effect of defining deviancy up and defining it down has been to normalize and legitimize what was once regarded as abnormal and illegitimate, and, conversely, to stigmatize and discredit what was once normal and respectable. This process, too, has occurred with startling rapidity. One might expect that attitudes and values would lag behind the reality, that people would continue to pay lip service to the moral principles they were brought up with, even while violating those principles in practice. What is striking about the 1960s "sexual revolution," as it has properly been called, is how revolutionary it was, in sensibility as well as reality. In 1965, 69 percent of American women and 65 percent of men under the age of thirty said that premarital sex was always or almost always wrong; by 1972, those figures had plummeted to 24 percent and 21 percent. For women over the age of thirty, the figures dropped from 91 percent to 62 percent, and for men from 62 percent to 47 percent—this in seven short years. . . .

Language, sensibility, and social policy conspire together to redefine deviancy. But the true effect may better be conveyed by an almost random array of facts. In his book on the underclass, Myron Magnet presents a sampling of statistics:

> By 1970 a baby born and raised in a big city had a greater chance of being murdered than a World War II GI had of dying in battle. Today, a twelve-year-old American boy has an 89% chance of becoming a victim of violent crime in his lifetime. . . . In mid-1989, one out of every four young black American males was either in jail or on probation—a larger proportion than was in college.

For a long time social critics and policy-makers have found it hard to face up to the realities of our moral condition, in spite of the statistical evidence. They criticize the statistics themselves or try to explain them away. . . .

⋯◉⋯

These realities have been difficult to confront because they violate the dominant ethos, which assumes that moral progress is a necessary by-product of material progress. It seems incomprehensible that in this age of free, compulsory education, illiteracy should be a problem, not among immigrants but among native-born Americans; or illegitimacy, at a time when sex education, birth control, and abortion are widely available; or drug addiction, once associated with primitive cultures and bohemian individuals. We rarely question that assumption about moral progress because we are suspicious of the very idea of morality. Moral principles, still more moral judgments, are thought to be at best an intellectual embarrassment, at worst evidence of an illiberal and repressive disposition. It is this reluctance to speak the language of morality, far more than any specific values, that separates us from the Victorians.

Most of us are uncomfortable with the idea of making moral judgments even in our private lives, let alone with the "intrusion," as we say, of moral judgments into public affairs. We are uncomfortable not only because we have come to feel that we have no right to make such judgments and impose them upon others, but because we have no confidence in the judgments themselves, no assurance that our principles are true and right for us, let alone for others. We are constantly beseeched to be "nonjudgmental," to be wary of crediting our beliefs with any greater validity than anyone else's, to be conscious of how "Eurocentric" and "culture-bound" we are. *"Chacun à son goût,"* we say of morals, as of taste; indeed, morals have become a matter of taste.

Public officials in particular shy away from the word "immoral," lest they be accused of racism, sexism, elitism, or simply a lack of compassion. When members of the president's cabinet were asked whether it is immoral for people to have children out of wedlock, they drew back from that distasteful word. The Secretary of Health and Human Services replied, "I don't like to put this in moral terms, but I do believe that having children out of wedlock is just wrong." The Surgeon General was more forthright: "No. Everyone has different moral standards.... You can't impose your standards on someone else."

It is not only our political and cultural leaders who are prone to this failure of moral nerve. Everyone has been infected by it, to one degree or another....

In Victorian England, moral principles and judgments were as much a part of social discourse as of private discourse, and as much a part of public policy as of personal life. They were not only deeply ingrained in tradition; they were also embedded in two powerful strains of Victorian thought: Utilitarianism on the one hand, Evangelicalism and Methodism on the other. These may not have been philosophically compatible, but in practice they complemented and reinforced each other, the Benthamite calculus of pleasure and pain, rewards and punishments, being the secular equivalent of the virtues and vices that Evangelicalism and Methodism derived from religion.

It was this alliance of a secular ethos and a religious one that determined social policy, so that every measure of poor relief or philanthropy, for example, had to justify itself by showing that it would promote the moral as well as the material well-being of the poor. The principle of "less eligibility," the "workhouse test," the distinction between "pauper" and "poor," the stigma attached to the "able-bodied pauper," indeed, the word "pauper" itself—all of which figured so largely in the New Poor Law—today seem invidious and inhumane. At the time, however, they were the result of a conscious moral decision: an effort to discourage dependency and preserve the respectability of the independent poor, while providing at least minimal sustenance for the indigent.

In recent decades we have so completely rejected any kind of moral calculus that we have deliberately, systematically divorced welfare—no longer called "relief"—from moral sanctions or incentives. This reflects in part the theory that society is responsible for all social problems and should therefore assume the task of solving them; and in part the prevailing spirit of relativism, which makes it difficult to pass any moral judgments or impose any moral conditions upon the recipients of relief. We are now confronting the consequences of this policy of moral neutrality. Having made the most valiant attempt to "objectify" the problem of poverty, to see it as the product of impersonal economic and social forces, we are discovering that the economic and social aspects of that problem are inseparable from the moral and personal ones. And having made the most determined effort to devise social policies that are "value-free," we find that these policies imperil both the moral and the material well-being of their intended beneficiaries.

In de-moralizing social policy—divorcing it from any moral criteria, requirements, even expectations—we have demoralized, in the more familiar sense, both the individuals receiving relief and society as a whole. Our welfare system is counterproductive not only because it aggravates the problem of welfare, creating more incentives to enter and remain within it than to try to avoid or escape from it. It also has the effect of exacerbating other more serious social problems. Chronic dependency is an integral part of the "social pathology" that now constitutes almost a single "social problem." . . .

Just as many intellectuals, social critics, and policymakers were reluctant for so long to credit the unpalatable facts about crime, illegitimacy, or dependency, so they find it difficult to appreciate the extent to which these facts themselves are a function of values—the extent to which "social pathology" is a function of "moral pathology" and social policy a function of moral principle.

⋅⟨◉⟩⋅

The moral divide has become a class divide. The "new class," as it has been called, is not in fact all that new; it is by now firmly established in the media, the academy, the professions, and the government. In a curious way, it is the mirror image of the "underclass." One might almost say that the two have a symbiotic relationship to each other. In its denigration of "bourgeois values" and the "Puritan ethic," the new class has legitimated, as it were, the values of the underclass and illegitimated those of the working class, who are still committed to bourgeois values and the Puritan ethic. . . .

By now this "liberated," anti-bourgeois ethic no longer seems so liberating. The moral and social statistics have become so egregious that it is now finally permissible to speak of the need for "family values." Under the headline "Courage to Say the Obvious," the black liberal columnist William Raspberry explained that he meant no disrespect for the many admirable single women who raise decent families, but he was worried about social policies that were likely to produce more single mothers. This column, and others like it, appeared in April 1993, soon after *The Atlantic* featured a long article by Barbara Dafoe Whitehead summarizing the recent work of social scientists about the family. The article created a sensation, partly because of the provocative title, "Dan Quayle Was Right," and partly because of the message encapsulated on the cover: "After decades of public dispute about so-called family diversity, the evidence from social-science research is coming in: The dissolution of two-parent families, though it may benefit the adults involved, is harmful to many children, and dramatically undermines our society." . . .

⋅⟨◉⟩⋅

One of the most effective weapons in the arsenal of the "counter-counterculture" is history—the memory not only of a time before the counterculture but also of the evolution of the counterculture itself. In 1968, the English playwright and member of Parliament A. P. Herbert had the satisfaction of witnessing the passage of the act he had sponsored abolishing censorship on the stage. Only two years later, he complained that what had started as a "worthy struggle for reasonable liberty for honest writers" had ended as the "right to represent copulation, veraciously, on the public stage." About the same time, a leading American civil-liberties lawyer, Morris Ernst, was moved to protest that he had meant to ensure the publication of Joyce's *Ulysses,* not the public performance of sodomy.

In the last two decades, the movements for cultural and sexual liberation in both countries have progressed far beyond their original intentions. Yet few people are able to resist their momentum or to recall their initial principles. In an unhistorical age such as ours, even the immediate past seems so remote as to be antediluvian; thus anything short of the present state of "liberation" is regarded as illiberal. And in a thoroughly relativistic age such as ours, any assertion of value—any distinction between the publication of *Ulysses* and the public performance of sodomy—is thought to be arbitrary and authoritarian....

The main thing the Victorians can teach us is the importance of values— or, as they would have said, "virtues"—in our public as well as private lives. And not so much the specifically Victorian virtues that we may well value today, as the importance of an ethos that does not denigrate or so thoroughly relativize values as to make them ineffectual and meaningless.

◦◦◦

The Victorians were, candidly and proudly, "moralists." In recent decades that has almost become a term of derision. Yet contemplating our own society, we may be more respectful of Victorian moralism. We may even be on the verge of assimilating some of that moralism into our own thinking. It is not only "values" that are being rediscovered, but "virtues" as well....

Industrialism and urbanism—"modernism," as it is now known—so far from contributing to the de-moralization of the poor, seems to have had the opposite effect. At the end of the nineteenth century, England was a more civil, more pacific, more humane society than it had been in the beginning. "Middle-class" manners and morals had penetrated into large sections of the working classes. The traditional family was as firmly established as ever, even as feminist movements proliferated and women began to be liberated from their "separate spheres." Voluntary associations and public agencies mitigated some of the worst effects of industrialism and urbanism. And religion continued to thrive, in spite of the premature reports of its death. (It even managed to beget two of the most important institutions of the twentieth century, the British trade-union movement and the Labour Party, both of which were virtually born in the chapel.)

If Victorian England did not succumb to the moral and cultural anarchy that is said to be the inevitable consequence of economic individualism, it is because of a powerful ethos that kept that individualism in check, as it also kept in check the anarchic impulses in human nature. For the Victorians, the individual, or "self," was the ally rather than the adversary of society. Self-help was seen in the context of the community as well as the family; among the working classes this was reflected in the virtue of "neighbourliness," among the middle classes, of philanthropy. Self-interest stood not in opposition to the general interest but, as Adam Smith had it, as the instrument of the general interest. Self-discipline and self-control were thought of as the source of self-respect and self-betterment; and self-respect as the precondition for the respect and approbation of others. The individual, in short, was assumed to have responsibilities as well as rights, duties as well as privileges.

That Victorian "self" was very different from the "self" that is celebrated today. Unlike "self-help," "self-esteem" does not depend upon the individual's actions or achievements; it is presumed to adhere to the individual regardless of how he behaves or what he accomplishes. Moreover, it adheres to him regardless of the esteem in which he is held by others, unlike the Victorian's self-respect which always entailed the respect of others. The current notions of self-fulfillment, self-expression, and self-realization derive from a self that does not have to prove itself by reference to any values, purposes, or persons outside itself—that simply is, and by reason of that alone deserves to be fulfilled and realized. This is truly a self divorced from others, narcissistic and solipsistic. It is this self that is extolled in the movement against "co-dependency," which aspires to free the self from any dependency upon others and, even more, from any responsibility to others. Where the interrelationship of dependency and responsibility was once regarded as a natural human condition, the source of such virtues as love, friendship, loyalty, and sociability, "co-dependency" is now seen as a pathological condition, a disease requiring a radical cure.

This is the final lesson we may learn from the Victorians: that the ethos of a society, its moral and spiritual character, cannot be reduced to economic, material, political, or other factors, that values—or better yet, virtues—are a determining factor in their own right. So far from being a "reflection," as the Marxist says, of the economic realities, they are themselves, as often as not, the crucial agent in shaping those realities. If in a period of rapid economic and social change, the Victorians managed to achieve a substantial improvement in their "condition" and "disposition," it may be that economic and social change do not necessarily result in personal and public disarray. If they could retain and even strengthen an ethos that had its roots in religion and tradition, it may be that we are not as constrained by the material circumstances of our time as we have thought. A post-industrial economy, we may conclude, does not necessarily entail a postmodernist society or culture.

It is often said that there is in human beings an irrepressible need for spiritual and moral sustenance. Just as England experienced a resurgence of religion when it seemed most unlikely (the rise of Puritanism in the aftermath of the Renaissance, or of Wesleyanism in the age of deism), so there emerged, at the very height of the Enlightenment, the movement for "moral reformation." Today, confronted with an increasingly de-moralized society, we may be ready for a new reformation, which will restore not so much Victorian values as a more abiding sense of moral and civic virtues.

NO ←

David Whitman

The Optimism Gap

Much of what everyone "knows" about the state of our nation is wrong. A large majority of Americans now believe that the nation is in decline. The causes of this decline are both familiar and disputed. Conservatives blame family breakdown, crime, and spiritual sloth for our national atrophy. Liberals attribute the decline to the forces of modern-day capitalism, racism, and greed; the poor and the working-class stiffs in the factories can no longer get ahead the way they once did, or so the argument goes. Yet while liberals and conservatives disagree about first causes, they nonetheless agree that the nation, like Rome before the fall, has already been compromised. The American Dream is now endangered. . . .

The Myth of Social Regression

> The trouble with this country is that there are too many people going about saying "the trouble with this country is . . ."
>
> — Sinclair Lewis

. . . Is America, in fact, in a state of decline? . . . To evaluate whether America is declining or advancing, it is necessary to look at whether the nation today is better or worse off in various respects than in the past. Yet the country's political leaders repeatedly duck the compared-to-what question. They are notorious for taking horrifying news stories and transmogrifying them into tales of national atrophy. In 1995, for example, Americans learned of the brutal murder of Deborah Evans and two of her children by three accomplices. One of the accomplices performed a crude C-section on Evans after she died in order to remove a 38-week-old baby whom the alleged murderer claimed for her own. Was the grisly, bizarre murder unusual?

Not according to Newt Gingrich. Here is how the House Speaker analyzed its meaning in a speech to the Republican Governors Association:

> This is not an isolated incident; there's barbarity after barbarity. There's brutality after brutality. And we shake our heads and say "well, what went wrong?" What's going wrong is the welfare system which subsidized people for doing nothing; a criminal system which tolerated drug dealers; an educational system which allows kids to not learn.... And then we end up with the final culmination of a drug-addicted underclass with no sense of humanity, no sense of civilization, and no sense of the rules of life in which human beings respect each other.... The child who was killed was endowed by God. And because we aren't willing to say that any more in a public place, and we're not willing to be tough about this any more, and we don't tell four-, five-, and six-year-olds "there are things you can't do, we will not tolerate drug dealing," we then turn around one day and find that we tolerated the decay of our entire civilization. And it's not just violence. In last year's National Assessment of Educational Progress, 74 percent of the fourth-graders could not read at fourth-grade level.... A civilization that only has 26 percent of its fourth-graders performing at fourth-grade level is a civilization in danger of simply falling apart.

...What is striking about all this is that Gingrich, the former history professor, makes no reference to history. When Gingrich's claims are placed in context, they evaporate. For example, the reading scores for fourth graders that Gingrich decried were all *lower* a quarter century ago when the NAEP tests began for white, black, and Hispanic students. If the current NAEP scores testify to a civilization in danger of falling apart, think of how endangered American society was a quarter century ago. (Gingrich also botched the test results. The test scores showed that about 60 percent of fourth graders were not "proficient" readers, not that 74 percent of them read below grade level. By definition, 50 percent of those tested read above "grade level.")

Similar questions might be posed about Gingrich's claims about the criminal justice system. Does law enforcement really "tolerate" drug dealers? More drug dealers are locked up, serving longer sentences, today than ever before. That does not mean drug dealing has been halted, but it does not suggest a policy of looking the other way. What about the notion that out streets are marked by barbarity after barbarity? Are Americans significantly more likely to murder each other today than a quarter century ago? Not really. The homicide rate was a hair higher in 1995 than in 1970 (8.2 homicides per 100,000 inhabitants in 1995 versus 7.9 homicides per 100,000 inhabitants in 1970). By 1971, and for the remainder of the 1970s in fact, the homicide rate was substantially *higher* than in 1995....

The Good News Surprise

Not all of the news about America is good. Yet most of the country's fundamental economic and social trends have improved over the last quarter century. That fact would surprise millions of Americans who feel as though they are living in Babylon.

Given that the Soviet Union has collapsed, that the threat of nuclear annihilation has almost vanished, and that the nation is now inundated with immigrants who cling to rafts, wade, swim, and run to reach our borders, it may seem an odd time to herald the demise of America. Quite apart from the question of America's standing in the world community, however, many domestic indexes have actually improved. In fact, much of what people presume about key social trends in America is wrong. Here are just a few examples at odds with the conventional wisdom:

Crime

Violent crime in the United States appears to be at its lowest level in a quarter century. There are two ways of tracking trends in crime. The first is to examine the Federal Bureau of Investigation's *Uniform Crime Reports,* which tabulate crimes reported to law enforcement agencies from around the nation. The second source of evidence is the Justice Department's annual national victimization surveys, which are huge polls that randomly sample approximately 100,000 people. The victimization surveys cover crimes not reported to police. (Only about a third of all crimes are reported to law enforcement agencies, and this fraction can change over time.) As a result, the victimization surveys are more representative than conventional crime statistics and are favored by many criminologists.

In 1996, violent crime rates were at their lowest levels since the victimization surveys started in 1973. According to the Justice Department reports, violent crime rates peaked 17 years ago, in 1981, and the rates of aggravated assault and rape are now lower than at any time in the previous 23 years. Meanwhile, property crime, which accounts for the bulk of all crime, had also plummeted to its lowest level since the federal surveys began. In 1996, the rates of household theft and burglary were about half of what they had been in 1973. The drop in property crime is so substantial that New York City now has a lower theft and burglary rate than London, and Los Angeles has fewer burglaries than Sydney, Australia.

Victimization surveys have one important gap: They do not track murders, since homicide victims cannot be interviewed after the fact. However, the FBI's *Uniform Crime Reports* do track homicides and the murder totals are considered accurate, because homicide is a crime that is hard to underreport. In 1996, the homicide rate of 7.4 murders per 100,000 inhabitants was well below the peak of 10.2 murders per 100,000 people in 1980. It was, in fact, virtually identical to the homicide rate in 1969, higher than in the 1950s, but lower than in 1931–34. Most of this well-publicized drop in violent crime has been concentrated in the nation's largest cities. In New York and Boston, fewer people were murdered in 1996 than at any time since the 1960s. In Los Angeles, fewer people were murdered in 1997 than in any year since 1977—even though the city now has 700,000 more residents....

Drugs

Annual government surveys show that illicit drug use among the general population is at levels far below those of a decade or more ago. Overall drug use peaked in 1979, when the nation had 25 million users, almost twice the current number. Since 1992, illicit drug use has essentially stabilized but at lower levels. Cocaine use hit its high in 1985, when 3 percent of adults, or 5.7 million Americans, reported they had used cocaine the previous month. By 1996, just 0.8 percent of Americans reported use of cocaine in the past month, and the number of current cocaine users had dropped by almost three-fourths since 1985, to 1.75 million. Among high school seniors, marijuana and LSD use has edged upward since 1992. But student use of marijuana remains well below the levels of the late 1970s and early 1980s, as does the use of most hard drugs. In 1981, 21.7 percent of high school seniors reported using an illicit drug other than marijuana during the month previous to when they were surveyed; in 1997, half as many (10.7 percent) did so. High school seniors were also three times more likely to use cocaine in 1985 than they are today....

Scholastic Achievement

Despite much-heralded reports of a nation at educational risk, high school students today do as well as or slightly better than their predecessors of the mid-1970s on both aptitude and achievement tests. As Derek Bok writes in his book *The State of the Nation,* "Contrary to all the alarmist talk, there are even some recent signs of modest improvement" in academic achievement.

The case that student aptitude has fallen rests largely on the fact that Scholastic Aptitude Test (SAT) scores declined between the early 1960s and 1970s and have never fully recovered. However, there are two reasons why those declines don't mean that today's students are performing worse than their parents.

First, only about half of all high school seniors take the SAT each year, and the sample is far from representative. In six states in 1993, more than 70 percent of high school seniors took the SAT, but in ten other states less than 10 percent of seniors did so. Unlike the SAT, the Preliminary Scholastic Aptitude Test (PSAT) is given to representative samples of high school juniors. Both the math and verbal PSAT scores have stayed the same from 1959 to the present....

Race

In the last quarter century, the black middle class has mushroomed. In 1996, black median family income, adjusted for inflation, was at an all-time high, and black poverty and infant mortality rates had edged downward to an all-time low. In 1970, about 1 out of every 17 blacks in the 25- to 34-year-old age group had earned a four-year college degree. By 1994, 1 in 8 had done so.

Orlando Patterson, a left-leaning Harvard sociologist, summarizes the import of these shifts in his 1997 book *The Ordeal of Integration.* "African Americans," he writes, "from a condition of mass illiteracy fifty years ago, are now among the most educated groups of people in the world, with median years of schooling and college completion rates higher than those of most European nations. Although some readers may think this observation is a shocking overstatement, it is not." ...

As Patterson acknowledges, a minority of blacks in urban ghettos have fared disastrously in the last 25 years. But the big picture is inescapable: Most blacks have prospered, and overt white racism has dramatically declined since the 1960s. Overwhelming majorities of whites today support the principle of equal treatment for the races in schools, jobs, housing, and other public spheres. Interracial friendships and marriages have blossomed as well. In 1970, just 2.6 percent of all new marriages involving an African-American mate were interracial marriages; today, more than 12 percent are interracial unions. Whites' greater openness to interracial marriages is one of the more dramatic attitudinal shifts in the last 25 years. In 1972, only a quarter of whites approved of marriages between blacks and whites. (In 1958, just 4 percent did so.) By 1997, however, over 60 percent of whites approved of interracial marriages....

The Myth of Moral Decline ...

The Family Values Conundrum

Since 1970, divorce and out-of-wedlock childbearing have skyrocketed in the United States. Many single-parent families manage to flourish, but on average, children raised by single parents are more likely than children raised by both their biological parents to be poor, drop out of school, become pregnant while in their teens, go to juvenile correction facilities, and be unemployed as adults.

... [M]any Americans, laypeople and scholars alike, exaggerate the consequences of family breakdown. The crude one-to-one correlation that exists in public discussion—more kids born out of wedlock automatically equals higher crime rates, weaker moral standards, worse schools, sicker children, and so on —has not been borne out in recent years. Crime rates have dropped, scholastic achievement has stabilized or edged upward, and infant mortality has declined, even as the out-of-wedlock birth ratio has risen. Nor is it clear that the ethical standards of Americans have declined.

Here again, when members of the public voice their distress about family breakdown, they are almost always referring to *other* people's families, not their own.

... Americans aren't just pleased with their own family life; they are delighted. In a 1997 Mother's Day survey, the Pew Research Center found that 93 percent of mothers with kids under 18 felt their children were a source of happiness all or most of the time; 90 percent said their marriage made them happy all or most of the time; and just 2 percent of moms reported being dissatisfied with the job they were doing rearing their children. In poll after poll, less than 10 percent of Americans say they are worse parents than were their own parents, and compared to the moms and dads of twenty years ago, today's parents are actually much more likely to rate traditional values, such as hard work, religion, patriotism, and having children as being "very important." In their own lives, three out of four adults don't find it difficult to meet their commitments to their families, kids, and employers—even though 90 percent also believe that a "major problem with society" is that people don't live up to their commitments....

The essential paradox is that while Americans believe today's moral breakdown was spawned by the permissiveness of the 1960s, they embrace, on a case-by-case basis, most of the liberties that were part of the 1960s revolution. When Americans are asked, as they were in a 1996 *Wall Street Journal* poll, what kind of impact various social movements have had on today's values, they almost invariably think they are beneficial. Roughly 80 percent of those surveyed by the *Journal* said that the civil rights movement, the environmental movement, and the women's movement all had a positive impact on people's values.

The previous year, the Gallup Organization also quizzed members of the public about whether they thought various changes had been good or bad for society. Hefty majorities of Americans thought the greater openness today toward divorced people was good for society, as was the greater openness about sex and the human body, changes in the role of women, greater cultural and ethnic diversity, the increased willingness to question government authority, and the greater attention paid to equality for racial and ethnic minorities. In only one instance (society's increased acceptance of homosexuality) did most people think social change had harmed society....

By All That's Holy

The problem of "family breakdown" can be thought of as a surrogate Rorschach test. Voters hear of its poignant consequences among divorced friends, or see news stories about latch-key kids and crack babies, and before long, every problem starts looking as though it can ultimately be traced back to family breakdown. One might, for example, infer that organized religion is slipping if out-of-wedlock childbearing and single-parenting are mushrooming. In fact, three in four Americans believe the nation is in spiritual decline. Yet the sway of organized religion is much greater in the United States today than in most Western nations, and the religiosity of Americans is at near record levels.

As Seymour Martin Lipset, a neoconservative intellectual, sums up in his 1996 book *American Exceptionalism,* "The historical evidence indicates that religious affiliation and belief in America are much higher in the twentieth century than in the nineteenth, and have not decreased in the post–World War II era.... The standard evidence marshalled to argue that America is experiencing a value crisis is unconvincing." Such counterconventional claims are hard for members of the public to accept, again, because of the optimism gap. Two-thirds of the electorate think that religion is losing its influence on American life. Yet 62 percent say that religion's influence is increasing in their own lives, according to a 1994 *U.S. News & World Report* poll.

Today, a solid majority of Americans belong to churches and synagogues, much as they have since the 1930s, when scientific polling began. In 1997, 68 percent of Americans reported belonging to a church or synagogue, not much below the 73 percent who said they belonged in both 1965 and 1952. Some members of the clergy have asserted that these high levels of church membership conceal a dip in religious commitment and belief. It's true that weekly attendance at religious services was "only" 41 percent in 1997. This was down a bit from its peak in 1958, when 49 percent of Americans said they had attended services the previous week. But attendance in 1997 was very similar to attendance in 1950, when 39 percent of Americans said they had attended a service the previous week. In 1997, the Gallup poll replicated one of its surveys on Americans' religious practices from 1947. The fifty-year update found that the same percentage of Americans pray today (90 percent), believe in God (96 percent), and attend church once a week. About the only difference between the two eras was that Americans were actually more likely to give grace or give thanks aloud in 1997 than in 1947 (63 percent compared to 43 percent).

George Gallup, Jr., summarizes the evidence by observing that "the religious beliefs and practices of Americans today look very much like those of the 1930s and 1940s. The percent of the populace who are active church members today closely matches the figures recorded in the 1930s." Nor is it the case, as Roger Finke and Rodney Stark point out in their influential book *The Churching of America, 1776–1990,* that acceptance of traditional religious doctrine is down. Most Americans still say that religion is central to their own lives: Roughly 60 percent of adults think that religion "can answer all or most of today's problems," and one in three view at least one religious TV show each week. After reviewing church membership records and other historical evidence, Finke and Stark conclude that "to the degree that denominations rejected traditional doctrines and ceased to make serious demands on their followers, they ceased to prosper. The churching of America was accomplished by aggressive churches committed to vivid otherworldliness."

The Ethics "Crisis"

Conceivably, the nation could still be in moral decline even when its citizens claim to be deeply religious. A skeptic might suggest that Americans are simply bigger hypocrites than ever. In 1993, Everett Carll Ladd, the president of the Roper Center for Public Opinion Research, attempted to assess that proposition by examining whether the unethical behavior of Americans had risen in recent decades. In an article titled "The Myth of Moral Decline," Ladd reports his findings: There is no compelling evidence that Americans' moral conduct or ethical standards are slipping, but ever since the introduction of polling in the mid-1930s, most Americans have felt moral standards were in decline. In 1963, for instance, only a third of all adults said they were satisfied "with the honesty and standards of behavior of people in the country today."

Ladd acknowledges there is abundant evidence that large numbers of modern-day Americans err and sin. Yet in tracking trends over time, there is little proof that the moral state of the country's citizenry has deteriorated. Philanthropic giving as a percentage of personal income declined slightly between 1969 and 1972 but has essentially remained steady ever since. However, because Americans' personal incomes have risen substantially since the 1950s, individual citizens are now donating more money to charities than their parents did, even after accounting for inflation. Volunteering seems to have become *more* common. When the Gallup poll first queried people in 1977 about their participation in charitable and social service activities that aid the poor, the sick, and the elderly, a quarter of the populace said they participated. By 1994, that number had doubled to almost half of all adults. . . .

William Bennett may have best summed up the zeitgeist of the day when he observed that "these are times in which conservatives are going to have to face the fact that there is some good news on the landscape. We're going to have to learn to live with it." In some measure, Bennett's curmudgeonly response to good news reflects the fact that conservatives are loath to credit Bill Clinton for progress. But his begrudging acceptance of the good news is also part of an age-old tradition. From era to era, the electorate's mood has swung from boosterish optimism—as during the first two decades after World War II—to the stubborn skepticism popular today. Over a century ago, Charles Dickens deftly captured this skeptical attitude toward politics and public life in his travel journal, *American Notes.* "It is an essential part of every national character to pique itself mightily upon its faults," he observed, "and to deduce tokens of its virtue or its wisdom from their very exaggeration." In America's case, Dickens argued, the "one great blemish in the popular mind ... and the prolific parent of an innumerable brood of evils, is Universal Distrust. Yet the American citizen plumes himself upon this spirit, even when he is sufficiently dispassionate to perceive the ruin it works; and will often adduce it ... as an instance of the great sagacity and acuteness of the people."

POSTSCRIPT

Is America in Moral Decline?

Handwringing over weakening morals has long been a favorite pastime. Yet are Americans less moral today than they were a century ago? Consider that slavery has been abolished, civil rights for minorities have been won and generally accepted, tolerant attitudes have greatly increased, and genocide toward Native Americans ceased a long time ago. How could Americans have made so much progress if they have been getting much worse for hundreds of years? Such reflections cast suspicion over the moral decline thesis. On the other hand, this thesis is supported by many trends, such as the recently stalled increases in crime and divorce. The issue is important because morality is a distinctive trait of the human species and essential to cooperative interactions. If morality declines, coercive restraint must increase to hold harmful behaviors in check, but self-restraint is much less costly than police restraint.

The issue of the trends in morality requires an examination of the blessings and curses of individualism and capitalism. One tenet of individualism is that we should be tolerant of each other's lifestyle choices. Though this may be kindly in the short run, according to Himmelfarb, it demoralizes social policy and weakens society in the long run. Capitalism would be another demoralizing factor because it encourages self-interest and the passion for personal gain. Higher education may be another culprit because it relativizes values. In general, the forces behind the demoralization of society as described by Himmelfarb are not likely to be reversed in the medium-term future.

Most of the relevant literature is on aspects of the moral decline. Few works challenge the decline thesis. Examples include Nicholas Lemann's "It's Not as Bad as You Think It Is," *The Washington Monthly* (March 1997) and Gregg Easterbrook's "America the O.K.," *The New Republic* (January 4 & 11, 1999). For an exposition of the moral decline thesis, see Charles Derber's *The Wilding of America: How Greed and Violence Are Eroding Our Nation's Character* (St. Martin's Press, 1996); Robert Bork's *Slouching Towards Gomorrah* (Regan Books, 1996); and Richard Sennett's *The Corrosion of Character* (W. W. Norton, 1998). Richard Stivers attributes the moral decline to a culture of cynicism in *The Culture of Cynicism: American Morality in Decline* (Basil Blackwell, 1994).

ISSUE 2

Does Television Violence Make Children Significantly More Violent?

YES: W. James Potter, from *On Media Violence* (Sage Publications, 1999)

NO: Jib Fowles, from *The Case for Television Violence* (Sage Publications, 1999)

ISSUE SUMMARY

YES: Professor of communication W. James Potter reviews the harmful influences of media violence and explains some of the mechanisms that cause these influences.

NO: Professor of communication Jib Fowles argues that the evidence on the negative influences of the media on children is weak and does not prove that television violence makes children significantly more violent.

$\mathbf{R}$andom shootings in schools and high murder rates by children demand explanations—and an often-suspected culprit is media violence, especially TV, movies, and video games. But like good detectives, we must not rush to judgment but carefully examine the evidence.

Throughout history children have been exposed to stories of violence, often for their moral education. Gretel pushing the witch into the oven and cooking her to death to save Hansel and the picture of the three blind mice having their tails cut off with the carving knife are vivid childhood images. Many a child's favorite experiences was to go to the local movie house on Saturday afternoons when it would show about three hours of funny—but violent —cartoons to a packed house of excited little children. Currently, literature on the impact of media violence on children suggests that these children were influenced and even harmed by the violence of the stories, cartoons, and poems that they viewed as youngsters. Were such children made more prone to violence when they laughed at the roadrunner tricking the coyote into running off the cliff and falling a mile to the floor of the canyon? The coyote got up with stars swirling in his eyes and soon was chasing the roadrunner again, so the violence can be said to be clearly farcical. Nevertheless, research does indicate that exposure to violence tends to make us act violently. How seriously should we take these results? How significant are the effects?

It has been reported that the average child will see more than 100,000 acts of violence on television before leaving elementary school. It is hard to imagine that this exposure will have no effect on children considering the fact that children have an instinctive desire to imitate behavior, and at a young age they have little discernment about what behavior is appropriate for imitating. The process starts early. Children as young as 14 months have been observed imitating behavior seen on television. Given the fact that the average impressionable preschooler watches over 27 hours of television per week, television programming gives children much to imitate, including much violence. But consider that most of the violence that past generations watched on television occurred in "westerns," with heroes like Roy Rogers and Tom Mix. They were simple morality plays that taught that it was good to be good and bad to be bad—and that the good guys win in the end. Such programs supported society's value system rather than challenging it. They taught bravery and commitment in doing what was good for society. Many say that television today is more complicated and somewhat less supportive of society's values, but most of television programming can still be said to be morality plays about good and evil. Examining our personal television watching experience, therefore, does not adequately lead to firm conclusions about the good or bad influences of television.

The selections that follow will provide us with much more information on which to base our conclusions. The selection by W. James Potter presents the more commonly accepted position that media violence is harming our children. His evidence of harmful influences and the reasons for them is both broad and detailed. Jib Fowles is not impressed with the evidence and argues that its methodological flaws lower our confidence in it. He maintains that the viewer is not controlled by television.

W. James Potter

On Media Violence

Overview and Introduction

Violence in American society is a public health problem. Although most people have never witnessed an act of serious violence in person, we are all constantly reminded of its presence by the media. The media constantly report news about individual violent crimes. The media also use violence as a staple in telling fictional stories to entertain us. Thus, the media amplify and reconfigure the violence in real life and continuously pump these messages into our culture.

The culture is responding with a range of negative effects. Each year about 25,000 people are murdered, and more than 2 million are injured in assaults. On the highways, aggressive behavior such as tailgating, weaving through busy lanes, honking or screaming at other drivers, exchanging insults, and even engaging in gunfire is a factor in nearly 28,000 traffic deaths annually, and the problem is getting worse at a rate of 7% per year. Gun-related deaths increased more than 60% from 1968 to 1994, to about 40,000 annually, and this problem is now considered a public health epidemic by 87% of surgeons and 94% of internists across the United States. Meanwhile, the number of pistols manufactured in the United States continues to increase—up 92% from 1985 to 1992.

Teenagers are living in fear. A Harris poll of 2,000 U.S. teenagers found that most of them fear violence and crime and that this fear is affecting their everyday behavior. About 46% of respondents said they have changed their daily behavior because of a fear of crime and violence; 12% said they carry a weapon to school for protection; 12% have altered their route to school; 20% said they have avoided particular parks or playgrounds; 20% said they have changed their circle of friends; and 33% have stayed away from school at times because of fear of violence. In addition, 25% said they did not feel safe in their own neighborhood, and 33% said they fear being a victim of a drive-by shooting. Nearly twice as many teenagers reported gangs in their school in 1995 compared to 1989, and this increase is seen in all types of neighborhoods; violent crime in schools increased 23.5% during the same period.

This problem has far-reaching economic implications. The U.S. Department of Justice estimates the total cost of crime and violence (such as child abuse and domestic violence, in addition to crimes such as murder, rape, and robbery) to be $500 billion per year, or about twice the annual budget of the Defense Department. The cost includes real expenses (such as legal fees, the cost of lost time from work, the cost of police work, and the cost of running the nation's prisons and parole systems) and intangibles (such as loss of affection from murdered family members). Violent crime is responsible for 14% of injury-related medical spending and up to 20% of mental health care expenditures.

The problem of violence in our culture has many apparent causes, including poverty, breakdown of the nuclear family, shift away from traditional morality to a situational pluralism, and the mass media. The media are especially interesting as a source of the problem. Because they are so visible, the media are an easy target for blame. In addition, they keep reminding us of the problem in their news stories. But there is also a more subtle and likely more powerful reason why the media should be regarded as a major cause of this public health problem: They manufacture a steady stream of fictional messages that convey to all of us in this culture what life is about. Media stories tell us how we should deal with conflict, how we should treat other people, what is risky, and what it means to be powerful. The media need to share the blame for this serious public health problem.

How do we address the problem? The path to remedies begins with a solid knowledge base. It is the task of social scientists to generate much of this knowledge. For the past five decades, social scientists and other scholars have been studying the topic of media violence. This topic has attracted researchers from many different disciplines, especially psychology, sociology, mental health science, cultural studies, law, and public policy. This research addresses questions such as these: How much media violence is there? What are the meanings conveyed in the way violence is portrayed? and What effect does violence have on viewers as individuals, as members of particular groups, and as members of society? Estimates of the number of studies conducted to answer these questions range as high as 3,000 and even 3,500. . . .

Effects of Exposure to Media Violence

Does exposure to violence in the media lead to effects? With each passing year, the answer is a stronger yes. The general finding from a great deal of research is that exposure to violent portrayals in the media increases the probability of an effect. The most often tested effect is referred to as *learning to behave aggressively*. This effect is also referred to as direct imitation of violence, instigation or triggering of aggressive impulses, and disinhibition of socialization against aggressive behavior. Two other negative effects—desensitization and fear—are also becoming prevalent in the literature.

Exposure to certain violent portrayals can lead to positive or prosocial effects. Intervention studies, especially with children, have shown that when a media-literate person talks through the action and asks questions of the viewer during the exposure, the viewer will be able to develop a counterreading of the violence; that is, the viewer may learn that violent actions are wrong even though those actions are shown as successful in the media portrayal.

The effects have been documented to occur immediately or over the long term. Immediate effects happen during exposure or shortly after the exposure (within about an hour). They might last only several minutes, or they might last weeks. Long-term effects do not occur after one or several exposures; they begin to show up only after an accumulation of exposures over weeks or years. Once a long-term effect eventually occurs, it usually lasts a very long period of time.

This [selection] focuses on the issues of both immediate effects and long-term effects of exposure to media violence. . . .

From the large body of effects research, I have assembled 10 major findings. These are the findings that consistently appear in quantitative meta-analyses and narrative reviews of this literature. Because these findings are so widespread in the literature and because they are so rarely disputed by scholars, they can be regarded as empirically established laws.

Immediate Effects of Violent Content

The first six laws illuminate the major findings of research into the immediate effects of exposure to media violence. Immediate effects occur during exposure or within several hours afterward.

1. Exposure to violent portrayals in the media can lead to subsequent viewer aggression through disinhibition.

This conclusion is found in most of the early reviews. For example, Stein and Friedrich closely analyzed 49 studies of the effects of antisocial and prosocial television content on people 3 to 18 years of age in the United States. They concluded that the correlational studies showed generally significant relationships ($r = .10$ to $.32$) and that the experiments generally showed an increase in aggression resulting from exposure to television violence across all age groups.

This conclusion gained major visibility in the 1972 Surgeon General's Report which stated that there was an influence, but this conclusion was softened by the industry members on the panel. . . .

Some of the early reviewers disagreed with this conclusion. . . .

In the two decades since this early disagreement, a great deal more empirical research has helped overcome these shortcomings, so most (but not all) of these critics have been convinced of the general finding that exposure to media violence can lead to an immediate disinhibition effect. All narrative reviews since 1980 have concluded that viewing of violence is consistently related to subsequent aggressiveness. This finding holds in surveys, laboratory experiments, and naturalistic experiments. For example, Roberts and Maccoby concluded that "the overwhelming proportion of results point to a causal relationship between exposure to mass communication portrayals of violence and an increased probability that viewers will behave violently at some subsequent time." Also, Friedrich-Cofer and Huston concluded that "the weight of the evidence from different methods of investigation supports the hypothesis that television violence affects aggression."

Meta-analytical studies that have reexamined the data quantitatively across sets of studies have also consistently concluded that viewing of aggression is likely to lead to antisocial behavior. For example, Paik and Comstock conducted a meta-analysis of 217 studies of the effects of television violence on antisocial behavior and reported finding a positive and significant correlation. They concluded that "regardless of age—whether nursery school, elementary school, college, or adult—results remain positive at a high significance level." Andison looked at 67 studies involving 30,000 participants (including 31 laboratory experiments) and found a relationship between viewing and subsequent aggression, with more than half of the studies showing a correlation (r) between .31 and .70. Hearold looked at 230 studies involving 100,000 participants to determine the effect of viewing violence on a wide range of antisocial behaviors in addition to aggression (including rule breaking, materialism, and perceiving oneself as powerless in society). Hearold concluded that for all ages and all measures, the majority of studies reported an association between exposure to violence and antisocial behavior. . . .

On balance, it is prudent to conclude that media portrayals of violence can lead to the immediate effect of aggressive behavior, that this can happen in response to as little as a single exposure, and that this effect can last up to several weeks. Furthermore, the effect is causal, with exposure leading to aggression. However, this causal link is part of a reciprocal process; that is, people with aggressive tendencies seek out violent portrayals in the media.

2. The immediate disinhibition effect is influenced by viewer demographics, viewer traits, viewer states, characteristics in the portrayals, and situational cues.

Each human is a complex being who brings to each exposure situation a unique set of motivations, traits, predispositions, exposure history, and personality factors. These characteristics work together incrementally to increase or decrease the probability of the person's being affected.

2.1 Viewer Demographics
The key characteristics of the viewer that have been found to be related to a disinhibition effect are age and gender, but social class and ethnic background have also been found to play a part.

Demographics of age and gender.   Boys and younger children are more affected. Part of the reason is that boys pay more attention to violence. Moreover, younger children have more trouble following story plots, so they are more likely to be drawn into high-action episodes without considering motives or consequences. Age by itself is not as good an explanation as is ability for cognitive processing.

Socioeconomic status.   Lower-class youth watch more television and therefore more violence.

Ethnicity.   Children from minority and immigrant groups are vulnerable because they are heavy viewers of television.

2.2 Viewer Traits

The key characteristics of viewer traits are socialization against aggression, ... cognitive processing, and personality type.

Socialization against aggression.   Family life is an important contributing factor. Children in households with strong norms against violence are not likely to experience enough disinhibition to exhibit aggressive behavior. The disinhibition effect is stronger in children living in households in which... children are abused by parents, watch more violence, and identify more with violent heroes; and in families that have high-stress environments.

Peer and adult role models have a strong effect in this socialization process. Male peers have the most immediate influence in shaping children's aggressive behaviors in the short term; adult males have the most lasting effect 6 months later....

Cognitive processing.   Viewers' reactions depend on their individual interpretations of the aggression. Rule and Ferguson (1986) said that viewers first must form a representation or cognitive structure consisting of general social knowledge about the positive value that can be attached to aggression. The process of developing such a structure requires that viewers attend to the material (depending on the salience and complexity of the program). Then viewers make attributions and form moral evaluations in the comprehension stage. Then they store their comprehension in memory.

Cognitive processing is related to age. Developmental psychologists have shown that children's minds mature cognitively and that in some early stages they are unable to process certain types of television content well....[U]ntil age 5, they are especially attracted to and influenced by vivid production features, such as rapid movement of characters, rapid changes of scenes, and unexpected sights and sounds. Children seek out and pay attention to cartoon violence, not because of the violence, but because of the vivid production features. By ages 6 to 11, children have developed the ability to lengthen their attention spans and make sense of continuous plots....

Personality type.   The more aggressive the person is, the more influence viewing of violence will have on that person's subsequent aggressive behavior (Comstock et al., 1978; Stein & Friedrich, 1972). And children who are emotionally disturbed are more susceptible to a disinhibition effect (Sprafkin et al., 1992)....

2.3. Viewer States

The degrees of physiological arousal, anger, and frustration have all been found to increase the probability of a negative effect.

Aroused state.   Portrayals (even if they are not violent) that leave viewers in an aroused state are more likely to lead to aggressive behavior (Berkowitz & Geen, 1966; Donnerstein & Berkowitz, 1981; Tannenbaum, 1972; Zillman, 1971).

Emotional reaction.   Viewers who are upset by the media exposure (negative hedonic value stimuli) are more likely to aggress (Rule & Ferguson, 1986; Zillmann et al., 1981). Such aggression is especially likely when people are left in a state of unresolved excitement (Comstock, 1985).... In his meta-analysis of 1,043 effects of television on social behavior, Hearold (1986) concluded that frustration... is not a necessary condition, but rather a contributory condition....

Degree of identity.   It has been well established that the more a person, especially a child, identifies with a character, the more likely the person will be influenced by that character's behavior.

Identity seems to be a multifaceted construct composed of similarity, attractiveness, and hero status. If the perpetrator of violence is perceived as *similar* to the viewer, the likelihood of learning to behave aggressively increases (Lieberman Research, 1975; Rosekrans & Hartup, 1967). When violence is performed by an *attractive* character, the probability of aggression increases (Comstock et al., 1978; Hearold, 1986). Attractiveness of a villain is also an important consideration (Health et al., 1989)....

2.4 Characteristics in the Portrayals

Reviews of the literature are clear on the point that people interpret the meaning of violent portrayals and use contextual information to construct that meaning.

In the media effects literature, there appear to be five notable contextual variables: rewards and punishments, consequences, justification, realism, and production techniques....

Rewards and punishments.   Rewards and punishments to perpetrators of violence provide important information to viewers about which actions are acceptable. However, there is reason to believe that the effect does not work with children younger than 10, who usually have difficulty linking violence presented early in a program with its punishment rendered later (Collins, 1973).

In repeated experiments, viewers who watch a model rewarded for performing violently in the media are more likely to experience a disinhibition effect and behave in a similar manner. But when violence is punished in the media portrayal, the aggressiveness of viewers is likely to be inhibited (Comstock et al., 1978). In addition, when nonaggressive characters are rewarded, viewers' levels of aggression can be reduced.

The absence of punishment also leads to disinhibition. That is, the perpetrators need not be rewarded in order for the disinhibition effect to occur. . . .

Consequences.   The way in which the consequences of violence are portrayed influences the disinhibition effect. . . . For example, Goranson showed people a film of a prize fight in which either there were no consequences or the loser of the fight received a bad beating and later died. The participants who did not see the negative consequences were more likely to behave aggressively after the viewing.

A key element in the consequences is whether the victim shows pain, because pain cues inhibit subsequent aggression. Moreover, Swart and Berkowitz (1976) showed that viewers could generalize pain cues to characters other than the victims.

Justification.   Reviews of the effects research conclude that justification of violent acts leads to higher aggression. For example, Bryan and Schwartz observed that "aggressive behavior in the service of morally commendable ends appears condoned. Apparently, the assumption is made that moral goals temper immoral actions. . . . Thus, both the imitation and interpersonal attraction of the transgressing model may be determined more by outcomes than by moral principles."

Several experiments offer support for these arguments. First, Berkowitz and Rawlings (1963) found that justification of filmed aggression lowers viewers' inhibitions to aggress in real life.

Justification is keyed to motives. Brown and Tedeschi (1976) found that offensive violence was regarded as more violent even when the actions themselves were not as violent. For example, a verbal threat that is made offensively is perceived as more violent than a punch that is delivered defensively.

The one motive that has been found to lead to the strongest disinhibition is vengeance. For example, Berkowitz and Alioto introduced a film of a sporting event (boxing and football) by saying that the participants were acting either as professionals wanting to win or as motivated by vengeance and wanting to hurt the other. They found that the vengeance film led to more shocks and longer duration of shocks in a subsequent test of participants. When violence was portrayed as vengeance, disinhibition was stronger than when violence was portrayed as self-defense or as a means of achieving altruistic goals.

Young children have difficulty understanding motives. For example, Collins (1973) ran an experiment on children aged 8 to 15 to see if a time lag from portrayal of motivation to portrayal of aggression changed participants' behaviors or interpretations. Participants were shown either a 30-minute film in which federal agents confronted some criminals or a control film of a travelogue. In the treatment film, the criminals hit and shot the federal agents, displaying negative motivation (desire to escape justice) and negative consequences (a criminal fell to his death while trying to escape). Some participants saw the sequence uninterrupted; others saw the motivation, followed by a 4-minute interruption of commercials, then the aggression. Both 18 days before the experiment and then again right after the viewing, participants were asked their responses to a wide range of hypothetical interpersonal conflict situations. There was a difference by age. Third graders displayed more aggressive choices on the postviewing measure when they had experienced the separation condition; sixth and 10th graders did not exhibit this effect. The author concluded that among younger children, temporal separation of story elements obscures the message that aggression was negatively motivated and punished. . . .

Realism.   When viewers believe that the aggression is portrayed in a realistic manner, they are more likely to try it in real life.

Production techniques.   Certain production techniques can capture and hold attention, potentially leading to differences in the way the action is perceived. Attention is increased when graphic and explicit acts are used to increase the dramatic nature of the narrative, to increase positive dispositions toward the characters using violence, and to increase levels of arousal, which is more likely to result in aggressive behavior. . . .

   3. Exposure to violence in the media can lead to fear effects.

   The best available review is by Cantor (1994), who defines fear effect as an immediate physiological effect of arousal, along with an emotional reaction of anxiety and distress.

   4. An immediate fear effect is influenced by a set of key factors about viewers and the portrayals.

4.1 Viewer Factors

Identification with the target.   The degree of identification with the target is associated with a fear effect. For example, characters who are attractive, who are heroic, or who are perceived as similar to the viewer evoke viewer empathy. When a character with whom viewers empathize is then the target of violence, viewers experience an increased feeling of fear.
   The identification with characters can lead to an enjoyment effect. For example, Tannenbaum and Gaer (1965) found that participants who identified more with the hero felt more stress and benefited more from a happy ending in which their stress was reduced. However, a sad or indeterminate ending increased participants' stress.

Prior real-life experience.   Prior experience with fearful events in real life leads viewers, especially children, to identify more strongly with the characters and events and thereby to involve them more emotionally.

Belief that the depicted violent action could happen to the viewer.   When viewers think there is a good chance that the violence they see could happen to them in real life, they are more likely to experience an immediate fear effect.

Motivations for exposure.   People expose themselves to media violence for many different reasons. Certain reasons for exposure can reduce a fear effect. If people's motivation to view violence is entertainment, they can employ a discounting procedure to lessen the effects of fear.

Level of arousal.   Higher levels of arousal lead to higher feelings of fear.

Ability to use coping strategies.   When people are able to remind themselves that the violence in the media cannot hurt them, they are less likely to experience a fear effect.

Developmental differences.   Children at lower levels of cognitive development are unable to follow plot lines well, so they are more influenced by individual violent episodes, which seem to appear randomly and without motivation.

Ability to perceive the reality of the portrayals.   Children are less able than older viewers to understand the fantasy nature of certain violent portrayals.

4.2 Portrayal Factors

Type of stimulus.   Cantor (1994) says that the fright effect is triggered by three categories of stimuli that usually are found in combination with many portrayals of violence in the media. First is the category of dangers and injuries, stimuli that depict events that threaten great harm. Included in this category are natural disasters, attacks by vicious animals, large-scale accidents, and violent encounters at levels ranging from interpersonal to intergalactic. Second is the category of distortions of natural forms. This category includes familiar organisms that are shown as deformed or unnatural through mutilation, accidents of birth, or conditioning. And third is the category of experience of endangerment and fear by others. This type of stimulus evokes empathy for particular characters, and the viewer then feels the fear that the characters in the narrative are portraying.

Unjustified violence.   When violence is portrayed as unjustified, viewers become more fearful.

Graphicness.   Higher levels of explicitness and graphicness increase viewer fear.

Rewards.   When violence goes unpunished, viewers become more fearful.

Realism.   Live-action violence provokes more intense fear than cartoon violence does. For example, Lazarus et al. found that showing gory accidents to adults aroused them physiologically less when the participants were told that the accidents were fake. This effect has also been found with children. In addition, fear is enhanced when elements in a portrayal resemble characteristics in a person's own life.

5. *Exposure to violence in the media can lead to desensitization.*

In the short term, viewers of repeated violence can show a lack of arousal and emotional response through habituation to the stimuli.

6. An immediate desensitization effect is influenced by a set of key factors about viewers and the portrayals.

Children and adults can become desensitized to violence upon multiple exposures through temporary habituation. But the habituation appears to be relatively short-term.

6.1 Viewer Factors
People who are exposed to larger amounts of television violence are usually found to be more susceptible to immediate desensitization.

6.2 Portrayal Factors
There appear to be two contextual variables that increase the likelihood of a desensitization effect: graphicness and humor.

Graphicness.   Graphicness of violence can lead to immediate desensitization. In experiments in which participants are exposed to graphic violence, initially they have strong physiological responses, but these responses steadily decline during the exposure. This effect has also been shown with children, especially among the heaviest viewers of TV violence.

Humor.   Humor contributes to the desensitization effect.

Long-Term Effects of Violent Content

Long-term effects of exposure to media violence are more difficult to measure than are immediate effects. The primary reason is that long-term effects occur so gradually that by the time an effect is clearly indicated, it is very difficult to trace that effect back to media exposures. It is not possible to argue that any single exposure triggers the effect. Instead, we must argue that the long-term pattern of exposure leads to the effect. A good analogy is the way in which an orthodontist straightens teeth. Orthodontists do not produce an immediate effect by yanking teeth into line in one appointment. Instead, they apply braces that exert very little pressure, but that weak pressure is constant. A person who begins wearing braces might experience sore gums initially, but even then there is no observable change to the alignment of the teeth. This change in alignment cannot be observed even after a week or a month. Only after many months is the change observable.

It is exceedingly difficult for social scientists to make a strong case that the media are responsible for long-term effects. The public, policymakers, and especially critics of social science research want to be persuaded that there is a causal connection. But with a matter of this complexity that requires the long-term evolution of often conflicting influences in the naturalistic environment of viewers' everyday lives, the case for causation cannot be made in any manner stronger than a tentative probabilistic one. Even then, a critic could point to a "third variable" as a potential alternative explanation.

7. Long-term exposure to media violence is related to aggression in a person's life.

Evidence suggests that this effect is causative and cumulative (Eron, 1982). This effect is also reciprocal: Exposure to violence leads to increased aggression, and people with higher levels of aggression usually seek out higher levels of exposure to aggression.

Huesmann, Eron, Guerra, and Crawshaw (1994) conclude from their longitudinal research that viewing violence as a child has a causal effect on patterns of higher aggressive behavior in adults. This finding has appeared in studies in the United States, Australia, Finland, Israel, Poland, the Netherlands, and South Africa. While recognizing that exposure to violence on TV is not the only cause of aggression in viewers, Huesmann et al. conclude that the research suggests that the effect of viewing television violence on aggression "is relatively independent of other likely influences and of a magnitude great enough to account for socially important differences."

The long-term disinhibition effect is influenced by "a variety of environmental, cultural, familial, and cognitive" factors. A major influence on this effect is the degree to which viewers identify with characters who behave violently. For example, Eron found that the learning effect is enhanced when children identify closely with aggressive TV characters. He argued that aggression is a learned behavior, that the continued viewing of television violence is a very likely cause of aggressive behavior, and that this is a long-lasting effect on children.

Once children reach adolescence, their behavioral dispositions and inhibitory controls have become crystallized to the extent that their aggressive habits are very difficult to change, and achievement [has] been found to be related to this effect. Huesmann et al. concluded that low IQ makes the learning of aggressive responses more likely at an early age, and this aggressive behavior makes continued intellectual development more difficult into adulthood.

Evidence also suggests that the effect is contingent on the type of family life. In Japan, for example, Kashiwagi and Munakata (1985) found no correlation between exposure to TV violence and aggressiveness of viewers in real life for children in general. But an effect was observed among young children living in families in which the parents did not get along well.

8. Media violence is related to subsequent violence in society.

When television is introduced into a country, the violence and crime rates in that country, especially crimes of theft, increase. Within a country, the amount of exposure to violence that a demographic group typically experiences in the media is related to the crime rate in neighborhoods where those demographic groups are concentrated. Finally, some evidence suggests that when a high-profile violent act is depicted in the news or in fictional programming, the incidents of criminal aggression increase subsequent to that coverage.

All these findings are subject to the criticism that the researchers have only demonstrated co-occurrence of media violence and real-life aggression. Researchers are asked to identify possible "third variables" that might be alternative explanations for the apparent relationship, and then to show that the relationship exists even after the effects of these third variables are controlled. Although researchers have been testing control variables, critics are still concerned that one or more important variables that have yet to be controlled may account for a possible alternative explanation of the effect.

9. People exposed to many violent portrayals over a long time will come to exaggerate their chances of being victimized.

This generalized fear effect has a great deal of empirical support in the survey literature. But this relationship is generally weak in magnitude, and it is sensitive to third variables in the form of controls and contingencies. The magnitude of the correlation coefficients (r) is usually low, typically in the range of .10 to .30, which means that exposure is able to explain only less than 10% of the variation in the responses of cultivation indicators. . . .

The magnitude of the cultivation effect is relatively weak even by social science standards. Cultivation theorists have defended their findings by saying that even though the effect is small, it is persistent. . . .

This cultivation effect is also remarkably robust. In the relatively large literature on cultivation, almost all the coefficients fall within a consistently narrow band. Not only is this effect remarkable in its consistency, but this consistency becomes truly startling when one realizes the wide variety of measures (of both television exposure and cultivation indicators) that are used in the computations of these coefficients.

10. People exposed to many violent portrayals over a long time will come to be more accepting of violence.

This effect is the gradual desensitizing of viewers to the plight of victims, as well as to violence in general. After repeated exposure to media violence over a long period of time, viewers lose a sense of sympathy with the victims of violence. Viewers also learn that violence is a "normal" part of society, that violence can be used successfully, and that violence is frequently rewarded.

The probability of this long-term effect is increased when people are continually exposed to graphic portrayals of violence. For example, Linz, Donnerstein, and Penrod (1988a) exposed male participants to five slasher movies during a 2-week period. After each film, the male participants exhibited decreasing perceptions that the films were violent or that they were degrading to women.

Conclusion

After more than five decades of research on the effects of exposure to media violence, we can be certain that there are both immediate and long-term effects.
The strongest supported immediate effect is the following: Exposure to violent
portrayals in the media increases subsequent viewer aggression. We also know
that there are other positive and negative immediate effects, such as fear and
desensitization. As for long-term effects, we can conclude that exposure to violence in the media is linked with long-term negative effects of trait aggression,
fearful worldview, and desensitization to violence. The effects process is highly
complex and is influenced by many factors about the viewers, situational cues,
and contextual characteristics of the violent portrayals.

NO

Jib Fowles

Violence Viewing and Science

Examining the Research

For the moment, it is prudent not to question the forces that gave rise to the violence effects literature and have sustained it for five decades nor to tease out the unarticulated assumptions enmeshed in it. Let us begin by taking this extensive literature entirely on its own terms. What will become clear is that although the majority of the published studies on the topic do report antisocial findings, the average extent of the findings is slight—often so much so that the findings are open to several interpretations. . . .

Those who pore over the violence effects literature agree that the case against televised fantasy viciousness is most broadly and clearly made in the large number of laboratory studies, such as those done by Bandura. Overall, these studies offer support for the imitative hypothesis—that younger viewers will exhibit a tendency to act out the aggression seen on the screen. In this group of studies, many find the issue reduced to a pristine clarity, parsed of all needless complexity and obscurity, and answered with sufficient experimental evidence. What is found in this literature can be rightfully generalized to the real world, some believe, to spark a host of inferences and even policies. However, the laboratory is not the real world, and may be so unreal as to discredit the results.

The unnaturalness of laboratory studies is frequently commented on by those who have reservations regarding this research (Buckingham, 1993, p. 11; Gunter & McAteer, 1990, p. 13; Noble, 1975, p. 125), but the extent of the artificiality is rarely defined, leaving those who are unfamiliar with these settings or the nature of these experiments with little sense of what is meant by "unnatural." . . .

[In a behavioral laboratory setting] in a room with other unmet children, the child may be unexpectedly frustrated or angered by the experimenters—shown toys but not allowed to touch them, perhaps, or spoken to brusquely. The child is then instructed to look at a video monitor. It would be highly unlikely for the young subject to sense that this experience in any way resembled television viewing as done at home. . . . Most signally, at home television viewing is an entirely voluntary activity: The child is in front of the set because the child has elected to do so and in most instances has elected the content, and he or she will elect other content if the current material does not satisfy. In the behavioral laboratory, the child is compelled to watch and, worse, compelled to watch material not of the child's choosing and probably not of the child's liking. The essential element of the domestic television-viewing experience, that of pleasure, has been methodically stripped away.

Furthermore, what the child views in a typical laboratory experiment will bear little resemblance to what the child views at home. The footage will comprise only a segment of a program and will feature only aggressive actions. The intermittent relief of commercials or changed channels is missing, as are television stories' routine endings bringing dramatic closure in which everything is set right, with the correct values ascendant.

The child then may be led to another room that resembles the one in the video segment and encouraged to play while being observed. This is the room that, in Bandura et al.'s (1963) famous experiment, contained the Bobo doll identical to the one shown on the screen. Is it any wonder that uneasy children, jockeying for notice and position in a newly convened peer group, having seen a videotaped adult strike the doll without repercussions, and being tacitly encouraged by hovering experimenters who do not seem to disapprove of such action, would also hit the doll? As Noble (1975) wryly asked, "What else can one do to a self-righting bobo doll except hit it?" (p. 133). There are typically only a limited number of options, all behavioral, for the young subjects. Certainly, no researcher is asking them about the meanings they may have taken from the screened violence.

In summary, laboratory experiments on violence viewing are concocted schemes that violate all the essential stipulations of actual viewing in the real world (Cook, Kendzierski, & Thomas, 1983, p. 180) and in doing so have nothing to teach about the television experience (although they may say much about the experimenters). Viewing in the laboratory setting is involuntary, public, choiceless, intense, uncomfortable, and single-minded, whereas actual viewing is voluntary, private, selective, nonchalant, comfortable, and in the context of competing activities. Laboratory research has taken the viewing experience and turned it inside out so that the viewer is no longer in charge. In this manner, experimenters have made a mockery out of the everyday act of television viewing. Distorted to this extent, laboratory viewing can be said to simulate household viewing only if one is determined to believe so....

The inadequacies of laboratory research on television violence effects are apparent in the small body of research on the matter of desensitization or, as Slaby (1994) called it, "the bystander effect." The few attempts to replicate the finding of the four Drabman and Thomas experiments (Drabman & Thomas 1974a, 1974b, 1976; Thomas & Drabman, 1975)—that children exposed to violent footage would take longer to call for the intercession of an adult supervisor —have produced inconsistent results. Horton and Santogrossi (1978) failed to replicate in that the scores for the control group did not differ from the scores for the experimental groups. In addition, Woodfield (1988) did not find statistically significant differences between children exposed to violent content and children exposed to nonviolent content....

A third attempt to replicate by Molitor and Hirsch (1994) did duplicate the original findings, apparently showing that children are more likely to tolerate aggression in others if they are first shown violent footage. An examination of their results, however, does give rise to questions about the rigor of the research. This experiment was set up with the active collaboration of the original researchers and may be less of an attempt to relicate (or not) than an attempt to vindicate. Forty-two Catholic school fourth- and fifth-grade children were assigned to two treatment groups (there was no control group). As for all laboratory experiments, the viewing conditions were so thoroughly alien that results may have been induced by subtle clues from the adult laboratory personnel, especially for obedient children from a parochial school setting. Children shown violent content (a segment from *Karate Kid*) waited longer on average before requesting adult intervention than did children shown nonviolent content (footage from the 1984 Olympic games). Again, this finding could be interpreted as evidence of catharsis: The violent content might have lowered levels of arousal and induced a momentary lassitude. The findings could also have resulted from a sense of ennui: Postexperiment interviews revealed that all the children shown *Karate Kid* had seen the movie before, some as many as 10 times (p. 201). By comparison, the Olympic contests might have seemed more exciting and stimulated swifter reactions to the videotaped misbehavior. The first author was one of the laboratory experimenters; therefore, the specter of expectancy bias cannot be dismissed.

Even if desensitization were to exist as a replicable laboratory finding, the pressing question is whether or not the effect generalizes to the real world. Are there any data in support of the notion that exposure to television violence makes people callous to hostility in everyday life? The evidence on this is scarce and in the negative. Studying many British youngsters, Belson (1978) could find no correlation between levels of television violence viewing and callousness to real violence or inconsiderateness to others (pp. 471–475, 511–516). Research by Hagell and Newburn (1994) can answer the question of whether some youngsters who view heightened hours of television become "desensitized" to violence and embark on criminal lives; unexpectedly, teenage criminals view on average less television, and less violent content, than their law-abiding peers.

Reviewers of the small desensitization literature conclude there is no empirical evidence that anything like the bystander effect actually exists in real life (Gauntlett, 1995, p. 39; Van der Voort, 1986, p. 327; Zillmann, 1991, p. 124). Even George Comstock (1989), normally sympathetic to the violence effects literature, concedes about desensitization studies that "what the research does not demonstrate is any likelihood that media portrayals would affect the response to injury, suffering, or violent death experienced firsthand" (p. 275).

I now turn from the contrivances of laboratory research to the more promising methodology of field experiments, in which typically children in circumstances familiar to them are rated on aggressiveness through the observation of their behavior, exposed to either violent or nonviolent footage, and then unobtrusively rated again. Although this literature holds out the hope of conclusive findings in natural settings, the actual results display a disquietingly

wide range of outcomes. Some of the data gathered indicate, instead of an eleva-
tion in aggressive behaviors, a diminishment in aggressive behaviors following
several weeks of high-violence viewing. Feshbach and Singer (1971) were able to
control the viewing diets of approximately 400 boys in three private boarding
schools and four homes for wayward boys. For 6 weeks, half the boys were randomly assigned to a viewing menu high in violent content, whereas the other
half made their selections from nonaggressive shows. Aggression levels were
determined by trained observers in the weeks before and after the controlled
viewing period. No behavioral differences were reported for the adolescents in
the private schools, but among the poorer, semidelinquent youths, those who
had been watching the more violent shows were calmer than their peers on the
blander viewing diet. The authors concluded that "exposure to aggressive content on television seems to reduce or control the expression of aggression in
aggressive boys from relatively low socioeconomic backgrounds" (p. 145).

Although Wood et al. (1991) report that the eight field experiments they
reviewed did, overall, demonstrate an imitative effect from watching televised
violence, other reviewers of this literature do not concur (Cumberbatch &
Howitt, 1989, p. 41; Freedman, 1988, p. 151). McGuire (1986) comments dis-
missively on "effects that range from the statistically trivial to practically
insubstantial" (p. 213). Most decisively, Gadow and Sprafkin (1989), themselves
contributors to the field experiment research, concluded their thorough review of the 20 studies they located by stating that "the findings from the field
experiments offer little support for the media aggression hypothesis" (p. 404).

In the aftermath of the thoroughgoing artificiality of the laboratory studies, and the equivocation of the field experiment results, the burden of proof
must fall on the third methodology, that of correlational studies. In the search
for statistical correlations (or not) between violence viewing and aggressive or
criminal behavior, this literature contains several studies impressive for their
naturalness and their size. Not all these studies uncover a parallel between,
on the one hand, increased levels of violence viewing and, on the other hand,
increased rates of misbehavior, by whatever measure. For example, for a sample of 2,000 11- to 16-year-olds, Lynn, Hampson, and Agahi (1989) found no
correlation between levels of violence viewing and levels of aggression. Nevertheless, many studies do report a positive correlation. It should be noted that
the magnitude of this co-occurrence is usually quite small, typically producing
a low correlation coefficient of 10 to 20 (Freedman, 1988, p. 153). Using these
correlations (small as they are), the question becomes one of the direction(s)
of possible causality. Does violence viewing lead to subsequent aggression as
is commonly assumed? Could more aggressive children prefer violent content,
perhaps as a vicarious outlet for their hostility? . . . Could any of a host of other
factors give rise to both elevated variables?

Following his substantial correlational study of 1,500 London adolescents,
Belson (1978) highlighted one of his findings—that boys with high levels of exposure to television violence commit 49% more acts of serious violence than
do those who view less—and on this basis issued a call for a reduction in video
carnage (p. 526). Closer examination of his data (pp. 380–382), however, reveals
that the relationship between the two variables is far more irregular than he

suggests in his text. Low viewers of television violence are more aggressive than moderate viewers, whereas very high violence viewers are less aggressive than those in the moderate to high range. Moreover, "acts of serious violence" constituted only one of Belson's four measures of real-life aggression; the other three were "total number of acts of violence," "total number of acts of violence weighted by degree of severity of the act," and "total number of violent acts excluding minor ones." Findings for these three variables cannot be said to substantiate Belson's conclusion. That is, for these measures, the linking of violence viewing to subsequent aggression was negated by reverse correlations —that aggressive youngsters sought out violent content (pp. 389–392). Three of his measures refuted his argument, but Belson chose to emphasize a fourth, itself a demonstrably inconsistent measure....

For the total television effects literature, whatever the methodology, the reviews ... bys Andison (1977), Hearold (1986), and Paik and Comstock (1994) are not the only ones that have been compiled. Other overviews reach very different summary judgments about this body of studies in its entirety. A review published contemporaneously with that of Andison considered the same research projects and derived a different conclusion (Kaplan & Singer, 1976). Kaplan and Singer examined whether the extant literature could support an activation view (that watching televised fantasy violence leads to aggression), a catharsis view (that such viewing leads to a decrease in aggression), or a null view, and they determined that the null position was the most judicious. They wrote, "Our review of the literature strongly suggests that the activating effects of television fantasy violence are marginal at best. The scientific data do not consistently link violent television fantasy programming to violent behavior" (p. 62).

In the same volume in which Susan Hearold's (1986) meta-analysis of violence studies appeared, there was also published a literature review by William McGuire (1986). In contrast to Hearold, it was McGuire's judgment that the evidence of untoward effects from violence viewing was not compelling. Throughout the 1980s, an assured critique of the violence effects literature [was] issued from Jonathan Freedman (1984, 1986, 1988). Freedman cautiously examined the major studies within each of the methodological categories.... Regarding correlational studies, he noted that "not one study produced strong consistent results, and most produced a substantial number of negative findings" (1988, p. 158). Freedman's general conclusion is that "considering all of the research —laboratory, field experiments, and correlational studies—the evidence does not support the idea that viewing television violence causes aggression" (1988, p. 158).

Freedman's dismissal of the violence effects literature is echoed in other literature reviews from British scholars, who may enjoy an objective distance on this largely American research agenda. Cumberbatch and Howitt (1989) discussed the shortcomings of most of the major studies and stated that the research data "are insufficiently robust to allow a firm conclusion about television violence as studied" (p. 51). David Gauntlett (1995) ... analyzed at length most of the consequential studies. He believes that "the work of effects researchers is done" (p. 1). "The search for direct 'effects' of television on behavior is over: Every effort has been made, and they simply cannot be found" (p. 120). Ian Vine (1997) concurs: "Turning now to the systemic evidence from hundreds of published studies of the relationship between viewing violence and subsequent problematic behaviors, the most certain conclusion is that there is *no* genuine consensus of findings" (p. 138)....

Discourse Within Discourse

Opened up for inspection, the sizable violence effects literature turns out to be an uneven discourse—inconsistent, flawed, pocked. This literature proves nothing conclusively, or equivalently, this literature proves everything in that support for any position can be drawn from its corpus. The upshot is that, no matter what some reformers affirm, the campaign against television violence is bereft of any strong, consensual scientific core. Flaws extend through to the very premises of the literature—flaws so total that they may crowd out alternative viewpoints and produce in some a mind-numbed acquiescence. Specifically, the literature's two main subjects—television and the viewer—are assumed to be what they are not.

Viewers are conceived of as feckless and vacuous, like jellyfish in video tides. Viewers have no intentions, no discretion, and no powers of interpretation. Into their minds can be stuffed all matter of content. Most often, the viewer postulated in the effects literature is young, epitomizing immaturity and malleability. This literature, wrote Carmen Luke (1990), "had constructed a set of scientifically validated truths about the child viewer as a behavioral response mechanism, as passive and devoid of cognitive abilities. The possibility that viewers bring anything other than demographic variables to the screen was conceptually excluded" (p. 281). Although there is ample evidence that the young are highly active, selective, and discriminating viewers (Buckingham, 1993; Clifford, Gunter, & McAleer, 1995; Durkin, 1985; Gunter & McAteer, 1990; Hawkins & Pingree, 1986; Hodge & Tripp, 1986; Noble, 1975), this is never the version in the violence effects literature.

Television, on the other hand, is seen as powerful, coercive, and sinister. The medium is not a servant but a tyrant. It rules rather than pleases. It is omnipotent; it cannot be regulated, switched, modulated, interpreted, belittled, welcomed, or ignored. All the things that television is in the real world it is not within the violence effects literature.

The relationship between television content and viewers, as implied in this research, is one way only, as television pounds its insidious message into a hapless audience; there is no conception of a return flow of information by which viewers via ratings indicate preferences for certain content rather than other content. The only result allowable from the viewing experience is that of direct and noxious effects. Other possibilities—of pleasures, relaxation, reinterpretations, therapy, and so on—are not to be considered. The television viewing experience, twisted beyond recognition, is conceived of in pathological terms; in fact, a large amount of the research throughout the past decades has been funded by national mental health budgets.

All these preconceptions apply before a bit of research is actually conducted. The surprising result is not that there have been worrisome findings reported but that, given these presuppositions, the negative findings were not much grander still. . . .

The war on television violence, the larger discourse, has united many allies with otherwise weak ties—prominent authorities and grassroots organizations, liberals and conservatives, and the religious and the secular. We must ask why they put aside their differences, lift their voices together, and join in this particular cause. This implausible alliance constitutes a force field that waxes and wanes throughout the decades, losing strength at one point and gaining it at another; it would seem to have a rhythm all its own. What can account for the regular reoccurrence of this public discourse denouncing television violence?

POSTSCRIPT

Does Television Violence Make Children Significantly More Violent?

Television has been blamed for many ills in our society, and many would argue that it is sometimes used as a scapegoat. But is it really as bad as many say it is? The federal government seems to think so. In 1972 the surgeon general released a report concluding that violence on television tends to make children who view it more aggressive. In 1982 the National Institute of Mental Health issued a report that concurred and pointed to additional harmful effects of television. In 1990 Congress was persuaded that television has a significant impact on children and passed the Children's Television Act, which regulates children's television. It obligates television broadcasters to provide educational programs for children, though it failed to require a minimum amount. In 1992 the American Psychological Association Task Force on Television and Society reached the same conclusion about the harmful effects of television. Most reviews of the literature reach similar conclusions. What is missing from these reports is comparable attention to the benefits of television. It is well known that *Sesame Street* has helped many children learn to read and provides many positive role models. One study showed that children who watched 12 episodes of *Mister Rogers' Neighborhood* became less aggressive, more cooperative, and more willing to share with other children. Little is known, however, about the effects of most programs. So the overall effect of television on children and on all of us remains an open question.

Most of the literature on television violence and aggression argues that these two factors are significantly connected. In addition to the studies mentioned above, see Robert Liebert and Joyce Sprafkin, *The Early Window: Effects of Television on Children and Youth*, 3rd ed. (Pergamon Press, 1988); S. Hearold, "A Synthesis of 1043 Effects of Television on Social Behavior," in G. Comstock ed., *Public Communication and Behavior, vol. 1* (Academic Press, 1986); A. C. Huston et al., *Big World, Small Screen: The Role of Television in American Society* (University of Nebraska Press, 1992); and W. Wood et al., "Effects of Media Violence on Viewers' Aggression in Unconstrained Social Interaction," *Psychological Bulletin* (vol. 109, no. 3, 1991). A fascinating field study on this issue is reported in *The Impact of Television: A Natural Experiment in Three Communities*, Tannis MacBeth, ed. (Academic Press, 1986). The major work arguing against the harmful effects of television is Jib Fowles, *The Case for Television Violence* (Sage, 1999). For a cross-national comparison of television impacts, see L. Rowell Huesmann and Leonard D. Eron, eds., *Television and the Aggressive Child: A Cross-National Comparison* (L. Erlbaum Associates, 1986). For an analysis of the impacts of different types of programming see A. H. Stein and L. K. Friedrich, "Television

Content and Young Children's Behavior," in John P. Murray et al., eds., *Television and Social Behavior, vol. 2, Television and Social Learning* (Government Printing Office, 1972). Another important question is how much violence is actually shown on television. The most extensive analyses of the incidence of violence on television are the annual studies by G. Gerbner and his colleagues from 1967–1989, which show consistently high levels of violence. For example, according to Gerbner, "Violence in Television Drama: Trends and Symbolic Functions," in G. A. Comstock and E. A. Rubenstein, eds., *Television and Social Behavior, vol. 1, Media Content and Control* (United States Government Printing Office, 1972), eight out of every ten plays broadcast in 1969 during the survey period contained some form of violence. For more data on violence on television, see the *National Television Violence Study* (Sage, 1997). For an attack on media violence see David Grossman et al., *Stop Teaching Our Kids to Kill: A Call to Action Against television, Movie, and Video Game Violence* (Crown Publishing Group, 1999). A political analysis of the issue is presented by Cynthia A. Cooper, *Violence in Television: Congressional Inquiry, Public Criticism, and Industry Response: A Policy Analysis* (University Press of America, 1996). See also James T. Hamilton, ed., *Television Violence and Public Policy* (University of Michigan Press, 1998).

ISSUE 3

Is Third World Immigration a Threat to America's Way of Life?

YES: Patrick Buchanan, from "Shields Up!" *The American Enterprise* (March 2002)

NO: Ben Wattenberg, from "Immigration Is Good," *The American Enterprise* (March 2002)

ISSUE SUMMARY

YES: Political analyst Patrick Buchanan asserts that the large influx of legal and illegal immigrants, especially from Mexico, threatens to undermine the cultural foundations of American unity.

NO: Ben Wattenberg, senior fellow at the American Enterprise Institute, argues that the United States needs a constant flow of immigrants to avoid population decline and also to avoid the diminishment of power and influence.

$\mathbf{B}$efore September 11, 2001, many Americans favored the reduction of immigration. After the terrorist attacks on the World Trade Center and the Pentagon by immigrants, some felt even stronger about limiting immigration. But is immigration bad for America, as this sentiment assumes, or does it strengthen America?

Today the number of legal immigrants to America is close to 1 million per year, and illegal ("undocumented") immigrants probably number well over that figure. In terms of numbers, immigration is now comparable to the level it reached during the early years of the twentieth century, when millions of immigrants arrived from southern and eastern Europe. A majority of the new immigrants, however, do not come from Europe but from what has been called the "Third World"—the underdeveloped nations. The largest percentages come from Mexico, the Philippines, Korea, and the islands of the Caribbean, while European immigration has shrunk to about 10 percent. Much of the reason for this shift has to do with changes made in U.S. immigration laws during the 1960s. Decades earlier, in the 1920s, America had narrowed its gate to people from certain regions of the world by imposing quotas designed to preserve the balance of races in America. But in 1965 a series of amendments to the Immigration Act put all the world's people on an equal footing in terms of immigration. The result, wrote journalist Theodore H. White, was "a stampede, almost an invasion" of Third World immigrants. Indeed, the 1965 amendments made it even easier for Third World immigrants to enter the country because the new law gave preference to those with a family member already living in the United States. Since most of the European immigrants who settled in the early part of the century had died off, and since few Europeans had immigrated in more recent years, a greater percentage of family-reuniting immigration came from the Third World.

Immigrants move to the United States for various reasons: to flee tyranny and terrorism, to escape war, or to join relatives who have already settled. Above all, they immigrate because in their eyes America is an island of affluence in a global sea of poverty; here they will earn many times what they could only hope to earn in their native countries. One hotly debated question is, What will these new immigrants do to the United States—or for it?

Part of the debate has to do with bread-and-butter issues: Will new immigrants take jobs away from American workers? Or will they fill jobs that American workers do not want anyway, which will help stimulate the economy? Behind these economic issues is a more profound cultural question: Will these new immigrants add healthy new strains to America's cultural inheritance, broadening and revitalizing it? Or will they cause the country to break up into separate cultural units, destroying America's unity? Of all the questions relating to immigration, this one seems to be the most sensitive.

In 1992 conservative columnist Patrick Buchanan set off a firestorm of controversy when he raised this question: "If we had to take a million immigrants next year, say Zulus or Englishmen, and put them in Virginia, which group would be easier to assimilate and cause less problems for the people of Virginia?" Although Buchanan later explained that his intention was not to denigrate Zulus or any other racial group but to simply talk about assimilation into Anglo-American culture, his remarks were widely characterized as racist and xenophobic (related to a fear of foreigners). Whether or not that characterization is justified, Buchanan's question goes to the heart of the cultural debate over immigration, which is the tension between unity and diversity.

In the selections that follow, Buchanan contends that immigrants are harming the United States both economically and culturally. He argues that the sheer number of immigrants from other cultures threatens to overwhelm traditional safeguards against cultural disintegration and that this foreign influx is changing America from a nation into a collection of separate nationalities. Ben Wattenberg counters that immigration will benefit the United States, especially by making it a "universal" nation that will be better able to compete in a future that is increasingly global.

Patrick Buchanan    **YES**

Shields Up!

In 1821, a newly independent Mexico invited Americans to settle in its northern province of Texas—on two conditions: Americans must embrace Roman Catholicism, and they must swear allegiance to Mexico. Thousands took up the offer. But, in 1835, after the tyrannical General Santa Anna seized power, the Texans, fed up with loyalty oaths and fake conversions, and outnumbering Mexicans in Texas ten to one, rebelled and kicked the tiny Mexican garrison back across the Rio Grande.

Santa Anna led an army north to recapture his lost province. At a mission called the Alamo, he massacred the first rebels who resisted. Then he executed the 400 Texans who surrendered at Goliad. But at San Jacinto, Santa Anna blundered straight into an ambush. His army was butchered, he was captured. The Texans demanded his execution for the Alamo massacre, but Texas army commander Sam Houston had another idea. He made the dictator an offer: his life for Texas. Santa Anna signed. And on his last day in office, Andrew Jackson recognized the independence of the Lone Star Republic.

Eight years later, the U.S. annexed the Texas republic. An enraged Mexico disputed the American claim to all land north of the Rio Grande, so President James Polk sent troops to the north bank of the river. When Mexican soldiers crossed and fired on a U.S. patrol, Congress declared war. By 1848, soldiers with names like Grant, Lee, and McClellan were in the city of Montezuma. A humiliated Mexico was forced to cede all of Texas, the Southwest, and California. The U.S. gave Mexico $15 million to ease the anguish of amputation.

Mexicans seethed with hatred and resentment, and in 1910 the troubles began anew. After a revolution that was anti-church and anti-American, U.S. sailors were roughed up and arrested in Tampico. In 1914, President Woodrow Wilson ordered the occupation of Vera Cruz by U.S. Marines. As Wilson explained to the British ambassador, "I am going to teach the South Americans to elect good men." When the bandit Pancho Villa led a murderous raid into New Mexico in 1916, Wilson sent General Pershing and 10,000 troops to do the tutoring.

From Patrick Buchanan, "Shields Up!" *The American Enterprise* (March 2002). Adapted from *The Death of the West: How Dying Populations and Immigrant Invasions Imperil Our Country and Civilization* (St. Martin's Press, 2002), pp. 123-133, 139, 141-146. Copyright © 2002 by Patrick J. Buchanan. Reprinted by permission of St. Martin's Press, LLC.

Despite FDR's Good Neighbor Policy, President Cárdenas nationalized U.S. oil companies in 1938—an event honored in Mexico to this day. Pemex was born, a state cartel that would collude with OPEC in 1999 to hike up oil prices to $35 a barrel. American consumers, whose tax dollars had supported a $50 billion bailout of a bankrupt Mexico in 1994, got gouged.

⋅⟨◉⟩⋅

The point of this history? Mexico has an historic grievance against the United States that is felt deeply by her people. This is one factor producing deep differences in attitudes toward America between today's immigrants from places like Mexico and the old immigrants from Ireland, Italy, and Eastern Europe. With fully one-fifth of all people of Mexican ancestry now residing in the United States, and up to 1 million more crossing the border every year, we need to understand these differences.

1. The number of people pouring in from Mexico is larger than any wave from any country ever before. In the 1990s alone, the number of people of Mexican heritage living in the U.S. grew by 50 percent to at least 21 million. The Founding Fathers wanted immigrants to spread out among the population to ensure assimilation, but Mexican Americans are highly concentrated in the Southwest.
2. Mexicans are not only from another culture, but of another race. History has taught that different races are far more difficult to assimilate than different cultures. The 60 million Americans who claim German ancestry are fully assimilated, while millions from Africa and Asia are still not full participants in American society.
3. Millions of Mexicans broke the law to get into the United States, and they break the law every day they remain here. Each year, 1.6 million illegal aliens are apprehended, almost all of them at our bleeding southern border.
4. Unlike the immigrants of old, who bade farewell to their native lands forever, millions of Mexicans have no desire to learn English or become U.S. citizens. America is not their home; they are here to earn money. They remain proud Mexicans. Rather than assimilate, they create their own radio and TV stations, newspapers, films, and magazines. They are becoming a nation within a nation.
5. These waves of Mexican immigrants are also arriving in a different America than did the old immigrants. A belief in racial rights and ethnic entitlements has taken root among America's minorities and liberal elites. Today, ethnic enclaves are encouraged and ethnic chauvinism is rife in the barrios. Anyone quoting Calvin Coolidge's declaration that "America must remain American" today would be charged with a hate crime.

Harvard professor Samuel P. Huntington, author of *The Clash of Civilizations*, calls migration "the central issue of our time." He has warned in the pages of this magazine:

> If 1 million Mexican soldiers crossed the border, Americans would treat it as a major threat to their national security.... The invasion of over 1 million Mexican civilians...would be a comparable threat to American societal security, and Americans should react against it with vigor.

Mexican immigration is a challenge to our cultural integrity, our national identity, and potentially to our future as a country. Yet, American leaders are far from reacting "with vigor," even though a Zogby poll found that 72 percent of Americans want less immigration, and a Rasmussen poll in July 2000 found that 89 percent support English as America's official language. The people want action. The elites disagree—and do nothing. Despite our braggadocio about being "the world's only remaining superpower," the U.S. lacks the fortitude to defend its borders and to demand, without apology, that immigrants assimilate to its society.

Perhaps our mutual love of the dollar can bridge the cultural chasm, and we shall all live happily in what Ben Wattenberg calls the First Universal Nation. But Uncle Sam is taking a hellish risk in importing a huge diaspora of tens of millions of people from a nation vastly different from our own. It is not a decision we can ever undo. Our children will live with the consequences. "If assimilation fails," Huntington recognizes, "the United States will become a cleft country with all the potentials for internal strife and disunion that entails." Is that a risk worth taking?

A North American Union of Canada, Mexico, and the United States has been proposed by Mexican President Fox, with a complete opening of borders to the goods and peoples of the three countries. *The Wall Street Journal* is enraptured. But Mexico's per capita GDP of $5,000 is only a fraction of America's —the largest income gap on earth between two adjoining countries. Half of all Mexicans live in poverty, and 18 million people exist on less than $2 a day, while the U.S. minimum wage is headed for $50 a day. Throw open the border, and millions could flood into the United States within months. Is America nothing more than an economic system?

⚜

Our old image is of Mexicans as amiable Catholics with traditional values. There are millions of hard-working, family-oriented Americans of Mexican heritage, who have been quick to answer the call to arms in several of America's wars. And, yes, history has shown that any man or woman, from any country on the planet, can be a good American.

But today's demographic sea change, especially in California, where a fourth of the residents are foreign-born and almost a third are Latino, has spawned a new ethnic chauvinism. When the U.S. soccer team played Mexico in Los Angeles a few years ago, the "Star-Spangled Banner" was jeered, an

American flag was torn down, and the U.S. team and its few fans were showered with beer bottles and garbage.

In the New Mexico legislature in 2001, a resolution was introduced to rename the state "Nuevo Mexico," the name it carried before it became a part of the American Union. When the bill was defeated, sponsor Representative Miguel Garcia suggested to reporters that "covert racism" may have been the cause.

A spirit of separatism, nationalism, and irredentism has come alive in the barrio. Charles Truxillo, a professor of Chicano Studies at the University of New Mexico, says a new "Aztlan," with Los Angeles as its capital, is inevitable. José Angel Gutierrez, a political science professor at the University of Texas at Arlington and director of the UTA Mexican-American Study Center, told a university crowd: "We have an aging white America. They are not making babies. They are dying. The explosion is in our population. They are shitting in their pants in fear! I love it."

More authoritative voices are sounding the same notes. The Mexican consul general José Pescador Osuna remarked in 1998, "Even though I am saying this part serious, part joking, I think we are practicing La Reconquista in California." California legislator Art Torres called Proposition 187, to cut off welfare to illegal aliens, "the last gasp of white America."

"California is going to be a Mexican State. We are going to control all the institutions. If people don't like it, they should leave," exults Mario Obledo, president of the League of United Latin American Citizens, and recipient of the Medal of Freedom from President Clinton. Former Mexican president Ernesto Zedillo told Mexican-Americans in Dallas: "You are Mexicans, Mexicans who live north of the border."

⋅⊙⋅

Why should nationalistic and patriotic Mexicans not dream of a *reconquista*? The Latino student organization known by its Spanish acronym MEChA states, "We declare the independence of our *mestizo* nation. We are a bronze people with a bronze culture. Before the world, before all of North America...we are a nation." MEChA demands U.S. "restitution" for "past economic slavery, political exploitation, ethnic and cultural psychological destruction and denial of civil and human rights."

MEChA, which claims 400 campus chapters across the country, is unabashedly racist and anti-American. Its slogan—Por la Raza todo. Fuera de La Raza nada.—translates as "For our race, everything. For those outside our race, nothing." Yet it now exerts real power in many places. The former chair of its UCLA chapter, Antonio Villaraigosa, came within a whisker of being elected mayor of Los Angeles in 2001.

That Villaraigosa could go through an entire campaign for control of America's second-largest city without having to explain his association with a Chicano version of the white-supremacist Aryan Nation proves that America's major media are morally intimidated by any minority that boasts past victimhood credentials, real or imagined.

Meanwhile, the invasion rolls on. America's once-sleepy 2,000-mile border with Mexico is now the scene of daily confrontations. Even the Mexican army shows its contempt for U.S. law. The State Department reported 55 military incursions in the five years before an incident in 2000 when truckloads of Mexican soldiers barreled through a barbed-wire fence, fired shots, and pursued two mounted officers and a U.S. Border Patrol vehicle. U.S. Border Patrol agents believe that some Mexican army units collaborate with their country's drug cartels.

America has become a spillway for an exploding population that Mexico is unable to employ. Mexico's population is growing by 10 million every decade. Mexican senator Adolfo Zinser conceded that Mexico's "economic policy is dependent on unlimited emigration to the United States." The *Yanqui*-baiting academic and "onetime Communist supporter" Jorge Casteñada warned in *The Atlantic Monthly* six years ago that any American effort to cut back immigration "will make social peace in…Mexico untenable…. Some Americans dislike immigration, but there is very little they can do about it." With Señor Casteñada now President Fox's foreign minister and Senator Zinser his national security adviser, these opinions carry weight.

The Mexican government openly supports illegal entry of its citizens into the United States. An Office for Mexicans Abroad helps Mexicans evade U.S. border guards in the deserts of Arizona and California by providing them with "survival kits" of water, dry meat, granola, Tylenol, anti-diarrhea pills, bandages, and condoms. The kits are distributed in Mexico's poorest towns, along with information on where illegal aliens can get free social services in California. Mexico is aiding and abetting an invasion of the United States, and the U.S. responds with intimidated silence and moral paralysis.

With California the preferred destination for this immigration flood, sociologist William Frey has documented an out-migration of African Americans and Anglo Americans from the Golden State in search of cities and towns like the ones in which they grew up. Other Californians are moving into gated communities. A country that cannot control its borders isn't really a country, Ronald Reagan warned some two decades ago.

Concerns about a radical change in America's ethnic composition have been called un-American. But they are as American as Benjamin Franklin, who once asked, "Why should Pennsylvania, founded by the English, become a Colony of Aliens, who will shortly be so numerous as to Germanize us instead of our Anglifying them?" Franklin would never find out if his fears were justified, because German immigration was halted during the Revolutionary War.

Theodore Roosevelt likewise warned that "The one absolutely certain way of bringing this nation to ruin, of preventing all possibility of its continuing to be a nation at all, would be to permit it to become a tangle of squabbling nationalities."

Immigration is a subject worthy of national debate, yet it has been deemed taboo by the forces of political correctness. Like the Mississippi, with its endless flow of life-giving water, immigration has enriched America throughout history.

But when the Mississippi floods its banks, the devastation can be enormous. What will become of our country if the levees do not hold?

⋅◦❁◦⋅

Harvard economist George Borjas has found no net economic benefit from mass migration from the Third World. In his study, the added costs of schooling, health care, welfare, prisons, plus the added pressure on land, water, and power resources, exceeded the taxes that immigrants pay. The National Bureau of Economic Research put the cost of immigration at $80 billion in 1995. What are the benefits, then, that justify the risk of the balkanization of America?

Today there are 28.4 million foreign-born persons living in the United States. Half are from Latin America and the Caribbean, one fourth from Asia. The rest are from Africa, the Middle East, and Europe. One in every five New Yorkers and Floridians is foreign-born, as is one of every four Californians. As the United States allots most of its immigrant visas to relatives of new arrivals, it is difficult for Europeans to be admitted to the U.S., while entire villages from El Salvador have settled here easily.

- A third of the legal immigrants who come to the United States have not finished high school. Some 22 percent do not even have a ninth-grade education, compared to less than 5 percent of our native-born.
- Of the immigrants who have arrived since 1980, 60 percent still do not earn $20,000 a year.
- Immigrant use of food stamps, Supplemental Security Income, and school lunch programs runs from 50 percent to 100 percent higher than use by the native born.
- By 1991, foreign nationals accounted for 24 percent of all arrests in Los Angeles and 36 percent of all arrests in Miami.
- In 1980, federal and state prisons housed 9,000 criminal aliens. By 1995, this number had soared to 59,000, a figure that does not include aliens who became citizens, or the criminals sent over from Cuba by Fidel Castro in the Mariel boat lift.

Mass emigration from poor Third World countries is good for business, especially businesses that employ large numbers of workers at low wages. But what is good for corporate America is not necessarily good for Middle America. When it comes to open borders, the corporate interest and the national interest do not coincide; they collide. Mass immigration raises more critical issues than jobs or wages—immigration is ultimately about America herself. Is the U.S. government, by deporting scarcely 1 percent of illegal aliens a year, failing in its Constitutional duty to protect the rights of American citizens?

Most of the people who leave their homelands to come to America, whether from Mexico or Mauritania, are good, decent people. They seek the same freedom and opportunities our ancestors sought.

But today's record number of immigrants arriving from cultures that have little in common with our own raises a question: What is a nation? Some define a nation as one people of common ancestry, language, literature, history, heritage, heroes, traditions, customs, mores, and faith who have lived together over time in the same land under the same rulers. Among those who pressed this definition were Secretary of State John Quincy Adams, who laid down these conditions on immigrants: "They must cast off the European skin, never to resume it. They must look forward to their posterity rather than backward to their ancestors." Woodrow Wilson, speaking to newly naturalized Americans in 1915 in Philadelphia, declared: "A man who thinks of himself as belonging to a particular national group in America has yet to become an American."

But Americans no longer agree on values, history, or heroes. What one half of America sees as a glorious past, the other views as shameful and wicked. Columbus, Washington, Jefferson, Jackson, Lincoln, and Lee—all of them heroes of the old America—are under attack. Equality and freedom, those most American of words, today hold different meanings for different Americans.

Nor is a shared belief in democracy sufficient to hold a people together. Half the nation did not even bother to vote in the Presidential election of 2000. Millions cannot name their congressman, senator, or the justices of the Supreme Court. They do not care. We live in the same country, we are governed by the same leaders. But are we one nation and one people?

It is hard to believe that over one million immigrants every year, from every country on earth, a third of them entering illegally, will reforge the bonds of our disuniting nation. John Stuart Mill cautioned that unified public opinion is "necessary to the working of representative government." We are about to find out if he was right.

NO ◂

Ben Wattenberg

Immigration Is Good

Many leading thinkers tell us we are now in a culture clash that will determine the course of history, that today's war is for Western civilization itself. There is a demographic dimension to this "clash of civilizations." While certain of today's demographic signals bode well for America, some look very bad. If we are to assess America's future prospects, we must start by asking, "Who are we?" "Who will we be?" and "How will we relate to the rest of the world?" The answers all involve immigration.

꩜

As data from the 2000 census trickled out, one item hit the headline jackpot. By the year 2050, we were told, America would be "majority non-white." The census count showed more Hispanics in America than had been expected, making them "America's largest minority." When blacks, Asians, and Native Americans are added to the Hispanic total, the "non-white" population emerges as a large minority, on the way to becoming a small majority around the middle of this century.

The first thing worth noting is that these rigid racial definitions are absurd. The whole concept of race as a biological category is becoming ever-more dubious in America. Consider:

Under the Clinton administration's census rules, any American who checks both the black and white boxes on the form inquiring about "race" is counted as black, even if his heritage is, say, one eighth black and seven eighths white. In effect, this enshrines the infamous segregationist view that one drop of black blood makes a person black.

Although most Americans of Hispanic heritage declare themselves "white," they are often inferentially counted as non-white, as in the erroneous *New York Times* headline which recently declared: "Census Confirms Whites Now a Minority" in California.

If those of Hispanic descent, hailing originally from about 40 nations, are counted as a minority, why aren't those of Eastern European descent, coming from about 10 nations, also counted as a minority? (In which case the Eastern European "minority" would be larger than the Hispanic minority.)

But within this jumble of numbers there lies a central truth: America is becoming a *universal nation,* with significant representation of nearly all human hues, creeds, ethnicities, and national ancestries. Continued moderate immigration will make us an even more universal nation as time goes on. And this process may well play a serious role in determining the outcome of the contest of civilizations taking place across the globe.

And current immigration rates are moderate, even though America admitted more legal immigrants from 1991 to 2000 than in any previous decade—between 10 and 11 million. The highest previous decade was 1901–1910, when 8.8 million people arrived. In addition, each decade now, several million illegal immigrants enter the U.S., thanks partly to ease of transportation.

Critics like Pat Buchanan say that absorbing all those immigrants will "swamp" the American culture and bring Third World chaos inside our borders. I disagree. Keep in mind: Those 8.8 million immigrants who arrived in the U.S. between 1901 and 1910 increased the total American population by 1 percent per year. (Our numbers grew from 76 million to 92 million during that decade.) In our most recent decade, on the other hand, the 10 million legal immigrants represented annual growth of only 0.36 percent (as the U.S. went from 249 million to 281 million).

Overall, nearly 15 percent of Americans were foreign-born in 1910. In 1999, our foreign-born were about 10 percent of our total. (In 1970, the foreign-born portion of our population was down to about 5 percent. Most of the rebound resulted from a more liberal immigration law enacted in 1965.) Or look at the "foreign stock" data. These figures combine Americans born in foreign lands and their offspring, even if those children have only one foreign-born parent. Today, America's "foreign stock" amounts to 21 percent of the population and heading up. But in 1910, the comparable figure was 34 percent —one third of the entire country—and the heavens did not collapse.

We can take in more immigrants, if we want to. Should we?

⋅⟨◉⟩⋅

Return to the idea that immigrants could swamp American culture. If that is true, we clearly should not increase our intake. But what if, instead of swamping us, immigration helps us become a stronger nation and a *swamper of others* in the global competition of civilizations?

Immigration is now what keeps America growing. According to the U.N., the typical American woman today bears an average of 1.93 children over the course of her childbearing years. That is mildly below the 2.1 "replacement" rate required to keep a population stable over time, absent immigration. The "medium variant" of the most recent Census Bureau projections posits that the U.S. population will grow from 281 million in 2000 to 397 million in 2050 with expected immigration, but only to 328 million should we choose a path of zero immigration. That is a difference of a population growth of 47 million versus 116 million. (The 47 million rise is due mostly to demographic momentum from previous higher birthrates.) If we have zero immigration with today's low birthrates indefinitely, the American population would eventually begin to *shrink*, albeit slowly.

Is more population good for America? When it comes to potential global power and influence, numbers can matter a great deal. Taxpayers, many of them, pay for a fleet of aircraft carriers. And on the economic side it is better to have a customer boom than a customer bust. (It may well be that Japan's stagnant demography is one cause of its decade-long slump.) The environmental case could be debated all day long, but remember that an immigrant does not add to the global population—he merely moves from one spot on the planet to another.

But will the current crop of immigrants acculturate? Immigrants to America always have. Some critics, like Mr. Buchanan, claim that this time, it's different. Mexicans seem to draw his particular ire, probably because they are currently our largest single source of immigration.

Yet only about a fifth (22 percent) of legal immigrants to America currently come from Mexico. Adding illegal immigrants might boost the figure to 30 percent, but the proportion of Mexican immigrants will almost surely shrink over time. Mexican fertility has diminished from 6.5 children per woman 30 years ago to 2.5 children now, and continues to fall. If high immigration continues under such circumstances, Mexico will run out of Mexicans.

California hosts a wide variety of immigrant groups in addition to Mexicans. And the children and grandchildren of Koreans, Chinese, Khmer, Russian Jews, Iranians, and Thai (to name a few) will speak English, not Spanish. Even among Mexican–Americans, many second- and third-generation offspring speak no Spanish at all, often to the dismay of their elders (a familiar American story).

Michael Barone's book *The New Americans* theorizes that Mexican immigrants are following roughly the same course of earlier Italian and Irish immigrants. Noel Ignatiev's book *How the Irish Became White* notes that it took a hundred years until Irish–Americans (who were routinely characterized as drunken "gorillas") reached full income parity with the rest of America.

California recently repealed its bilingual education programs. Nearly half of Latino voters supported the proposition, even though it was demonized by opponents as being anti-Hispanic. Latina mothers reportedly tell their children, with no intent to disparage the Spanish language, that "Spanish is the language of busboys"—stressing that in America you have to speak English to get ahead.

⌘

The huge immigration wave at the dawn of the twentieth century undeniably brought tumult to America. Many early social scientists promoted theories of what is now called "scientific racism," which "proved" that persons from Northwest Europe were biologically superior. The new immigrants—Jews, Poles, and Italians—were considered racially apart and far down the totem pole of human character and intelligence. Blacks and Asians were hardly worth measuring. The immigration wave sparked a resurgence of the Ku Klux Klan, peaking in the early 1920s. At that time, the biggest KKK state was not in the South; it was Indiana, where Catholics, Jews, and immigrants, as well as blacks, were targets.

Francis Walker, superintendent of the U.S. Bureau of the Census in the late 1890s, and later president of MIT, wrote in 1896 that "the entrance of such vast masses of peasantry degraded below our utmost conceptions is a matter which no intelligent patriot can look upon without the gravest apprehension and alarm. They are beaten men from beaten races. They have none of the ideas and aptitudes such as belong to those who were descended from the tribes that met under the oak trees of old Germany to make laws and choose chiefs." (Sorry, Francis, but Germany did not have a good twentieth century.)

Fast-forward to the present. By high margins, Americans now tell pollsters it was a very good thing that Poles, Italians, and Jews emigrated to America. Once again, it's the *newcomers* who are viewed with suspicion. This time, it's the Mexicans, Filipinos, and people from the Caribbean who make Americans nervous. But such views change over time. The newer immigrant groups are typically more popular now than they were even a decade ago.

Look at the high rates of intermarriage. Most Americans have long since lost their qualms about marriage between people of different European ethnicities. That is spreading across new boundaries. In 1990, 64 percent of Asian Americans married outside their heritage, as did 37 percent of Hispanics. Black-white intermarriage is much lower, but it climbed from 3 percent in 1980 to 9 percent in 1998. (One reason to do away with the race question on the census is that within a few decades we won't be able to know who's what.)

⋯◉⋯

Can the West, led by America, prevail in a world full of sometimes unfriendly neighbors? Substantial numbers of people are necessary (though not sufficient) for a country, or a civilization, to be globally influential. Will America and its Western allies have enough people to keep their ideas and principles alive?

On the surface, it doesn't look good. In 1986, I wrote a book called *The Birth Dearth*. My thesis was that birth rates in developed parts of the world —Europe, North America, Australia, and Japan, nations where liberal Western values are rooted—had sunk so low that there was danger ahead. At that time, women in those modern countries were bearing a lifetime average of 1.83 children, the lowest rate ever absent war, famine, economic depression, or epidemic illness. It was, in fact, 15 percent below the long-term population replacement level.

Those trendlines have now plummeted even further. Today, the fertility rate in the modern countries averages 1.5 children per woman, 28 percent below the replacement level. The European rate, astonishingly, is 1.34 children per woman—radically below replacement level. The Japanese rate is similar. The United States is the exceptional country in the current demographic scene.

As a whole, the nations of the Western world will soon be less populous, and a substantially smaller fraction of the world population. Demographer Samuel Preston estimates that even if European fertility rates jump back to replacement level immediately (which won't happen) the continent would still lose 100 million people by 2060. Should the rate not level off fairly soon, the ramifications are incalculable, or, as the Italian demographer Antonio Golini likes to mutter at demographic meetings, "unsustainable... unsustainable." (Shockingly, the current Italian fertility rate is 1.2 children per woman, and it has been at or below 1.5 for 20 years—a full generation.)

The modern countries of the world, the bearers of Western civilization, made up one third of the global population in 1950, and one fifth in 2000, and are projected to represent one eighth by 2050. If we end up in a world with nine competing civilizations, as Samuel Huntington maintains, this will make it that much harder for Western values to prevail in the cultural and political arenas.

The good news is that fertility rates have also plunged in the less developed countries—from 6 children in 1970 to 2.9 today. By the middle to end of this century, there should be a rough global convergence of fertility rates and population growth.

⚜

Since September 11, immigration has gotten bad press in America. The terrorist villains, indeed, were foreigners. Not only in the U.S. but in many other nations as well, governments are suddenly cracking down on illegal entry. This is understandable for the moment. But an enduring turn away from legal immigration would be foolhardy for America and its allies.

If America doesn't continue to take in immigrants, it won't continue to grow in the long run. If the Europeans and Japanese don't start to accept more immigrants they will evaporate. Who will empty the bedpans in Italy's retirement homes? The only major pool of immigrants available to Western countries hails from the less developed world, i.e., non-white, and non-Western countries.

The West as a whole is in a deep demographic ditch. Accordingly, Western countries should try to make it easier for couples who want to have children. In America, the advent of tax credits for children (which went from zero to $1,000 per child per year over the last decade) is a small step in the direction of fertility reflation. Some European nations are enacting similar pro-natal policies. But their fertility rates are so low, and their economies so constrained, that any such actions can only be of limited help.

That leaves immigration. I suggest America should make immigration safer (by more carefully investigating new entrants), but not cut it back. It may even be wise to make a small increase in our current immigration rate. America needs to keep growing, and we can fruitfully use both high- and low-skill immigrants. Pluralism works here, as it does in Canada and Australia.

Can pluralism work in Europe? I don't know, and neither do the Europeans. They hate the idea, but they will depopulate if they don't embrace pluralism, via immigration. Perhaps our example can help Europeans see that pluralism might work in the admittedly more complex European context. Japan is probably a hopeless case; perhaps the Japanese should just change the name of their country to Dwindle.

Our non-pluralist Western allies will likely diminish in population, relative power, and influence during this century. They will become much grayer. Nevertheless, by 2050 there will still be 750 million of them left, so the U.S.

needs to keep the Western alliance strong. For all our bickering, let us not forget that the European story in the second half of the twentieth century was a wonderful one; Western Europeans stopped killing each other. Now they are joining hands politically. The next big prize may be Russia. If the Russians choose our path, we will see what Tocqueville saw: that America and Russia are natural allies.

We must enlist other allies as well. America and India, for instance, are logical partners—pluralist, large, English-speaking, and democratic. We must tell our story. And our immigrants, who come to our land by choice, are our best salesmen. We should extend our radio services to the Islamic world, as we have to the unliberated nations of Asia through Radio Free Asia. The people at the microphones will be U.S. immigrants.

We can lose the contest of civilizations if the developing countries don't evolve toward Western values. One of the best forms of "public diplomacy" is immigration. New immigrants send money home, bypassing corrupt governments—the best kind of foreign aid there is. They go back home to visit and tell their families and friends in the motherland that American modernism, while not perfect, ain't half-bad. Some return home permanently, but they bring with them Western expectations of open government, economic efficiency, and personal liberty. They know that Westernism need not be restricted to the West, and they often have an influence on local politics when they return to their home countries.

Still, because of Europe and Japan, the demographic slide of Western civilization will continue. And so, America must be prepared to go it alone. If we keep admitting immigrants at our current levels there will be almost 400 million Americans by 2050. That can keep us strong enough to defend and perhaps extend our views and values. And the civilization we will be advancing may not just be Western, but even more universal: American.

POSTSCRIPT

Is Third World Immigration a Threat to America's Way of Life?

F ormer representative Silvio Conte (R-Massachusetts) said at a citizenship ceremony, "You can go to France, but you will never be a Frenchman. You can go to Germany but you will never be a German. Today you are all Americans, and that is why this is the greatest country on the face of the earth." At one time America's open door to immigrants was one of the prides of America. For some people, like Wattenberg, it still is. He thinks that an integrated, multicultural society is a culturally rich society and that immigration is making America stronger. Many people disagree because they fear the consequences of today's immigration. Buchanan worries that, although the new immigrants may want to assimilate, they have reached such a critical mass that the United States has lost the ability to absorb everyone into its own, slowly dissipating culture. The result is that immigrants are encouraged to maintain and promote the cultures that they arrive with, which further dilutes the original culture of America. The issue is based on what one thinks will happen as America becomes more diverse. Buchanan sees America as coming apart and Wattenberg sees America as leading the world.

For a fascinating study of the roots of American traditional culture, see David Hackett Fischer, *Albion's Seed: Four British Folkways in America* (Oxford University Press, 1989). Stanley Lieberson and Mary C. Waters, in *From Many Strands* (Russell Sage Foundation, 1988), argue that ethnic groups with European origins are assimilating, marrying outside their groups, and losing their ethnic identities. Richard D. Alba's study "Assimilation's Quiet Tide," *The Public Interest* (Spring 1995) confirms these findings.

Several major works debate whether or not immigrants, on average, economically benefit America and can assimilate. Sources that argue that immigrants largely benefit America include Julian L. Simon, *The Economic Consequences of Immigration,* 2d ed. (University of Michigan Press, 1999) and *Immigration: The Demographic and Economic Facts* (Cato Institute, 1995).

Sources that argue that immigrants have more negative than positive impacts include George Borjas, *Heaven's Door: Immigration Policy and the American Economy* (Princeton University Press, 1999); Roy Beck, *The Case Against Immigration* (W. W. Norton, 1996); and Patrick Buchanan, *The Death of the West: How Dying Populations and Immigrant Invasions Imperil Our Country and Civilization* (Thomas Dunne Books, 2002).

American Men's Studies Association

The American Men's Studies Association is a not-for-profit professional organization of scholars, therapists, and others interested in the exploration of masculinity in modern society.

http://mensstudies.org

American Studies Web

The American Studies Web site is an eclectic site that provides links to a wealth of resources on the Internet related to gender studies.

http://www.georgetown.edu/crossroads/asw/

Feminist Majority Foundation

The Feminist Majority Foundation Web site provides affirmative action links, resources from women's professional organizations, information for empowering women in business, sexual harassment information, and much more.

http://www.feminist.org/gateway/sd_exec2.html

GLAAD: Gay and Lesbian Alliance Against Defamation

The Gay and Lesbian Alliance Against Defamation (GLAAD), formed in New York in 1985, seeks to improve the public's attitudes toward homosexuality and to put an end to discrimination against lesbians and gay men.

http://www.glaad.org/org.index.html

International Lesbian and Gay Association

The resources on the International Lesbian and Gay Association Web site are provided by a worldwide network of lesbian, gay, bisexual, and transgendered groups.

http://www.ilga.org

SocioSite: Feminism and Women's Issues

The Feminism and Women's Issues SocioSite provides insights into a number of issues that affect family relationships. It covers wide-ranging issues regarding women and men, family and children, and much more.

http://www.pscw.uva.nl/sociosite/TOPICS/Women.html

PART 2

Sex Roles, Gender, and the Family

*T*he modern feminist movement has advanced the causes of women to the point where there are now more women in the workforce in the United States than ever before. Professions and trades that were traditionally regarded as the provinces of men have opened up to women, and women now have easier access to the education and training necessary to excel in these new areas. But what is happening to sex roles, and what are the effects of changing sex roles? How has stress caused by current sex roles, male-female communication difficulties, the demand for the right to same-sex marriages, and the deterioration of the traditional family structure affected men and women? The issues in this part address these sorts of questions.

- Do the New Sex Roles Burden Women More Than Men?

- Are Communication Problems Between Men and Women Largely Due to Radically Different Conversation Styles?

- Should Same-Sex Marriages Be Legally Recognized?

- Is the Decline of the Traditional Family a National Crisis?

ISSUE 4

Do the New Sex Roles Burden Women More Than Men?

YES: Jeff Grabmeier, from "The Burden Women Bear: Why They Suffer More Distress Than Men," *USA Today Magazine* (July 1995)

NO: Susan Faludi, from *Stiffed: The Betrayal of the American Man* (William Morrow and Company, 1999)

ISSUE SUMMARY

YES: Editor and author Jeff Grabmeier presents evidence showing that women experience more stress than men and then analyzes why.

NO: Author Susan Faludi argues that men have been socialized into a sex role that cannot be successfully fulfilled due to current conditions.

The publication of Betty Friedan's *The Feminine Mystique* (W. W. Norton, 1963) is generally thought of as launching the modern women's movement, and since that time significant changes have occurred in American society. Occupations and professions, schools, clubs, associations, and governmental positions that were by tradition or law previously reserved for men only are now open to women. Women are found in increasing numbers among lawyers, judges, physicians, and elected officials. In 1981 President Ronald Reagan appointed the first woman, Sandra Day O'Connor, to the Supreme Court. In 1983 the first American woman astronaut, Sally Ride, was included in the crew of a space shuttle, and women have been on more recent space shuttle missions, as well. The service academies have accepted women since 1976, and women in the military participated in the U.S. invasion of Panama in December 1989 and in the Persian Gulf War in 1990. Elizabeth Watson became the first woman to head a big-city police department when the mayor of Houston appointed her as chief of police in January 1990.

These sorts of changes—quantifiable and highly publicized—may signal a change in women's roles. Women now engage in occupations that were previously exclusive to men, and can pursue the necessary training and education required to do so. Paula Span, in "It's a Girl's World," *The Washington Post Magazine* (June 22, 1997), quotes her daughter as saying, "Most of my girlfriends and I feel like we could do anything.... Being female isn't a restriction." Now most women of working age are either in school or the labor force, even those with children. As a result, the problem for women today has less to do with occupational exclusion than with the stress of inclusion.

But what about men today? To the extent that sex bias remains they are the advantaged sex. However, do they really have it made? Some would argue that they do not. Men may experience less stress as Jeff Grabmeier, author of the first selection, asserts, but they die younger. In fact, between the ages of 15 and 24, when sex roles take full hold, the death rate for men is over three times the death rate for women. Furthermore, if death by heart disease is likely to be related to stress, it should be noted that men die of heart disease at almost twice the age-adjusted death rate as women. One reason may be that men who work full time on average spend substantially more time working and commuting than women who work full time.

Neither stress data nor death-rate data can tell us the extent that sex roles affect the differential rates. Biological differences also play a role and the extent of this role is not clear. At this point, therefore, the discussion should focus on what burdens sex roles create for women and men. Current sex roles for women give them primary responsibility for household and child care so they end up with a second work shift if they choose to have a career as well as a family. According to Grabmeier, women are not too happy about this. He states that, based on his interviews with women, "well over half the women expressed anger, hostility, and resentment toward their husbands or partners for failing to share child care and household responsibilities." The aggravation is due in large part to differential sex role changes. Women's roles have changed due to the women's movement, the increasing financial need for two paychecks, and the opportunities of an expanding white-collar economy. However, the sex roles for men have not changed very much. Men's sex role problem can be seen as two-sided. One side of the problem is that men are still socialized to conform to masculine sex roles but are not given real opportunities to fulfill these roles in today's society. This is why Susan Faludi, in her selection, states that men are made to feel like failures. The other side of the problem is that men experience expectations from women to be more feminine and to increasingly perform what many men think of as women's tasks. On the one side they are failures in their own eyes and on the other side they are failures in women's eyes.

In the following selection, Grabmeier argues that women suffer a greater burden than men and uses data on stress to support his conclusions. He discusses the biological reasons for this, but emphasizes that roles for women have changed dramatically without a commensurate change in the traditional dominant roles for men. Women often blame themselves for their problems, which worsens them, according to Grabmeier. Faludi counters that men, particularly working-class men, are frustrated by a world for which their socialization has not prepared them. In combination with mortality and disease statistics, Faludi's analysis supports the conclusion that men are more burdened by modern sex roles than women.

Jeff Grabmeier

YES

The Burden Women Bear: Why They Suffer More Distress Than Men

Who suffers more in life, men or women? This was a great issue to bring up around the office coffee machine or at cocktail parties because it not only made for lively conversation, it also was one of those questions that couldn't be settled simply by calling the reference desk at the local library.

Recently, though, evidence is growing that women, in fact, do suffer more than men. Blame it on biology, the stress of combining parenthood and career, living in a male-centered society, or all of the above. A study at Ohio State University by sociologists John Mirowsky and Catherine Ross shows that females experience symptoms of psychological distress—including sadness, anger, anxiety, malaise, and physical aches and pains—about 30% more often than males. Their work complements earlier research that found women about twice as likely as men to experience major clinical depression.

"Women genuinely suffered more distress than men by all the measures in our study," Mirowsky indicates. He and Ross interviewed 1,282 women and 749 men aged 18 to 90 and asked them on how many of the last seven days they had experienced various emotions. In each case, women reported more days with symptoms of distress than men. Don't assume women feel more of everything than men, however. The female participants experienced happiness 3.3% less often than the males.

In the past, assertions about women's surplus of suffering have been dismissed because they were thought to be more emotional than men. In other words, females simply complained more than males, who hid their pain behind a stoic facade. Mirowsky and Ross examined that possibility and found that women did indeed express their emotions more than men. About 68% of the males in the study agreed or strongly agreed that they kept their emotions to themselves, compared to 50% of the females who responded similarly. Even after the researchers took these differences into account, women still showed more signs of distress than men. "Women do express their emotions more, but that doesn't mean they aren't truly more depressed," Mirowsky maintains.

There is no simple explanation for why women suffer more distress than men. Most experts believe a combination of factors, including biological differences, puts females at greater risk for some psychological troubles. Scientists

From Jeff Grabmeier, "The Burden Women Bear: Why They Suffer More Distress Than Men," *USA Today Magazine*, vol. 124, no. 2602 (July 1995). Copyright © 1995 by The Society for the Advancement of Education, Inc. Reprinted by permission of *USA Today Magazine*.

have discovered that imbalances of certain neurotransmitters in the brain—particularly norepinepherine and serotonin—are related to depression. Low levels of serotonin may lead to depression, anxiety, anger, eating disorders, and impulsive behavior, points out Henry Nasrallah, chairperson of psychiatry. "We don't know why, but women may have less stable brain systems for regulating these neurotransmitters. Female hormones are believed to play a role in the regulation of neurotransmitters that affect mood and that may explain why females are more likely to experience clinical depression. Fluctuations in hormone levels, for example, have been associated with the well-known premenstrual syndrome, which afflicts some women."

Just how much of a role biology plays in women's distress remains unclear. "There is usually an interplay between biological, psychological, and social factors," says Nasrallah. "Clearly there are biological factors that contribute a great deal to behavior and mood in men and women."

Blaming biology for distress can be a two-edged sword. It can help to mobilize medical resources and make physicians take such problems seriously, but also may take the focus off social factors that contribute to the situation.

This two-edged sword is painfully apparent for those with a uniquely female form of distress—postpartum depression. Women suffering from this syndrome have formed national interest groups seeking, in part, to get more medical attention for their problems, notes Verta Taylor, a professor of sociology who has studied their cause. However, these women walk a fine line between looking for medical solutions and pushing for their partners to provide more help in caring for children.

For a book she is writing, Taylor interviewed more than 100 women who said they suffered emotional problems—ranging from "baby blues" to clinical depression—after the birth or adoption of a baby. This illness, which afflicts more than three-quarters of new mothers, may last weeks or, as one woman told Taylor, it "didn't end until [my son] left home for college."

Taylor indicates that the question of whether postpartum depression has biological roots is a hotly debated topic. She found that women physicians who suffered from it were more likely than male doctors to believe that the disorder is the result of a deficiency in the hormone progesterone. Accordingly, women physicians were more likely to advocate progesterone therapy to treat the biochemical basis of the illness.

Nasrallah says most medical professionals believe that postpartum depression is an illness with biochemical causes that must be treated with antidepressants. However, the less serious postpartum blues usually can be treated with rest, family support, and reassurance.

Even women who believe their postpartum depression has a biochemical aspect don't blame their condition simply on hormonal imbalances, Taylor points out. They echo the grievances of many working mothers—with and without postpartum depression—who complain of not getting enough support from husbands and partners. "A majority of the women I interviewed saw their excessive worry and irritability as the inevitable result of trying to combine and balance the demands of a 'second shift' of child care, housework, and a marriage with a paid job. Well over half the women expressed anger, hostility, and resentment toward their husbands or partners for failing to share child care and household responsibilities."

The problem, according to history professor Susan Hartmann, is that women now have more opportunities outside the home, but still do most of the household chores. "The old norms haven't changed that much. Women are still expected to take care of the home and children. But a majority of women also have taken on the responsibility of work. They've added new roles and responsibilities without significant changes in their old ones."

Although men sometimes may help out, there usually isn't a true sharing of household and child care responsibilities in American society. When men care for their children, for instance, it often is seen as "babysitting." When women do it, that simply is part of being a mother.

There is ample evidence that women still shoulder most of the responsibility of caring for kids, housework, and day-to-day chores. Margaret Mietus Sanik, an associate professor of family resource management, conducts studies of time use in families. She has found that, in couples with a new child, mothers spend about 4.6 hours per day in infant care, compared to about 1.3 for fathers. New mothers also lose more of their leisure time—about 3.8 hours a day—than their husbands, who give up approximately one hour. The result is that women often feel overworked and underappreciated.

A recent U.S. government survey of 250,000 working women found that stress was the most mentioned problem by respondents. The number-one issue females would like to talk about with Pres. Clinton is their inability to balance work and family, the survey found.

With the often overwhelming demands of juggling a career and family, it is no wonder that employed women suffer more depression than men. That doesn't mean that full-time homemakers have it better; in fact, research suggests they actually have higher levels of psychological distress than employed women. While working women can derive satisfaction from multiple roles at home and in the workplace, stay-at-home moms have only their homemaker role, Mirowsky indicates. They may feel isolated and out of step with the rest of society because parenting apparently is not highly valued in American culture.

Moreover, whether they want to work or not, housewives are economically dependent on their husbands, which is a powerful cause of distress. "In our culture, economic independence gives you status in the eyes of the community and a sense of security and self-worth," Mirowsky explains. "Housewives don't have that economic security. What we have found is that women are psychologically better off if they are employed."

In her studies of postpartum depression, Taylor has found that society's expectations of mothers also can put a suffocating burden on women. It is expected that a new mother will be happy, overjoyed even, and more than willing to put her baby's needs above her own. "But motherhood is often difficult, and women can find that their feelings are out of sync with societal expectations. They may feel as though their negative feelings are proof that they're not being a good mother, which compounds their feelings of distress, depression, anger, anxiety, and guilt."

If the stress of work and caring for children contributes to women's higher levels of distress, what about single, childless females? According to Mirowsky, they show less evidence of distress than other women, but more than men. That is because females face more than just role overload, she maintains. Women in the U.S. are paid about 75% of what men receive, are more likely to live in poverty, face a greater threat of physical and sexual abuse, and live in a culture that often promotes near-unattainable ideals for physical perfection. "Women just face a lot of problems and obstacles that men don't have to deal with. I'm surprised women don't feel more distress."

Psychological Strategies

Adding to the situation is the fact that women tend to use psychological strategies that amplify and prolong their distress. Psychologists have found that, when females are faced with problems, they are more likely than males to think continually about troubling issues. They also are more apt to blame themselves. The result is that women can be caught in a cycle of worry and depression instead of working to find a way out. Men, on the other hand, tend to take action in dealing with problems. They are more likely to place the blame elsewhere and find activities such as sports or hobbies to distract them.

All of this ruminating about their troubles leads women to more than just depression. One of the key findings about women's distress is the amount of anger they feel, Mirowsky and Ross discovered. The stereotype has been that women get depressed and men get angry, but their study revealed that the female subjects actually experienced anger about 29% more often than the males. "Anger is depression's companion—not its substitute," Mirowsky notes.

The anger gap actually was larger than the difference in depression. The researchers found that women were more angry and anxious than men who were equally depressed. Females in the study also were more likely to express their anger through yelling at others. "We thought this was particularly interesting because yelling is crossing the line between an emotion and an action," Mirowsky says. "Our interpretation is that women are yelling at their children more often than their husbands do."

While women are at home getting angry and depressed, maybe men are handling their distress another way—by drinking alcohol and taking drugs. Research has shown that males are more likely than females to abuse alcohol and drugs, but Mirowsky doesn't think that explains the distress gap. "In one sense, if alcohol and drugs really did help eliminate distress, then our findings would make sense—it would explain why men feel less distressed than women. In actuality, there's no evidence that alcohol or drugs help people, or men in particular, feel better." One study, for instance, found that alcoholism and drug abuse increase the odds of a major depressive episode more than fourfold. "Alcohol and drug use probably produces more distress than it prevents," Mirowsky claims.

No matter how you look at the evidence, he suggests, it seems clear that women really do suffer more psychological distress. Is there anything that can be done about it? There is not much females can change concerning their biology, although serious depression often can be treated with anti-depressant drugs. Many of the problems require fundamental changes in how government, business, and society treat women. Taylor says they want their concerns taken seriously. Because females traditionally have been seen as emotional, their problems haven't been given much weight. "Whatever causes higher rates of distress in women, it's not treated. If women feel it and suffer from it, then it should be seen as real."

One thing they are doing is organizing to make their voices heard. Some groups, such as the National Organization for Women, are well-known for their efforts to improve the lot of females. Taylor notes that women with postpartum depression have organized two national groups to present their issues to the public and the medical community. Their efforts, while specifically for the benefit of those with postpartum depression, really involve issues of concern to many females, she states. "The leaders of these groups argue all the time in their speeches that we need men to get more involved in parenting. Women are under this tremendous strain because they are almost solely responsible for parenting. Men have to assume a larger role, and that's a societal problem that requires changing how we structure gender roles."

Working women face special problems that need to be addressed by business and government, experts say. A recent survey by the U.S. government of 250,000 working women has put the spotlight on some of the issues women face, such as lack of adequate child care and unequal pay with men. "I think that more and more businesses are trying to recognize the needs of women in the workforce, yet the progress has been slow," Hartmann points out. "The situation for working women may get incrementally better, but I don't see any major improvements soon."

Social change is always slow and uneven, Mirowsky feels, but it is necessary if the distress gap is to be eased. "People may debate whether there's a difference in the quality of life for men and women in the United States. The evidence, however, suggests the quality of life is poorer for many women, and it's something that needs to be addressed."

NO

Susan Faludi

Stiffed: The Betrayal of the American Man

The American Century Versus the Century of the Common Man

... [A]s the nation wobbled toward the millennium, its pulse-takers seemed to agree that a domestic apocalypse was under way: American manhood was under siege....

If so many concurred in the existence of a male crisis, consensus collapsed as soon as anyone asked the question: Why? Not that there was a shortage of responses. Everyone proposed a favorite whipping boy—or, more often, whipping girl—and blame-seekers on all sides went after their selected culprits with righteous and bitter relish.

As a feminist and a journalist, I began investigating this crisis where you might expect a feminist journalist to begin: at the weekly meetings of a domestic-violence group.... What did I expect to divine about the broader male condition by monitoring a weekly counseling session for batterers?... I can see now that I was operating from an assumption both underexamined and dubious: that the male crisis in America was caused by something men were *doing* unrelated to something being done to them, and that its cure was surely to be found in figuring out how to get men to *stop* whatever it was. I had my own favorite whipping boy, suspecting that the crisis of masculinity was caused by masculinity on the rampage. If male violence was the quintessential expression of masculinity run amok, out of control and trying to control everything in its path, then a domestic-violence therapy group must be at the very heart of this particular darkness.

... The two counselors who ran the group, which was called Alternatives to Violence, worked hard to make "control" a central issue. Each new member would be asked to describe to the group what he had done to a woman, a request that was generally met with sullen reluctance, vague references to "the incident," and invariably the disclaimer "I was out of control." The counselors would then expend much energy showing him how he had, in fact, been in control the entire time. He had chosen his fists, not a knife; he had hit her in the stomach, not the face; he had stopped before landing a permanently injurious blow, and so forth. One session was devoted to reviewing "The Power and

From Susan Faludi, *Stiffed: The Betrayal of the American Man* (William Morrow and Company, 1999). Copyright © 1999 by Susan Faludi. Reprinted by permission of HarperCollins Publishers, Inc. Notes omitted.

71

Control Wheel," a mimeographed chart that enumerated the myriad ways men could victimize their mates. No doubt the moment of physical contact for these men had grown out of a desire for supreme control fueled by a need to dominate. I cannot conceive of a circumstance that would exonerate such violence. By making the abusive spouse take responsibility for his actions, the counselors were pursuing a worthy goal. But the logic behind the violence still remained elusive.

A serviceman who had turned to nightclub bouncer jobs and pastry catering after his military base shut down seemed to confirm the counselors' position one evening shortly before his "graduation" from the group. "I denied it before," he said of the night he pummeled his girlfriend, who had also worked on the base. As he spoke he studied his massive, callused hands, lying uselessly on his lap. "I thought I'd blacked out. But looking back at that night when I beat her with an open hand, I didn't black out. I was feeling good. I was in power, I was strong, I was in control. I felt like a *man*." But what struck me most strongly was what he said next: that moment of control had been the only one in his recent life. "That feeling of power," he said, "didn't last long. Only until they put the cuffs on. Then I was feeling again like I was no man at all."

He was typical in this regard. The men I got to know in the group had without exception lost their compass in the world. They had lost or were losing jobs, homes, cars, families. They had been labeled outlaws but felt like castoffs. Their strongest desire was to be dutiful and to belong, to adhere with precision to the roles society had set out for them as men. In this respect, they were prototypical modern wife beaters, who, demographic research suggests, are commonly ill equipped to fulfill the requirements of expected stereotypical sex roles, men who are socially isolated, afflicted with a sense of ineffectuality, and have nothing but the gender rule book to fall back on....

There was something almost absurd about these men struggling, week after week, to recognize themselves as dominators when they were so clearly dominated, done in by the world. "That 'wheel' is misnamed," a laid-off engineer ruefully told the counselors. "It should be called the Powerlessness and Out-of-Control Wheel." The men had probably felt in control when they beat their wives, but their everyday experience was of feeling controlled—a feeling they had no way of expressing because to reveal it was less than masculine, would make each of them, in fact, "no man at all." For such men, the desire to be in charge was what they felt they must do to survive in a nation that *expected* them to dominate....

More than a quarter century ago, women began to suspect in their own lives "a problem with no name." Even the most fortunate woman in postwar, suburban America, maneuvering her gleaming Hoovermatic across an expansive rec room, sensed that she'd been had. Eventually, this suspicion would be expressed in books—most notably Betty Friedan's *The Feminine Mystique*—that traced this uneasiness back to its source: the cultural forces of the mass media, advertising, pop psychology, and all the other "helpful" advice industries. Women began to free themselves from the box in which they were trapped by feeling their way along its contours, figuring out how it had been constructed around them, how it was shaped and how it shaped them, how their reflections on its mirrored walls distorted who they were or might be. Women were able to take action, paradoxically, by understanding how they were acted upon. "Women have been largely man-made," Eva Figes wrote in 1970 in *Patriarchal Attitudes*. What had been made by others women themselves could unmake. Once their problems could be traced to external forces generated by a male society and culture, they could see them more clearly and so challenge them.

Men feel the contours of a box, too, but they are told that box is of their own manufacture, designed to their specifications. Who are they to complain? The box is there to showcase the man, not to confine him. After all, didn't he build it—and can't he destroy it if he pleases, if he is a *man*? For men to say they feel boxed in is regarded not as laudable political protest but as childish and indecent whining. How dare the kings complain about their castles?

Women's basic grievances are seen as essentially reasonable; even the most blustery antifeminist these days is quick to say that, of course, he favors equal pay and equal opportunity. What women are challenging is something that everyone can see. Men's grievances, by contrast, seem hyperbolic, almost hysterical; so many men seem to be doing battle with phantoms and witches that exist only in their own overheated imaginations. Women see men as guarding the fort, so they don't see how the culture of the fort shapes men. Men don't see how they are influenced by the culture either; in fact, they prefer not to. If they did, they would have to let go of the illusion of control....

The very paradigm of modern masculinity—that it is all about being the master of your universe—prevents men from thinking their way out of their dilemma, from taking active political steps to resolve their crisis. If they are the makers of history, not the subjects of historical forces, then how can they rise up?

... Yet clearly masculinity is shaped by society. Anyone wondering how mutable it is need only look at how differently it is expressed under the Taliban in Kabul or on the streets of Paris. Witness men walking with their arms wrapped around each other in Istanbul or observe the Mexican immigrant to Los Angeles whose manhood is so linked to supporting a family that any job, even a busboy's, holds a masculine pride. As anthropologist David D. Gilmore demonstrated in *Manhood in the Making,* his comprehensive cross-cultural survey of masculine ideals, manliness has been expressed as laboring-class loyalty in Spain, as diligence and discipline in Japan, as dependence on life outside the home in the company of men in Cyprus, as gift-giving among Sikhs, as the restraint of temper and the expression of "creative energy" among the Gisu of Uganda, and as entirely without significance to the Tahitians. "Manliness is a symbolic script," Gilmore concluded, "a cultural construct, endlessly variable and not always necessary."

It should be self-evident that ideas of manhood vary and are contingent on the times and the culture. Despite that, contemporary discussion about what bedevils men fixes almost exclusively on the psychological and the biological....

Cause Without a Rebel

A question that has plagued feminists like myself is the nature of male resistance to female change. Why are so many men so disturbed by the prospect of women's independence? Why do so many men seem to begrudge it, resent it, fear it, fight it with an unholy passion? The question launched my inquiry. But in the end, much to my surprise, it was not the question that most compelled me. It is not the question, finally, that drives this [selection]. Because the more I explored the predicament of postwar men, the more familiar it seemed to me. The more I consider what men have lost—a useful role in public life, a way of earning a decent and reliable living, appreciation in the home, respectful treatment in the culture—the more it seems that men of the late twentieth century are falling into a status oddly similar to that of women at mid-century. The fifties housewife, stripped of her connections to a wider world and invited to fill the void with shopping and the ornamental display of her ultrafeminity, could be said to have morphed into the nineties man, stripped of his connections to a wider world and invited to fill the void with consumption and a gym-bred display of his ultra-masculinity. The empty compensations of a "feminine mystique" are transforming into the empty compensations of a masculine mystique; with a gentlemen's cigar club no more satisfying than a ladies' bake-off, the Nike Air Jordan no more meaningful than the Dior New Look.

And so my question changed. Instead of wondering why men resist women's struggle for a freer and healthier life, I began to wonder why men refrain from engaging in their own struggle. Why, despite a crescendo of random tantrums, have they offered no methodical, reasoned response to their predicament? Given the untenable and insulting nature of the demands placed on men to prove themselves in our culture, why don't men revolt?

Like many women, I was drawn to feminism out of a desire to challenge the silence of my sex. It has come to seem to me that, under all the rantings of men seeking to drown out the female voice, theirs is as resounding a silence. Why haven't men responded to the series of betrayals in their own lives—to the failures of their fathers to make good on their promises—with something co-equal to feminism? When the frontier that their fathers offered them proved to be a wasteland, when the enemy their fathers sent them to crush turned out often to be women and children trembling in thatched huts, when the institutions their fathers claimed would buoy them downsized them, when the women their fathers said wanted their support got their own jobs, when the whole deal turned out to be a crock and it was clear that they had been thoroughly stiffed, why did the sons do nothing?

The feminine mystique's collapse a generation earlier was not just a crisis but a historic opportunity for women. Women responded to their "problem with no name" by naming it and founding a political movement, by beginning the process of freeing themselves. Why haven't men done the same? This seems to me to be the real question that lurks behind the "masculinity crisis" facing American society: not that men are fighting against women's liberation, but that they have refused to mobilize for their own—or their society's—liberation.

Not that traditional male roles are endangered, but that men themselves are in danger of not acting.

Many in the women's movement and in the mass media complain that men just "don't want to give up the reins of power." But that would seem to have little applicability to the situations of most men, who individually feel not the reins of power in their hands but its bit in their mouths. What's more likely is that they are clinging to a phantom status. A number of men I interviewed, as they argued for the importance of having a male head of the household, tellingly demoted that to an honorary post: it's important, they would say, that every home have a "figurehead." But even the natural reluctance to give up a position of putative superiority, no matter how compromised, is not enough to explain a deeper male silence.

To understand why men are so reluctant to break with the codes of manhood sanctioned in their childhood, perhaps we need to understand how strong the social constraints on them are. It's not just women who are bombarded by cultural messages about appropriate gender behavior. In the past half century, Madison Avenue, Hollywood, and the mass media have operated relentlessly on men, too. The level of mockery, suspicion, and animosity directed at men who step out of line is profound, and men respond profoundly—with acquiescence. But that is not a wholly satisfying explanation either, for haven't women, the object of such commercial and political manipulation, kicked over these traces successfully?

If men do not respond, then maybe it is because their society has proposed no route for them to venture down. Surely the culture has not offered an alternative vision of manhood. No one has: not the so-called men's movement, which clings to its dusted-off copies of *Grimms' Fairy Tales* and its caveman clichés; not conservative or liberal political leaders who call for a remilitarized model of manhood with work camps and schools run by former generals; not the Promise Keepers or Nation of Islam ministers, whose programs of male contrition and resurrection are fantasies of past fantasies; not a gay culture, which, as it gets increasingly absorbed into the larger commercial culture, becomes increasingly muted in its challenge of masculine roles; not even the women's movement, which clamors for men to change but has yet to conceptualize that change. But then, did feminists wait upon men to craft their revolution for them? Didn't the women's movement make its own way, without any assistance —no, with much resistance—from the dominant culture? So why can't men act? The ultimate answer has deep ramifications not only for men but for feminists. Eventually I came to believe that, far from being antagonists, they were each poised at this hour to be vital in the other's advance. But that answer came at the end. First I had to begin....

My travels led me to a final question: Why don't contemporary men rise up in protest against their betrayal? If they have experienced so many of the same injuries as women, the same humiliations, why don't they challenge the culture as women did? Why can't men seem to act?

The stock answers that have been offered to explain men's reluctance to break out of stereotypical male models don't suffice. Men aren't simply refusing to "give up the reins of power," as some feminists have argued. The reins have already slipped from most of their hands, anyway.... While the pressures on men to imagine themselves in power and in control of their emotions are impediment to male revolt, a more fundamental obstacle overshadows them. If men have feared to tread where women have rushed in, then maybe that's because women have had it easier in one very simple regard: women could frame their struggle as a battle against men....

Because the women who engaged in the feminist campaigns of the seventies were fighting the face of "male domination," they were able to take advantage of a ready-made model for revolt. To wage their battle, they could unfurl a well-worn map and follow a reliable strategy. Ironically, it was a male strategy—feminists grabbed hold of the blueprint for the American male paradigm and made good use of it. They had at the ready all the elements required to make that paradigm work. They had a clearly defined oppressive enemy: the "patriarchy." They had a real frontier to conquer and clear for other women: all those patriarchal institutions, both the old ones that still rebuffed women, like the U.S. Congress or U.S. Steel, and the new ones that tried to remold women, like Madison Avenue or the glamour and media-pimp kingdoms of Bert Parks and Hugh Hefner. Feminists also had their own army of "brothers": sisterhood. Each GI Jane who participated in this struggle felt she was useful. Whether she was distributing leaflets or working in a women's-health clinic, whether she was lobbying legislators to pass a child-care bill or tossing her bottles of Clairol in a "freedom trash can," she was part of a greater glory, the advancement of her entire sex. Many women whose lives were touched by feminism felt in some way that they had reclaimed an essential usefulness; together, they had charged the barricades that kept each of them from a fruitful, thriving life. Women had discovered a good fight, and a flight path to adult womanhood. Traveling along with trajectory of feminism, each "small step" for a woman would add up finally to a giant leap for womankind, not to mention humankind.

The male paradigm of confrontation, in which an enemy could be identified, contested, and defeated, was endlessly transferable. It proved useful as well to activists in the civil-rights movement and the antiwar movement, the gay-rights movement and the environmental movement. It was, in fact, the fundamental organizing principle of virtually every concerted countercultural campaign of the last half century. Yet it could launch no "men's movement." Herein lies the bedeviling paradox, and the source of male inaction: the model women have used to revolt is the exact one men not only can't use but are trapped in. The solution for women has proved the problem for men.

The male paradigm is peculiarly unsuited to mounting a challenge to men's predicament. Men have no clearly defined enemy who is oppressing them. How can men be oppressed when the culture has already identified them as the oppressors, and when they see themselves that way? As one man wrote plaintively to Promise Keepers, "I'm like a kite with a broken string, but I'm also holding the tail." In an attempt to employ the old paradigm, men have invented antagonists to make their problems visible, but with the passage of time, these culprits—scheming feminists, affirmative-action proponents, job-grabbing illegal aliens, the wife of a president—have come to seem increasingly unconvincing as explanations for their situation. Defeating such paper tigers offers no sense of victory. Nor do men have a clear frontier on which to challenge their intangible enemies. What new realms should they be gaining—the media, entertainment, and image-making institutions of corporate America? But these are institutions, they are told, that are already run by men; how can men invade their own territory?...

Social responsibility is not the special province of masculinity; it's the lifelong work of all citizens in a community where people are knit together by meaningful and mutual concerns. But if husbanding a society is not the exclusive calling of "husbands," all the better for men's future. Because as men struggle to free themselves from their crisis, their task is not, in the end, to figure out how to be masculine—rather, their masculinity lies in figuring out how to be human. The men who worked at the Long Beach Naval Shipyard didn't come there and learn their crafts as riggers, welders, and boilermakers to *be* masculine; they were seeking something worthwhile to *do*. Their sense of their own manhood flowed out of their utility in a society, not the other way around. Conceiving of masculinity as something to *be* turns manliness into a detachable entity, at which point it instantly becomes ornamental, and about as innately "masculine" as fake eyelashes are inherently "feminine." Michael Bernhardt was one man who came to understand this in his difficult years after he returned from Vietnam. "All these years I was trying to be all these stereotypes" of manhood, he said, "and what was the use?... I'm beginning to think now of not even defining it anymore. I'm beginning to think now just in terms of people." From this discovery follow others, like the knowledge that he no longer has to live by the "scorecard" his nation handed him. He can begin to conceive of other ways of being "human," and hence, of being a man.

And so with the mystery of men's nonrebellion comes the glimmer of an opening, an opportunity for men to forge a rebellion commensurate with women's and, in the course of it, to create a new paradigm for human progress that will open doors for both sexes. That was, and continues to be, feminism's dream, to create a freer, more humane world. Feminists have pursued it, particularly in the last two centuries, with great determination and passion. In the end, though, it will remain a dream without the strength and courage of men who are today faced with a historic opportunity: to learn to wage a battle against no enemy, to own a frontier of human liberty, to act in the service of a brotherhood that includes us all.

POSTSCRIPT

Do the New Sex Roles Burden Women More Than Men?

Sex roles are currently in transition. At the moment both men and women face challenges in fulfilling their sex roles. Much of this has to do with the pace of life. Both men and women are overwhelmed because they are short on time and loaded with choices and demands. But notice that most people do not want to go back to earlier days. A few men may long for frontier challenges and many women want to stay home while their children are young, but most want sex roles to continue to evolve in the direction they are going. The major influence on the changes in sex roles has been feminism and the women's movement.

Over the past 30 years, there has been a deluge of books, articles, and periodicals devoted to expounding feminist positions. Important recent statements by feminist leaders are Barbara A. Crow ed., *Radical Feminism: A Documentary Reader* (New York University Press, 2000); Gloria Steinem's book, *Outrageous Acts and Everyday Rebellions,* 2d ed. (Henry Holt, 1995) and article "Revving Up for the Next 25 Years," *Ms.* magazine (September/October 1997); and Patricia Ireland, *What Women Want* (Penguin, 1996). For a history of the women's movement see Kathleen C. Berkeley, *The Women's Liberation Movement in America* (Greenwood Press, 1999). For the impact of the women's movement on American society and culture see Cassandra L. Langer, *A Feminist Critique: How Feminism Has Changed American Society, Culture, and How We Live From the 1940's to the Present* (IconEditions, 1996) and Ruth Rosen, *The World Split Open: How the Modern Women's Movement Changed America* (Viking, 2000). For some recent discussions of the demands of work and family on women see Arlie Russell Hochschild, *The Second Shift* (Avon Books, 1997); Daphne Spain and Suzanne M. Bianchi, *Balancing Act: Motherhood, Marriage, and Employment Among American Women* (Russell Sage Foundation, 1996); and Nancy Kaltreider ed., *Dilemmas of a Double Life: Women Balancing Careers and Relationships* (Jason Aronson, 1997). For some analyses of the sex role problems of men see Michael S. Kimmel, *Manhood in America: A Cultural History* (Free Press, 1996); Stephen Wicks, *Warriors and Wildmen: Men, Masculinity, and Gender* (Bergin & Carvey, 1996); Joseph A. Kuypers, ed., *Men and Power* (Prometheus Books, 1999); John MacInnes, *The End of Masculinity: The Confusion of Sexual Genesis and Sexual Difference in Modern Society* (Open University Press, 1998); and Warren Farrell, *The Myth of Male Power* (Simon & Schuster, 1993). Perhaps the final resolution of this issue is described in Pepper Schwartz' *Peer Marriage: How Love Between Equals Really Works* (Free Press, 1994).

ISSUE 5

Are Communication Problems Between Men and Women Largely Due to Radically Different Conversation Styles?

YES: Philip Yancey, from "Do Men and Women Speak the Same Language?" *Marriage Partnership* (Fall 1993)

NO: Mary Crawford, from *Talking Difference: On Gender and Language* (Sage Publications, 1995)

ISSUE SUMMARY

YES: Author Philip Yancey argues that men and women have strikingly different communication styles because they grow up in different cultures. A man is usually concerned about enhancing or maintaining status as he communicates, while a woman will usually communicate in ways that gain or maintain closeness.

NO: Professor of psychology Mary Crawford contends that the thesis that men and women have radically different communication styles is greatly exaggerated in the media and is based on simplistic stereotypes.

In 1992 John Gray published his best-selling book *Men Are From Mars, Women Are From Venus* (HarperCollins), which promises greatly improved relationships between men and women if they understand that men and women are different and if they accept rather than resent their differences. Here are some selections from the book:

> One of the biggest differences between men and women is how they cope with stress. Men become increasingly focused and withdrawn while women become increasingly overwhelmed and emotionally involved. At these times, a man's needs for feeling good are different from a woman's. He feels better by solving problems while she feels better by talking about problems. Not understanding and accepting these differences creates unnecessary friction in our relationships (p. 29).

When a Martian gets upset he never talks about what is bothering him. He would never burden another Martian with his problem unless his friend's assistance was necessary to solve the problem. Instead he becomes very quiet and goes to his private cave to think about his problem, mulling it over to find a solution. When he has found a solution, he feels much better and comes out of his cave (p. 30).

When a Venusian becomes upset or is stressed by her day, to find relief, she seeks out someone she trusts and then talks in great detail about the problems of her day. When Venusians share feelings of being overwhelmed, they suddenly feel better. This is the Venusian way.

On Venus sharing your problems with another actually is considered a sign of love and trust and not a burden. Venusians are not ashamed of having problems. Their egos are dependent not on looking "competent" but rather on being in loving relationships....

A Venusian feels good about herself when she has loving friends with whom to share her feelings and problems. A Martian feels good when he can solve his problems on his own in his cave (p. 31).

Some claim to be greatly helped by Gray's message. Others find it demeaning to characterize women as irrational, passive, and overly dependent on others. Critics also feel that it counsels women to accept boorish and uncaring behavior in men, while telling men that they only have to listen to women more to make them happy. Gray's message gets a strong reaction because it addresses a very important issue: how can men and women better understand each other?

This issue fascinates sociologists because it plunges them into questions about the construction of reality, perceptions of reality, differential socialization, and power in male-female relationships. Gray himself is constructing reality as he sees it in his book, and according to his reality many difficulties between men and women are not anyone's fault but are just misunderstandings. His reality leaves power out, but a sociologist will always take it into account. In fact, sociologists would note that men and women differ not only in their socialization but also in their relative power in their relationships. The person with greater income, education, and job status will feel freer to determine when, where, how, and about what the pair talks.

The differences in male-female communication styles that Philip Yancey identifies in the following selection are similar to Gray's. He says that men are more concerned about hierarchy and that women are more concerned about relationships, but it is a matter of degree. He, like Gray, works for better understanding between men and women. In the second selection, Mary Crawford reacts strongly to the proponents of gender differences in communication because she feels that their construction of gendered reality is superficial and puts women down.

Philip Yancey

 **YES**

Do Men and Women Speak the Same Language?

For five years my wife, Janet, and I met in a small group with three other couples. Sometimes we studied the Bible, sometimes we read books together, sometimes we spontaneously discussed topics like money and sex. Almost always we ended up talking about our marriages. Finally we decided the time had come to investigate an explosive topic we had always avoided: the differences between men and women. We used the book *You Just Don't Understand* [William Morrow & Company, 1990], by Deborah Tannen, as the springboard for our discussions. That study of the different communication styles of men and women had risen to the top of The New York Times bestseller list. Books on gender differences tend to portray one party as the "right" party. Women are sensitive, compassionate, peace-loving, responsible, nurturing; men are boorish slobs whose idea of "bonding" is to slouch in front of a TV with their buddies watching other men chase little round balls. Or, men are rational, organizational geniuses who run the world because they are "hardwired" with leadership skills that women can never hope to master. But in her book, Tannen strives to avoid such bias, focusing instead on what it takes for men and women to understand each other.

She sees males as more competitive, aggressive, hierarchical and emotionally withdrawn. Females, she concludes, are quieter, more relational and mutually supportive. Naturally, any generalities about gender differences do not apply to all men or all women. Yet we found one point of commonality that helped us all: Male/female relationships represent a classic case of cross-cultural communication. The key to effective relationships is to understand the vast "cultural" gap between male and female.

Anyone who has traveled overseas knows that barriers exist between cultures, language being the most obvious. The barriers between men and women can be just as real, and just as frustrating. Typically, says Tannen, men and women don't recognize these differences; they tend to repeat the same patterns of miscommunication, only more forcefully. As a result, marriages often resemble the stereotypical tourist encounter: One party speaks loudly and slowly in a language the other does not comprehend.

From Philip Yancey, "Do Men and Women Speak the Same Language?" *Marriage Partnership*, vol. 10, no. 4 (Fall 1993). Copyright © 1993 by Philip Yancey. Reprinted by permission of the author.

The Male/Female Culture Gap

"Shared meaning" is a good, concise definition of culture. By virtue of growing up in the United States, I share the meaning of things like Bart Simpson, baseball and the Fourth of July with 250 million other people, and no one else in the world. Our couples group found that some problems come about because one spouse enters marriage with a different set of "shared meanings" than the other. Consider routine dinner conversation. For some of us, interrupting another's conversation seems an act of impoliteness or hostility; for others, it expresses friendly engagement. Angie, one of the women in our group, said, "When Greg first came to my Italian family's get-togethers he would hardly speak. We usually had a fight on the way home. We later figured out he felt shut down whenever someone interrupted him in the middle of a story or a comment. Well, in my family interrupting is a sign of involvement. It means we're listening to you, egging you on.

"Greg comes from a German family where everyone politely takes turns responding to the previous comment. I go crazy—their conversation seems so boring and stilted. It helped us both to realize there is no 'right' or 'wrong' style of conversation—we were simply acting out of different cultural styles."

Everyone grows up with "rules" or assumptions about how life is supposed to operate. Marriage forces into close contact two people with different sets of shared meanings and then requires them to negotiate a common ground. Bill and Holly told of a disagreement that nearly ruined their Christmas vacation. Bill said, "We visited Holly's family, which is huge and intimidating. That Christmas, one of the sisters bought a VCR and television to present to the parents, without consulting the rest of the family. 'You guys can chip in anything you want,' she told her siblings and in-laws. 'I'll sign the card and present the gift as being from all of us.'

"To me this looked like a set-up job," Bill continued. "I felt pressure to come up with our fair share, which was a lot more than we would have spent on our own. I felt manipulated and angry, and Holly couldn't understand my feelings. She said her sister was absolutely sincere. 'Our family doesn't keep score,' she said. 'Ellen spontaneously felt like buying a present, and she'll be content whether everyone chips in one-eighth or if no one contributes anything. It's not 'tit-for-tat' like your family.'

"Holly was probably right. My family does keep score. You send a letter, you expect one in return. You give a gift, you expect one of equal value. I'm finally coming to grasp that Holly's family doesn't operate like mine."

Another couple, Gayle and Don, identified on-timeness as their major cross-cultural disagreement. Gayle grew up in a family that didn't notice if they were 10 or 15 minutes late, but Don wears a digital watch and follows it punctually. Several times a week they clash over this common cross-cultural difference. In Germany the trains run on time; in Mexico they get there—eventually.

Cross-cultural differences may seem trivial but, as many couples learn, on small rocks great ships wreck. It helps to know in advance where the rocks are.

Cross-Gender Communication

Communication can either span—or widen—the gender gap. Research shows that boys and girls grow up learning different styles of communicating. Boys tend to play in large groups that are hierarchically structured, with a leader who tells the others what to do and how to do it. Boys reinforce status by giving orders and enforcing them; their games have winners and losers and are run by elaborate rules. In contrast, girls play in small groups or in pairs, with "best friends." They strive for intimacy, not status.

These gender patterns continue into adulthood. A man relates to the world as an individual within a hierarchy; he measures himself against others and judges success or failure by his movement up or down the ladder. A woman approaches the world as a network of many social connections. For women, writes Deborah Tannen, "conversations are negotiations for closeness in which people try to seek and give confirmation and support, and to reach consensus."

Tannen's studies of the corporate world show it to be a male-dominated culture where men tend to make pronouncements, to surround themselves with symbols of status, to position themselves against one another, and to improve their standing by opposition. Women, though, tend to seek approval from others and thereby gain their sense of worth. Women are more inclined to be givers of praise than givers of information.

Our couples group agreed that Tannen's observations about the corporate world ring true. "I feel trapped," said Gayle, a management consultant. "At work I find myself changing in order to meet male expectations. I can't be tentative or solicit other people's reactions. I have to appear strong and confident whether I genuinely feel that way or not. I feel I'm losing my femininity."

Because women rely so strongly on feedback from others, they may hesitate to express themselves in a forthright, direct manner. As one psychologist says, "A man might ask a woman, 'Will you please go the store?' where a woman might say, 'I really need a few things from the store, but I'm so tired.' " A man might judge such behavior sneaky or underhanded, but such indirectness is actually the norm in many cultures.

For example, a direct approach such as, "I want to buy that cabbage for 50 cents" will get you nowhere in a Middle Eastern or African market. Both parties expect an elaborate social dance of bluff and innuendo. "If indirectness is understood by both parties, then there is nothing covert about it," Tannen concludes. The challenge in marriage is for both parties to recognize a communication style and learn to work within it.

Battle of the Sexes

We discovered that each couple in our group had what we called a Blamer and a Blamee; two of the Blamers were husbands, two were wives. The Blamer was usually a perfectionist, very detail-and task-oriented, who expected unrealistically high standards of the spouse. "No matter what I do," said one Blamee, "I can never measure up to my husband's standard of cooking or housekeeping or reading or sex, or anything. It's like I'm constantly being graded on my perfor-mance. And it doesn't motivate me to improve. I figure I'm not going to satisfy him anyway, so why try?"

All of us would like to make a few changes in the person we live with, but attempts to coax those changes often lead to conflict. And in conflict, gender differences rise quickly to the surface. Men, who grow up in a hierar-chical environment, are accustomed to conflict. Women, concerned more with relationship and connection, prefer the role of peacemaker.

In my own marriage, for example, Janet and I view conflict through dif-ferent eyes. As a writer, I thrive on criticism. I exchange manuscripts with other writers, and I've learned the best editors are the least diplomatic ones. I have two friends who pepper my manuscripts with words like "Ugh!" and "Awk!", and I would hesitate to publish any book without first running it through their gauntlet. In addition, I've gotten used to receiving heated letters from readers. Complimentary letters sound alike; angry letters fascinate me.

Janet, though, tends to feel criticism as a personal attack. I have learned much by watching her manage other people. Sensitive to criticism herself, she has become masterful at communicating criticism to others. When I managed employees in an office setting I would tend to blunder in with a straightforward approach: "There are five things you're doing right and five things you're doing wrong." After numerous failures, I began to see that the goal in criticism is to help the other person see the problem and desire to change. I have learned the necessity of communicating cross-culturally in my conflicts. When dealing with gluttons for punishment like me, I can be as direct as I want. For more sensitive persons, I need to exercise the skills I've gleaned from diplomats like my wife.

As our small group discussed various styles, we arrived at the following "guidelines" for conflict:

First, identify your fighting style. We tend to learn fighting styles from the family we grow up in. In Angie's Italian family, the fighting style was obvious: yell, argue and, if necessary, punch your brother in the nose. She approached marriage much the same way, only without the punches. Meanwhile, her hus-band would clam up and walk away from an argument. Angie thought Greg was deliberately ignoring her, and their conflicts never got resolved until they sought counseling. There, they realized that Greg was walking away because he knew he had no chance against Angie's well-honed fighting skills. Once both of them realized the dynamics behind their dead-end conflicts, they were able to make appropriate adjustments and change the "rules of engagement."

Second, agree on rules of engagement. Every couple needs to negotiate what constitutes "fighting fair." The couples in our group agreed to avoid these things: fighting in public, straying from the topic at hand, bringing up old his-tory, threatening divorce and using sex as a way to paper over conflict. It's also helpful to consider additional rules, such as "Don't pretend to go along with a decision and then bring it up later as a matter of blame;" and "Don't resort to 'guerrilla warfare'—getting revenge by taking cheap shots after an argument is over."

Third, identify the real issue behind the conflict. A hidden message often underlies conflict. For example, women are sometimes accused of "nagging." On the surface, their message is the specific complaint at hand: not spending enough time with the kids, not helping with housework, coming home late from work. Actually, Deborah Tannen writes, there is another message at work:

"That women have been labeled 'nags' may result from the interplay of men's and women's styles, whereby many women are inclined to do what is asked of them and many men are inclined to resist even the slightest hint that anyone, especially a woman, is telling them what to do. A woman will be inclined to repeat a request that doesn't get a response because she is convinced that her husband would do what she asks if he only understood that she really wants him to do it. But a man who wants to avoid feeling that he is following orders may instinctively wait before doing what she asked in order to imagine that he is doing it of his own free will. Nagging is the result, because each time she repeats the request, he again puts off fulfilling it."

Spouses need to ask themselves questions like, "Is taking out the garbage really the issue, or is it a husband's crusty resistance to anything that infringes on his independence?"

Man Talk, and Woman Talk

In conversation, men and women appear to be doing the same thing—they open their mouths and produce noise. However, they actually use conversation for quite different purposes. Women use conversation primarily to form and solidify connections with other people. Men, on the other hand, tend to use words to navigate their way within the hierarchy. They do so by communicating their knowledge and skill, imparting information to others.

Women excel at what Tannen calls "private speaking" or "rapport-talk." Men feel most comfortable in "public speaking" or "report talk." Even though women may have more confidence in verbal ability (aptitude tests prove their superior skill), they are less likely to use that ability in a public context. Men feel comfortable giving reports to groups or interrupting a speaker with an objection—these are skills learned in the male hierarchy. Many women might perceive the same behavior as putting themselves on display. For example, at a party the men tell stories, share their expertise and tell jokes while the women usually converse in smaller groups about more personal subjects. They are busy connecting while the men are positioning themselves.

Our couples' group discussion became heated when we brought up another female trait that commonly goes by the name "bitching" (Tanner substituted the much more respectable term "ritual lament"). "Yeah, let's talk about this!" Greg said. "I remember one ski trip when I met some of my buddies in Colorado. We spent three days together before our wives joined us. We guys were having a great time, but when the women showed up everything changed. Nothing was right: The weather was too cold and the snow too crusty, the condo was drafty, the grocery store understocked, the hot tub dirty. Every night we heard them complain about sore muscles and raw places where the ski boots rubbed.

"The guys would listen to the griping, then just look at each other and say, 'The women are here!' It was incredible. We were living and skiing in exactly the same conditions. But before the women arrived, we had peace. Afterward, we heard nothing but gripes."

Tannen's explanation is that women tend to bond in pain. Through griping, they reaffirm connections with each other. For men, the immediate response to a complaint is to fix the problem. Otherwise, why complain? Women don't necessarily want the problem solved—who can "fix" the weather, for example? They merely want to feel understood and sympathized with.

Coming Together

Over several months our couples group gained an appreciation for the profound differences between male and female, but also a respect for how difficult it can be to pin down those differences.

Talking Difference: On Gender and Language

Talking Across the Gender Gap

People believe in sex differences. As one best-selling book puts it, when it comes to communication, *Men are from Mars, Women are from Venus* (Gray, 1992). Social scientists have helped to create and confirm that belief by conducting innumerable studies of every conceivable linguistic and stylistic variation between the sexes and by developing theories that stress differences rather than similarities and overlap (West and Zimmerman, 1985). In *Language and Woman's Place* (1975) the linguist Robin Lakoff proposed that women use a speech style that is ineffectual because it is overly polite, hesitant, and deferent. The assertiveness training movement of the 1970s and 1980s—a therapeutic fad led by psychologists whose clients were largely women—engaged perhaps hundreds of thousands of people in attempts to change their way of communicating. A rationale for the movement was that some people (especially women) suffer from poor communication skills and irrational beliefs that prevent them from expressing themselves clearly and directly. More recently, linguists and communication experts have created another conceptual bandwagon by applying theories of cross-cultural communication to women and men. According to this view, 'men from Mars' and 'women from Venus' are fated to misunderstand each other unless they recognize their deeply socialized differences.

The view of gender and language encoded in these writings and therapies is that fundamental differences between women and men shape the way they talk. The differences are conceived as located within individuals and prior to the talk—as differences in personality traits, skills, beliefs, attitudes, or goals. For the millions of people who have become acquainted with issues of gender and language through reading best-selling books telling women how to be more assertive or how to understand the 'opposite' sex, or through watching television talk shows featuring communication experts who claim that talk between women and men is cross-cultural communication, a powerful narrative frame is provided and validated: that gender is difference, and difference is static, bipolar, and categorical. Absorbing such messages, it would be very difficult *not* to believe that women and men are indeed opposite sexes when it comes to talk. . . .

Two Sexes, Two Cultures

Cross-Cultural Talk . . .

Talking Across the Gender Divide

. . . When we think of distinct female and male subcultures we tend to think of societies in which women and men spend virtually their entire lives spatially and interactionally segregated; for example, those which practice purdah. In Western societies, however, girls and boys are brought up together. They share the use of common space in their homes; eat, work, and play with their siblings of both sexes; generally attend co-educational schools in which they are aggregated in many classes and activities. Both sexes are supervised, cared for, and taught largely by women in infancy and early childhood, with male teachers and other authority figures becoming more visible as children grow older. Moreover, they see these social patterns mirrored and even exaggerated in the mass media. How can the talk of Western women and men be seen as talk across cultures?

The two-cultures model was first applied to the speech of North American women and men by Daniel Maltz and Ruth Borker, who proposed that difficulties in cross-sex and cross-ethnic communication are 'two examples of the same larger phenomenon: cultural difference and miscommunication' (1982: 196). Maltz and Borker acknowledge the argument that American women and men interact with each other far too much to be characterized as living in different subcultures. However, they maintain that the social rules for friendly conversation are learned between the ages of approximately 5 and 15, precisely the time when children's play groups are maximally segregated by sex. Not only do children voluntarily choose to play in same-sex groups, they consciously exaggerate differences as they differentiate themselves from the other sex. Because of the very different social contexts in which they learn the meanings and goals of conversational interaction, boys and girls learn to use language in different ways.

Citing research on children's play, Maltz and Borker (1982) argue that girls learn to do three things with words:

1. to create and maintain relationships of closeness and equality;
2. to criticize others in acceptable (indirect) ways;
3. to interpret accurately and sensitively the speech of other girls.

In contrast, boys learn to do three very different things with words:

1. to assert one's position of dominance;
2. to attract and maintain an audience;
3. to assert oneself when another person has the floor.

The Two-Cultures Approach as Bandwagon

... The new twist in the two-cultures model of communication is to conceive relationship difficulties not as women's deficiencies but as an inevitable result of deeply ingrained male–female differences. The self-help books that encode a two-cultures model make the paradoxical claim that difference between the sexes is deeply socialized and/or fundamental to masculine and feminine natures, and at the same time subject to change and manipulation if the reader only follows prescribed ways of talking. Instead of catchy slogans and metaphors that stigmatize women (*Women who Love too Much,* Doris Doormat v. Agatha Aggressive) the equally catchy new metaphors glorify difference.

... Deborah Tannen's *You just don't Understand: Women and Men in Conversation* (1990)... has become a phenomenal success in the US. Acclaimed in the popular press as the 'Rosetta Stone that at last deciphers the miscommunication between the sexes' and as 'a Berlitz guidebook to the language and customs of the opposite gender [sic]'... Tannen claims that childhood play has shaped world views so that, when adult women and men are in relationships 'women speak and hear a language of connection and intimacy, while men speak and hear a language of status and independence' (1990:42). The contrasting conversational goals of intimacy and independence lead to contrasting conversational styles. Women tell each other of their troubles, freely ask for information and help, and show appreciation of others' helping efforts. Men prefer to solve problems rather than talk about them, are reluctant to ask for help or advice, and are more comfortable in the roles of expert, lecturer, and teacher than learner or listener. Men are more talkative in public, women in private. These different styles are labelled 'report talk' (men's) and 'rapport talk' (women's).

Given the stylistic dichotomy between the sexes, miscommunication is almost inevitable; however, no one is to blame. Rather, another banner proclaims, 'The Key is Understanding:' 'Although each style is valid on its own terms, misunderstandings arise because the styles are different. Taking a cross-cultural approach to male–female conversations makes it possible to explain why dissatisfactions are justified without accusing anyone of being wrong or crazy' (1990:47).

You just don't Understand makes its case for the two-cultures model skillfully and well using techniques that have become standard in popular writing about behavior: characterizations of 'most' women and men, entertaining anecdotes, and the presentation of research findings as fact.... Instead of advocating conversational formulae or regimented training programs for one sex, it recommends simply that people try to understand and accept sex differences and to be as flexible in style as possible....

The Two-Cultures Approach: An Evaluation

Beyond Deficiencies and Blame

Proponents of the two-cultures model maintain that it is an advance over approaches that blame particular groups for miscommunication....

Unlike earlier approaches, the two-cultures model does not characterize women's talk as deficient in comparison to a male norm. In contrast to the notion of an ineffectual 'female register' or the prescriptive masculine ideals of the assertiveness training movement, the two-cultures model problematizes the behavior of men as well as women. To John Gray, neither Mars nor Venus is a superior home. To Deborah Tannen, 'report talk' and 'rapport talk' are equally limiting for their users in cross-sex communication. The speech style attributed to men is no longer 'standard' speech or 'the language,' but merely one way of negotiating the social landscape.

A model of talk that transcends woman-blaming is less likely to lead to woman-as-problem research programs or to widespread attempts to change women through therapy and skills training. Moreover, ways of talking thought to characterize women can be positively revalued within this framework. In a chapter on gossip, Tannen notes that the negative connotation of the word reflects men's interpretation of women's ways of talking. But gossip can be thought of as 'talking about' rather than 'talking against.' It can serve crucial functions of establishing intimacy and rapport....

Doing Gender, Doing Power

The two-cultures approach fails to theorize how power relations at the structural level are recreated and maintained at the interactional level. The *consequences* of 'miscommunication' are not the same for powerful and powerless groups. As Deborah Cameron (1985: 150) points out, 'The right to represent and stereotype is not mutual.' Stereotypes of less powerful groups (immigrants, people of color) as inadequate speakers serve to ensure that no one need take seriously what these people say. People of color may have their own set of negative stereotypes of white people, but 'these are the ideas of people without power. They do not serve as a base for administrative procedures and decisions, nor do they get expressed routinely in mass media.' Recent research on the relationship between power and stereotyping suggests that people in power stereotype others partly as a cognitive 'shortcut' that minimizes the need to attend to them as individuals. People without power, of course, must attend carefully to their 'superiors' in order to avoid negative judgment or actual harm and cannot afford to use schematic shortcuts (Fiske, 1993).

'Negotiating status' is an evaluatively neutral term for interpersonal behaviors that consolidate power and maintain dominance. Ignoring the enactment of power and how it connects to structural power in gender relations does a disservice to sociolinguistics, distorting its knowledge base and undermining other more legitimate research approaches (Freed, 1992). Moreover, it badly misrepresents communication phenomena. Nancy Henley and Cheris Kramarae (1991) provide a detailed analysis of six 'cultural differences' in female–male speech styles taken from Maltz and Borker (1982), showing that they may be more plausibly interpreted as manifestations and exercises of power. For example, men's tendency to interpret questions as requests for information, and problem-sharing as an opportunity to give expert advice, can be viewed as prerogatives of power. In choosing these speech strategies, men take to themselves the voice of authority.

This failure to recognize structural power and connect it with international power has provoked the strongest criticisms of the two-cultures approach. In a review of *You just don't Understand,* Senta Troemel-Ploetz (1991) pointed out that if the majority of relationships between women and men in our society were not fundamentally asymmetrical to the advantage of men,

> we would not need a women's liberation movement, women's commissions, houses for battered women, legislation for equal opportunity, antidiscrimination laws, family therapy, couple therapy, divorce . . . If you leave out power, you do not understand any talk, be it the discussion after your speech, the conversation at your own dinner-table, in a doctor's office, in the back yards of West Philadelphia, in an Italian village, on a street in Turkey, in a court room or in a day-care center, in a women's group or at a UN conference. It is like saying Black English and Oxford English are just two different varieties of English, each valid on its own; it just so happens that the speakers of one variety find themselves in high-paying positions with a lot of prestige and power of decision-making, and the others are found more in low-paying jobs, or on the streets and in prisons. They don't always understand each other, but they both have the best intentions; if they could only learn a bit from each other and understand their differences as a matter of style, all would be well. (Troemel-Ploetz, 1991: 497–8)

No one involved in debating the two-cultures approach denies that men have more social and political power than women. Maltz and Borker (1982: 199) acknowledge that power differentials 'may make some contribution' to communication patterns. However, they do not theorize the workings of power in interaction or advocate structural changes to reduce inequity.

The Bandwagon Revisited

There is no inherent limitation to the two-cultures approach that would prevent its development as a theory of difference *and* dominance, a theory that could encompass the construction of gendered subjectivities, the reproduction of inequality in interaction, and the role of interaction in sustaining gendered social structures. It is therefore the more disappointing that in the popularized versions that have influenced perhaps millions of people, it is flattened into an account of sex dichotomies. And this is why the model has been so harshly evaluated by feminist scholars. Perhaps unfortunately, the more egregious versions have been largely ignored and the more scholarly one attacked. Deborah Tannen's critics have charged that, despite the absence of overt women-blaming and the positive evaluation of 'feminine' modes of talk, the interpretations she offers often disguise or gloss over inequity, and privilege men's interpretations (Freed, 1992; Troemel-Ploetz, 1991). They have accused her of being an apologist for men, excusing their insensitivity, rudeness, and dominance as mere stylistic quirks, and encouraging women to make the adjustments when needs conflict (Freed, 1992). Indeed, the interpretations Tannen offers for the many anecdotes that enliven her book often read as though the past two decades of women's studies scholarship had never occurred, and there were no feminist analyses available with which to contextualize gendered behavior (Troemel-Ploetz, 1991).

You just don't Understand is apolitical—a choice which is in itself a political act, and a significant one at that, given that the book has sold well over a million copies. Like the popular psychology of the assertiveness training movement, it does not threaten the status quo (Troemel-Ploetz, 1991). Like its pop-psychology companions on the bookstore shelves, it offers something to both the powerful and those over whom they have power: to men, a compelling rationale of blame-free difference and to women a comforting promise of mutual accommodation.

Let us consider [two] examples, from [two] types of conversational setting, to illustrate how the accounts of interaction in *You just don't Understand* might be reinterpreted in light of research on women and gender. The first is an anecdote about Josh and Linda. When an old friend calls Josh at work with plans for a visit nearby on business, Josh invites him to spend the weekend and makes plans to go out with him Friday night. These plans are made without consulting with Linda, who protests that Josh should have checked with her, especially since she will be returning from a business trip herself that day. Tannen's explanation of the misunderstanding is in terms of an autonomy/intimacy dichotomy. Linda likes to have her life entwined with Josh's, to consult and be consulted about plans. Josh feels that checking with her implies a loss of independence. 'Linda was hurt because she sensed a failure of closeness in their relationship... he was hurt because he felt she was trying to control him and limit his freedom' (1990: 27).

No resolution of the conflict is provided in the anecdote; the implication is that Josh's plans prevail. Interpreting this story in terms of women's needs for intimacy and men's for autonomy glosses the fact that Josh has committed mutual resources (living space, food, the time and work required to entertain a houseguest) on behalf of himself and his partner without acknowledgement that the partner should have a voice in that decision. His behavior seems to reflect the belief that the time and energy of others (women) are to be accommodated to men. As a test of the fairness of his behavior, imagine that Josh were living with a male housemate. To invite a mutual weekend guest without consulting the housemate would be considered overtly rude. The housemate (but not the woman in a heterosexual couple) would be warranted in refusing to cooperate, because he is seen as entitled to make his own plans and control his own resources. A sense of entitlement to act entirely on one's own and make decisions unilaterally is 'part of the social empowerment that men enjoy. It has precious little to do with communicative style or language' (Freed, 1992: 4)....

In a section titled 'First Me, Then Me,' Tannen describes her own experience of discourse in a professional setting. Seated at a faculty dinner next to a woman, she enjoyed a mutually informative and pleasant discussion in which each talked about her research and explored connections and overlaps. Turning to a male guest, she initiated a conversation in a similar way. However, the conversation proceeded very differently:

> During the next half hour, I learned a lot about his job, his research, and his background. Shortly before the dinner ended there was a lull, and he asked me what I did. When I said I was a linguist, he became excited and told me about a research project he had conducted that was related to neurolinguistics. He was still telling me about his research when we all got up to leave the table. (1990: 126)

Lecturing, says Tannen, is part of a male style. And women let them get away with it. Because women's style includes listening attentively and not interrupting, they do not jump in, challenge, or attempt to deflect the lecturer. Men assume that if their partner had anything important to say, she would say it. The two styles interact to produce silent women, who nod and smile although they are bored, and talkative men, who lecture at length though they themselves may be bored and frustrated by the lack of dialogue. Thus, apparent conversational dominance is not something men deliberately do to women. Neither is it something women culpably permit. The imbalance is created by 'habitual styles.'

The stylistic interpretation discounts the possibility that the male academic in this example did not want to hear about his female dinner companion's research because he did not care about it. That women and what they do are valued less than men and what they do is one of the fundamental insights of feminism. The history of women in the professions provides ample evidence of exclusion, discrimination, and marginalization. Methods vary: plagiarizing women's work (Spender, 1989), denigrating them as unfeminine while stealing their ideas (Sayre, 1975), denying them employment (Crawford, 1981; Scarborough and Furumoto, 1987) and recognition (Nochlin, 1971). When women compete successfully in male domains, they are undermined by sexual harassment (Gutek, 1985) and by being represented as sex objects (a long-running 1980s ad campaign featured female physicians and attorneys making medical rounds and appearing in court in their underwear) (Lott, 1985). In short, there is not yet much reason to believe that women in the professions are routinely taken as seriously as their male peers. And the academy is no exception. What Tannen explains as mere stylistic differences have the effect of keeping women and their work invisible, and have had documented consequences on women's hiring, promotion, and tenure (Caplan, 1993)....

A Rhetoric of Reassurance

The rhetoric of difference makes everyone—and no one—responsible for interpersonal problems. Men are not to blame for communication difficulties; neither is a social system in which gender governs access to resources. Instead, difference is reified: 'The culprit, then is not an individual man or even men's styles alone, but the difference between women and men's styles' (Tannen, 1990: 95).

One of the most striking effects achieved in these books is to reassure women that their lot in heterosexual relationships is normal. Again and again, it is stressed that no one is to blame, that miscommunication is inevitable, that unsatisfactory results may stem from the best of intentions. As these explanations dominate the public realm of discourse about gender, they provide 'one more pseudo-explanation' and 'one more ingenious strategy for not tackling the root causes of women's subordinate status' (Cameron, in press).

Its very ubiquity has made inequality of status and power in heterosexual relationships seem unremarkable, and one of the most important contributions of feminist research has been to make it visible (Wilkinson and Kitzinger,

1993). In the discourse of miscommunication the language feminists have developed to theorize status and power is neutralized. Concepts such as sexism, sex discrimination, patriarchy, and gender inequity are barely mentioned, and conversational strategies that have the effect of silencing women are euphemized as stylistic 'asymmetries.' For example, Tannen explains that when men do most of the talking in a group, it is not because they intend to prevent women from speaking or believe that women have nothing important to say. Rather, they see the women as *equals,* and expect them to compete in the same style they themselves use. Thus, an inequity that feminists have conceptualized in terms of power differentials is acknowledged, but explained as an accidental imbalance created by style and having little to do with a gendered social order.

Power dynamics in heterosexual relationships are obscured by the kinds of intentions imputed to speakers. Both books presume an innocence of communicative intent. In the separate and simplistic worlds of Martians and Venusians, women just want to be cherished and men just want to be needed and admired. In the separate worlds of 'report talk' and 'rapport talk', the goal may be sex-specific but the desire is the same: to be understood and responded to in kind. In *You just don't Understand,* each anecdote is followed by an analysis of the intentions of *both* speakers, a practice that Tannen (1992) feels reflects her fairness to both sexes. But this symmetry is false, because the one kind of intention that is never imputed to any speaker is the intent to dominate. Yet people are aware of such intentions in their talk, and, when asked, can readily describe the verbal tactics they use to 'get their own way' in heterosexual interactions (Falbo, 1982; Falbo and Peplau, 1980; Kelley et al., 1978). Tannen acknowledges the role of power in conversational dynamics (cf. p. 283, 'We enact and create our gender, and our inequality, with every move we make'). But the rhetorical force of the anecdotes is about difference. When an anecdote seems obviously explainable in terms of dominance strategies, the possibility of such an account is often acknowledged but discounted. The characteristics that the two-cultures model posit for females' speech are ones appropriate to friendly conversation, while the characteristics posited for men's speech are not neutral, but indicate uncooperative, dominating and disruptive interaction (Henley and Kramarae, 1991). Whose needs are being served when intent to dominate is ruled out *a priori* in accounting for cross-sex conversation?

Many of the most compelling anecdotes describe situations in which a woman is hurt, frustrated or angered by a man's apparently selfish or dominating behavior, only to find that her feelings were unwarranted because the man's intentions were good. This is psychologically naive. There is no reason to believe that *post hoc* stated intentions are a complete and sufficient description of conversational motives....

The emphasis on interpreting a partner's intentions is problematic in other ways as well. As Nancy Henley and Cheris Kramarae (1991: 42) point out, '[F]emales are required to develop special sensitivity to interpret males' silence, lack of emotional expressiveness, or brutality, and to help men express themselves, while men often seem to be trained deliberately to misinterpret much of women's meaning.' Young girls are told that hitting, teasing, and insults are to be read as signs of boys' 'liking.' Adolescent girls are taught to take responsibility for boys' inexpressiveness by drawing them out in conversation, steering talk to topics that will make them feel comfortable, and being a good listener. . . .

Analyzing conversation in terms of intentions has a very important implication: it deflects attention from *effects,* including the ways that everyday action and talk serve to recreate and maintain current gender arrangements.

POSTSCRIPT

Are Communication Problems Between Men and Women Largely Due to Radically Different Conversation Styles?

One of Crawford's concerns is the demeaning picture of women that the literature on gender differences in communication styles often suggests. Men are problem solvers and stand on their own two feet, while women are people pleasers and dependent. Men, however, could also feel put down. According to the theory, men are predominantly interested in defending and advancing their status, even to the point of stepping on toes and jeopardizing closeness. This makes men out to be rather immoral. Self-promotion and the need to dominate others is not sanctioned by most religions or appreciated much by most people. Women come closer to religious and popular ideals than men do. To their credit, they bond, love, and share more through communication than men do, and women do so without necessarily sacrificing their competence in the process.

Many issues regarding gender differences in communication styles remain murky. Everyone, including Crawford, acknowledges that there are talking differences between genders, but how big are these differences? This relates to the large question of how different men and women are on other significant dimensions. What causes these differences? To what extent are they biological and hormonal, and to what extent are they due to differential socialization and different positions in society? How changeable are these differences? Should they be changed?

The past two decades have produced considerable research on gender differences in communication styles, which is reflected in several readers and academic works. Deborah Tannen is prominent in this literature, see Tannen's *You Just Don't Understand: Women and Men in Conversation* (Ballantine Books, 1991); *Gender and Discourse* (Oxford University Press, 1994); and her edited book *Gender and Conversational Interaction* (Oxford University Press, 1993). See also Deborah Cameron, ed., *The Feminist Critique of Language: A Reader,* 2d ed. (Routledge, 1998); Jennifer Coates, ed., *Language and Gender: A Reader* (Blackwell, 1998); Ruth Wodak, ed., *Gender and Discourse* (Sage Publications, 1997); Mary Bucholtz, A. C. Liang, and Laurel A. Sutton, eds., *Reinventing Identities: The Gendered Self in Discourse* (Oxford University Press, 1999); Mary Ritchie Key, *Male/Female Language* (Scarecrow Press, 1996); and Victoria L. Bergwall, Janet M. Bing, and Alice F. Freed, eds., *Rethinking Language and Gender Research: Theory and Practice* (Longman, 1996).

Should Same-Sex Marriages Be Legally Recognized?

YES: Andrew Sullivan, from *Virtually Normal: An Argument About Homosexuality* (Alfred A. Knopf, 1995)

NO: James Q. Wilson, from "Against Homosexual Marriage," *Commentary* (March 1996)

ISSUE SUMMARY

YES: Editor and author Andrew Sullivan argues that the secular liberal state must grant the right of same-sex partners to marry. To not do so would be blatant discrimination.

NO: Professor of management and public policy James Q. Wilson presents arguments against legally recognizing same-sex marriages.

In 1979 in Sioux Falls, South Dakota, Randy Rohl and Grady Quinn became the first acknowledged homosexual couple in America to receive permission from their high school principal to attend the senior prom together. The National Gay Task Force hailed the event as a milestone in the progress of human rights. It is unclear what the voters of Sioux Falls thought about it, since it was not put up to a vote. However, if their views were similar to those of voters in Dade County, Florida; Houston, Texas; Wichita, Kansas; and various localities in the state of Oregon, they probably were not pleased. In referenda held in these and other areas, voters have reversed decisions by legislators and local boards that banned discrimination by sexual preference.

Yet the attitude of Americans toward the rights of homosexuals is not easy to pin down. Voters have also defeated resolutions such as the one in California in 1978 that would have banned the hiring of homosexual schoolteachers, or the one on the Oregon ballot in 1992 identifying homosexuality as "abnormal, wrong, unnatural and perverse." In some states, notably Colorado, voters have approved initiatives widely perceived as antihomosexual. But, almost invariably, these resolutions have been carefully worded so as to appear to oppose "special" rights for homosexuals. In general, polls show that a large majority of Americans believe that homosexuals should have equal rights with heterosexuals with regard to job opportunities. On the other hand, many view homosexuality as morally wrong.

Currently, same-sex marriages are not legally recognized by Congress. In the Defense of Marriage Act of 1996, Congress defined marriage as heterosexual. A state does not have to recognize another state's nonheterosexual marriage. The legal situation is constantly changing because several states are experimenting with new laws. A few states permit same-sex marriage but most do not.

The issue of same-sex marriage fascinates sociologists because it represents a basic change in a major social institution and is being played out on several fields: legal, cultural/moral, and behavioral. The legal debate will be decided by courts and legislatures; the cultural/moral debate is open to all of us; and the behavioral debate will be conducted by the activists on both sides. In the readings that follow, Andrew Sullivan presents some of the arguments in favor of same-sex marriages and James Q. Wilson responds to Sullivan's assertions with his counterarguments.

Andrew Sullivan  **YES**

Virtually Normal

> In everyone there sleeps
> A Sense of life lived according to love.
> To some it means the difference they could make
> By loving others, but across most it sweeps
> As all they might have been had they been loved.
> That nothing cures.

— Philip Larkin

If there were no alternative to today's conflicted politics of homosexuality, we might be condemned to see the proponents of the four major positions fight noisily while society stumbles from one awkward compromise to another. But there is an alternative: a politics that can reconcile the best arguments of liberals and conservatives, and find a way to marry the two. In accord with liberalism, this politics respects the law, its limits, and its austerity. It places a high premium on liberty, and on a strict limit to the regulation of people's minds and actions. And in sympathy with conservatism, this politics acknowledges that in order to create a world of equality, broader arguments may often be needed to persuade people of the need for change, apart from those of rights and government neutrality. It sees that beneath politics, human beings exist whose private lives may indeed be shaped by a shift in public mores.

This politics begins with the view that for a small minority of people, from a young age, homosexuality is an essentially involuntary condition that can neither be denied nor permanently repressed. It is a function of both nature and nurture, but the forces of nurture are formed so early and are so complex that they amount to an involuntary condition. It is *as if* it were a function of nature. Moreover, so long as homosexual adults as citizens insist on the involuntary nature of their condition, it becomes politically impossible simply to deny or ignore the fact of homosexuality.

This politics adheres to an understanding that there is a limit to what politics can achieve in such a fraught area as homosexuality, and trains its focus not on the behavior of citizens in civil society but on the actions of the public and allegedly neutral state. While it eschews the use of law to legislate culture, it strongly believes that law can affect culture indirectly by its insistence on the equality of all citizens. Its goal in the area of homosexuality is simply to ensure that the liberal state live up to its promises for all its citizens. It would seek full public equality for those who, through no fault of their own, happen to be homosexual; and it would not deny homosexuals, as the other four politics do, their existence, integrity, dignity, or distinctness. It would attempt neither to patronize nor to exclude.

This politics affirms a simple and limited principle: that all *public* (as opposed to private) discrimination against homosexuals be ended and that every right and responsibility that heterosexuals enjoy as public citizens be extended to those who grow up and find themselves emotionally different. *And that is all.* No cures or re-educations, no wrenching private litigation, no political imposition of tolerance; merely a political attempt to enshrine formal public equality, whatever happens in the culture and society at large. For these reasons, it is the only politics that actually tackles the *political* problem of homosexuality; the only one that fully respects liberalism's public-private distinction; and, ironically, as we shall see, the only one that cuts the Gordian knot of the shame and despair and isolation that many homosexuals feel. For these reasons, perhaps, it has the least chance of being adopted by homosexuals and heterosexuals alike.

What would it mean in practice? Quite simply, an end to all proactive discrimination by the state against homosexuals. That means an end to sodomy laws that apply only to homosexuals; a recourse to the courts if there is not equal protection of heterosexuals and homosexuals in law enforcement; an equal legal age of consent to sexual activity for heterosexuals and homosexuals, where such regulations apply; inclusion of the facts about homosexuality in the curriculum of every government-funded school, in terms no more and no less clear than those applied to heterosexuality (although almost certainly with far less emphasis, because of homosexuality's relative rareness when compared with heterosexuality); recourse to the courts if any government body or agency can be proven to be engaged in discrimination against homosexual employees; equal opportunity and inclusion in the military; and legal homosexual marriage and divorce....

Its most powerful and important elements are equal access to the military and marriage. The military ban is by far the most egregious example of proactive public discrimination in the Western democracies. By conceding the excellent service that many gay and lesbian soldiers have given to their country, the U.S. military in recent years has elegantly clarified the specificity of the government's unfairness. By focusing on the mere public admission of homosexuality in its 1993 "don't ask, don't tell" compromise, the military isolated the core issue at the heart of the equality of homosexual persons. It argued that homosexuals could serve in the military; that others could know they were homosexuals; that *they* could know they were homosexuals; but that if they ever so much as mentioned this fact, they were to be discharged. The prohibition was not against homosexual acts as such—occasional lapses by heterosexuals were not to be grounds for expulsion. The prohibition was not even against homosexuality. The prohibition was against homosexuals' being honest about their sexuality, because that honesty allegedly lowered the morale of others.

Once the debate has been constructed this way, it will eventually, surely, be won by those advocating the admission of open homosexuals in the military. When this is the sole argument advanced by the military—it became the crux of the debate on Capitol Hill—it has the intellectual solidity of a pack of cards. One group is arbitrarily silenced to protect not the rights but the sensibilities of the others. To be sure, it won the political battle; but it clearly lost the moral and intellectual war, as subsequent court tests demonstrated. It required one of the most respected institutions in American society to impose upon its members a rule of fundamental dishonesty in order for them to perform their duties. It formally introduced hypocrisy as a rule of combat....

If this politics is feasible, both liberal and conservative dead ends become new beginnings. The liberal can campaign for formal public equality—for the abolition of sodomy laws, equal protection in public employment and institutions, the end of the ban on openly gay men and lesbians in the military—and rightly claim that he is merely seeing that all citizens in their public capacity are treated equally. But he can also argue fervently for freedom of expression—for those on both sides of the cultural war—and for freedom of economic contract. And he can concentrate his efforts on the work of transforming civil society, the place where every liberal longs to be.

And the conservative, while opposing "special rights," is able to formulate a vision of what values the society wants to inculcate. He can point to the virtues of a loyal and dedicated soldier, homosexual or heterosexual, and celebrate his patriotism; he can involve another minority group in the collective social good. He can talk about relations between heterosexuals and homosexuals not under the rubric of a minority group seeking preferences from a majority group, but as equal citizens, each prepared and willing to contribute to the common good, so long as they are treated equally by the state.

But the centerpiece of this new politics goes further than this. The critical measure for this politics of public equality-private freedom is something deeper and more emotional, perhaps, than the military.

It is equal access to civil marriage.

As with the military, this is a question of formal public discrimination, since only the state can grant and recognize marriage. If the military ban deals with the heart of what it means to be a citizen, marriage does even more so, since, in peace and war, it affects everyone. Marriage is not simply a private contract; it is a social and public recognition of a private commitment. As such, it is the highest public recognition of personal integrity. Denying it to homosexuals is the most public affront possible to their public equality.

This point may be the hardest for many heterosexuals to accept. Even those tolerant of homosexuals may find this institution so wedded to the notion of heterosexual commitment that to extend it would be to undo its very essence. And there may be religious reasons for resisting this that, within certain traditions, are unanswerable. But I am not here discussing what churches do in their private affairs. I am discussing what the allegedly neutral liberal state should do in public matters. For liberals, the case for homosexual marriage is overwhelming. As a classic public institution, it should be available to any two citizens.

Some might argue that marriage is by definition between a man and a woman; and it is difficult to argue with a definition. But if marriage is articulated beyond this circular fiat, then the argument for its exclusivity to one man and one woman disappears. The center of the public contract is an emotional, financial, and psychological bond between two people; in this respect, heterosexuals and homosexuals are identical. The heterosexuality of marriage is intrinsic only if it is understood to be intrinsically procreative; but that definition has long been abandoned in Western society. No civil marriage license is granted on the condition that the couple bear children; and the marriage is no less legal and no less defensible if it remains childless. In the contemporary West, marriage has become a way in which the state recognizes an emotional commitment by two people to each other for life. And within that definition, there is no public way, if one believes in equal rights under the law, in which it should legally be denied homosexuals....

But perhaps surprisingly... one of the strongest arguments for gay marriage is a conservative one. It's perhaps best illustrated by a comparison with the alternative often offered by liberals and liberationists to legal gay marriage, the concept of "domestic partnership." Several cities in the United States have domestic partnership laws, which allow relationships that do not fit into the category of heterosexual marriage to be registered with the city and qualify for benefits that had previously been reserved for heterosexual married couples. In these cities, a variety of interpersonal arrangements qualify for health insurance, bereavement leave, insurance, annuity and pension rights, housing rights (such as rent-control apartments), adoption and inheritance rights. Eventually, the aim is to include federal income tax and veterans' benefits as well. Homosexuals are not the only beneficiaries; heterosexual "live-togethers" also qualify.

The conservative's worries start with the ease of the relationship. To be sure, potential domestic partners have to prove financial interdependence, shared living arrangements, and a commitment to mutual caring. But they don't need to have a sexual relationship or even closely mirror old-style marriage. In principle, an elderly woman and her live-in nurse could qualify, or a pair of frat buddies. Left as it is, the concept of domestic partnership could open a Pandora's box of litigation and subjective judicial decision making about who qualifies. You either are or you're not married; it's not a complex question. Whether you are in a domestic partnership is not so clear.

More important for conservatives, the concept of domestic partnership chips away at the prestige of traditional relationships and undermines the priority we give them. Society, after all, has good reasons to extend legal advantages to heterosexuals who choose the formal sanction of marriage over simply living together. They make a deeper commitment to one another and to society; in exchange, society extends certain benefits to them. Marriage provides an anchor, if an arbitrary and often weak one, in the maelstrom of sex and relationships to which we are all prone. It provides a mechanism for emotional stability and economic security. We rig the law in its favor not because we disparage all forms of relationship other than the nuclear family, but because we recognize that not to promote marriage would be to ask too much of human virtue....

Any heterosexual man who takes a few moments to consider what his life would be like if he were never allowed a formal institution to cement his relationships will see the truth of what I am saying. Imagine life without a recognized family; imagine dating without even the possibility of marriage. Any heterosexual woman who can imagine being told at a young age that her attraction to men was wrong, that her loves and crushes were illicit, that her destiny was single-hood and shame, will also appreciate the point. Gay marriage is not a radical step; it is a profoundly humanizing, traditionalizing step. It is the first step in any resolution of the homosexual question—more important than any other institution, since it is the most central institution to the nature of the problem, which is to say, the emotional and sexual bond between one human being and another. If nothing else were done at all, and gay marriage were legalized, ninety percent of the political work necessary to achieve gay and lesbian equality would have been achieved. It is ultimately the only reform that truly matters.

... It has become a truism that in the field of emotional development, homosexuals have much to learn from the heterosexual culture. The values of commitment, of monogamy, of marriage, of stability are all posited as models for homosexual existence. And, indeed, of course, they are. Without an architectonic institution like that of marriage, it is difficult to create the conditions for nurturing such virtues, but that doesn't belie their importance.

It is also true, however, that homosexual relationships, even in their current, somewhat eclectic form, may contain features that could nourish the broader society as well. Precisely because there is no institutional model, gay relationships are often sustained more powerfully by genuine commitment. The mutual nurturing and sexual expressiveness of many lesbian relationships, the solidity and space of many adult gay male relationships, are qualities sometimes lacking in more rote, heterosexual couplings. Same-sex unions often incorporate the virtues of friendship more effectively than traditional marriages; and at times, among gay male relationships, the openness of the contract makes it more likely to survive than many heterosexual bonds. Some of this is unavailable to the male-female union: there is more likely to be greater understanding of the need for extramarital outlets between two men than between a man and a woman; and again, the lack of children gives gay couples greater freedom. Their failures entail fewer consequences for others. But something of the gay relationship's necessary honesty, its flexibility, and its equality could undoubtedly help strengthen and inform many heterosexual bonds....

As I've just argued, I believe strongly that marriage should be made available to everyone, in a politics of strict public neutrality. But within this model, there is plenty of scope for cultural difference. There is something baleful about the attempt of some gay conservatives to educate homosexuals and lesbians into an uncritical acceptance of a stifling model of heterosexual normality. The truth is, homosexuals are not entirely normal; and to flatten their varied and complicated lives into a single, moralistic model is to miss what is essential and exhilarating about their otherness.

NO ↩

James Q. Wilson

Against Homosexual Marriage

Our courts, which have mishandled abortion, may be on the verge of mishandling homosexuality. As a consequence of two pending decisions, we may be about to accept homosexual marriage.

In 1993 the supreme court of Hawaii ruled that, under the equal-protection clause of that state's constitution, any law based on distinctions of sex was suspect, and thus subject to strict judicial scrutiny. Accordingly, it reversed the denial of a marriage permit to a same-sex couple, unless the state could first demonstrate a "compelling state interest" that would justify limiting marriages to men and women.... [I]n the meantime, the executive branch of Hawaii appointed a commission to examine the question of same-sex marriages; its report, by a vote of five to two, supports them. The legislature, for its part, holds a different view of the matter, having responded to the court's decision by passing a law unambiguously reaffirming the limitation of marriage to male-female couples.

... [S]ince the United States Constitution has a clause requiring that "full faith and credit shall be given to the public acts, records, and judicial proceedings of every other state," a homosexual couple in a state like Texas, where the population is overwhelmingly opposed to such unions, may soon be able to fly to Hawaii, get married, and then return to live in Texas as lawfully wedded....

Contemporaneous with these events, an important book has appeared under the title *Virtually Normal*. In it, Andrew Sullivan, the editor of the *New Republic*, makes a strong case for a new policy toward homosexuals. He argues that "all *public* (as opposed to private) discrimination against homosexuals be ended.... *And that is all.*" The two key areas where this change is necessary are the military and marriage law. Lifting bans in those areas, while also disallowing antisodomy laws and providing information about homosexuality in publicly supported schools, would put an end to the harm that gays have endured. Beyond these changes, Sullivan writes, American society would need no "cures [of homophobia] or reeducations, no wrenching private litigation, no political imposition of tolerance."

It is hard to imagine how Sullivan's proposals would, in fact, end efforts to change private behavior toward homosexuals, or why the next, inevitable, step would not involve attempts to accomplish just that purpose by using cures

From James Q. Wilson, "Against Homosexual Marriage," *Commentary* (March 1996). Copyright © 1996 by The American Jewish Committee. Reprinted by permission. Notes omitted.

and reeducations, private litigation, and the political imposition of tolerance. But apart from this, Sullivan—an English Catholic, a homosexual, and someone who has on occasion referred to himself as a conservative—has given us the most sensible and coherent view of a program to put homosexuals and heterosexuals on the same public footing. . . .

⋅⟨◉⟩⋅

Sullivan recounts three main arguments concerning homosexual marriage, two against and one for. He labels them prohibitionist, conservative, and liberal. (A fourth camp, the "liberationist," which advocates abolishing all distinctions between heterosexuals and homosexuals, is also described—and scorched for its "strange confluence of political abdication and psychological violence.") I think it easier to grasp the origins of the three main arguments by referring to the principles on which they are based.

The prohibitionist argument is in fact a biblical one; the heart of it was stated by Dennis Prager in an essay in the *Public Interest* ("Homosexuality, the Bible, and Us," Summer 1993). When the first books of the Bible were written, and for a long time thereafter, heterosexual love is what seemed at risk. In many cultures—not only in Egypt or among the Canaanite tribes surrounding ancient Israel but later in Greece, Rome, and the Arab world, to say nothing of large parts of China, Japan, and elsewhere—homosexual practices were common and widely tolerated or even exalted. The Torah reversed this, making the family the central unit of life, the obligation to marry one of the first responsibilities of man, and the linkage of sex to procreation the highest standard by which to judge sexual relations. Leviticus puts the matter sharply and apparently beyond quibble:

> Thou shalt not live with mankind as with womankind; it is an abomination. . . . If a man also lie with mankind, as he lieth with a woman, both of them have committed an abomination; they shall surely be put to death; their blood shall be upon them.

Sullivan acknowledges the power of Leviticus but deals with it by placing it in a relative context. What is the nature of this "abomination"? Is it like killing your mother or stealing a neighbor's bread, or is it more like refusing to eat shellfish or having sex during menstruation? Sullivan suggests that all of these injunctions were written on the same moral level and hence can be accepted or ignored *as a whole*. He does not fully sustain this view, and in fact a refutation of it can be found in Prager's essay. In Prager's opinion and mine, people at the time of Moses, and for centuries before him, understood that there was a fundamental difference between whom you killed and what you ate, and in all likelihood people then and for centuries earlier linked whom you could marry closer to the principles that defined life than they did to the rules that defined diets.

The New Testament contains an equally vigorous attack on homosexuality by St. Paul. Sullivan partially deflects it by noting Paul's conviction that the earth was about to end and the Second Coming was near; under these conditions, all forms of sex were suspect. But Sullivan cannot deny that Paul singled out homosexuality as deserving of special criticism. He seems to pass over this obstacle without effective retort.

Instead, he takes up a different theme, namely, that on grounds of consistency many heterosexual practices—adultery, sodomy, premarital sex, and divorce, among others—should be outlawed equally with homosexual acts of the same character. The difficulty with this is that it mistakes the distinction alive in most people's minds between marriage as an institution and marriage as a practice. As an institution, it deserves unqualified support; as a practice, we recognize that married people are as imperfect as anyone else. Sullivan's understanding of the prohibitionist argument suffers from his unwillingness to acknowledge this distinction.

⋅⟨⊙⟩⋅

The second argument against homosexual marriage—Sullivan's conservative category—is based on natural law as originally set forth by Aristotle and Thomas Aquinas and more recently restated by Hadley Arkes, John Finnis, Robert George, Harry V. Jaffa, and others. How it is phrased varies a bit, but in general its advocates support a position like the following: man cannot live without the care and support of other people; natural law is the distillation of what thoughtful people have learned about the conditions of that care. The first thing they have learned is the supreme importance of marriage, for without it the newborn infant is unlikely to survive or, if he survives, to prosper. The necessary conditions of a decent family life are the acknowledgement by its members that a man will not sleep with his daughter or a woman with her son and that neither will openly choose sex outside marriage.

Now, some of these conditions are violated, but there is a penalty in each case that is supported by the moral convictions of almost all who witness the violation. On simple utilitarian grounds it may be hard to object to incest or adultery; if both parties to such an act welcome it and if it is secret, what differences does it make? But very few people, and then only ones among the overeducated, seem to care much about mounting a utilitarian assault on the family. To this assault, natural-law theorists respond much as would the average citizen—never mind "utility," what counts is what is right. In particular, homosexual uses of the reproductive organs violate the condition that sex serve solely as the basis of heterosexual marriage.

To Sullivan, what is defective about the natural-law thesis is that it assumes different purposes in heterosexual and homosexual love: moral consummation in the first case and pure utility or pleasure alone in the second. But in fact, Sullivan suggests, homosexual love can be as consummatory as heterosexual. He notes that as the Roman Catholic Church has deepened its understanding of the involuntary—that is, in some sense genetic—basis of homosexuality, it has attempted to keep homosexuals in the church as objects of affection and nurture, while banning homosexual acts as perverse.

But this, though better than nothing, will not work, Sullivan writes. To show why, he adduces an analogy to a sterile person. Such a person is permitted to serve in the military or enter an unproductive marriage; why not homosexuals? If homosexuals marry without procreation, they are no different (he suggests) from a sterile man or woman who marries without hope of procreation. Yet people, I think, want the form observed even when the practice varies; a sterile marriage, whether from choice or necessity, remains a marriage of a man and a woman. To this Sullivan offers essentially an aesthetic response. Just as albinos remind us of the brilliance of color and genius teaches us about moderation, homosexuals are a "natural foil" to the heterosexual union, "a variation that does not eclipse the theme." Moreover, the threat posed by the foil to the theme is slight as compared to the threats posed by adultery, divorce, and prostitution. To be consistent, Sullivan once again reminds us, society would have to ban adulterers from the military as it now bans confessed homosexuals.

But again this misses the point. It would make more sense to ask why an alternative to marriage should be invented and praised when we are having enough trouble maintaining the institution at all. Suppose that gay or lesbian marriage were authorized; rather than producing a "natural foil" that would "not eclipse the theme," I suspect such a move would call even more seriously into question the role of marriage at a time when the threats to it, ranging from single-parent families to common divorces, have hit record highs. Kenneth Minogue recently wrote of Sullivans's book that support for homosexual marriage would strike most people as "mere parody," one that could further weaken an already strained institution.

To me, the chief limitation of Sullivan's view is that it presupposes that marriage would have the same, domesticating effect on homosexual members as it has on heterosexuals, while leaving the latter largely unaffected. Those are very large assumptions that no modern society has ever tested.

Nor does it seem plausible to me that a modern society resists homosexual marriages entirely out of irrational prejudice. Marriage is a union, sacred to most, that unites a man and woman together for life. It is a sacrament of the Catholic Church and central to every other faith. Is it out of misinformation that every modern society has embraced this view and rejected the alternative? Societies differ greatly in their attitude toward the income people may have, the relations among their various races, and the distribution of political power. But they differ scarcely at all over the distinctions between heterosexual and homosexual couples. The former are overwhelmingly preferred over the latter. The reason, I believe, is that these distinctions involve the nature of marriage and thus the very meaning—even more, the very possibility—of society....

◦◦◉◦◦

Let us assume for the moment that a chance to live openly and legally with another homosexual is desirable. To believe that, we must set aside biblical injunctions, a difficult matter in a profoundly religious nation. But suppose we manage the diversion, perhaps on the grounds that if most Americans skip church, they can as readily avoid other errors of (possibly) equal magnitude.

Then we must ask on what terms the union shall be arranged. There are two alternatives—marriage or domestic partnership.

Sullivan acknowledges the choice, but disparages the domestic-partnership laws that have evolved in some foreign countries and in some American localities. His reasons, essentially conservative ones, are that domestic partnerships are too easily formed and too easily broken. Only real marriages matter. But—aside from the fact that marriage is in serious decline, and that only slightly more than half of all marriages performed in the United States this year will be between never-before-married heterosexuals—what is distinctive about marriage is that it is an institution created to sustain child-rearing. Whatever losses it has suffered in *this* respect, its function remains what it has always been.

The role of raising children is entrusted in principle to married heterosexual couples because after much experimentation—several thousand years, more or less—we have found nothing else that works as well. Neither a gay nor a lesbian couple can of its own resources produce a child; another party must be involved. What do we call this third party? A friend? A sperm or egg bank? An anonymous donor? There is no settled language for even describing, much less approving of, such persons.

Suppose we allowed homosexual couples to raise children who were created out of a prior heterosexual union or adopted from someone else's heterosexual contact. What would we think of this? There is very little research on the matter. Charlotte Patterson's famous essay, "Children of Gay and Lesbian Parents" (*Journal of Child and Development*, 1992), begins by conceding that the existing studies focus on children born into a heterosexual union that ended in divorce or that was transformed when the mother or father "came out" as a homosexual. Hardly any research has been done on children acquired at the outset by a homosexual couple. We therefore have no way of knowing how they would behave. And even if we had such studies, they might tell us rather little unless they were conducted over a very long period of time.

But it is one thing to be born into an apparently heterosexual family and then many years later to learn that one of your parents is homosexual. It is quite another to be acquired as an infant from an adoption agency or a parent-for-hire and learn from the first years of life that you are, because of your family's position, radically different from almost all other children you will meet. No one can now say how grievous this would be. We know that young children tease one another unmercifully; adding this dimension does not seem to be a step in the right direction.

Of course, homosexual "families," with or without children, might be rather few in number. Just how few, it is hard to say. Perhaps Sullivan himself would marry, but, given the great tendency of homosexual males to be promiscuous, many more like him would not, or if they did, would not marry with as much seriousness.

That is problematic in itself. At one point, Sullivan suggests that most homosexuals would enter a marriage "with as much (if not more) commitment as heterosexuals." Toward the end of this book, however, he seems to withdraw from so optimistic a view. He admits that the label "virtually" in the title of his book is deliberately ambiguous, because homosexuals as a group are *not* "normal." At another point, he writes that the "openness of the contract" between two homosexual males means that such a union will in fact be more durable than a heterosexual marriage because the contract contains an *"understanding of the need for extramarital outlets"* (emphasis added). But no such "understanding" exists in heterosexual marriage; to suggest that it might in homosexual ones is tantamount to saying that we are now referring to two different kinds of arrangements. To justify this difference, perhaps, Sullivan adds that the very "lack of children" will give "gay couples greater freedom." Freedom for what? Freedom, I think, to do more of those things that heterosexual couples do less of because they might hurt the children.

⋅⟨∘⟩⋅

The courts in Hawaii and in the nation's capital must struggle with all these issues under the added encumbrance of a contemporary outlook that makes law the search for rights, and responsibility the recognition of rights. Indeed, thinking of laws about marriage as documents that confer or withhold rights is itself an error of fundamental importance—one that the highest court in Hawaii has already committed. "Marriage," it wrote, "is a state-conferred legal-partnership status, the existence of which gives rise to a multiplicity of rights and benefits. . . ." A state-conferred legal partnership? To lawyers, perhaps; to mankind, I think not. . . .

Our challenge is to find a way of formulating a policy with respect to homosexual unions that is not the result of a reflexive act of judicial rights-conferring, but is instead a considered expression of the moral convictions of a people.

POSTSCRIPT

Should Same-Sex Marriages Be Legally Recognized?

The issue of the rights of homosexuals creates a social dilemma. Most people would agree that all members of society should have equal rights. However, the majority may disapprove of the lifestyles of a minority group and pass laws against some of their behaviors. The question is: When do these laws violate civil rights? Are laws against same-sex marriage such a violation?

There is a considerable literature on homosexuality. Recent works on the history of the gay rights movement include Dudley Clendinen and Adam Nagourney, *Out for Good: The Struggle to Build a Gay Rights Movement in America* (Simon & Schuster, 1999); Ronald J. Hunt, *Historical Dictionary of the Gay Liberation Movement* (Scarecrow Press, 1999); and John Loughery, *The Other Side of Silence: Men's Lives and Gay Identities: A Twentieth-Century History* (Henry Holt, 1998). For broad academic works on homosexuality see Kath Weston, *Long Slow Burn: Sexuality and Social Science* (Routledge, 1998); Alan Sinfield, *Gay and After* (Serpent's Tail, 1998); and Michael Ruse, *Homosexuality: A Philosophical Inquiry* (Blackwell, 1998). Recent works that focus on homosexual rights include David A. J. Richards, *Identity and the Case for Gay Rights* (University of Chicago Press, 1999); Morris B. Kaplan, *Sexual Justice* (Routledge, 1997); James Button, et al., *Private Lives, Public Conflicts: Battles Over Gay Rights in American Communities* (CQ Press, 1997); and Carl F. Stychin, *A Nation by Rights: National Cultures, Sexual Identity Politics, and the Discourse of Rights* (Temple University Press, 1998). On the antigay rights movement see Stephanie L. Whitt and Suzanne McCorkle, eds., *Anti-Gay Rights: Assessing Voter Initiatives* (Praeger, 1997). For an examination of prejudice against homosexuals see Gregory M. Herek, ed., *Stigma and Sexual Orientation: Understanding Prejudice Against Lesbians, Gay Men, and Bisexuals* (Sage, 1998). For a reader on same-sex marriage see Andrew Sullivan, *Same-Sex Marriage, Pro and Con: A Reader* (Random House, 1997). The best work on human sexual practices is Edward O. Laumann, John H. Gagnon, Robert T. Michael, and Stuart Michaels, *The Social Organization of Sexuality: Sexual Practices in the United States* (University of Chicago Press, 1994).

ISSUE 7

Is the Decline of the Traditional Family a National Crisis?

YES: David Popenoe, from "The American Family Crisis," *National Forum: The Phi Kappa Phi Journal* (Summer 1995)

NO: Stephanie Coontz, from "The American Family," *Life* (November 1999)

ISSUE SUMMARY

YES: Sociologist David Popenoe contends that families play important roles in society but how the traditional family functions in these roles has declined dramatically in the last several decades, with very adverse effects on children.

NO: Family historian Stephanie Coontz argues that current discussion of family decline includes a false idealization of the traditional family of the past and misleading interpretations of current data on families. She finds that the trends are both positive and negative.

T he state of the American family deeply concerns many Americans. About 40 percent of marriages end in divorce, and only 27 percent of children born in 1990 are expected to be living with both parents by the time they reach age 17. Most Americans, therefore, are affected personally or are close to people who are affected by structural changes in the family. Few people can avoid being exposed to the issue: violence in the family and celebrity divorces are standard fare for news programs, and magazine articles decrying the breakdown of the family appear frequently. Politicians today try to address the problems of the family. Academics have affirmed that the family crisis has numerous significant negative effects on children, spouses, and the rest of society.

Sociologists pay attention to the role that the family plays in the functioning of society. For a society to survive, its population must reproduce (or take in many immigrants), and its young must be trained to perform adult roles and to have the values and attitudes that will motivate them to contribute to society. Procreation and socialization are two vital roles that families traditionally have performed. In addition, the family provides economic and emotional support for its members, which is vital to their effective functioning in society.

Today the performance of the family is disappointing in all of these areas. Procreation outside of marriage has become common, and it has been found to lead to less than ideal conditions for raising children. The scorecard on American family socialization is hard to assess, but there is concern about such issues as parents' declining time with and influence on their children and latchkey children whose parents work and who must therefore spend part of the day unsupervised. The economic performance of two-parent families is improving because more mothers are entering the labor force, but this gain is often related to a decline in emotional support. Single-parent families tend to perform less well on both counts. Overall, the high divorce rate and the frequency of child and spousal abuse indicate that the modern family fails to provide adequate social and emotional support.

Although most experts agree that the American family is in crisis, there is little agreement about what, if anything, should be done about it. After all, most of these problems result from the choices that people make to try to increase their happiness. People end unhappy marriages. Married women work for fulfillment or financial gain. Unwed mothers decide to keep their children. The number of couples who choose to remain childless is growing rapidly. These trends cannot be changed unless people start choosing differently. As yet there is no sign of this happening. Does this mean that the weakening of the family is desirable? Few would advocate such an idea, but perhaps some weakening must be accepted as the consequence of embracing other cherished values.

In the selections that follow, David Popenoe argues that the family is the key institution in society. Since it plays many important roles, its functional decline, which is largely due to cultural trends, has many adverse social impacts, including greatly harming children. He concludes by suggesting what needs to be done to strengthen families and family life. Stephanie Coontz provides a much different assessment of the present state of the family as compared with earlier times. She maintains that the family crisis thesis ignores the many strengths of American families today, overemphasizes certain negative trends, and misinterprets several of them. She tries to set the record straight and to counter much of the misinformation that the media produces.

David Popenoe

 **YES**

The American Family Crisis

Throughout our nation's history, we have depended heavily on the family to provide both social order and economic success. Families have provided for the survival and development of children, for the emotional and physical health of adults, for the special care of the sick, injured, handicapped, and elderly, and for the reinforcement of society's values. Today, America's families face growing problems in each of these areas, and by many measures are functioning less well than ever before—less well, in fact, than in other advanced, industrialized nations.

The most serious negative effects of the functional decline of families have been on children. Evidence suggests that today's generation of children is the first in our nation's history to be less well-off psychologically and socially than their parents were at the same age. Alarming increases have occurred in such pathologies as juvenile delinquency, violence, suicide, substance abuse, eating disorders, nonmarital births, psychological stress, anxiety, and unipolar depression.

Such increases are especially troubling because many conditions for child well-being have improved. Fewer children are in each family today; therefore, more adults are theoretically available to care for them. Children are in some respects healthier and materially better off; they have completed more years in school, as have their parents. Greater national concern for children's rights, for child abuse, and for psychologically sound childrearing practices is also evident.

Family Origins and History

As the first social institution in human history, the family probably arose because of the need for adults to devote a great amount of time to childrearing. Coming into the world totally dependent, human infants must, for a larger portion of their lives than for any other species, be cared for and taught by adults. To a unique degree, humans nurture, protect, and educate their offspring. It is hard to conceive of a successful society, therefore, that does not have families that are able to raise children to become adults who have the capacity to love and to work, who are committed to such positive social values as honesty, respect, and responsibility, and who pass these values on to the next generation.

Infants and children need, at minimum, one adult to care for them. Yet, given the complexities of the task, childrearing in all societies until recent years has been shared by many adults. The institutional bond of marriage between biological parents, with the essential function of tying the father to the mother and child, is found in virtually every society. Marriage is the most universal social institution known; in no society has nonmarital childbirth, or the single parent, been the cultural norm. In all societies the biological father is identified where possible, and in almost all societies he plays an important role in his children's upbringing, even though his primary task is often that of protector and breadwinner.

In the preindustrial era, however, adult family members did not necessarily consider childrearing to be their primary task. As a unit of rural economic production, the family's main focus typically was economic survival. According to some scholars, rather than the family being for the sake of the children, the children, as needed workers, were for the sake of the family. One of the most important family transitions in history was the rise in industrial societies of what we now refer to as the "traditional nuclear family": husband away at work during the day and wife taking care of the home and children full time. This transition took place in the United States beginning in the early 1800s. The primary focus of this historically new family form was indeed the care and nurturing of children, and parents dedicated themselves to this effort.

Over the past thirty years, the United States (along with other modern societies) has witnessed another major family transformation—the beginning of the end of the traditional nuclear family. Three important changes have occurred:

- The divorce rate increased sharply (to a level currently exceeding 50 percent), and parents increasingly decided to forgo marriage, with the consequence that a sizable number of children are being raised in single-parent households, apart from other relatives.
- Married women in large numbers left the role of full-time mother and housewife to go into the labor market, and the activities of their former role have not been fully replaced.
- The focus of many families shifted away from childrearing to the psychological well-being and self-development of their adult members. One indication of this latter focus is that, even when they have young children to raise, parents increasingly break up if their psychological and self-fulfillment needs are unmet in the marriage relationship.

We can never return to the era of the traditional nuclear family, even if we wanted to, and many women and men emphatically do not. The conditions of life that generated that family form have changed. Yet the one thing that has not changed through all the years and all the family transformations is the need for children to be raised by mothers and fathers. Indeed, in modern, complex societies in which children need an enormous amount of education and psychological security to succeed, active and nurturing relationships with adults may be more critical for children than ever.

Unfortunately, the amount of time children spend with adults, especially their parents, has been dropping dramatically. Absent fathers, working mothers, distant grandparents, anonymous schools, and transient communities have become hallmarks of our era. Associated with this trend in many families, and in society as a whole, is a weakening of the fundamental assumption that children are to be loved and valued at the highest level of priority.

The Individualism Trend

To understand fully what has happened to the family, we must look at the broader cultural changes that have taken place, especially changes in the values and norms that condition everyday choices. Over recent centuries in industrialized and industrializing societies, a gradual shift has occurred from a "collectivist" culture (I am using this term with a cultural and not a political meaning) toward an individualistic culture. In the former, group goals take precedence over individual ones. "Doing one's duty," for example, is more important than "self-fulfillment," and "social bonds" are more important than "personal choice." In individualistic cultures, the welfare of the group is secondary to the importance of such personal goals as self-expression, independence, and competitiveness.

Not surprisingly, individualistic societies rank higher than collectivist societies in political democracy and individual development. But the shift from collectivism to individualism involves social costs as well as personal gains—especially when it proceeds too far. Along with political democracy and individual development, individualistic societies tend to have high rates of individual deviance, juvenile delinquency, crime, loneliness, depression, suicide, and social alienation. In short, these societies have more free and independent citizens but less social order and probably a lower level of psychological well-being.

"Communitarian" Individualism

The United States has long been known as the world's most individualistic society. Certainly, we place a high value on this aspect of our society, and it is a major reason why so many people from other countries want to come here. Yet for most of our history, this individualism has been balanced, or tempered, by a strong belief in the sanctity of accepted social organizations and institutions, such as the family, religion, voluntary associations, local communities, and even the nation as a whole. While individualistic in spirit, people's identities were rooted in these social units, and their lives were directed toward the social goals that they represented. Thus, the United States has been marked for much of its history, not by a pure form of individualism, but by what could be termed a "communitarian" or balanced individualism.

"Expressive" Individualism

As the individualism trend has advanced, however, a more radical or "expressive" individualism has emerged, one that is largely devoted to "self-indulgence" or "self-fulfillment" at the expense of the group. Today, we see a large number of people who are narcissistic or self-oriented, and who show concern for social institutions only when these directly affect their own well-being. Unfortunately, these people have a tendency to distance themselves from the social and community groupings that have long been the basis for personal security and social order. Since the 1950s, the number of people being married, visiting informally with others, and belonging to voluntary associations has decreased, and the number of people living alone has increased.

In turn, the traditional community groupings have been weakened. More people are viewing our once accepted social institutions with considerable skepticism. As measured by public opinion polls, confidence in such public institutions as medicine, higher education, the law, the press, and organized religion has declined dramatically. As measured by people voting with their feet, trust in the institution of marriage also had declined dramatically. And, as we see almost every night on the news, our sense of cultural solidarity seems to be diminishing.

The highly disturbing actions of inner-city residents that we have witnessed in the urban riots of recent years could be considered less a departure from everyday American cultural reality than a gross intensification of it. Few social and cultural trends found in the inner city are not also present in the rest of the nation. Indeed, with respect to the family, the characteristics of the African American family pronounced by President Lyndon Johnson in 1965 to be in a state of "breakdown" are very similar to the family characteristics of America as a whole in 1994!

In summary, for the good of both the individual and society, the individualism trend in the United States has advanced too far. The family holds the key. People need strong families to provide them with the identity, belonging, discipline, and values that are essential for full individual development. The social institutions of the surrounding community depend on strong families to teach those "civic" values—honesty, trust, self-sacrifice, personal responsibility, respect for others—that enable them to thrive. But let us not forget that strong families depend heavily on cultural and social supports. Family life in an unsupportive community is always precarious and the social stresses can be overwhelming.

Not to Forget the Gains

While I have presented a fairly grim picture in describing these cultural changes, it is important to add that not every aspect of our society has deteriorated. In several key areas, this nation has seen significant social progress. For instance, we are a much more inclusive society today—segregation and racism have diminished, and we now accept more African Americans, Hispanics, and other minority groups into the mainstream. The legal, sexual, and financial emancipation of women has become a reality as never before in history. With advances in medicine, we have greater longevity and, on the whole, better physical health. And our average material standard of living, especially in the possession of consumer durables, has increased significantly.

The Nuclear Family and Marriage

Given our nation's past ability to accept positive social change, we can have some confidence in our capacity to solve the problem of family decline. In seeking solutions, we should first consider what family structure is best able to raise children who are autonomous and socially responsible, and also able to meet adult needs for intimacy and personal attachment. Considering the available evidence, as well as the lessons of recent human experience, unquestionably the family structure that works best is the nuclear family. I am not referring to the traditional nuclear family, but rather to the nuclear family that consists of a male and a female who marry and live together and share responsibility for their children and for each other.

Let us look, for a moment, at other family forms. No advanced, Western society exists where the three-generation extended family is very important and where it is not also on the wane. Some scholars suggest that a new extended family has emerged with the trend toward "step" and "blended" families. "Isn't it nice," they say, "that we now have so many new relatives!" The final verdict is not yet in on stepfamilies, but preliminary evidence from the few empirical studies that have been done sends quite the opposite message, and it is a chilling one. For example, a recent British study of 17,000 children born in 1958 concluded that "the chances of stepchildren suffering social deprivation before reaching twenty-one are even greater than those left living after divorce with a lone parent." Similar findings are turning up in the United States.

How are the single-parent families doing? Accumulating evidence on the personal and social consequences of this family type paints an equally grim picture. A 1988 survey by the National Center for Health Statistics found, for example, that children from single-parent families are two to three times more likely to have emotional and behavioral problems than children from intact families, and reduced family income is by no means the only factor involved. In their new book *Growing Up With a Single Parent*, Sara McLanahan and Gary Sandefur, after examining six nationally representative data sets containing over 25,000 children from a variety of racial and social class backgrounds, conclude that "children who grow up with only one of their biological parents are disadvantaged across a broad array of outcomes ... they are twice as likely to drop out of high school, 2.5 times as likely to become teen mothers, and 1.4 times as likely to be idle—out of school and out of work—as children who grow up with both parents." The loss of economic resources, they report, accounts for only about 50 percent of the disadvantages associated with single parenthood.

Toward Solutions

Of course, many people have no other choice than to live in step- and single-parent families. These families can be successful, and their members deserve our continuing support. Nevertheless, the benefits that strong nuclear families bring to a high-achieving, individualistic, and democratic society are absolutely clear. For example, a committed marriage, which is the basis of the strong nuclear family, brings enormous benefits to adults. It is ironic in this age of self-fulfillment, when people are being pulled away from marriage, that a happy marriage seems to provide the best source of self-fulfillment. By virtually every measure, married individuals are better off than single individuals.

Another reason for supporting strong nuclear families is that society gains enormously when a high percentage of men are married. While unmarried women take relatively good care of themselves, unmarried men often have difficulty in this regard. In general, every society must be wary of the unattached male, for he is universally the cause of numerous social ills. Healthy societies are heavily dependent on men being attached to a strong moral order, which is centered in families, both to discipline sexual behavior and to reduce competitive aggression. Men need the moral and emotional instruction of women more than vice versa. Family life, especially having children, is for men a civilizing force of no mean proportions.

We should be seriously concerned, therefore, that men currently spend more time living apart from families than at probably any other time in American history. About a quarter of all men aged twenty-five to thirty-four live in nonfamily households, either alone or with an unrelated individual. In 1960, average Americans spent 62 percent of their adult lives with spouse and children, which was the highest in our history; by 1980, they spent 43 percent, the lowest in our history. This trend alone may help to account for the high and rising crime rates over the past three decades. During this period, the number of reported violent crimes per capita, largely committed by unattached males, increased by 355 percent.

Today, a growing portion of American men are highly involved in child care, providing more help with the children than their own fathers did. Yet, because they did not stay with or marry the mothers of their children, or because of divorce, a large number of men have abandoned their children entirely.

Between 1960 and 1990 the percentage of children living apart from their biological fathers more than doubled, from 17 percent to 36 percent. In general, childrearing women have become increasingly isolated from men. This is one of the main reasons why nothing would benefit the nation more than a national drive to promote strong marriages.

The New Familism: A Hopeful Trend

One bright spot in this picture is what some of us have called "the new familism," a growing realization in America that, "yes, the family really is in trouble and needs help." Public opinion polls indicate that nearly two-thirds of Americans believe "family values have gotten weaker in the United States." Both major political parties and our President now seem to be in agreement.

Two primary groups are involved in this cultural mini-shift: the maturing baby boomers, now at the family stage of their life cycle, and the "baby-boom echo" children of the divorce revolution. The middle-aged baby boomers, spurred by growing evidence that children have been hurt by recent family changes, have been instrumental in shifting the media in a profamily direction. And many of the echo children of the 1970s, with their troubled childhoods, are coming into adulthood with a resolve not to repeat their parents' mistakes. They tend to put a high premium on marital permanence, perhaps because they have been unable to take the family for granted as many of their parents—the children of the familistic 1950s—did. But one concern is this: will they have the psychological stability to sustain an intimate relationship, or will their insecure childhoods make it impossible for them to fulfill their commitment to a lasting marriage?

Unfortunately, studies of the long-term effects of divorce on children and adolescents provide no optimism in this regard.

A couple of other factors seem to be working in a profamily direction. One is AIDS, which has now noticeably slowed the sexual revolution. As one entertainment figure recently said (with obvious dismay), "dating in Hollywood just isn't what it used to be." Neither, I must add, is dating what it used to be on the college campus, but the changes so far have not been very remarkable. Another factor is that cultural change is often reflected in cycles, and some cycles of change are patterned in generational terms. We know that not all cultural values can be maximized simultaneously. What one generation comes to value because they have less of it, their parents' generation rejected. This factor leads us to believe that the nation as a whole may be primed in the 1990s to run away from the values of radical individualism and more fully embrace the ideals of family and other social bonds.

Conclusion

In thinking about how to solve America's family crisis, we should keep the following considerations uppermost in mind:

- As a society, we cannot return to the era of the traditional nuclear family. But, we must do everything possible to strengthen the husband-wife nuclear family that stays together and takes responsibility for its children. Every child both wants—and needs—a mother and a father.
- Fundamental to strengthening the nuclear family is a renewed emphasis on the importance of marriage, which is the social institution designed primarily to hold men to the mother-child unit. It is extremely important for our children, and for our society, that men are attached to childrearing families.

- With even the strongest of marriages, parents have great difficulty raising children in an unsupportive and hostile environment. We must seek to renew the sinews of community life that can support families, maintain social order, and promote the common good. We should give as much attention to recreating a "family culture" as we are now giving to strengthening a "work culture."
- As an overall approach to promoting family life, nothing is more important than trying to diminish and even turn back the trend toward radical individualism. Social bonds, rather than personal choice, and community needs, rather than individual autonomy, must be accorded a higher priority in our culture—and in our lives.

The American Family

As the century comes to an end, many observers fear for the future of America's families. Our divorce rate is the highest in the world, and the percentage of unmarried women is significantly higher than in 1960. Educated women are having fewer babies, while immigrant children flood the schools, demanding to be taught in their native language. Harvard University reports that only 4 percent of its applicants can write a proper sentence.

There's an epidemic of sexually transmitted diseases among men. Many streets in urban neighborhoods are littered with cocaine vials. Youths call heroin "happy dust." Even in small towns, people have easy access to addictive drugs, and drug abuse by middle-class wives is skyrocketing. Police see 16-year-old killers, 12-year-old prostitutes, and gang members as young as 11.

America at the end of the 1990s? No, America at the end of the 1890s.

The litany of complaints may sound familiar, but the truth is that many things were worse at the start of this century than they are today. Then, thousands of children worked full-time in mines, mills and sweatshops. Most workers labored 10 hours a day, often six days a week, which left them little time or energy for family life. Race riots were more frequent and more deadly than those experienced by recent generations. Women couldn't vote, and their wages were so low that many turned to prostitution.

In 1900 a white child had one chance in three of losing a brother or sister before age 15, and a black child had a fifty-fifty chance of seeing a sibling die. Children's-aid groups reported widespread abuse and neglect by parents. Men who deserted or divorced their wives rarely paid child support. And only 6 percent of the children graduated from high school, compared with 88 percent today.

Why do so many people think American families are facing worse problems now than in the past? Partly it's because we compare the complex and diverse families of the 1990s with the seemingly more standard-issue ones of the 1950s, a unique decade when every long-term trend of the 20th century was temporarily reversed. In the 1950s, for the first time in 100 years, the divorce rate fell while marriage and fertility rates soared, creating a boom in nuclear-family living. The percentage of foreign-born individuals in the country decreased. And the debates over social and cultural issues that had divided

Americans for 150 years were silenced, suggesting a national consensus on family values and norms.

Some nostalgia for the 1950s is understandable: Life looked pretty good in comparison with the hardship of the Great Depression and World War II. The GI Bill gave a generation of young fathers a college education and a subsidized mortgage on a new house. For the first time, a majority of men could support a family and buy a home without pooling their earnings with those of other family members. Many Americans built a stable family life on these foundations.

But much nostalgia for the 1950s is a result of selective amnesia—the same process that makes childhood memories of summer vacations grow sunnier with each passing year. The superficial sameness of 1950s family life was achieved through censorship, coercion and discrimination. People with unconventional beliefs faced governmental investigation and arbitrary firings. African Americans and Mexican Americans were prevented from voting in some states by literacy tests that were not administered to whites. Individuals who didn't follow the rigid gender and sexual rules of the day were ostracized.

Leave It to Beaver did not reflect the real-life experience of most American families. While many moved into the middle class during the 1950s, poverty remained more widespread than in the worse of our last three recessions. More children went hungry, and poverty rates for the elderly were more than twice as high as today's.

Even in the white middle class, not every woman was as serenely happy with her lot as June Cleaver was on TV. Housewives of the 1950s may have been less rushed than today's working mothers, but they were more likely to suffer anxiety and depression. In many states, women couldn't serve on juries or get loans or credit cards in their own names.

And not every kid was as wholesome as Beaver Cleaver, whose mischievous antics could be handled by Dad at the dinner table. In 1955 alone, Congress discussed 200 bills aimed at curbing juvenile delinquency. Three years later, LIFE reported that urban teachers were being terrorized by their students. The drugs that were so freely available in 1900 had been outlawed, but many children grew up in families ravaged by alcohol and barbiturate abuse.

Rates of unwed childbearing tripled between 1940 and 1958, but most Americans didn't notice because unwed mothers generally left town, gave their babies up for adoption and returned home as if nothing had happened. Troubled youths were encouraged to drop out of high school. Mentally handicapped children were warehoused in institutions like the Home for Idiotic and Imbecilic Children in Kansas, where a woman whose sister had lived there for most of the 1950s once took me. Wives routinely told pollsters that being disparaged or ignored by their husbands was a normal part of a happier-than-average marriage.

Denial extended to other areas of life as well. In the early 1900s, doctors refused to believe that the cases of gonorrhea and syphilis they saw in young girls could have been caused by sexual abuse. Instead, they reasoned, girls could get these diseases from toilet seats, a myth that terrified generations of mothers and daughters. In the 1950s, psychiatrists dismissed incest reports as Oedipal fantasies on the part of children.

Spousal rape was legal throughout the period and wife beating was not taken seriously by authorities. Much of what we now label child abuse was accepted as a normal part of parental discipline. Physicians saw no reason to question parents who claimed that their child's broken bones had been caused by a fall from a tree.

There are plenty of stresses in modern family life, but one reason they seem worse is that we no longer sweep them under the rug. Another is that we have higher expectations of parenting and marriage. That's a good thing. We're right to be concerned about inattentive parents, conflicted marriages, antisocial values, teen violence and child abuse. But we need to realize that many of our worries reflect how much better we *want* to be, not how much better we *used* to be.

AMERICAN MIRROR

M uncie, Ind. (pop. 67,476), calls itself America's Hometown. But to generations of sociologists it is better known as America's Middletown—the most studied place in the 20th century American landscape. "Muncie has nothing extraordinary about it," says University of Virginia professor Theodore Caplow, which is why, for the past 75 years, researchers have gone there to observe the typical American family. Muncie's averageness first drew sociologists Robert and Helen Lynd in 1924. They returned in 1935 (their follow-up study was featured in a LIFE photo essay by Margaret Bourke-White). And in 1976, armed with the Lynds' original questionnaires, Caplow launched yet another survey of the town's citizens.

Caplow discovered that family life in Muncie was much healthier in the 1970s than in the 1920s. Not only were husbands and wives communicating more, but unlike married couples in the 1920s, they were also shopping, eating out, exercising and going to movies and concerts together. More than 90 percent of Muncie's couples characterized their marriages as "happy" or "very happy." In 1929 the Lynds had described partnerships of a drearier kind, "marked by sober accommodation of each partner to his share in the joint undertaking of children, paying off the mortgage and generally 'getting on.'"

Caplow's five-year study, which inspired a six-part PBS series, found that even though more moms were working outside the home, two thirds of them spent at least two hours a day with their children; in 1924 fewer than half did. In 1924 most children expected their mothers to be good cooks and housekeepers, and wanted their fathers to spend time with them and respect their opinions. Fifty years later, expectations of fathers were unchanged, but children wanted the same—time and respect—from their mothers.

This year, Caplow went back to survey the town again. The results (and another TV documentary) won't be released until December 2000.

—Sora Song

Fathers in intact families are spending more time with their children than at any other point in the past 100 years. Although the number of hours the average woman spends at home with her children has declined since the early 1900s, there has been a decrease in the number of children per family and an increase in individual attention to each child. As a result, mothers today, including working moms, spend almost twice as much time with each child as mothers did in the 1920s. People who raised children in the 1940s and 1950s typically report that their own adult children and grandchildren communicate far better with their kids and spend more time helping with homework than they did—even as they complain that other parents today are doing a worse job than in the past.

Despite the rise in youth violence from the 1960s to the early 1990s, America's children are also safer now than they've ever been. An infant was four times more likely to die in the 1950s than today. A parent then was three times more likely than a modern one to preside at the funeral of a child under the age of 15, and 27 percent more likely to lose an older teen to death.

If we look back over the last millennium, we can see that families have always been diverse and in flux. In each period, families have solved one set of problems only to face a new array of challenges. What works for a family in one economic and cultural setting doesn't work for a family in another. What's helpful at one stage of a family's life may be destructive at the next stage. If there is one lesson to be drawn from the last millennium of family history, it's that families are always having to play catch-up with a changing world.

Take the issue of working mothers. Families in which mothers spend as much time earning a living as they do raising children are nothing new. They were the norm throughout most of the last two millennia. In the 19th century, married women in the United States began a withdrawal from the workforce, but for most families this was made possible only by sending their children out to work instead. When child labor was abolished, married women began reentering the workforce in ever large numbers.

For a few decades, the decline in child labor was greater than the growth of women's employment. The result was an aberration: the male-breadwinner family. In the 1920s, for the first time, a bare majority of American children grew up in families where the husband provided all the income, the wife stayed home full-time, and they and their siblings went to school instead of work. During the 1950s, almost two thirds of children grew up in such families, an all-time high. Yet that same decade saw an acceleration of workforce participation by wives and mothers that soon made the dual-earner family the norm, a trend not likely to be reversed in the next century.

What's new is not that women make half their families' living, but that for the first time they have substantial control over their own income, along with the social freedom to remain single or to leave an unsatisfactory marriage. Also new is the declining proportion of their lives that people devote to rearing children, both because they have fewer kids and because they are living longer. Until about 1940, the typical marriage was broken by the death of one partner within a few years after the last child left home. Today, couples can look forward to spending more than two decades together after the children leave.

The growing length of time partners spend with only each other for company has made many individuals less willing to put up with an unhappy marriage, while women's economic independence makes it less essential for them to do so. It is no wonder that divorce has risen steadily since 1900. Disregarding a spurt in 1946, a dip in the 1950s and another peak around 1980, the divorce rate is just where you'd expect to find it, based on the rate of increase from 1900 to 1950. Today, 40 percent of all marriages will end in divorce before a couple's 40th anniversary. Yet despite this high divorce rate, expanded life expectancies mean that more couples are reaching that anniversary than ever before.

Families and individuals in contemporary America have more life choices than in the past. That makes it easier for some to consider dangerous or unpopular options. But it also makes success easier for many families that never would have had a chance before—interracial, gay or lesbian, and single-mother families, for example. And it expands horizons for most families.

Women's new options are good not just for themselves but for their children. While some people say that women who choose to work are selfish, it turns out that maternal self-sacrifice is not good for children. Kids do better when their mothers are happy with their lives, whether their satisfaction comes from being a full-time homemaker or from having a job.

Largely because of women's new roles at work, men are doing more at home. Although most men still do less housework than their wives, the gap has been halved since the 1960s. Today, 49 percent of couples say they share childcare equally, compared with 25 percent of 1985.

Men's greater involvement at home is good for their relationships with their parents, and also good for their children. Hands-on fathers make better parents than men who let their wives do all the nurturing and childcare: They raise sons who are more expressive and daughters who are more likely to do well in school, especially in math and science.

In 1900, life expectancy was 47 years, and only 4 percent of the population was 65 or older. Today, life expectancy is 76 years, and by 2025, about 20 percent of Americans will be 65 or older. For the first time, a generation of adults must plan for the needs of both their parents and their children. Most Americans are responding with remarkable grace. One in four households gives the equivalent of a full day a week or more in unpaid care to an aging relative, and more than half say they expect to do so in the next 10 years. Older people are less likely to be impoverished or incapacitated by illness than in the past, and they have more opportunity to develop a relationship with their grandchildren.

Even some of the choices that worry us the most are turning out to be manageable. Divorce rates are likely to remain high, but more non-custodial parents are staying in touch with their children. Child-support receipts are up. And a lower proportion of kids from divorced families are exhibiting problems than in earlier decades. Stepfamilies are learning to maximize children's access to supportive adults rather than cutting them of from one side of the family.

Out-of-wedlock births are also high, however, and this will probably continue because the age of first marriage for women has risen to an all-time high of 25, almost five years above what it was in the 1950s. Women who marry at an older age are less likely to divorce, but they have more years when they are at risk—or at choice—for a nonmarital birth.

Nevertheless, births to teenagers have fallen from 50 percent of all non-marital births in the late 1970s to just 30 percent today. A growing proportion of women who have a nonmarital birth are in their twenties and thirties and usually have more economic and educational resources than unwed mothers of the past. While two involved parents are generally better than one, a mother's personal maturity, along with her educational and economic status, is a better predictor of how well her child will turn out than her marital status. We should no longer assume that children raised by single parents face debilitating disadvantages.

As we begin to understand the range of sizes, shapes and colors that today's families come in, we find that the differences *within* family types are more important than the differences *between* them. No particular family form guarantees success, and no particular form is doomed to fail. How a family functions on the inside is more important than how it looks from the outside.

The biggest problem facing most families as this century draws to a close is not that our families have changed too much but that our institutions have changed too little. America's work policies are 50 years out of date, designed for a time when most moms weren't in the workforce and most dads didn't understand the joys of being involved in childcare. Our school schedules are 150 years out of date, designed for a time when kids needed to be home to help with the milking and haying. And many political leaders feel they have to decide whether to help parents stay home longer with their kids or invest in better childcare, preschool and afterschool programs, when most industrialized nations have long since learned it's possible to do both.

So America's social institutions have some Y2K bugs to iron out. But for the most part, our families are ready for the next millennium.

POSTSCRIPT

Is the Decline of the Traditional Family a National Crisis?

P openoe admits that there are many positive aspects to the recent changes that have affected families, but he sees the negative consequences, especially for children, as necessitating actions to counter them. He recommends a return to family values and speaks out against the individualistic ethos. Coontz contends that the traditional family form that people like Popenoe are nostalgic for was atypical in American history and cannot be re-created. Furthermore, a closer look at the data indicates that the institution of the family is not in crisis. While admitting that many marriages fail, Coontz asserts that many families are strong.

Support for Coontz's point of view can be found in E. L. Kain, *The Myth of Family Decline* (D. C. Heath, 1990); J. F. Gubrium and J. A. Holstein, *What Is a Family?* (Mayfield, 1990); and Rosalind C. Barnett and Caryl Rivers, *She Works/He Works: How Two-Income Families Are Happier, Healthier, and Better Off* (HarperCollins, 1997). Recent works describing the weakening of the family and marriage include Richard T. Gill, *Posterity Lost: Progress, Ideology, and the Decline of the American Family* (Rowman & Littlefield, 1997); Dana Mack, *The Assault on Parenthood: How Our Culture Undermines the Family* (Simon & Schuster, 1997); Maggie Gallagher, *The Abolition of Marriage: How We Destroy Lasting Love* (Regnery, 1996); and Barbara Dafoe Whitehead, *The Divorce Culture: How Divorce Became an Entitlement and How It Is Blighting the Lives of Our Children* (Alfred A. Knopf, 1997).The work dealing with divorce and its consequences that is currently in the spotlight is Judith Wallerstein, *The Unexpected Legacy of Divorce* (Hyperion, 2000). David Popenoe and Jean Bethke Elshtain's book *Promises to Keep: Decline and Renewal of Marriage in America* (Rowman & Littlefield, 1996) discusses the decline but also signs of renewal of marriage.

Works that analyze changes in marriage and the family include Andrew Cherlin's *Marriage, Divorce, Remarriage,* rev. ed. (Harvard University Press, 1992); Betty Farrell's *Family: The Making of an Idea, an Institution, and a Controversy in American Culture* (Westview Press, 1999); Karla B. Hackstaff's *Marriage in a Culture of Divorce* (Temple University Press, 1999); Jessica Weiss's *To Have and to Hold: Marriage, the Baby Boom, and Social Change* (University of Chicago Press, 2000); Barbara J. Risman's *Gender Vertigo: American Families in Transition* (Yale University Press, 1998); Ronald D. Taylor and Margaret C. Wang, eds., *Resilience Across Contexts: Family, Work, Culture, and Community* (Lawrence Erlbaum, 2000); and Linda J. Waite and Maggie Gallagher, *The Case for Marriage: Why Married People Are Happier, Healthier, and Better Off Financially* (Doubleday, 2000).

For two major works on aspects of familial changes, see David Blankenhorn, *Fatherless America: Confronting Our Most Urgent Social Problem* (Basic Books, 1995) and Sara McLanahan and Gary Sandefur, *Growing up With a Single Parent: What Hurts and What Helps* (Harvard University Press, 1994).

On the Internet ...

Statistical Resources on the Web: Sociology

This Statistical Resources on the Web site provides links to data on poverty in the United States. Included is a link that contains both current and historical poverty data.

http://www.lib.umich.edu/govdocs/stats.html

Institute for Research on Poverty (IRP)

The Institute for Research on Poverty researches the causes and consequences of social inequality and poverty in the United States. This Web site includes frequently asked questions about poverty and links to other Internet resources on the subject.

http://www.ssc.wisc.edu/irp/

About.com: Affirmative Action

About.com's Web site on affirmative action contains information about resources and organizations that focus on affirmative action policies and current events. This site also enables you to search other topics related to race relations.

http://www.racerelations.about.com/cs/affirmativeaction

Yahoo! Full Coverage: Affirmative Action

This Web site links you to the Yahoo! search engine for the topic of affirmative action.

http://fullcoverage.yahoo.com/fc/US/Affirmative_Action

PART 3

Stratification and Inequality

*W*hy *is there so much poverty in a society as rich as ours? Why has there been such a noticeable increase in inequality over the past quarter century? Although the ideal of equal opportunity for all is strong in the United States, many charge that the American political and economic system is unfair. Does extensive poverty demonstrate that policymakers have failed to live up to United States egalitarian principles? Are American institutions deeply flawed in that they provide fabulous opportunities for the educated and rich and meager opportunities for the uneducated and poor? Is the American stratification system at fault or are the poor themselves at fault? And what about the racial gap? The civil rights movement and the Civil Rights Act have made America more fair than it was, so why does a sizeable racial gap remain? Various affirmative action programs have been implemented to remedy unequal opportunities, but some argue that this is discrimination in reverse. In fact, California passed a referendum banning affirmative action. Where should America go from here? Social scientists debate these questions in this part.*

- Is Increasing Economic Inequality a Serious Problem?

- Is the Underclass the Major Threat to American Ideals?

- Has Affirmative Action Outlived Its Usefulness?

ISSUE 8

Is Increasing Economic Inequality a Serious Problem?

YES: Christopher Jencks, from "Does Inequality Matter?" *Daedalus* (Winter 2002)

NO: Christopher C. DeMuth, from "The New Wealth of Nations," *Commentary* (October 1997)

ISSUE SUMMARY

YES: Christopher Jencks, professor of social policy at the Kennedy School at Harvard University, presents data on how large the income inequality is in the United States and describes the consequences of this inequality.

NO: Christopher C. DeMuth, president of the American Enterprise Institute for Public Policy Research, argues that the "recent increase in income inequality... is a very small tick in the massive and unprecedented leveling of material circumstances that has been proceeding now for almost three centuries and in this century has accelerated dramatically."

T he cover of the January 29, 1996, issue of *Time* magazine bears a picture of 1996 Republican presidential candidate Steve Forbes and large letters reading: "DOES A FLAT TAX MAKE SENSE?" During his campaign Forbes expressed his willingness to spend $25 million of his own wealth in pursuit of the presidency, with the major focus of his presidential campaign being a flat tax, which would reduce taxes substantially for the rich. It seems reasonable to say that if the rich pay less in taxes, others would have to pay more. Is it acceptable for the tax burden to be shifted away from the rich in America? Forbes believed that the flat tax would benefit the poor as well as the rich. He theorized that the economy would surge ahead because investors would shift their money from relatively nonproductive, but tax-exempt, investments to productive investments. Although Forbes has disappeared from the political scene, his basic argument still thrives today. It is an example of the trickle-down theory, which states that helping the rich stimulates the economy, which helps the poor. In fact, the trickle-down theory is the major rationalization for the view that great economic inequality benefits all of society.

Inequality is not a simple subject. For example, America is commonly viewed as having more social equality than the more hierarchical societies of Europe and Japan, but America has more income inequality than almost all other industrial societies. This apparent contradiction is explained when one recognizes that American equality is not in income but in the opportunity to obtain higher incomes. The issue of economic inequality is further complicated by other categories of equality/inequality, which include political power, social status, and legal rights.

Americans believe that everyone should have an equal opportunity to compete for jobs and awards. This belief is backed up by free public school education, which provides poor children with a ladder to success, and by laws that forbid discrimination. Americans, however, do not agree on many specific issues regarding opportunities or rights. For example, should society compensate for handicaps such as disadvantaged family backgrounds or the legacy of past discrimination? This issue has divided the country. Americans do not agree on programs such as income-based scholarships, quotas, affirmative action, or the Head Start compensatory education program for poor preschoolers.

America's commitment to political equality is strong in principle, though less strong in practice. Everyone over 18 years old gets one vote, and all votes are counted equally. However, the political system tilts in the direction of special interest groups; those who do not belong to such groups are seldom heard. Furthermore, as in the case of Forbes, money plays an increasingly important role in political campaigns.

The final dimension of equality/inequality is status. Inequality of status involves differences in prestige, and it cannot be eliminated by legislation. Ideally, the people who contribute the most to society are the most highly esteemed. To what extent does this principle hold true in the United States?

The Declaration of Independence proclaims that "all men are created equal," and the Founding Fathers who wrote the Declaration of Independence went on to base the laws of the land on the principle of equality. The equality they were referring to was equality of opportunity and legal and political rights for white, property-owning males. In the two centuries following the signing of the Declaration, nonwhites and women struggled for and won considerable equality of opportunity and rights. Meanwhile, income gaps in the United States have been widening.

In the readings that follow, Christopher Jencks points out how extreme the inequality has become and how bad off the lowest fifth of the country is. He is cautious in asserting what the impacts are of extreme inequality because he requires hard data that is difficult to get. Nevertheless, he concludes, "My bottom line is that the social consequences of economic inequality are sometimes negative, sometimes neutral, but seldom—as far as I can discover—positive." Christopher C. DeMuth admits that incomes have become more unequally distributed, but he argues that consumption, a better indicator of living conditions, has become much more equally distributed.

Christopher Jencks  **YES**

Does Inequality Matter?

The economic gap between rich and poor has grown dramatically in the United States over the past generation and is now considerably wider than in any other affluent nation. This increase in economic inequality has no recent precedent, at least in America. The distribution of family income was remarkably stable from 1947 to 1980. We do not have good data on family incomes before 1947, but the wage gap between skilled and unskilled workers narrowed dramatically between 1910 and 1947, which probably means that family incomes also became more equal. The last protracted increase in economic inequality occurred between 1870 and 1910.

The gap between the rich and the rest of America has widened steadily since 1979. The Census Bureau, which is America's principal source of data on household incomes, does not collect good data from the rich, but the Congressional Budget Office (CBO) has recently combined census data with tax records to track income trends near the top of the distribution. Figure 1 shows that the share of after-tax income going to the top 1 percent of American households almost doubled between 1979 and 1997. The top 1 percent included all households with after-tax incomes above $246,000 in 1997. The estimated purchasing power of the top 1 percent rose by 157 percent between 1979 and 1997, while the median household's purchasing power rose only 10 percent. The gap between the poorest fifth of American households and the median household also widened between 1979 and 1997, but the trend was far less dramatic....

❧❦❧

Some of the potential costs and benefits of inequality emerge when we contrast the United States with other rich democracies. One simple way to describe income inequality in different countries is to compute what is called the "90/10 ratio." To calculate this ratio we rank households from richest to poorest. Then we divide the income of the household at the ninetieth percentile by the income of the household at the tenth percentile. (Comparing the ninetieth percentile to the tenth percentile is better than, say, comparing the ninety-ninth percentile to the first percentile, because few countries collect reliable data on the incomes of either the very rich or the very poor.)

Excerpted from Christopher Jencks, "Does Inequality Matter?" *Daedalus* (Winter 2002), pp. 49–53, 55–60, 64–65. Copyright © 2002 by Christopher Jencks. Reprinted by permission of the author. Notes omitted.

Figure 1

Percent of Household Income Going to the Richest One Percent

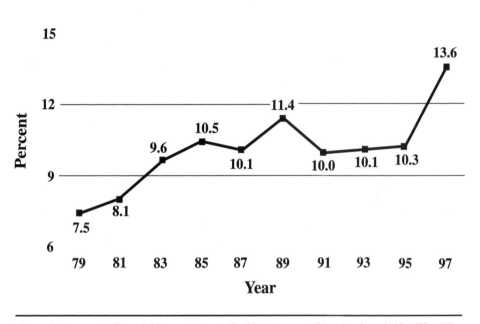

Changes in the percent of household income going to the richest 1 percent of American households, 1979—1977.
Source: Congressional Budget Office, *Historical Effective Tax Rates, 1979-1977.* September 2001, Table G-1 C.

The Luxembourg Income Study (LIS), which is the best current source of data on economic inequality in different countries, has calculated 90/10 ratios for fourteen rich democracies in the mid-1990s. Table 1 shows the results. To keep differences between these fourteen countries in perspective I have also included data on two poorer and less democratic countries, Mexico and Russia. If we set aside Mexico and Russia, the big English-speaking democracies are the most unequal, the Scandinavian democracies are the most equal, and Western European democracies fall in the middle. (Italy looks more unequal than the other continental democracies, but the Italian data is somewhat suspect.) Within the English-speaking world the United States is the most unequal of all. The 90/10 ratio in the United States is twice that in Scandinavia. But even the United States is nothing like as unequal as Russia, Mexico, or many other Latin American countries.

America's unusually high level of inequality is not attributable to its unusually diverse labor force. Years of schooling are more equally distributed in the United States than in the European countries for which we have comparable data (Sweden, the Netherlands, and Germany). Adult test scores are more unequally distributed in the United States than Europe, partly because American immigrants score so poorly on tests given in English. But disparities in cogni-

Table 1

Income Inequality and Economic Output in Various Countries During the 1990s

Country (and year of the ninetieth to the tenth percentile)	Ratio of household income at the 90th to 10th percentile[a]	GDP per capita as a percent of U.S. level in 1998[b]	Life expectancy at birth (1995 est.)[c]
Scandinavia[d]	2.8	75	77.2
Sweden (1995)	2.6	68	78.9
Finland (1995)	2.7	68	76.6
Norway (1995)	2.8	85	77.8
Denmark (1992)	2.9	79	75.4
Western Europe	3.6	73	77.5
Nether. (1994)	3.2	75	77.5
Germany (1994)	3.2	71	76.6
Belgium (1996)	3.2	74	76.4
France (1994)	3.5	66	78.4
Switz. (1992)	3.6	84	78.5
Italy (1995)	4.8	67	77.6
Brit. Com.	4.3	73	77.7
Canada (1994)	4.0	78	78.2
Australia (1994)	4.3	75	78.0
U.K. (1995)	4.6	67	77.0[e]
U.S. (1997)	5.6	100	75.7
Middle-income nations			
Russia (1995)	9.4	21(?)	65.0
Mexico (1998)	11.6	25	NA

a From http://lisweb.ceps.lu/key/figures/inqtable.htm.
b From U.S. Bureau of the Census *Statistical Abstract of the United States,* 2000, Government Printing Office, Table 1365. GDP is converted to $U.S. using purchasing power parity.
c National Center for Health Statistics, *Health, United States,* 2000. Government Printing Office 2000, Table 27.
d All area averages are unweighted arithmetic means.
e England and Wales.

tive skills turn out to play a tiny role in explaining cross-national differences in the distribution of earnings. If one compares American workers with the same test scores and the same amount of schooling, the Americans' wages vary more than the wages of *all* Swedish, Dutch, or German workers.

Almost everyone who studies the causes of economic inequality agrees that by far the most important reason for the differences between rich democracies is that their governments adopt different economic policies. There is no agreement about *which* policies are crucial, but there is a fairly standard list of suspects. A number of rich countries have centralized wage bargaining, which almost always compresses the distribution of earnings. Many rich democracies also make unionization easy, which also tends to compress the wage distribution. Some rich democracies transfer a lot of money to people who are retired, unemployed, sick, or permanently disabled, while others are far less generous. The United States is unusually unequal partly because it makes little effort to limit wage inequality: the minimum wage is low, and American law makes unionization relatively difficult. In addition, the United States transfers less money to those who are not working than most other rich democracies.

The fact that the American government makes so little effort to reduce economic inequality may seem surprising in a country where social equality is so important. American politicians present themselves to the public as being just like everyone else, and once they step outside their offices, Americans all wear jeans. The way Americans talk and the music they listen to are also affected by egalitarian impulses. But while the tenor of American culture may be democratic, Americans are also far more hostile to government than the citizens of other rich democracies. Since egalitarian economic policies require governmental action, they win far less support in the United States than in most other rich democracies....

Conservatives often blame American poverty on the existence of an "underclass" that rejects mainstream social norms, does little paid work, and has children whom neither parent can support. It is certainly true that poor American households include fewer working adults than affluent American households. This is true in every rich country for which we have data. But when Lars Osberg, an economist at Dalhousie University, compared poor households in the United States, Canada, Britain, Sweden, France, and Germany, he found that the poor American households worked far more hours per year than their counterparts in the other five countries. This finding suggests that what distinguishes the United States from the other rich democracies is not the idleness of the American poor but the anger that idleness inspires in more affluent Americans, which helps explain the stinginess of the American welfare state....

~◈~

Up to this point I have been focusing exclusively on what people can afford to buy. While economic goods and services are obviously important, many people believe that inequality also affects human welfare in ways that are independent of any given household's purchasing power. Even if my family income remains constant, the distribution of income in my neighborhood or my nation may influence my children's educational opportunities, my life expectancy, my chance of being robbed, the probability that I will vote, and perhaps even my overall happiness. The remainder of this article tries to summarize what we know about such effects.

Table 2

Purchasing Power of Households at the 10th and 90th Percentiles of Each
Nation's Distribution Relative to Households at the Same Percentile
in the United States in the Same Year, 1992–1997

Country (and year)	Purchasing power as a percent of the U.S. level in the same year		
	10th percentile	90th percentile	Average of all percentiles
Scandinavia	112	57	77
Sweden (1995)	103	49	67
Finland (1995)	105	53	73
Norway (1995)	128	68	88
Denmark (1995)	110	59	80
Western Europe	119	73	88
Neth. (1994)	110	64	76
Germany (1994)	113	67	82
Belgium (1996)	121	73	80
France (1994)	110	71	84
Switz. (1992)	141	89	116
Commonwealth	94	73	80
Canada (1994)	105	80	92
U.K. (1995)	85	68	72
Australia (1994)	87	71	76
U.S. (1997)	100	100	100

Source: Columns 1 and 2 are from Timothy Smeeding and Lee Rainwater, "Comparing Living Standards Across Countries: Real Incomes at the Top, the Bottom, and the Middle" (paper prepared for a conference on "What Has Happened to the Quality of Life in America and Other Advanced Industrial Nations?" Levy Institute, Bard College, Annandale-on-Hudson, N.Y., June 2001). Local currencies were converted to dollars using their estimated purchasing power parity. Area averages are unweighted arithmetic means. Column 3 is calculated from the national means of the logarithms of after-tax household income, using data provided by Rainwater.

Educational opportunities.   Increases in economic inequality have raised the value of a college degree in the United States. If all else had remained equal, making a college degree more valuable should increase both teenagers' interest in attending college and their parents' willingness to pay for college. But the growth of economic inequality in America has been accompanied by a change in the way we finance public higher education. Tax subsidies play a smaller role than they once did, and tuition plays a larger role. Since 1979 tuition at America's public colleges and universities has risen faster than most parents' income.

...[S]tudents are likely to be far more sensitive to changes in tuition than to a change in the hypothetical lifetime value of a BA. Tuition is easily observed and has to be paid now. The lifetime value of a BA is always uncertain and cannot be realized for a long time. Among students who pay their own bills, higher tuition could easily reduce college attendance even when the long-run returns of a college degree are rising.

Table 3 is taken from work by two economists, David Ellwood at Harvard and Thomas Kane at UCLA. It shows changes between 1980–1982 and 1992 in the fraction of high-school graduates from different economic backgrounds entering four-year colleges. Among students from the most affluent families, the proportion entering a four-year college rose substantially. Among students from middle-income families, whose families often help with children's college expenses but seldom pay the whole bill, attendance rose more modestly. Students from the poorest quartile were no more likely to attend a four-year college in 1992 than in 1980–1982. . . .

Table 3

Percent of High-School Graduates Enrolling in a 4-year-College or Some Other Form of Postsecondary Education Within 20 months of Graduation, by Income Quartile: 1980–1982 and 1992

Income quartile	Entered a 4-year college			Entered some other form of post-secondary education		
	1980-82	1992	Change	1980-82	1992	Change
Lowest	29	28	-1	28	32	4
Second	33	38	5	30	32	2
Third	39	48	9	33	32	-1
Highest	55	66	11	26	24	-2
All	39	45	6	29	30	1

Source: David Ellwood and Thomas Kane, "Who Is Getting a College Education? Family Background and the Growing Gaps in Enrollment," in Sheldon Danziger and Jane Waldfogel, eds., *Securing the Future* (New York: Russell Sage, 2000).

Life expectancy.   People live longer in rich countries than in poor countries, but the relationship flattens out as national income rises. Indeed, the statistics in Table 1 show that life expectancy and GDP per capita are not strongly related in rich democracies. In particular, life expectancy is lower in the United States than in almost any other rich democracy.

Within any given country people with higher incomes also live longer. This relationship flattens out near the top of the income distribution, but the gap between richer and poorer families does not seem to narrow when everyone's standard of living rises. Despite both rising incomes and the introduction of Medicare and Medicaid, for example, the effects of both income and education on mortality increased in the United States between 1960 and 1986. . . .

In 1992 Richard Wilkinson wrote an influential article arguing that a more equal distribution of income improved life expectancy in rich countries. Subsequent work showed that mortality was also lower in American states and metropolitan areas where incomes were more equal.…

Wilkinson and his followers believe that inequality also lowers life expectancy independent of its effect on any given household's income, because it changes the social context in which people live. According to Wilkinson, inequality erodes the social bonds that make people care about one another and accentuates feelings of relative deprivation (the social-science term for what people used to call envy). Other epidemiologists take what they call a "materialist" position, arguing that inequality kills because it affects public policy, altering the distribution of education, health care, environmental protection, and other material resources.…

⚘

I began this inquiry by arguing that American does less than almost any other rich democracy to limit economic inequality. As a result, the rich can buy a lot more in America than in other affluent democracies, while the poor can buy a little less. If you evaluate this situation by Rawlsian standards, America's policies are clearly inferior to those of most rich European countries. If you evaluate the same situation using a utilitarian calculus, you are likely to conclude that most American consumers do better than their counterparts in other large democracies. Much of this advantage is due to the fact that Americans spend more time working than Europeans do, but that may not be the whole story.

I also looked at evidence on whether economic inequality affects people's lives independent of its effects on their material standard of living. At least in the United States, the growth of inequality appears to have made more people attend college but also made educational opportunities more unequal. Growing inequality may also have lowered life expectancy, but the evidence for such an effect is weak and the effect, if there was one, was probably small. There is some evidence that changes in equality affect happiness in Europe, but not much evidence that this is the case in the United States. If inequality affects violent crime, these effects are swamped by other factors. There is no evidence that changes in economic inequality affect political participation, but declining political participation among the less affluent may help explain why American politicians remained so passive when inequality began to grow after 1980.

My bottom line is that the social consequences of economic inequality are sometimes negative, sometimes neutral, but seldom—as far as I can discover—positive. The case for inequality seems to rest entirely on the claim that it promotes efficiency, and the evidence for that claim is thin. All these judgments are very tentative, however, and they are likely to change as more work is done. Still, it is worthwhile to ask what they would imply about the wisdom of trying to limit economic inequality if they were, in fact, correct.

Readers' answers to that question should, I think, depend on four value judgments. First, readers need to decide how much weight they assign to improving the lot of the least advantaged compared with improving the average level of well-being. Second, they need to decide how much weight they assign to increasing material well-being compared with increasing "family time" or "leisure." Third, they need to decide how much weight they assign to equalizing opportunities for the young as against maximizing the welfare of adults. Fourth, they need to decide how much value they assign to admitting more people from poor countries such as Mexico to the United States, since this almost inevitably makes the distribution of income more unequal.

If you are a hard-core Rawlsian who thinks that society's sole economic goal should be to improve the position of the least advantaged, European experience suggests that limiting inequality can benefit the poor. If you are a hard-core utilitarian, European experiences suggests—though it certainly does not prove—that limiting inequality lowers consumption. But European experience also suggests that lowering inequality reduces consumption partly by encouraging people to work fewer hours, which many Europeans see as a good thing. If you care more about equal opportunity for children than about consumption among adults, limiting economic inequality among parents probably reduces disparities in the opportunities open to their children.

All things considered, the case for limiting inequality seems to me strong but not overwhelming. That is one reason why most rich societies are deeply divided about the issue. Yet given the centrality of redistribution in modern politics, it is remarkable how little effort rich societies have made to assemble the kinds of evidence they would need to assess the costs and benefits of limiting inequality. Even societies that redistribute a far larger fraction of their GDP than the United States spend almost nothing on answering questions of this kind. Answering such questions would require collecting better evidence, which costs real money. It would also require politicians to run the risk of being proven wrong. Nonetheless, moral sentiments uninformed by evidence have done incalculable damage over the past few centuries, and their malign influence shows no sign of abating. Rich democracies can do better if they try.

Christopher C. DeMuth

 **NO**

The New Wealth of Nations

The Nations of North America, Western Europe, Australia, and Japan are wealthier today than they have ever been, wealthier than any others on the planet, wealthier by far than any societies in human history. Yet their governments appear to be impoverished—saddled with large accumulated debts and facing annual deficits that will grow explosively over the coming decades. As a result, government spending programs, especially the big social-insurance programs like Social Security and Medicare in the United States, are facing drastic cuts in order to avert looming insolvency (and, in France and some other European nations, in order to meet the Maastricht treaty's criteria of fiscal rectitude). American politics has been dominated for several years now by contentious negotiations over deficit reduction between the Clinton administration and the Republican Congress. This past June, first at the European Community summit in Amsterdam and then at the Group of Eight meeting in Denver, most of the talk was of hardship and constraint and the need for governmental austerity ("Economic Unease Looms Over Talks at Denver Summit," read the *New York Times* headline).

These bloodless problems of governmental accounting are said, moreover, to reflect real social ills: growing economic inequality in the United States; high unemployment in Europe; an aging, burdensome, and medically needy population everywhere; and the globalization of commerce, which is destroying jobs and national autonomy and forcing bitter measures to keep up with the bruising demands of international competitiveness.

How can it be that societies so surpassingly wealthy have governments whose core domestic-welfare programs are on the verge of bankruptcy? The answer is as paradoxical as the question. We have become not only the richest but also the freest and most egalitarian societies that have ever existed, and it is our very wealth, freedom, and equality that are causing the welfare state to unravel.

❦

That we have become very rich is clear enough in the aggregate. That we have become very equal in the enjoyment of our riches is an idea strongly resisted by many. Certainly there has been a profusion of reports in the media and political speeches about increasing income inequality: the rich, it is said, are getting richer, the poor are getting poorer, and the middle and working classes are under the relentless pressure of disappearing jobs in manufacturing and middle management.

Although these claims have been greatly exaggerated, and some have been disproved by events, it is true that, by some measures, there has been a recent increase in income inequality in the United States. But it is a very small tick in the massive and unprecedented leveling of material circumstances that has been proceeding now for almost three centuries and in this century has accelerated dramatically. In fact, the much-noticed increase in measured-income inequality is in part a result of the increase in real social equality. Here are a few pieces of this important but neglected story.

• First, progress in agriculture, construction, manufacturing, and other key sectors of economic production has made the material necessities of life—food, shelter, and clothing—available to essentially everyone. To be sure, many people, including the seriously handicapped and the mentally incompetent, remain dependent on the public purse for their necessities. And many people continue to live in terrible squalor. But the problem of poverty, defined as material scarcity, has been solved. If poverty today remains a serious problem, it is a problem of individual behavior, social organization, and public policy. This was not so 50 years ago, or ever before.

• Second, progress in public health, in nutrition, and in the biological sciences and medical arts has produced dramatic improvements in longevity, health, and physical well-being. Many of these improvements—resulting, for example, from better public sanitation and water supplies, the conquest of dread diseases, and the abundance of nutritious food—have affected entire populations, producing an equalization of real personal welfare more powerful than any government redistribution of income.

The Nobel prize-winning economist Robert Fogel has focused on our improved mastery of the biological environment—leading over the past 300 years to a doubling of the average human life span and to large gains in physical stature, strength, and energy—as the key to what he calls "the egalitarian revolution of the 20th century." He considers this so profound an advance as to constitute a distinct new level of human evolution. Gains in stature, health, and longevity are continuing today and even accelerating. Their outward effects may be observed, in evolutionary fast-forward, in the booming nations of Asia (where, for example, the physical difference between older and younger South Koreans is strikingly evident on the streets of Seoul).

• Third, the critical *source* of social wealth has shifted over the last few hundred years from land (at the end of the 18th century) to physical capital (at the end of the 19th) to, today, human capital—education and cognitive ability. This development is not an unmixed gain from the standpoint of economic equality. The ability to acquire and deploy human capital is a function of intelligence, and intelligence is not only unequally distributed but also, to a significant degree, heritable. As Charles Murray and the late Richard J. Herrnstein argue in *The Bell Curve,* an economy that rewards sheer brainpower replaces one old source of inequality, socioeconomic advantage, with a new one, cognitive advantage.

৵৹৵

But an economy that rewards human capital also tears down far more artificial barriers than it erects. For most people who inhabit the vast middle range of the bell curve, intelligence is much more equally distributed than land or physical capital ever was. Most people, that is, possess ample intelligence to pursue all but a handful of specialized callings. If in the past many were held back by lack of education and closed social institutions, the opportunities to use one's human capital have blossomed with the advent of universal education and the erosion of social barriers.

Furthermore, the material benefits of the knowledge-based economy are by no means limited to those whom Murray and Herrnstein call the cognitive elite. Many of the newest industries, from fast food to finance to communications, have succeeded in part by opening up employment opportunities for those of modest ability and training—occupations much less arduous and physically much less risky than those they have replaced. And these new industries have created enormous, widely shared economic benefits in consumption; I will return to this subject below.

• Fourth, recent decades have seen a dramatic reduction in one of the greatest historical sources of inequality: the social and economic inequality of the sexes. Today, younger cohorts of working men and women with comparable education and job tenure earn essentially the same incomes. The popular view would have it that the entry of women into the workforce has been driven by falling male earnings and the need "to make ends meet" in middle-class families. But the popular view is largely mistaken. Among married women (as the economist Chinhui Juhn has demonstrated), it is wives of men with high incomes who have been responsible for most of the recent growth in employment.

• Fifth, in the wealthy Western democracies, material needs and desires have been so thoroughly fulfilled for so many people that, for the first time in history, we are seeing large-scale voluntary reductions in the amount of time spent at paid employment. This development manifests itself in different forms: longer periods of education and training for the young; earlier retirement despite longer life spans; and, in between, many more hours devoted to leisure, recreation, entertainment, family, community and religious activities, charitable and other nonremunerative pursuits, and so forth. The dramatic growth of the sports, entertainment, and travel industries captures only a small slice of what has happened. In Fogel's estimation, the time devoted to nonwork activities by the average male head of household has grown from 10.5 hours per week in 1880 to 40 hours today, while time per week at work has fallen from 61.6 hours to 33.6 hours. Among women, the reduction in work (including not only outside employment but also household work, food preparation, childbearing and attendant health problems, and child rearing) and the growth in nonwork have been still greater.

There is a tendency to overlook these momentous developments because of the often frenetic pace of modern life. But our busy-ness actually demonstrates the point: time, and not material things, has become the scarce and valued commodity in modern society.

❧

One implication of these trends is that in very wealthy societies, income has become a less useful gauge of economic welfare and hence of economic equality. When income becomes to some degree discretionary, and when many peoples' incomes change from year to year for reasons unrelated to their life circumstances, *consumption* becomes a better measure of material welfare. And by this measure, welfare appears much more evenly distributed: people of higher income spend progressively smaller shares on consumption, while in the bottom ranges, annual consumption often exceeds income. (In fact, government statistics suggest that in the bottom 20 percent of the income scale, average annual consumption is about twice annual income—probably a reflection of a substantial underreporting of earnings in this group.) According to the economist Daniel Slesnick, the distribution of consumption, unlike the distribution of reported income, has become measurably *more* equal in recent decades.

If we include leisure-time pursuits as a form of consumption, the distribution of material welfare appears flatter still. Many such activities, being informal by definition, are difficult to track, but Dora Costa of MIT has recently studied one measurable aspect—expenditures on recreation—and found that these have become strikingly more equal as people of lower income have increased the amount of time and money they devote to entertainment, reading, sports, and related enjoyments.

Television, videocassettes, CD's, and home computers have brought musical, theatrical, and other entertainments (both high and low) to everyone, and have enormously narrowed the differences in cultural opportunities between wealthy urban centers and everywhere else. Formerly upper-crust sports like golf, tennis, skiing, and boating have become mass pursuits (boosted by increased public spending on parks and other recreational facilities as well as on environmental quality), and health clubs and full-line book stores have become as plentiful as gas stations. As some of the best things in life become free or nearly so, the price of pursuing them becomes, to that extent, the "opportunity cost" of time itself.

The substitution of leisure activities for income-producing work even appears to have become significant enough to be contributing to the recently much-lamented increase in inequality in measured income. In a new AEI study, Robert Haveman finds that most of the increase in earnings inequality among U.S. males since the mid-1970's can be attributed not to changing labor-market opportunities but to voluntary choice—to the free pursuit of nonwork activities at the expense of income-producing work.

Most of us can see this trend in our own families and communities. A major factor in income inequality in a wealthy knowledge economy is age—many people whose earnings put them at the top of the income curve in their late fifties were well down the curve in their twenties, when they were just getting out of school and beginning their working careers. Fogel again: today the average household in the top 10 percent might consist of a professor or accountant married to a nurse or secretary, both in their peak years of earning. As for the stratospheric top 1 percent, it includes not only very rich people like Bill Cosby but also people like Cosby's fictional Huxtable family: an obstetrician married to a corporate lawyer. All these individuals would have appeared well down the income distribution as young singles, and that is where their young counterparts appear today.

That more young people are spending more time in college or graduate school, taking time off for travel and "finding themselves," and pursuing interesting but low- or non-paying jobs or apprenticeships before knuckling down to lifelong careers is a significant factor in "income inequality" measured in the aggregate. But this form of economic inequality is in fact the social equality of the modern age. It is progress, not regress, to be cherished and celebrated, not feared and fretted over.

POSTSCRIPT

Is Increasing Economic Inequality a Serious Problem?

This debate can be posed in terms of contradictory statements by the two authors: "The economic gap between rich and poor has grown dramatically in the United States over the past generation and is now considerably wider than in any other affluent nation" (Jencks). "We have become very equal in the enjoyment of our riches" (DeMuth). Both authors support their statements with indicators that measure trends, but they select different indicators. The reader has to decide which set of indicators better describes his or her idea of inequality.

Inequality, stratification, and social mobility are central concerns of sociology, and they are addressed by a large literature. Important discussions of income inequality are *The Inequality Paradox: Growth of Income Disparity* edited by James A. Auerbach and Richard S. Belous (National Policy Association, 1998); Barry Bluestone and Bennett Harrison, *Growing Prosperity: The Battle for Growth With Equity in the Twenty-First Century* (Houghton Mifflin, 2000); D. G. Champernowne and F. A. Cowell, *Economic Inequality and Income Distribution* (Cambridge University Press, 1998); Sheldon Danziger and Peter Gottschalk, *America Unequal* (Harvard University Press, 1995); Richard B. Freeman, *When Earnings Diverge: Causes, Consequences, and Cures for the New Inequality in the U.S.* (National Policy Association, 1997); Andrew Hacker, *Money: Who Has How Much and Why* (Scribner's Reference, 1997); Frank Levy, *The New Dollars and Dreams: American Income and Economic Change* (Russell Sage Foundation, 1998); and Paul Ryscavage, *Income Inequality in America: An Analysis of Trends* (M. E. Sharpe, 1999). For a major structural analysis of inequality, see Peter M. Blau's *Structural Contexts of Opportunities* (University of Chicago Press, 1994). Richard J. Herrnstein and Charles Murray's *The Bell Curve: Intelligence and Class Structure in American Life* (Free Press, 1994) is a controversial work in which the authors conclude that the major cause of income inequality is differences in intelligence. This book is vigorously attacked by Claude S. Fischer et al. in *Inequality by Design: Cracking the Bell Curve Myth* (Princeton University Press, 1996). For a poignant ethnographic study of the poor and their disadvantages, see Elliot Liebow, *Tell Them Who I Am: The Lives of Homeless Women* (Free Press, 1993).

ISSUE 9

Is the Underclass the Major Threat to American Ideals?

YES: Charles Murray, from "And Now for the Bad News," *Society* (November/December 1999)

NO: Barry Schwartz, from "Capitalism, the Market, the 'Underclass,' and the Future," *Society* (November/December 1999)

ISSUE SUMMARY

YES: Author Charles Murray describes destructive behavior among the underclass. Murray asserts that this type of behavior will result in serious trouble for society even though, according to statistics, the number of crimes committed has decreased.

NO: Psychology professor Barry Schwartz states that the underclass is not the major threat to American ideals. He counters that "the theory and practice of free-market economics have done more to undermine traditional moral values than any other social force."

T he Declaration of Independence proclaims the right of every human being to "life, liberty, and the pursuit of happiness." It never defines happiness, but Americans tend to agree that happiness includes doing well financially, getting ahead in life, and maintaining a comfortable standard of living.

The fact is that millions of Americans do not do well and do not live comfortably. They are mired in poverty and seem unable to get out. On the face of it, this fact poses no contradiction to America's commitment to the pursuit of happiness. To pursue is not necessarily to catch.

The real difficulty in reconciling the American ideal with American reality is not the problem of income differentials but the *persistence* of poverty from generation to generation. There are two basic explanations for this problem. One largely blames the poor and the other largely blames the circumstances of the poor and, thus, society.

The explanation that blames the poor is most strongly identified with the culture-of-poverty thesis, according to which a large segment of the poor does not really try to get out of poverty. In its more extreme form this view portrays the poor as lazy, stupid, or base. Poverty is not to be blamed on defects of American society but on personal defects. After all, many successful Americans have worked their way up from humble beginnings, and many immigrant groups have made progress in one generation. Therefore, some believe that the United States provides ample opportunities for those who work hard.

According to this view, available opportunities are ignored by the portion of the poor that embraces what is known as the *culture of poverty*. In other words, the poor have a culture all their own that is at variance with middle-class culture and that hinders their success. Although it may keep people locked into what seems to be an intolerable life, some would assert that this culture nevertheless has its own compensations and pleasures. It does not demand that people postpone pleasure, save money, or work hard.

However, the culture of poverty does not play a major role in today's version of the poor-are-to-blame theory. According to recent versions of this theory, having children out of wedlock, teenage pregnancy, divorce, absent fathers, crime, welfare dependency, and child abuse are what contribute to poverty. The culture of poverty contributes to these practices by being permissive or even condoning. This culture, however, is not antithetical to but is rather shared in part by much of the middle class. The difference is that in the middle class its consequences are usually not as extreme.

According to the second explanation of poverty, the poor have few opportunities and many obstacles to overcome to climb out of poverty. Most of the poor will become self-supporting if they are given the chance. Their most important need is for decent jobs that have the potential for advancement. Many poor people cannot find jobs, and when they do, the jobs are degrading or lack further opportunity.

These two perspectives are expressed in the two selections that follow. Charles Murray blames a segment of the poor that he calls the underclass for their poverty and for much of the harm done to society. Barry Schwartz blames the functioning of capitalism and the stock market for creating obstacles to the poor for getting ahead. Values such as sympathy, fairness, and self control, which sustain a productive and humane society, are undermined, according to Schwartz.

Charles Murray

 **YES**

And Now for the Bad News

Good news is everywhere. Crime rates are falling; welfare rolls are plunging; unemployment is at rock bottom; teenage births are down. Name an indicator, economic or social, and chances are it has taken a turn in the right direction. This happy story is worth celebrating. It is also a story that begs to be disentangled. For what is happening to the nation as a whole is not happening to the sub-population that we have come to call the underclass.

To make the case, I return to three indicators I first selected in the late 1980s to track the course of the underclass: criminality, dropout from the labor force among young men, and illegitimate births among young women. Then and now, these three seemed to me key outcroppings of what we mean by the underclass: people living outside the mainstream, often preying on the mainstream, in a world where the building blocks of a life—work, family and community—exist in fragmented and corrupt forms. Crime offers the most obvious example of a story that needs disentangling. After seven straight years of decline, the crime rate is at its lowest in a quarter-century. Almost everyone feels safer, especially in big cities. But suppose we ask not how many crimes are committed, but how many Americans demonstrate chronic criminality. That number is larger than ever. We don't notice, because so many of the chronically criminal are in jail.

Off the Street

For the past 20 years the United States has engaged in a massive effort to take criminals off the street. As of 1997, more than 1.8 million people were in prisons, jails and juvenile facilities. It has not been an efficient process—many who should be behind bars aren't and vice versa—but the great majority of prisoners are there because they have been a menace to their fellow citizens. To see how our appraisal of the crime problem depends on the imprisonment binge, suppose that in 1997 we imprisoned at the same rate relative to crime that we did in 1980, the year that the crime rate hit its all-time high. At the 1980 rate, 567,000 people would have been incarcerated in 1997, roughly 1.3 million fewer than the actual number. Now suppose that tomorrow we freed 1.3 million prisoners. Recent scholarly estimates of the average number of crimes prevented per year of incarceration range from 12 to 21. Even if these numbers are too high, it is clear that if we set free 1.3 million people now in prison, we would no longer be bragging about a falling crime rate. The only uncertainty is how sky-high the crime rate would be. It is a major accomplishment that crime has gone down. It has been achieved not by socializing the underclass, but by putting large numbers of its members behind bars.

Unemployment is another success story for the nation as a whole. Unemployment rates have dropped for just about any group of people who have been in the labor market, including blacks, and young black males in particular. Suppose we turn instead to a less-publicized statistic, but one of the most significant in trying to track the course of the underclass, the percentage of young males not in the labor force. When large numbers of young men neither work nor look for work, most are living off the underground economy or are dependent on handouts, perhaps moving into the labor force periodically, getting a job, and then quitting or getting fired a few weeks later, consigning themselves to a life at the margins of the economy.

Sudden and unexpected increases in the labor force dropout rates of young black males in the mid-1960s heralded the deterioration of the inner city. The 1990s have seen a new jump in dropout from the labor force that is just as ominous. The increased dropout has occurred selectively, among a subgroup that should have virtually 100% labor-force participation: young men who are no longer in school. The increase in labor force dropout is largest among young black males. Among 16- to 24-year-old black males not in school, the proportion who are not working or looking for work averaged 17% during the 1980s. It first hit 20% in 1992. As of 1997, it stood at 23%. The magnitude of dropout among white males the same age not in school is smaller, 9% in 1997. But the proportional increase since 1990 is substantial, up 25% overall, and concentrated among white teenagers (up 33% since 1990). That these increases in labor-force dropout have occurred despite a sustained period of high demand for workers at all skill levels is astonishing and troubling.

As for illegitimacy, confusion reigns. Headlines declare that "Illegitimacy is Falling," but the referent is birthrates, illegitimate births per 1,000 unmarried women. The referent for the headlines is also usually blacks, because that's where the dramatic change has occurred: The black illegitimate birth rate for women 15 to 44 fell 18% from 1990 to 1996; the black teenage birth rate fell by even more. But what is happening to the illegitimacy *ratio*—the percentage of babies who are born to unmarried women? The two measures need not track with each other, as the black experience vividly illustrates. Birthrates for unmarried black women and for black teenagers did not begin to drop in 1990. They dropped further and for much longer from 1960 to 1985. But the black illegitimacy ratio rose relentlessly throughout that period. The ratio also rose from 1990 to 1994 as birth rates fell. The good news about the black illegitimacy ratio is that it has since leveled off, even dropping a percentage point—meaning that as of 1997 it stood at a catastrophic 69% instead of a catastrophic 70%.

Most analysts, including me, have focused on the ratio rather than the rate because it is the prevalence of mother-only homes that determines the nature of a neighborhood and the socialization of the next generation. But when we turn from blacks to the national numbers for all races, it doesn't make much difference which measure you think is important. The rate and ratio have both risen substantially over the past few decades. Since 1994 the rate has fallen slightly, while the ratio has been flat at 32%. That is, almost one out of three American babies is now born to an unmarried woman.

The problems associated with illegitimacy have not really leveled off. Because the illegitimacy ratio is so much higher today than 18 years ago, the proportion of American children under 18 who were born to unmarried women will continue to increase. The problems associated with illegitimacy will also continue to increase well into the next century as the babies born in the 1990s grow up. That illegitimacy has stopped rising is a genuinely hopeful sign, but for practical purposes we are at the peak of the problem.

The size of the welfare population was not one of my 1989 indicators for tracking the underclass (it tends to double-count the role of illegitimacy), but recent success on this front has been so dramatic that it should be acknowledged. By "welfare reform" I mean the movement that began in the states in the early 1990s and culminated in the national welfare reform law of 1996. The change has been stunning: In 1993, slightly more than five million families were on welfare. By 1998, that number had dropped to about three million—a 40% drop in five years. The economy gets only a modest part of the credit. During the two preceding booms, welfare soared (in the 1960s) and declined fractionally (in the 1980s).

But once again, disentangling is crucial. For years, liberals defending welfare stressed that half of all women who ever go on welfare exit within a few years (and thus are ordinary women who have hit a rough patch), while conservatives attacking welfare stressed that half the welfare caseload at any point in time consists of women who have been on the rolls for many years (and thus are likely candidates for the underclass). So the crucial question is: How has the 40% reduction in caseload split between the two groups? No one yet knows. Past experience with workfare programs has been that the effect is concentrated on women who fit the profile of the short-term recipient. Answers about the current situation should be forthcoming soon.

The more profound question is what difference it makes if single mothers go to work. Is a community without fathers importantly different just because more mothers are earning a paycheck? One line of argument says yes. Jobs provide regularity, structure and dignity to family life, even if the father is not around. But we know from recent research that the bad effects of single parenting persist for women not on welfare. No counterbalancing body of research demonstrates that it is good for children when a single mother works (rather the opposite). I like to think children who see their mothers working for a living grow up better equipped to make their way in the world than children who watch their mothers live off a welfare check, even if there are no fathers in their lives. But this is a hope, not a finding.

In net, the underclass is as large as or larger than it has ever been. It is probably still growing among males, level or perhaps falling among females. We know for sure that the underclass today is substantially larger than it was at any time in the 1980s when the Reagan administration was being excoriated for ignoring the underclass. Yet the underclass is no longer a political issue. Why? I propose an ignoble explanation. Whatever we might tell ourselves, mainstream Americans used to worry about the underclass primarily insofar as it intruded on our lives. Busing sent children from the wrong side of the tracks into our schools; the homeless infested our public spaces; the pervasive presence of graffiti, street hustlers and clusters of glowering teenagers made us anxious. Most of all, high crime rates twisted urban life into a variety of knots.

It took the better part of three decades, but we dealt with those intrusions. Busing is so far in the past that the word has an archaic ring to it. Revitalized vagrancy laws and shelters took most homeless off the streets. Most of all, we figured out what to do with criminals. Innovations in policing helped, but the key insight was an old one: lock 'em up.

Why is the underclass no longer an issue? Because what bothered us wasn't that the underclass existed, but that it was in our face. Now it is not. So we can forget about it. "For the time being" is the crucial hedge. What about the long term? Can the United States retain its political and social culture in the presence of a permanent underclass? The answer is certainly yes, if an underclass is sufficiently small. As long as it is only a fragment, the disorganization and violence of its culture do not spill over into the mainstream. The answer is certainly no if the underclass is sufficiently large. Trying to decide where the American underclass stands on that continuum raises two questions without clear answers.

First, how much has the culture of the underclass already spilled over into the mainstream? So far, the American underclass has been predominantly urban and black. Urban black culture has been spilling over into mainstream American culture for more than a century now, to America's great advantage. But during the past three decades it has increasingly been infiltrated by an underclass subculture that celebrates a bastardized social code—predatory sex and "getting paid." The violence and misogyny that pervade certain forms of popular music reflect these values. So does the hooker look in fashion, and the flaunting of obscenity and vulgarity in comedy.

Perhaps most disturbing is the widening expression, often approving, of underclass ethics: Take what you want. Respond violently to anyone who antagonizes you. Despise courtesy as weakness. Take pride in cheating (stealing, lying, exploiting) successfully. I do not know how to measure how broadly such principles have spread, but it's hard to deny that they are more openly espoused in television, films and recordings than they used to be. Among the many complicated explanations for this deterioration in culture, cultural spill-over from the underclass is implicated.

Implicated—that's all. There are many culprits behind the coarsening of American life. It should also go without saying that vulgarity, violence and the rest were part of mainstream America before the underclass came along. But these things always used to be universally condemned in public discourse. Now they are not. It is not just that America has been defining deviancy down, slackening old moral codes. Inner-city street life has provided an alternative code and it is attracting converts.

The converts are mainly adolescents, which makes sense. The street ethics of the underclass subculture are not "black." They are the ethics of male adolescents who haven't been taught any better. For that matter, the problem of the underclass itself is, ultimately, a problem of adolescents who haven't been taught any better. There are a lot more white adolescents than black ones, leading to the second question: How fast will the white underclass grow?

National statistics tell us that in the past decade white criminality has not only increased but gotten more violent, that white teenage males are increasingly dropping out of the labor force, and that white illegitimacy has increased rapidly. Anecdotal evidence about changes in white working-class neighborhoods points to increased drug use, worse school performance and a breakdown of neighborhood norms—recalling accounts of black working-class neighborhoods three decades ago. (Systematic documentation of these trends is still lacking.)

Looking ahead, much depends on whether illegitimacy among whites has already reached critical mass—the point at which we can expect accelerated and sustained growth in white crime, labor force dropout and illegitimacy rates. The good news is that the growth in the white illegitimacy ratio has slowed. The bad news is that it stands at 26%–22% for non-Latino whites—which, judging from the black experience in the early 1960s, may be near that point of critical mass. No one knows, of course, whether the subsequent trajectory of events for whites will be the same as it was for blacks, but there is ample cause for worry. European countries with high white illegitimacy ratios offer no comfort. Juvenile crime is increasing rapidly across Europe, along with other indicators of social deterioration in low-income groups.

Jamesian Directions

The most striking aspect of the current situation, and one that makes predictions very dicey, is the degree to which the United States is culturally compartmentalizing itself. America in the 1990s is a place where the local movie theater may play *Sense and Sensibility* next door to *Natural Born Killers*. Brian Lamb (on C-SPAN) is a few channels away from Jerry Springer. Formal balls are in vogue in some circles; mosh pits in others. Name just about any aspect of American life, and a case can be made that the country is going in different directions simultaneously, some of them Jamesian, others Hogarthian.

The Jamesian elements are not confined to a cultured remnant. Broad swaths of American society are becoming more civil and less vulgar, more responsible and less self-indulgent. The good news is truly good, and it extends beyond the statistics. What's more, the bad news may prove manageable. One way to interpret the nation's success in re-establishing public order is that we have learned how to cope with our current underclass. One may then argue that the size of the underclass is stabilizing, meaning that we can keep this up indefinitely. It requires only that we set aside moral considerations and accept that the huge growth of the underclass since 1960 cannot now be reversed.

Welfare reform and the growing school-voucher movement are heartening signs that many are not ready to accept the status quo. But they struggle against a larger movement toward what I have called "custodial democracy," in which the mainstream subsidizes but also walls off the underclass. In effect, custodial democracy takes as its premise that a substantial portion of the population cannot be expected to function as citizens.

At this moment, elated by falling crime rates and shrinking welfare rolls, we haven't had to acknowledge how far we have already traveled on the road to custodial democracy. I assume the next recession will disabuse us. But suppose that our new *modus vivendi* keeps working? We just increase the number of homeless shelters, restore the welfare guarantee, build more prison cells, and life for the rest of us goes on, pleasantly. At some point we will be unable to avoid recognizing that custodial democracy has arrived. This will mark a fundamental change in how we conceive of America. Will anyone mind?

Capitalism, the Market, the "Underclass," and the Future

I share Charles Murray's concern that there is bad news lurking in the shadows of what seems to be unalloyed prosperity in millennial America. I share his concerns about urban crime, employment, the fragility of the family, and the coarseness of the culture. But I am also angry. I am angry at the resolute refusal of conservatives like Murray, William Bennett, and James Q. Wilson to face squarely what their colleague Pat Buchanan is willing to face, when he writes:

> Reaganism and its twin sister, Thatcherism, create fortunes among the highly educated, but in the middle and working classes, they generate anxiety, insecurity and disparities.... Tax cuts, the slashing of safety nets and welfare benefits, and global free trade... unleash the powerful engines of capitalism that go on a tear. Factories and businesses open and close with startling speed.... As companies merge, downsize and disappear, the labor force must always be ready to pick up and move on.... The cost is paid in social upheaval and family breakdown.... Deserted factories mean gutted neighborhoods, ghost towns, ravaged communities and regions that go from boom to bust... Conservatism is being confronted with its own contradictions for unbridled capitalism is an awesome destructive force.

Murray's message is that things have not been working nearly as well as we think they have. Crime is down only because we have locked all the hardened criminals away; the tendency to commit crime has not changed. Unemployment is down, but those who remain unemployed are contemptuous of work. Illegitimate births are down, but legitimate births are down even more, as growing numbers of people seem disdainful of marriage. All these signs of moral decay Murray traces to the underclass, and he is especially worried because the middle class seems increasingly to approve of what he calls "underclass ethics." He says that "among the many complicated explanations for this deterioration in culture, cultural spill-over [from the underclass to the rest of us] is implicated."

But Murray also says this: "There are many culprits behind the coarsening of American life. It should also go without saying that vulgarity, violence and the rest were part of mainstream America before the underclass came along.

But these things always used to be universally condemned in public discourse. Now they are not. It is not just that America has been defining deviancy down, slackening old moral codes. Inner-city street life has provided an alternative code and it is attracting converts."

The idea that middle America needs to look at the underclass for examples of coarseness is preposterous. It turns a willful blind eye to what the conservative revolution has brought us. The conservatism that captured America's fancy in the 1980s was actually two distinct conservatisms. It was an *economic* conservatism committed to dismantling the welfare state and turning as many facets of life as possible over to the private sector. And it was a *moral* conservatism committed to strengthening traditional values and the social institutions that foster them. These two conservatisms corresponded to the economic and social agendas that guided the policies of both the Reagan and the Bush administrations. These Presidents and their supporters seemed to share not only the belief that free-market economics and traditional moral values are good, but that they go together.

This has proven to be a serious mistake. The theory and practice of free-market economics have done more to undermine traditional moral values than any other social force. It is not permissive parents, unwed mothers, undisciplined teachers, multicultural curricula, fanatical civil libertarians, feminists, rock musicians, or drug pushers who are the primary sources of the corrosion that moral conservatives are trying to repair. Instead, it is the operation of the market system itself, along with an ideology that justifies the pursuit of economic self-interest as the "American way." And so, I acknowledge that Murray's concerns about the "problem of the underclass" are not being solved by our current prosperity. But I insist that they will never be solved unless we face up squarely to what causes them. And what causes them, I believe, is in large part what is responsible for our current prosperity.

I am not going to argue here that the evils of market capitalism demand that we all gather to storm the barricades and wrest the means of production out of the hands of evil capitalists and turn them over to the state. As everyone says, "the Cold War is over, and we won." State ownership of the means of production is a non-issue. We are all capitalists now. The issues before us really are two. First, what kind of capitalism? Is it the capitalism of Reagan and Thatcher —of unregulated markets and privatization of everything, with government involvement viewed as a cause of waste and inefficiency? Or is it the capitalism of John Maynard Keynes and of Franklin Roosevelt, with significant state regulation of the market and state guarantees of life's necessities? I'm going to argue for the latter—old-fashioned capitalism. The boom we are in the midst of has created perhaps the greatest degree of income inequality in the history of the developed world. What the free market teaches us is that what *anyone* can have not *everyone* can have, often with very painful consequences for the have-nots. And second, if we must live with capitalism, what are we prepared to do to correct the moral corrosion that it brings as a side effect? For in addition to asking what free-market capitalism does *for* people, we must ask what it does *to* people. And I will suggest that it turns people into nasty, self-absorbed, self-interested competitors—that it demands this of people, and celebrates it.

The Market and Inequality

One would think that if the problem is the underclass, the solution—or *a* solution—is to reduce its numbers. What do we know about the great economic "boom" we are living in the midst of? The income of the average wage-earning worker in 1997 was 3.1% lower than it was in 1989. Median family income was $1000 less in 1997 than in 1989. The typical couple worked 250 more hours in 1997 than in 1989. So to the extent that average people have been able to hold their own at all, it is because they worked harder. The median wage of high school graduates fell 6% between 1980 and 1996 while the median wage of college graduates rose 12%.

And this picture looks worse if you include benefits. Benefits used to be the "great equalizer," distributed equally among employees despite huge disparities in salary. For example, the $20,000/year employee and the $500,000/year employee got the same $4000 medical insurance. But despite IRS efforts to prevent differential benefits based on income (by making such benefits taxable), employers have invented all kinds of tricks. They have introduced lengthy employment "trial periods" with no benefits. They have resorted to hiring temporary workers who get no benefits. The result is that while 80% of workers received paid vacations and holidays in 1996, less than 10% in the bottom tenth of the income distribution did. The result is that while 70% of workers have some sort of employer funded pension, less than 10% of those in the bottom tenth of the income distribution do. The result is that while 90% of high wage employees have health insurance, only 26% of low wage employees do. All told, about 40 million Americans have no health insurance. The picture looks still worse if you consider *wealth* rather than income. The richest 1% of Americans have almost 50% of the nation's wealth. The next 9% have about a third. And the remaining 90% have about a sixth.

America now has the greatest wealth and income inequality in the developed world, and it is getting bigger every day. Efforts to implement even modest increases in the minimum wage are met with intense resistance. Further, as pointed out in a recent analysis in the *Left Business Observer,* the United States has the highest poverty rate of any developed nation, and uses government income transfers to reduce poverty less than any developed nation. Our two main rivals in these categories are Thatcher's England, and postcommunist, gangster-capitalist Russia.

Is this massive inequality an accident—an imperfection in an otherwise wonderful system? I don't think so. Modern capitalism depends on inequality. Modern capitalism is consumer capitalism. People have to buy things. In 1997, $120 billion was spent in the United States on advertising, more than was spent on all forms of education. Consumer debt, excluding home mortgages, exceeded $1 trillion in 1995—more than $10,000 per household. But people also need to save, to accumulate money for investment, especially now, in these days of ferocious global competition. How can you save and spend at the same time? The answer is that some must spend while others save. Income and wealth inequality allow a few to accumulate, and invest, while most of us spend—even more than we earn. And this is not an accident, but a structural necessity. There must be some people who despite society-wide exhortation to spend just cannot spend all they make. These people will provide the capital for investment.

Perhaps this kind of inequality is just the price we pay for prosperity. Concentrating wealth in the hands of the few gives them the opportunity to invest. This investment "trickles down" to improve the lives of all, by improving the products we buy and creating employment opportunities. There is no question that the current political leadership in the U.S.—of both parties—thinks that keeping Wall Street happy is essential to the nation's financial well-being. By encouraging people to buy stocks we put money in the hands of investors who then produce innovation and improvement in economic efficiency. Thus, we reduce capital gains taxes. And we eliminate the deficit to make Wall Street happy, even if it means neglecting the social safety net.

But who gains? It is true that what's good for Wall Street is good for America? On investment, more than 90% of all stock market trades involve just shuffling of paper as shares move from my hands to yours, or vice versa. Almost none of the activity on Wall Street puts capital in the hands of folks who invest in plant and equipment. Similarly, most corporate debt is used to finance mergers and acquisitions, or to buy back stock that later goes to chief executives as performance bonuses.

Why is it that when a company announces major layoffs, its stock goes up? The answer is that layoffs signal higher profits, good news for investors. Why is it that when unemployment rates go down, stock prices go down? The answer is that low unemployment signals potential inflation, bad news for investors. Why is it that banks bailed out a highly speculative hedge fund—for rich folks only—that was able to invest borrowed money (20 times its actual assets) while at the same time lobbying to crack down on personal bankruptcy laws, when the overwhelming majority of those facing personal bankruptcy make less than $20,000/year? The evidence is clear and compelling: the stock market operates to benefit the few at the expense of the many.

So if, as Murray contends (correctly, I think), the underclass is a social problem for America that is not going away, why isn't Murray demanding a set of policies that make it smaller rather than larger? Why isn't he demanding a minimum wage that is a *living* wage, so that parents can *afford* to take care of their children? And in addition, why isn't he demanding high-quality day care, so that the children of single mothers, or of two worker households, won't be neglected? How is it that a set of economic policies that has made the underclass bigger glides by free of Murray's wrath, as he chooses to condemn instead the nation's growing enthusiasm for underclass values?

The Market and Morality

... [R]ecent thinkers have realized that we can't take the bourgeois values that support capitalism for granted. Indeed, as Karl Polanyi, in *The Great Transformation*, and Fred Hirsch, in *Social Limits to Growth* argue persuasively, not only can we not take these values for granted, but market capitalism—the very thing that so desperately depends on them—actively undermines them. This, I believe, is the lesson that Murray and his cohort refuses to accept. The so-called "underclass" may threaten the comfort and safety of the middle class, but it is the overclass that threatens the stability and the future prospects of society.

One sees this dramatically in James Q. Wilson's . . . book *The Moral Sense.* In that book, Wilson argues for a biologically based moral sense in human beings—a sense that almost guarantees such moral traits as sympathy, duty, self-control, and fairness. . . .

Having made the sweeping claim that the market contributes more to the erosion of our moral sense than any other modern social force, I want to defend that claim with some more specific arguments. In particular, I want to discuss the market's negative effects on some of the moral sentiments that Wilson emphasizes and on some of the social institutions that nurture those sentiments.

One of the moral sentiments that is central to Wilson's argument is sympathy, the ability to feel and understand the misfortune of others and the desire to do something to ameliorate that misfortune. Wilson notes correctly that other-regarding sentiments and actions, including sympathy and altruism, are extremely common human phenomena, notwithstanding the efforts of many cynical social scientists to explain them away as subtle forms of self-interested behavior. What the literature on sympathy and altruism have made clear is that they depend on a person's ability to take the perspective of another (to "walk a mile in her shoes"). This perspective-taking ability in turn depends on a certain general cognitive sophistication, on familiarity with the other, and on proximity to the other. What does the market do to sympathy? Well, the market thrives on anonymity. One of its great virtues is that buyers are interchangeable with other buyers and sellers with other sellers. All that matters is price and quality and the ability to pay. Increasingly, in the modern market, transactions occur over long distances. Indeed, increasingly, they occur over telephone lines, as "e-commerce" joins the lexicon. Thus, the social institution that dominates modern American society is one that fosters, both in principle and in fact, social relations that are distant and impersonal—social relations that are the antithesis of what sympathy seems to require.

A second moral sentiment that attracts Wilson's attention is fairness. He correctly notes (as any parent will confirm) that concern about fairness appears early in human development and that it runs deep. Even four-year-olds have a powerful, if imperfect conception of what is and is not fair. What does fairness look like in adults?

[Professors] Daniel Kahneman, Jack Knetsch, and Richard Thaler asked this question by posing a variety of hypothetical business transactions to randomly chosen informants and asking the informants to judge whether the transactions were fair. What these hypothetical transactions had in common was that they all involved legal, profit-maximizing actions that were of questionable moral character. What these researchers found is that the overwhelming majority of people have a very strong sense of what is fair. While people believe that business people are entitled to make a profit, they do not think it fair for producers to charge what the market will bear (for example, to price gouge during shortages) or to lower wages during periods of slack employment. In short, most people think that concerns for fairness should be a constraint on profit-seeking. So far, so good; this study clearly supports Wilson's contention that fairness is one of our moral sentiments.

But here's the bad news. Another investigator posed these same hypotheticals to students in a nationally prominent MBA program. The overwhelming majority of these informants thought that anything was fair, as long as it was legal. Maximizing profit was the point; fairness was irrelevant. In another study, these same hypotheticals were posed to a group of CEOs. What the authors of the study concluded was that their executive sample was less inclined than those in the original study to find the actions posed in the survey to be unfair. In addition, often when CEOs did rate actions as unfair, they indicated in unsolicited comments that they did not think the actions were unfair so much as they were unwise, that is, bad business practice....

To summarize, people care about fairness, but if they are participants in the market, or are preparing to be participants in the market, they care much less about fairness than others do. Is it the ideology of relativism that is undermining this moral sentiment or the ideology of the market?

Another of the moral sentiments Wilson discusses is self-control. What does the market do to self-control? As many have pointed out, modern corporate management is hardly a paradigm of self-control. The combination of short-termism and me-first management that have saddled large companies with inefficiency and debt are a cautionary tale on the evils of self-indulgence. Short-termism is in part structural; managers must answer to shareholders, and in the financial markets, you're only as good as your last quarter. Me-first management seems to be pure greed. Some of the excesses of modern executive compensation have recently been documented by Derek Bok, in his book *The Cost of Talent*. Further, *The Economist*, in a survey of pay published in May of 1999, makes it quite clear that the pay scale of American executives is in another universe from that in any other nation, and heavily loaded with stock options that reward the executive for the company's performance in the stock market rather than the actual markets in goods and services in which the company operates....

The final moral sentiment that Wilson identifies and discusses is duty, "a disposition to honor obligations even without hope of reward or fear of punishment." Wilson is quite right about the importance of duty. If we must rely on threat of punishment to enforce obligations, they become unenforceable. Punishment works only as long as most people will do the right thing most of the time even if they can get away with transgressing....

The enemy of duty is free-riding, taking cost-free advantage of the dutiful actions of others. The more people are willing to be free-riders, the higher the cost to those who remain dutiful, and the higher the cost of enforcement to society as a whole. How does the market affect duty and free-riding? Well, one of the studies of fairness I mentioned above included a report of an investigation of free-riding. Economics students are more likely to be free riders than students in other disciplines. And this should come as no surprise. Free-riding is the "rational, self-interested" thing to do. Indeed, if you are the head of a company, free-riding may even be your fiduciary responsibility. So if free-riding is the enemy of duty, then the market is the enemy of duty.

... In my view, this is what market activity does to all the virtues that Wilson, and Murray long for—it submerges them with calculations of personal preference and self-interest.

If Wilson fails to acknowledge the influence of the market on our moral sense, where then does he look? As I said earlier, he thinks a good deal of human morality reflects innate predisposition. But that disposition must be nurtured, and it is nurtured, according to Wilson, in the family, by what might be described as "constrained socialization." The child is not a miniature adult (socialization is required), but nor is she a blank slate (not anything is possible; there are predispositions on the part of both parents and children for socialization to take one of a few "canonical" forms.) One of the primary mechanisms through which socialization occurs is imitation: "There can be little doubt that we learn a lot about how we ought to behave from watching others, especially others to whom we are strongly attached....

So let us accept Wilson's position about socialization and ask what the adults who the young child will be imitating look like. I believe, following the work of [economist] Fred Hirsch, that in the last few decades there has been an enormous upsurge in what might be called the "commercialization of social relations"—that choice has replaced duty and utility maximization replaced fairness in relations among family members....

Wilson seems mindful of all this. He decries the modern emphasis on rights and the neglect of duty. He acknowledges that modern society has posed a real challenge to the family by substituting labor markets for householding. And he deplores the ideology of choice as applied to the family:

> Not even the family has been immune to the ideology of choice. In the 1960s and 1970s (but less so today) books were written advocating "alternative" families and "open" marriages. A couple could choose to have a trial marriage, a regular marriage but without an obligation to sexual fidelity, or a revocable marriage with an easy exit provided by no-fault divorce. A woman could choose to have a child out of wedlock and to raise it alone. Marriage was but one of several "options" by which men and women could manage their intimate needs, an option that ought to be carefully negotiated in order to preserve the rights of each contracting party. The family, in this view, was no longer the cornerstone of human life, it was one of several "relationships" from which individuals could choose so as to maximize their personal goals.

But instead of attributing this ideology of choice to the market, from which I think it clearly arises, Wilson attributes it to the weakening of cultural standards—to relativism. Indeed he even adopts a Becker-like economic analysis of the family himself, apparently unaware that if people actually thought about their families in the way that he and [economist Gary] Becker claim they do, the family would hardly be a source of any of the moral sentiments that are important to him:

> But powerful as they are, the expression of these [familial] instincts has been modified by contemporary circumstances. When children have less economic value, then, at the margin, fewer children will be produced, marriage (and childbearing) will be postponed, and more marriages will end in

divorce. And those children who are produced will be raised, at the margin, in ways that reflect their higher opportunity cost. Some will be neglected and others will be cared for in ways that minimize the parental cost in personal freedom, extra income, or career opportunities.

Let me be clear that I think Wilson is right about changes that have occurred in the family, and that he is also right about the unfortunate social consequences of those changes. His mistake is in failing to see the responsibility for these changes that must be borne by the spread of market thinking into the domain of our intimate social relations. As I have said elsewhere, there is an opportunity cost to thinking about one's social relations in terms of opportunity costs. In Wilson's terms, that opportunity cost will be paid in sympathy, fairness, and duty. Sociologist Arlie Hochschild has written that "each marriage bears the footprints of economic and cultural trends which originate far outside marriage." Wilson has emphasized the cultural and overlooked the economic. And so, alas, has Murray.

What Economies Do to People

In Arthur Miller's play, *All My Sons,* much of the drama centers around the belated discovery by a son that his father knowingly shipped defective airplane parts to fulfill a government contract during World War II. The parts were installed, some of the planes crashed, and pilots and their crews were killed. The man responsible, the father, is a good man, a kind man, a man who cares deeply about his family and would do anything to protect them and provide for them. His son simply can't imagine that a man like his father is capable of such an act—but he is. As he explains, he was under enormous pressure to deliver the goods. The military needed the parts right away, and failure to deliver would have destroyed his business. He had a responsibility to take care of his family. And anyway, there was no certainty that the parts would not hold up when in use. As the truth slowly comes out, the audience has the same incredulity as the son. How could it be? If a man like that could do a thing like that, then anyone is capable of doing anything.

This, of course, is one of the play's major points. Almost anyone *is* capable of almost anything. A monstrous system can make a monster of anyone, or perhaps more accurately, can make almost anyone do monstrous things. We see this as drama like Miller's are played out in real life, with horrifyingly tragic consequences.

- All too close to the story of *All My Sons,* military contractors have been caught knowingly making and selling defective brake systems for U.S. jet fighters, defective machine gun parts that cause the guns to jam when used, and defective fire-fighting equipment for navy ships.
- An automobile manufacturer knowingly made and sold a dangerous car, whose gas tank was alarmingly likely to explode in rear end collisions. This defect could have been corrected at a cost of a few dollars per car.

- A chemical company continued operating a chemical plant in Bhopal, India long after it knew the plant was unsafe. A gas leak killed more than 2000 people, and seriously injured more than 30,000. The $5 billion company responded to this tragedy by sending $1 million in disaster relief and a shipment of medicines sufficient for about 400 people.
- Other drug and chemical manufacturers make and sell to the Third World products known to be sufficiently dangerous that their sale is banned in the U.S.
- The asbestos industry knowingly concealed the hazardous nature of their products for years from workers who were exposed to carcinogens on a daily basis.
- Trucking companies put trucks on the road more than 30% of which would fail safety inspections and are thus hazards to their drivers as well as to other motorists.
- And of course, we all know now about the tobacco industry.

And it isn't just about dramatic death and destruction. The death and destruction can be slow and torturous:

- Firms get closed down, people put out of work, and communities destroyed, not because they aren't profitable, but because they aren't *as* profitable as other parts of the business.
- People are put to work in illegal sweatshops, or the work is sent offshore, where the working conditions are even worse, but not illegal.

Why does all this abuse occur? What makes people seek to exploit every advantage over their customers? What makes bosses abuse their employees? Do the people who do these things take pleasure from hurting their unsuspecting customers? Do they relish the opportunity to take advantage of people? It does not seem so. When bosses are challenged about their unscrupulous practices, they typically argue that "everybody does it." Understand, the argument is not that since everybody does it, it is all right. The argument is that since everybody does it, you have to do it also, in self-defense. In competitive situations, it seems inevitable that dishonest, inhumane practices will drive out the honest and humane ones; to be humane becomes a luxury that few business people can afford.

I find it unimaginable as I talk to the talented, ambitious, enthusiastic students with whom I work that any of them aspires to a future in which he or she will oversee the production of cars, drugs, chemicals, foods, military supplies, or anything else that will imperil the lives of thousands of people. I even find it unimaginable that any of them will accept such a future. They are good, decent people, as far removed from those who seek to turn human weakness and vulnerability into profit as anyone could be. And yet, I know that some of my former students already have, and some of my current students surely will accept such positions. They will also marry, have families, and raise wonderful children who won't believe their parents could ever do such things.

Surely there is an urgent need to figure out what it is that makes good people do such bad things, and stop it.

The leaders of corporations tell themselves that they have only one mission—to do whatever they can to further the interests of the shareholders, the owners of the company that these leaders have been hired to manage. When the leaders of corporations say these things to themselves, they are telling themselves the truth. They work within a system that asks—even requires—them to be single-minded, no matter how much they wish they could be different. As long as the system has this character, we can expect that only the single-minded will rise to the top. Only rarely will people whose intentions are to change corporate practices go far enough to implement those intentions.

Several years ago United States Catholic Bishops drafted a position paper, a pastoral letter, on the economy. In it they said, "every perspective on economic life that is human, moral, and Christian must be shaped by two questions: What does the economy do *for* people? What does the economy do *to* people?" I have been suggesting that our economy does terrible things *to* people, even to those people who succeed. It makes them into people that they should not and do not want to be, and it encourages them to do things that they should not and do not want to do. No matter what an economy does *for* these people, it cannot be justified if it does these things *to* them. And it seems to me that in the face of massive, antisocial practices like these, blaming the underclass for teaching mainstream America the lessons of incivility is perverse.

POSTSCRIPT

Is the Underclass the Major Threat to American Ideals?

In *Reducing Poverty in America* edited by Michael R. Darby (Sage Publications, 1996), James Q. Wilson summarizes the debate on the causes of poverty as the clash between two views: "The first is incentives or objective factors: jobs, incomes, opportunities. The second is culture: single-parent families, out-of-wedlock births, and a decaying work ethic." Sociologists expect the structural versus individual explanations of poverty to be debated for a long time because both can be seen as at least partially true. The cultural explanation derives from the anthropological studies of Oscar Lewis and was proposed as a major cause of urban poverty in America by Edward Banfield in *The Unheavenly City* (Little, Brown, 1970). Today, the most vigorous proponent of the culture-of-poverty thesis today is Lawrence E. Harrison, who wrote *Who Prospers? How Cultural Values Shape Economic and Political Success* (Basic Books, 1992). In *The Dream and the Nightmare: The Sixties' Legacy to the Underclass* (William Morrow, 1993), Myron Magnet blames the culture of the underclass for their poverty, but he also blames the upper classes for contributing greatly to the underclass's culture. Charles Murray, in *Losing Ground* (Basic Books, 1984), provides empirical support for the idea that welfare is a cause of poverty and not its solution, and concludes that welfare should be abolished.

The counter to the cultural explanation of poverty is the structural explanation. Its most current version focuses on the loss of unskilled jobs. This is the thrust of William Julius Wilson's analysis of the macroeconomic forces that impact so heavily on the urban poor in *The Truly Disadvantaged* (University of Chicago Press, 1987) and in *When Work Disappears: The World of the New Urban Poor* (Alfred A. Knopf, 1996). If Jeremy Rifkin's analysis in *The End of Work: The Decline of the Global Labor Force and the Dawn of the Post-Market Era* (Putnam, 1995) is correct, then this situation will get worse, not better, because new technologies will lengthen unemployment lines unless the economy or the working world is radically restructured. For a similar view, see Stanley Aronowitz and William DiFazio, *The Jobless Future: Sci-Tech and the Dogma of Work* (University of Minnesota Press, 1994).

There are countless works that describe the adverse conditions of the poor. The nineteenth-century English novelist Charles Dickens was a crusader for the poor, and many of his novels, still in print and certainly considered classics, graphically depict the wretchedness of poverty. Michael Harrington described poverty in America in his influential nonfiction book *The Other America* (Macmillan, 1963) at a time when a substantial portion of the country was affluent.

ISSUE 10

Has Affirmative Action Outlived Its Usefulness?

YES: Walter E. Williams, from "Affirmative Action Can't Be Mended," *Cato Journal* (Spring/Summer 1997)

NO: Wilbert Jenkins, from "Why We Must Retain Affirmative Action," *USA Today Magazine* (September 1999)

ISSUE SUMMARY

YES: Professor of economics Walter E. Williams asserts that "the civil rights struggle for blacks is over and won," so affirmative action policies are unjust and adversely affect society.

NO: History professor Wilbert Jenkins dismisses the arguments against affirmative action as founded on the false logic that since the promised land has been reached, continuing affirmative action would be reverse discrimination. Jenkins maintains that an honest look at the facts reveals that affirmative action is still needed.

In America, equality is a principle as basic as liberty. "All men are created equal" is perhaps the most well known phrase in the Declaration of Independence. More than half a century after the signing of the Declaration, the French social philosopher Alexis de Tocqueville examined democracy in America and concluded that its most essential ingredient was the equality of condition. Today we know that the "equality of condition" that Tocqueville perceived did not exist for women, blacks, Native Americans, and other racial minorities, nor for other disadvantaged social classes. Nevertheless, the ideal persisted.

When slavery was abolished after the Civil War, the Constitution's newly ratified Fourteenth Amendment proclaimed, "No State shall . . . deny to any person within its jurisdiction the equal protection of the laws." Equality has been a long time coming. For nearly a century after the abolition of slavery, American blacks were denied equal protection by law in some states and by social practice nearly everywhere. One-third of the states either permitted or forced schools to become racially segregated, and segregation was achieved elsewhere through housing policy and social behavior. In 1954 the Supreme Court reversed a 58-year-old standard that had found "separate but equal" schools compatible with equal protection of the law. A unanimous decision in *Brown v. Board of Education* held that separate is *not* equal for the members of the discriminated-against group when the segregation "generates a feeling of inferiority as to their status in the community that may affect their hearts and minds in a way unlikely ever to be undone." The 1954 ruling on public elementary education has been extended to other areas of both governmental and private conduct, including housing and employment.

Even if judicial decisions and congressional statutes could end all segregation and racial discrimination, would this achieve equality—or simply perpetuate the status quo? Consider that the unemployment rate for blacks today is much higher than that of whites. Disproportionately higher numbers of blacks experience poverty, brutality, broken homes, physical and mental illness, and early deaths, while disproportionately lower numbers of them reach positions of affluence and prestige. It seems possible that much of this inequality has resulted from 300 years of slavery and segregation. Is termination of this ill treatment enough to end the injustices? No, say the proponents of affirmative action.

Affirmative action—the effort to improve the educational and employment opportunities for minorities—has had an uneven history in U.S. federal courts. In *Regents of the University of California v. Allan Bakke* (1978), which marked the first time the Supreme Court dealt directly with the merits of affirmative action, a 5–4 majority ruled that a white applicant to a medical school had been wrongly excluded in favor of a less qualified black applicant due to the school's affirmative action policy. Yet the majority also agreed that "race-conscious" policies may be used in admitting candidates—as long as they do not amount to fixed quotas. The ambivalence of *Bakke* has run through the Court's treatment of the issue since 1978. More recent decisions suggest that the Court is beginning to take a dim view of affirmative action. In 1989, for example, the Court ruled that a city council could *not* set aside a fixed percentage of public construction projects for minority contractors.

Affirmative action is hotly debated outside the courts, and white males have recently been vocal on talk shows and in print about being treated unjustly because of affirmative action policies. In the following selections, Walter E. Williams and Wilbert Jenkins debate the merits of affirmative action. In Williams's view, affirmative action has outlived its usefulness, and the government should follow a policy of strict race neutrality. Jenkins, on the other hand, considers affirmative action an essential means for bringing about the equality that both sides ostensibly want.

Walter E. Williams

 **YES**

Affirmative Action Can't Be Mended

For the last several decades, affirmative action has been the basic compo-
nent of the civil rights agenda. But affirmative action, in the form of racial
preferences, has worn out its political welcome. In Gallup Polls, between 1987
and 1990, people were asked if they agreed with the statement: "We should
make every effort to improve the position of blacks and other minorities even
if it means giving them preferential treatment." More than 70 percent of the
respondents opposed preferential treatment while only 24 percent supported
it. Among blacks, 66 percent opposed preferential treatment and 32 percent
supported it (Lipset 1992: 66–69).

The rejection of racial preferences by the broad public and increasingly
by the Supreme Court has been partially recognized by even supporters of affirmative action. While they have not forsaken their goals, they have begun
to distance themselves from some of the language of affirmative action. Thus,
many business, government, and university affirmative action offices have been
renamed "equity offices." Racial preferences are increasingly referred to as "diversity multiculturalism." What is it about affirmative action that gives rise to
its contentiousness?

For the most part, post–World War II America has supported civil rights
for blacks. Indeed, if we stick to the uncorrupted concept of civil rights, we
can safely say that the civil rights struggle for blacks is over and won. Civil
rights properly refer to rights, held simultaneously among individuals, to be
treated equally in the eyes of the law, make contracts, sue and be sued, give
evidence, associate and travel freely, and vote. There was a time when blacks
did not fully enjoy those rights. With the yeoman-like work of civil rights organizations and decent Americans, both black and white, who fought lengthy
court, legislative, and street battles, civil rights have been successfully secured
for blacks. No small part of that success was due to a morally compelling appeal to America's civil libertarian tradition of private property, rule of law, and
limited government.

Today's corrupted vision of civil rights attacks that civil libertarian tradition. Principles of private property rights, rule of law, freedom of association,
and limited government are greeted with contempt. As such, the agenda of
today's civil rights organizations conceptually differs little from yesteryear's

From Walter E. Williams, "Affirmative Action Can't Be Mended," *Cato Journal,* vol. 17, no. 1 (Spring/
Summer 1997). Copyright © 1997 by The Cato Institute. Reprinted by permission. Notes and some
references omitted.

restrictions that were the targets of the earlier civil rights struggle. Yesteryear civil rights organizations fought *against* the use of race in hiring, access to public schools, and university admissions. Today, civil rights organizations fight *for* the use of race in hiring, access to public schools, and university admissions. Yesteryear, civil rights organizations fought *against* restricted association in the forms of racially segregated schools, libraries, and private organizations. Today, they fight *for* restricted associations. They use state power, not unlike the racists they fought, to enforce racial associations they deem desirable. They protest that blacks should be a certain percentage of a company's workforce or clientele, a certain percentage of a student body, and even a certain percentage of an advertiser's models.

Civil rights organizations, in their successful struggle against state-sanctioned segregation, have lost sight of what it means to be truly committed to liberty, especially the freedom of association. The true test of that commitment does not come when we allow people to be free to associate in ways we deem appropriate. The true test is when we allow people to form those voluntary associations we deem offensive. It is the same principle we apply to our commitment to free speech. What tests our commitment to free speech is our willingness to permit people the freedom to say things we find offensive.

Zero-Sum Games

The tragedy of America's civil rights movement is that it has substituted today's government-backed racial favoritism in the allocation of resources for yesterday's legal and extra-legal racial favoritism. In doing so, civil rights leaders fail to realize that government allocation of resources produces the kind of conflict that does not arise with market allocation of resources. Part of the reason is that any government allocation of resources, including racial preferential treatment, is a zero-sum game.

A zero-sum game is defined as any transaction where one person's gain necessarily results in another person's loss. The simplest example of a zero-sum game is poker. A winner's gain is matched precisely by the losses of one or more persons. In this respect, the only essential difference between affirmative action and poker is that in poker participation is voluntary. Another difference is the loser is readily identifiable, a point to which I will return later.

The University of California, Berkeley's affirmative action program for blacks captures the essence of a zero-sum game. Blacks are admitted with considerably lower average SAT scores (952) than the typical white (1232) and Asian student (1254) (Sowell 1993: 144). Between UCLA and UC Berkeley, more than 2,000 white and Asian straight A students are turned away in order to provide spaces for black and Hispanic students (Lynch 1989: 163). The admissions gains by blacks are exactly matched by admissions losses by white and Asian students. Thus, any preferential treatment program results in a zero-sum game almost by definition.

More generally, government allocation of resources is a zero-sum game primarily because government has no resources of its very own. When government gives some citizens food stamps, crop subsidies, or disaster relief payments, the recipients of the largesse gain. Losers are identified by asking: where does government acquire the resources to confer the largesse? In order for government to give to some citizens, it must through intimidation, threats, and coercion take from other citizens. Those who lose the rights to their earnings, to finance government largesse, are the losers.

Government-mandated racial preferential treatment programs produce a similar result. When government creates a special advantage for one ethnic group, it necessarily comes at the expense of other ethnic groups for whom government simultaneously creates a special disadvantage in the form of reduced alternatives. If a college or employer has X amount of positions, and R of them have been set aside for blacks or some other group, that necessarily means there are $(X - R)$ fewer positions for which other ethnic groups might compete. At a time when there were restrictions against blacks, that operated in favor of whites, those restrictions translated into a reduced opportunity set for blacks. It is a zero-sum game independent of the race or ethnicity of the winners and losers.

Our courts have a blind-sided vision of the zero-sum game. They have upheld discriminatory racial preferences in hiring but have resisted discriminatory racial preferences in job layoffs. An example is the U.S. Supreme Court's ruling in *Wygant v. Jackson Board of Education* (1986), where a teacher union's collective-bargaining agreement protected black teachers from job layoffs in order to maintain racial balance. Subsequently, as a result of that agreement, the Jackson County School Board laid off white teachers having greater seniority while black teachers with less seniority were retained.

A lower court upheld the constitutionality of the collective bargaining agreement by finding that racial preferences in layoffs were a permissible means to remedy societal discrimination (*Wygant* 1982: 1195, 1201). White teachers petitioned the U.S. Supreme Court, claiming their constitutional rights under the Equal Protection clause were violated. The Court found in their favor. Justice Lewis F. Powell delivered the opinion saying, "While hiring goals impose a diffuse burden, only closing one of several opportunities, layoffs impose the entire burden of achieving racial equity on particular individuals, often resulting in serious disruption of their lives. The burden is too intrusive" (*Wygant* 1986: 283)....

There is no conceptual distinction in the outcome of the zero-sum game whether it is played on the layoff or the hiring side of the labor market.... The diffuseness to which Justice Powell refers is not diffuseness at all. It is simply that the victims of hiring preferences are less visible than victims of layoff preferences as in the case of *Wygant*. The petitioners in *Wygant* were identifiable people who could not be covered up as "society." That differs from the cases of hiring and college admissions racial preferences where those who face a reduced opportunity set tend to be unidentifiable to the courts, other people, and even to themselves. Since they are invisible victims, the Supreme Court and others can blithely say racial hiring goals (and admission goals) impose a diffuse burden.

Tentative Victim Identification

In California, voters passed the California Civil Rights Initiative of 1996 (CCRI) that says: "The state shall not discriminate against, or grant preferential treatment to, any individual or group on the basis of race, sex, color, ethnicity, or national origin in the operation of public employment, public education, or public contracting." Therefore, California public universities can no longer have preferential admission policies that include race as a factor in deciding whom to admit. As a result, the UCLA School of Law reported accepting only 21 black applicants for its fall 1997 class—a drop of 80 percent from the previous year, in which 108 black applicants were accepted. At the UC Berkeley Boalt Hall School of Law, only 14 of the 792 students accepted for the fall 1997 class are black, down from 76 the previous year. At the UCLA School of Law, white enrollment increased by 14 percent for the fall 1997 term and Asian enrollment rose by 7 percent. At UC Berkeley, enrollment of white law students increased by 12 percent and Asian law students increased by 18 percent (Weiss 1997)....

In the case of UC Berkeley's preferential admissions for blacks, those whites and Asians who have significantly higher SAT scores and grades than the admitted blacks are victims of reverse discrimination. However, in the eyes of the courts, others, and possibly themselves, they are invisible victims. In other words, no one can tell for sure who among those turned away would have gained entry to UC Berkeley were it not for the preferential treatment given to blacks....

Affirmative Action and Supply

An important focus of affirmative action is statistical underrepresentation of different racial and ethnic groups on college and university campuses. If the percentages of blacks and Mexican-Americans, for example, are not at a level deemed appropriate by a court, administrative agency, or university administrator, racial preference programs are instituted. The inference made from the underrepresentation argument is that, in the absence of racial discrimination, groups would be represented on college campuses in proportion to their numbers in the relevant population. In making that argument, little attention is paid to the supply issue—that is, to the pool of students available that meet the standards or qualifications of the university in question.

In 1985, fewer than 1,032 blacks scored 600 and above on the verbal portion of the SAT and 1,907 scored 600 and above on the quantitative portion of the examination. There are roughly 58 elite colleges and universities with student body average composite SAT scores of 1200 and above (Sowell 1993: 142). If blacks scoring 600 or higher on the quantitative portion of the SAT (assuming their performance on the verbal portion of the examination gave them a composite SAT score of 1200 or higher) were recruited to elite colleges and universities, there would be less than 33 black students available per university. At none of those universities would blacks be represented according to their numbers in the population.

There is no evidence that suggests that university admissions offices practice racial discrimination by turning away blacks with SAT scores of 1200 or higher. In reality, there are not enough blacks to be admitted to leading colleges and universities on the same terms as other students, such that their numbers in the campus population bear any resemblance to their numbers in the general population.

Attempts by affirmative action programs to increase the percent of blacks admitted to top schools, regardless of whether blacks match the academic characteristics of the general student body, often produce disastrous results. In order to meet affirmative action guidelines, leading colleges and universities recruit and admit black students whose academic qualifications are well below the norm for other students. For example, of the 317 black students admitted to UC Berkeley in 1985, all were admitted under affirmative action criteria rather than academic qualifications. Those students had an average SAT score of 952 compared to the national average of 900 among all students. However, their SAT scores were well below UC Berkeley's average of nearly 1200. More than 70 percent of the black students failed to graduate from UC Berkeley (Sowell 1993: 144).

Not far from UC Berkeley is San Jose State University, not one of the top-tier colleges, but nonetheless respectable. More than 70 percent of its black students fail to graduate. The black students who might have been successful at San Jose State University have been recruited to UC Berkeley and elsewhere where they have been made artificial failures. This pattern is one of the consequences of trying to use racial preferences to make a student body reflect the relative importance of different ethnic groups in the general population. There is a mismatch between black student qualifications and those of other students when the wrong students are recruited to the wrong universities.

There is no question that preferential admissions is unjust to both white and Asian students who may be qualified but are turned away to make room for less-qualified students in the "right" ethnic group. However, viewed from a solely black self-interest point of view, the question should be asked whether such affirmative action programs serve the best interests of blacks. Is there such an abundance of black students who score above the national average on the SAT, such as those admitted to UC Berkeley, that blacks as a group can afford to have those students turned into artificial failures in the name of diversity, multiculturalism, or racial justice? The affirmative action debate needs to go beyond simply an issue of whether blacks are benefited at the expense of whites. Whites and Asians who are turned away to accommodate blacks are still better off than the blacks who were admitted. After all, graduating from the university of one's second choice is preferable to flunking out of the university of one's first choice.

To the extent racial preferences in admission produce an academic mismatch of students, the critics of California's Proposition 209 may be unnecessarily alarmed, assuming their concern is with black students actually graduating from college. If black students, who score 952 on the SAT, are not admitted to UC Berkeley, that does not mean that they cannot gain admittance to one of America's 3,000 other colleges. It means that they will gain admittance to some other college where their academic characteristics will be more similar to those of their peers. There will not be as much of an academic mismatch. To the extent this is true, we may see an *increase* in black graduation rates. Moreover, if black students find themselves more similar to their white peers in terms of college grades and graduation honors, they are less likely to feel academically isolated and harbor feelings of low self-esteem.

Affirmative Action and Justice

Aside from any other question, we might ask what case can be made for the morality or justice of turning away more highly credentialed white and Asian students so as to be able to admit more blacks? Clearly, blacks as a group have suffered past injustices, including discrimination in college and university admissions. However, that fact does not spontaneously yield sensible policy proposals for today. The fact is that a special privilege cannot be created for one person without creating a special disadvantage for another. In the case of preferential admissions at UCLA and UC Berkeley, a special privilege for black students translates into a special disadvantage for white and Asian students. Thus, we must ask what have those individual white and Asian students done to deserve punishment? Were they at all responsible for the injustices, either in the past or present, suffered by blacks? If, as so often is the case, the justification for preferential treatment is to redress past grievances, how just is it to have a policy where a black of today is helped by punishing a white of today for what a white of yesterday did to a black of yesterday? Such an idea becomes even more questionable in light of the fact that so many whites and Asians cannot trace the American part of their ancestry back as much as two or three generations.

Affirmative Action and Racial Resentment

In addition to the injustices that are a result of preferential treatment, such treatment has given rise to racial resentment where it otherwise might not exist. While few people support racial resentment and its manifestations, if one sees some of affirmative action's flagrant attacks on fairness and equality before the law, one can readily understand why resentment is on the rise.

In the summer of 1995, the Federal Aviation Administration (FAA) published a "diversity handbook" that said, "The merit promotion process is but one means of filling vacancies, which need not be utilized if it will not promote your diversity goals." In that spirit, one FAA job announcement said, "Applicants who meet the qualification requirements ... cannot be considered for this position. ... Only those applicants who do not meet the Office of Personnel Management requirements ... will be eligible to compete" (Roberts and Stratton 1995: 141).

According to a General Accounting Office report that evaluated complaints of discrimination by Asian-Americans, prestigious universities such as UCLA, UC Berkeley, MIT, and the University of Wisconsin have engaged in systematic discrimination in the failure to admit highly qualified Asian students in order to admit relatively unqualified black and Hispanic students (U.S. GAO 1995).

In Memphis, Tennessee, a white police officer ranked 59th out of 209 applicants for 75 available positions as police sergeant, but he did not get promoted. Black officers, with lower overall test scores than he, were moved ahead of him and promoted to sergeant. Over a two-year period, 43 candidates with lower scores were moved ahead of him and made sergeant (Eastland 1996: 1–2).

There is little need to recite the litany of racial preference instances that are clear violations of commonly agreed upon standards of justice and fair play. But the dangers of racial preferences go beyond matters of justice and fair play. They lead to increased group polarization ranging from political backlash to mob violence and civil war as seen in other countries. The difference between the United States and those countries is that racial preferences have not produced the same level of violence (Sowell 1990). However, they have produced polarization and resentment.

Affirmative action proponents cling to the notion that racial discrimination satisfactorily explains black/white socioeconomic differences. While every vestige of racial discrimination has not been eliminated in our society, current social discrimination cannot begin to explain all that affirmative action proponents purport it explains. Rather than focusing our attention on discrimination, a higher payoff can be realized by focusing on real factors such as fraudulent education, family disintegration, and hostile economic climates in black neighborhoods. Even if affirmative action was not a violation of justice and fair play, was not a zero-sum game, was not racially polarizing, it is a poor cover-up for the real work that needs to be done.

References

Eastland, T. (1996) *Ending Affirmative Action: The Case for Colorblind Justice*. New York: Basic Books.

Lipset, S. M. (1992) "Equal Chances Versus Equal Results." In H. Orlans and J. O'Neill (eds.) *Affirmative Action Revisited; Annals of the American Academy of Political and Social Science* 523 (September): 63–74.

Lynch, F. R. (1989) *Invisible Victims: White Males and the Crisis of Affirmative Action*. New York: Greenwood Press.

Roberts, P. C., and Stratton, L. M. (1995) *The Color Line: How Quotas and Privilege Destroy Democracy*. Washington, D.C.: Regnery.

Sowell, T. (1990) *Preferential Policies: An International Perspective*. New York: William Morrow.

Sowell, T. (1993) *Inside American Education: The Decline, The Deception, The Dogmas*. New York: The Free Press.

United States General Accounting Office (1995) *Efforts by the Office for Civil Rights to Resolve Asian-American Complaints*. Washington, D.C.: Government Printing Office. (December).

Weiss, K. R. (1997) "UC Law Schools' New Rules Cost Minorities Spots." *Los Angeles Times*, 15 May.

Wygant v. Jackson Board of Education (1982) 546 F. Supp. 1195.

Wygant v. Jackson Board of Education (1986) 476 U.S. 267.

NO ✐

Wilbert Jenkins

Why We Must Retain Affirmative Action

The historical origins of affirmative action can be found in the 14th and 15th Amendments to the Constitution, the Enforcement Acts of 1870 and 1871, and the Civil Rights Acts of 1866 and 1875, which were passed by Republican-dominated Congresses during the Reconstruction period. This legislation set the precedent for many of the civil rights laws of the 1950s and 1960s—such as the Civil Rights Act of 1957, the Civil Rights Act of 1964, and the Voting Rights Act of 1965—and paved the way for what would become known as affirmative action.

In spite of the fact that laws designed to promote and protect the civil and political rights of African-Americans were enacted by Congress in the 1950s and 1960s, it was obvious that racism and discrimination against blacks in the area of education and, by extension, the workplace were huge obstacles that needed to be overcome if African-Americans were ever going to be able to carve an economic foundation. Thus, in the 1960s, affirmative action became a part of a larger design by Pres. Lyndon Johnson's War on Poverty program. In a historic 1965 speech at Howard University, the nation's top black school, Johnson illustrated the thinking that led to affirmative action: "You do not take a person who for years has been hobbled by chains and liberate him, bring him to the starting line and say you are free to compete with all the others." Civil rights leader Martin Luther King, Jr., also underscored this belief when he stated that "one cannot ask people who don't have boots to pull themselves up by their own bootstraps."

Policymakers fervently believed that more than three centuries of enslavement, oppression, and discrimination had so economically deprived African-Americans that some mechanism had to be put in place that would at least allow them a fighting chance. Blacks were locked out of the highest paid positions and made considerably fewer dollars than their white counterparts in the same jobs. Moreover, the number of African-Americans enrolling in the nation's undergraduate and graduate schools was extremely low. Affirmative action became a vehicle to correct this injustice. The original intent of affirmative action was not to provide jobs and other advantages to blacks solely because of the color of their skin, but to provide economic opportunities for those who are competent and qualified. Due to a history of discrimination, even those with outstanding credentials were often locked out. As the years wore on, it was deemed necessary to add other minorities—such as Native Americans, Hispanics, and Asian-Americans—as well as women to the list of those requiring affirmative action in order to achieve a measure of economic justice.

A number of conservatives—black and white—such as Armstrong Williams, Linda Chavez, Patrick Buchanan, Robert Novak, Ward Connerly, Clarence Thomas, Clint Bolick, Alan Keyes, and others argue that it is time to scrap affirmative action. This is necessary, they maintain, if the country is truly going to become a color-blind society like King envisioned. People would be judged by the content of their character, not by the color of their skin. Many among these conservatives also maintain that affirmative action is destructive to minorities because it is demeaning, saps drive, and leads to the development of a welfare dependency mentality. Minorities often come to believe that something is owed them.

Thus, conservatives argue against race-based admissions requirements to undergraduate and graduate schools, labeling them preferential treatment and an insult to anyone who is the beneficiary of this practice. In their opinion, it is psychologically, emotionally, and personally degrading for individuals to have to go through life realizing they were not admitted to school or given employment because of their credentials, but in order to fill some quota or to satisfy appearances. It is rather ironic, however, that they are so concerned about this apparent harm to black self-esteem, since there is little evidence that those who have been aided by affirmative action policies feel many doubts or misgivings. The vast majority of them believe they are entitled to whatever opportunities they have received—opportunities, in their estimation, which are long overdue because of racism and discrimination. Consequently, America is only providing them with a few economic crumbs which are rightfully theirs.

Although a number of affirmative action critics argue that lowering admissions standards for minorities creates a class of incompetent professionals —if they are somehow fortunate enough to graduate—the facts run counter to their arguments. For instance, a study conducted by Robert C. Davidson and Ernest L. Lewis of affirmative action students admitted to the University of California at Davis Medical School with low grades and test scores concluded that these students became doctors just as qualified as the higher-scoring applicants. The graduation rate of 94% for special-admissions students compared favorably to that of regular-admissions students (98%). Moreover, despite the fact that regular-admissions students were more likely to receive honors or A grades, there was no difference in the rates at which students failed core courses.

Many whites have been the recipients of some form of preferential treatment. For many years, so-called selective colleges have set less-demanding standards for admitting offspring of alumni or the children of the rich and famous. For example, though former Vice Pres. Dan Quayle's grade-point average was minuscule and his score on the LSAT very low, he was admitted to Indiana University's Law School. There is little evidence that Quayle or other recipients of this practice have developed low self-esteem or have felt any remorse for those whose credentials were better, but nonetheless were rejected because less-qualified others took their slots. The following example further underscores this practice. A number of opponents of affirmative action were embarrassed during 1996 in the midst of passage of Proposition 209, which eliminated affirmative action in California, when the *Los Angeles Times* broke a story documenting the fact that many of them and their children had received preferential treatment in acquiring certain jobs and gaining entry to some colleges.

Some opponents of affirmative action go so far as to suggest that it aggravates racial tensions and leads, in essence, to an increase in violence between whites and people of color. This simply does not mesh with historical reality. Discrimination against and violence toward the powerless always has increased during periods of economic downturns, as witnessed by the depressions of 1873 and 1893. There was nothing akin to affirmative action in this country for nearly two centuries of its existence, yet African-American women were physically and sexually assaulted by whites, and people of color were brutalized, murdered, and lynched on an unprecedented scale. Moreover, there were so many race riots in the summer of 1919 that the author of the black national anthem, James Weldon Johnson, referred to it as "the red summer." The 1920s witnessed the reemergence of a reinvigorated Ku Klux Klan. Many state politicians even went public with their memberships, and the governor of Indiana during this period was an avowed member of the Klan. The 1930s and 1940s did not bring much relief, as attested to by several race riots and Pres. Franklin D. Roosevelt's refusal to promote an anti-lynching bill.

Some of the African-American critics of affirmative action have actually been beneficiaries of such a program. It is unlikely that Clarence Thomas would have been able to attend Yale University Law School or become a justice on the U.S. Supreme Court without affirmative action. Yet, Thomas hates it with a passion, once saying he would be violating "God's law" if he ever signed his name to an opinion that approved the use of race—even for benign reasons—in hiring or admissions.

Opponents of affirmative action from various racial and ethnic backgrounds argue that it may lead to reverse discrimination, whereby qualified whites fail to acquire admission to school, secure employment, or are fired because of their race since prospective slots have to be preserved solely for minorities. It is difficult to say with any degree of certainty how many whites may have been bypassed or displaced because preferences have been given to blacks and other minorities. What can be said, though, with a large measure of accuracy is that whites have not lost ground in medicine and college teaching, despite considerable efforts to open up those fields. In addition, contrary to popular myth, there is little need for talented and successful advertising executives, lawyers, physicians, engineers, accountants, college professors, movie executives, chemists, physicists, airline pilots, architects, etc. to fear minority preference. Whites who lose out are more generally blue-collar workers or persons at lower administrative levels, whose skills are not greatly in demand.

Furthermore, some whites who are passed over for promotion under these circumstances may simply not be viewed as the best person available for the job. It is human nature that those not receiving promotions that go to minorities or not gaining admission to colleges and universities prefer to believe that they have been discriminated against. They refuse to consider the possibility that the minorities could be better qualified. Although some highly qualified white students may be rejected by the University of California at Berkeley, Duke, Yale, Harvard, Stanford, or Princeton, the same students often are offered slots at Brown, Dartmouth, Cornell, Columbia, Michigan, the University of Pennsylvania, and the University of North Carolina at Chapel Hill—all first-rate institutions of higher learning.

Although some white women have been the victims of affirmative action, females, for the most part, arguably have been the largest beneficiaries of it. Over the last quarter-century, their numbers have increased dramatically in such fields as law, medicine, accounting, engineering, broadcasting, architecture, higher education, etc. Nonetheless, many white women vehemently have attacked affirmative action. For example, according to an ABC News poll taken in November, 1996, 52% of white women in California voted to support Proposition 209, which sought to eliminate racial and gender preferences in hiring, college admissions, and Federal contracts. What explains this behavior?

White women believe affirmative action is denying their sons admission to some schools and taking jobs away from their sons and husbands. Many worry about the psychological and emotional toll this could have on their loved ones. In fact, a bipartisan Federal panel found in 1995 that white men hold 95% of the nation's top management jobs although they represent just 43% of the workforce. It thus is apparent that much ground still has to be covered in terms of providing adequate economic opportunities for minorities. Yet, when most critics of affirmative action who favor destroying it are asked the question of what they would replace it with, they are silent.

Tangible Benefits

Affirmative action has produced some tangible benefits for the nation as a whole. As a result of it, the number of minorities attending and receiving degrees from colleges and universities rose in the 1970s and 1980s. This led to an increase in the size of the African-American middle class. An attainment of higher levels of education, as well as affirmative action policies in hiring, helped blacks gain access to some professions that earlier had been virtually closed to them. For instance, it traditionally had been nearly impossible for African-Americans and other minorities to receive professorships at predominantly white schools. Some departments at these schools actively began to recruit and hire minority faculty as their campuses became more diverse.

As expected, African-American, Hispanic, Native American, and Asian-American students demanded that not only should more minority faculty be hired, but that the curriculum be expanded to include courses that deal with the cultural and historical experiences of their past. Some school administrators granted their demands, which has borne fruit in a number of ways. First, given the fact that the U.S. is steadily becoming even more multicultural, it is imperative that Americans learn about and develop an appreciation and respect for various cultures. This could enable those who plan to teach students from several different racial, cultural, and ethnic backgrounds in the public school system to approach their jobs with more sensitivity and understanding. Second, it is often crucial for minority faculty to act as role models, particularly on white campuses. Third, white students could profit by being taught by professors of color. Since a white skin provides everyday advantages, having to face people of color in positions of authority may awaken some whites to realities about themselves and their society they previously have failed to recognize. It also might become obvious to them that certain racial stereotypes fly out of the window in light of intellectual exchanges with professors and peers of color.

Since education is crucial to acquiring economic advancement, it is of paramount importance that as many educational opportunities as possible be extended to the nation's minorities, which many studies indicate will total 50% of the population by 2050. Although much more is needed than affirmative action in order for minorities to gain the necessary access to higher levels of education and hiring, it nevertheless is the best mechanism to ensure at least a small measure of success in this regard. However, it currently is under attack in the areas of higher education, hiring, and Federal contracts. Now is the perfect time to find ways of improving affirmative action, rather than developing strategies aimed at destroying it.

Although a large number of minorities were attending and graduating from colleges and universities in the 1970s and 1980s, this trend had subsided by the 1990s. Tougher admission requirements, rising college costs, cutbacks of scholarships and fellowships or their direct elimination, as well as a reduction of grants and loans to students are contributing factors. Budgetary cuts have had a devastating effect on faculty in general, and minority faculty in particular, since they are often the first to be released from jobs. At a time when tenure and promotion are difficult to attain for most academics, it is almost impossible for some minority faculty.

Indeed, the attack on affirmative action is real. In California, without a commitment to affirmative action, the number of black students has dipped sharply. Applications from "underrepresented" minorities in 1997 on the nine campuses of the University of California dropped five percent, while overall applications rose 2.6%. The losses were even more dramatic at Ues Boalt Hall Law School, where admissions of African-Americans dropped 81% and Hispanics 50%. What are the implications of this for the nation? Certainly there will not be as many choices or opportunities for students and employers who have learned the value of a diverse workforce. This onslaught is contributing to the creation of an atmosphere in which many whites feel comfortable making racially derogatory remarks they would not have dared make a few years ago. For example, a University of Texas law professor remarked that "Blacks and Mexican-Americans are not academically competitive with whites in selective institutions. It is the result primarily of cultural effects. They have a culture that seems not to encourage achievement. Failure is not looked upon with disgrace."

Impact

Three questions beg answering in this racially charged environment: What impact will the attack on affirmative action have on the recruitment of minority student-athletes? Will they eventually be subjected to the same rigorous admissions standards as other students? Even if they are not, will they continue to enroll in large numbers at predominantly white state-supported colleges and universities with steadily decreasing numbers of minority students and faculty? Since minority athletes bring millions of dollars to schools, which, in turn, are used to subsidize the education of whites, I seriously doubt that tougher admission standards will be applied to them so rigorously that they eventually will be driven away from these schools. Administrators could not afford to lose millions of dollars.

Let's for a second imagine what would happen to state colleges that tried to recruit minority athletes to their campuses if they were all white in terms of faculty and student body. Those schools would have a difficult time convincing them to come. Furthermore, private schools not subjected to the same admission requirements would be all too happy to offer minority athletes lucrative financial aid packages.

Many industries began downsizing in the late 1980s and the practice has continued in the 1990s, helping to reverse some of the earlier gains made by minorities. With American society steadily becoming even more multicultural, it makes good business sense to have a workforce that is reflective of this development. In order to make this a reality, affirmative action policies need to be kept in place, not abandoned. Why not use the expertise of African-Americans to target African-American audiences for business purposes or Asian-Americans to tap into potential Asian-American consumers? Businessmen who believe minorities will purchase products as readily from all-white companies as those which are perceived as diverse are seriously misguided.

A diverse workforce also can yield huge economic dividends in the international business sector, as became obvious in 1996 to Republicans who hoped to increase their majority in Congress and ride into the White House by attacking affirmative action policies in hiring. Rep. Dan Burton of Indiana, Speaker of the House Newt Gingrich, and presidential candidate Bob Dole, to name a few, applied pressure on businesses to end affirmative action policies in hiring. Executives informed them that this would be bad business and that the losses in revenue potentially would be staggering. In addition, it would be foolish public relations and substantially would reduce the pool of fine applicants. For the time being, the Republicans eased off.

A diverse workforce in a multicultural society makes practical and ethical sense. With all of the problems that need to be solved—such as disease, hunger, poverty, homelessness, lack of health care, racism, anti-Semitism, sexism, teenage pregnancy, crime, drugs, etc.—why should anyone's input be limited because of sex, race, color, class, or ethnic background? All Americans should be working together in this endeavor. It can best be accomplished by creating a truly diverse workforce through a continuation of affirmative action policies.

In spite of the fact that affirmative action has helped some African-Americans and other minorities achieve a middle-class status, not all have witnessed a significant improvement in their economic condition. For the most part, it has only helped the last generation of minorities. In order to make a significant impact, affirmative action policies need to be in place for several generations. Between 1970 and 1992, the median income for white families, computed in constant dollars, rose from $34,773 to $38,909, an increase of 11.9%. Black family income declined during this period, from $21,330 to $21,162. In relative terms, black incomes dropped from $613 to $544 for each $1,000 received by whites. Moreover, in 1992, black men with bachelor's degrees made $764 for each $1,000 received by white men with such degrees, and black males with master's degrees earned $870 for each $1,000 their white counterparts earned. Overall, black men received $721 for every $1,000 earned by white men.

Even more depressing for blacks is the fact that unemployment rates for them have remained at double-digit levels since 1975, averaging 14.9% for the 1980s, while the average was 6.3% for whites. The number of black children living below the poverty line reached 46.3% by 1992, compared to 12.3% of white children. At the same time, the overall poverty rate among Hispanics increased to 28.2%. Even in professions where blacks made breakthroughs by the early 1990s, they remained underrepresented. This was the case in engineering, law, medicine, dentistry, architecture, and higher education. Although blacks represented 10.2% of the workforce in 1992, they constituted just 3.7% of engineers, 2.7% of dentists, 3.1% of architects, and held 4.8% of university faculty positions.

Furthermore, while 27,713 doctoral degrees were awarded in 1992 to U.S. citizens and aliens who indicated their intention is to remain in America, 1,081, or 3.9%, of these doctorates went to blacks. Given the low percentage of African-Americans receiving doctoral degrees, most college departments in all likelihood will find it difficult to recruit black faculty. With the hatchet steadily chopping affirmative action programs, this may become virtually impossible in the near future. The same holds true for other professions.

The most feasible way to ensure that colleges, universities, and various occupations will not become lily-white again is by the continuation of affirmative action. It gives minority groups that traditionally have been locked out of the education system and the workforce the best opportunity to carve out a solid economic foundation in America. I agree with Pres. Clinton, who said, "Don't end it; mend it."

America has had over 200 years to deliver true justice, freedom, and equality to women and people of color. To believe that it now will make good the promise of equality without some kind of legislation to assist it is to engage in fantasy.

In advocating for affirmative action policies, people of color are not looking for government handouts. They merely are asking that some mechanism be kept in place to help provide the same social and economic opportunities most whites have had and continue to have access to.

POSTSCRIPT

Has Affirmative Action Outlived Its Usefulness?

Despite their basic disagreement, both Williams and Jenkins desire a just society. The authors' main disagreement is on whether or not affirmative action is needed today to achieve this goal. Jenkins suggests that to abandon affirmative action before opportunities are much more equal is to perpetuate injustice. Williams contends that progress in racial justice has advanced to the point that some affirmative action programs are now unjust to whites. He observes that Americans support "soft affirmative action" but are opposed to more aggressive affirmative action. Could less aggressive affirmative action be the way to greater national unity on the race issue?

The writings on this subject are diverse and numerous. For an in-depth discussion of the legal standing of affirmative action, see Girardeau A. Spann, *The Law of Affirmative Action: Twenty-Five Years of Supreme Court Decisions on Race and Remedies* (New York University Press, 2000). For a review of affirmative action programs, see M. Ali Raza et al., *The Ups and Downs of Affirmative Action Preferences* (Greenwood, 1999). William G. Bowen and Derek Bok review affirmative action in college admissions in *The Shape of the River: Long-Term Consequences of Considering Race in College and University Admissions* (Princeton University Press, 1998). For a history of affirmative action, see Philip F. Rubio, *A History of Affirmative Action* (University Press of Mississippi, 2001). For a personal reading of black and white attitudes, see Studs Terkel, *Race: How Blacks and Whites Think and Feel About the American Obsession* (New Press, 1992). For a more academic reading of white racial attitudes, see Paul M. Sniderman and Thomas Piazza, *The Scar of Race* (Harvard University Press, 1993). One way to learn about racism is to read Gregory Howard Williams's story about living as a black after years as a white in *Life on the Color Line: The True Story of a White Boy Who Discovered He Was Black* (E. P. Dutton, 1995). Two works that portray the experiences of racism by the black middle class are Ellis Close, *The Rage of a Privileged Class* (HarperCollins, 1993) and Joe R. Feagin and Melvin P. Sikes, *Living With Racism: The Black Middle-Class Experience* (Beacon, 1994). Two personal accounts of this experience are Brent Staples, *Parallel Time: Growing Up in Black and White* (Pantheon, 1994) and Henry Louis Gates, *Colored People* (Free Press, 1994). Andrew Hacker argues that affirmative action has relatively minor adverse consequences for whites in *Two Nations: Black and White, Separate, Hostile, Unequal* (Charles Scribner's Sons, 1992). Dinesh D'Souza, in *The End of Racism* (Free Press, 1995), argues that white racism has pretty much disappeared in the United States. The opposite is argued by Joe R. Feagin and Hernan Vera in *White Racism: The Basics* (Routledge, 1995) and by Stephen Steinberg in *Turning Back* (Beacon Press, 1995).

Economic Report of the President

The Economic Report of the President Web site includes current and anticipated trends in the United States and annual numerical goals concerning topics
such as employment, production, real income, and federal budget outlays. The
database notes employment objectives for significant groups of the labor force,
annual numeric goals, and a plan for carrying out program objectives.

`http://www.library.nwu.edu/gpo/help/econr.html`

National Center for Policy Analysis

Through the National Center for Policy Analysis site you can read discussions
that are of major interest in the study of American politics and government from
a sociological perspective.

`http://www.ncpa.org`

Speakout.com

The Speakout.com Web site contains a library of online information and links
related to public policy issues, primarily those in the United States. The issues
are organized into topics and subtopics for easy searching.

`http://www.speakout.com/activism/issues`

Policy.com

Visit Policy.com, the site of the "policy community," to examine major issues
related to social welfare, welfare reform, social work, and many other topics.
The site includes substantial resources for researching issues online.

`http://www.policy.com`

PART 4

Political Economy and Institutions

*A*re political power and economic power merged within a "power elite" that dominates the U.S. political system? The first issue in this part explores that debate. The second issue concerns the proper role of government in the economy. Some believe that the government must correct for the many failures of the market, while others think that the government usually complicates the workings of the free market. The next debate concerns public policy: What is the impact of the end of the Federal AFDC program? The fourth issue examines alternative educational policies for significantly improving public education. Finally, the last issue in this part looks at doctor-assisted suicide for terminally ill patients.

- Is Government Dominated by Big Business?

- Should Government Intervene in a Capitalist Economy?

- Has Welfare Reform Benefited the Poor?

- Is Competition the Solution to the Ills of Public Education?

- Should Doctor-Assisted Suicide Be Legalized for the Terminally Ill?

ISSUE 11

Is Government Dominated
by Big Business?

YES: G. William Domhoff, from *Who Rules America? Power and Politics in the Year 2000*, 3rd ed. (Mayfield Publishing, 1998)

NO: Jeffrey M. Berry, from "Citizen Groups and the Changing Nature of Interest Group Politics in America," *The Annals of the American Academy of Political and Social Science* (July 1993)

ISSUE SUMMARY

YES: Political sociologist G. William Domhoff argues that the "owners and top-level managers in large income-producing properties are far and away the dominant power figures in the United States" and that they have inordinate influence in the federal government.

NO: Jeffrey M. Berry, a professor of political science, contends that public interest pressure groups that have entered the political arena since the end of the 1960s have effectively challenged the political power of big business.

Since the framing of the U.S. Constitution in 1787, there have been periodic charges that America is unduly influenced by wealthy financial interests. Richard Henry Lee, a signer of the Declaration of Independence, spoke for many Anti-Federalists (those who opposed ratification of the Constitution) when he warned that the proposed charter shifted power away from the people and into the hands of the "aristocrats" and "moneyites."

Before the Civil War, Jacksonian Democrats denounced the eastern merchants and bankers who, they charged, were usurping the power of the people. After the Civil War, a number of radical parties and movements revived this theme of antielitism. The ferment—which was brought about by the rise of industrial monopolies, government corruption, and economic hardship for western farmers—culminated in the founding of the People's Party at the beginning of the 1890s. The Populists, as they were more commonly called, wanted economic and political reforms aimed at transferring power away from the rich and back to "the plain people."

By the early 1900s the People's Party had disintegrated, but many writers and activists have continued to echo the Populists' central thesis: that the U.S. democratic political system is in fact dominated by business elites. Yet the thesis has not gone unchallenged. During the 1950s and the early 1960s, many social scientists subscribed to the *pluralist* view of America.

Pluralists argue that because there are many influential elites in America, each group is limited to some extent by the others. There are some groups, like the business elites, that are more powerful than their opponents, but even the more powerful groups are denied their objectives at times. Labor groups are often opposed to business groups; conservative interests challenge liberal interests, and vice versa; and organized civil libertarians sometimes fight with groups that seek government-imposed bans on pornography or groups that demand tougher criminal laws. No single group, the pluralists argue, can dominate the political system.

Pluralists readily acknowledge that American government is not democratic in the full sense of the word; it is not driven by the majority. But neither, they insist, is it run by a conspiratorial "power elite." In the pluralist view, the closest description of the American form of government would be neither majority rule nor minority rule but *minorities* rule. (Note that in this context, "minorities" does not necessarily refer to race or ethnicity but to any organized group of people with something in common—including race, religion, or economic interests—not constituting a majority of the population.) Each organized minority enjoys some degree of power in the making of public policy. In extreme cases, when a minority feels threatened, its power may take a negative form: the power to derail policy. When the majority—or, more accurately, a coalition of other minorities—attempts to pass a measure that threatens the vital interests of an organized minority, that group may use its power to obstruct their efforts. (Often cited in this connection is the use of the Senate filibuster, which is the practice of using tactics during the legislative process that cause extreme delays or prevent action, thus enabling a group to "talk to death" a bill that threatens its vital interests.) But in the pluralist view negative power is not the only driving force: when minorities work together and reach consensus on certain issues, they can institute new laws and policy initiatives that enjoy broad public support. Pluralism, though capable of producing temporary gridlock, ultimately leads to compromise, consensus, and moderation.

Critics of pluralism argue that pluralism is an idealized depiction of a political system that is in the grip of powerful elite groups. Critics fault pluralist theory for failing to recognize the extent to which big business dominates the policy-making process. In the selections that follow, G. William Domhoff supports this view, identifies the groups that compose the power elite, and details the way they control or support social, political, and knowledge-producing associations and organizations that advance their interests. Jeffrey M. Berry, in opposition, argues that, thanks to new consumer, environmental, and other citizen groups, big business no longer enjoys the cozy relationship it once had with Washington policymakers.

G. William Domhoff

 **YES**

Who Rules America?

Power and Class in the United States

... [T]he owners and top-level managers in large income-producing properties are far and away the dominant power figures in the United States. Their corporations, banks, and agribusinesses come together as a *corporate community* that dominates the federal government in Washington. Their real estate, construction, and land development companies form *growth coalitions* that dominate most local governments. Granted, there is competition within both the corporate community and the local growth coalitions for profits and investment opportunities, and there are sometimes tensions between national corporations and local growth coalitions, but both are cohesive on policy issues affecting their general welfare, and in the face of demands by organized workers, liberals, environmentalists, and neighborhoods.

As a result of their ability to organize and defend their interests, the owners and managers of large income-producing properties have a very great share of all income and wealth in the United States, greater than in any other industrial democracy. Making up at best 1 percent of the total population, by the early 1990s they earned 15.7 percent of the nation's yearly income and owned 37.2 percent of all privately held wealth, including 49.6 percent of all corporate stocks and 62.4 percent of all bonds. Due to their wealth and the lifestyle it makes possible, these owners and managers draw closer as a common social group. They belong to the same exclusive social clubs, frequent the same summer and winter resorts, and send their children to a relative handful of private schools. Members of the corporate community thereby become a *corporate rich* who create a nationwide *social upper class* through their social interaction.... Members of the growth coalitions, on the other hand, are *place entrepreneurs,* people who sell locations and buildings. They come together as local upper classes in their respective cities and sometimes mingle with the corporate rich in educational or resort settings.

The corporate rich and the growth entrepreneurs supplement their small numbers by developing and directing a wide variety of nonprofit organizations, the most important of which are a set of tax-free charitable foundations, think

From G. William Domhoff, *Who Rules America? Power and Politics in the Year 2000,* 3rd ed. (Mayfield Publishing, 1998). Notes omitted.

tanks, and policy-discussion groups. These specialized nonprofit groups constitute a *policy-formation network* at the national level. Chambers of commerce and policy groups affiliated with them form similar policy-formation networks at the local level, aided by a few national-level city development organizations that are available for local consulting.

Those corporate owners who have the interest and ability to take part in general governance join with top-level executives in the corporate community and the policy-formation network to form the *power elite,* which is the leadership group for the corporate rich as a whole. The concept of a power elite makes clear that not all members of the upper class are involved in governance; some of them simply enjoy the lifestyle that their great wealth affords them. At the same time, the focus on a leadership group allows for the fact that not all those in the power elite are members of the upper class; many of them are high-level employees in profit and nonprofit organizations controlled by the corporate rich. . . .

The power elite is not united on all issues because it includes both moderate conservatives and ultraconservatives. Although both factions favor minimal reliance on government on all domestic issues, the moderate conservatives sometimes agree to legislation advocated by liberal elements of the society, especially in times of social upheaval like the Great Depression of the 1930s and the Civil Rights Movement of the early 1960s. Except on defense spending, ultraconservatives are characterized by a complete distaste for any kind of government programs under any circumstances—even to the point of opposing government support for corporations on some issues. Moderate conservatives often favor foreign aid, working through the United Nations, and making attempts to win over foreign enemies through patient diplomacy, treaties, and trade agreements. Historically, ultraconservatives have opposed most forms of foreign involvement, although they have become more tolerant of foreign trade agreements over the past thirty or forty years. At the same time, their hostility to the United Nations continues unabated.

Members of the power elite enter into the electoral arena as the leaders within a *corporate-conservative coalition,* where they are aided by a wide variety of patriotic, antitax, and other single-issue organizations. These conservative advocacy organizations are funded in varying degrees by the corporate rich, direct-mail appeals, and middle-class conservatives. This coalition has played a large role in both political parties at the presidential level and usually succeeds in electing a conservative majority to both houses of Congress. Historically, the conservative majority in Congress was made up of most Northern Republicans and most Southern Democrats, but that arrangement has been changing gradually since the 1960s as the conservative Democrats of the South are replaced by even more conservative Southern Republicans. The corporate-conservative coalition also has access to the federal government in Washington through lobbying and the appointment of its members to top positions in the executive branch. . . .

Despite their preponderant power within the federal government and the many useful policies it carries out for them, members of the power elite are constantly critical of government as an alleged enemy of freedom and economic growth. Although their wariness toward government is expressed in terms of a dislike for taxes and government regulations, I believe their underlying concern is that government could change the power relations in the private sphere by aiding average Americans through a number of different avenues: (1) creating government jobs for the unemployed; (2) making health, unemployment, and welfare benefits more generous; (3) helping employees gain greater workplace rights and protections; and (4) helping workers organize unions. All of these initiatives are opposed by members of the power elite because they would increase wages and taxes, but the deepest opposition is toward any government support for unions because unions are a potential organizational base for advocating the whole range of issues opposed by the corporate rich....

Where Does Democracy Fit In?

... [T]o claim that the corporate rich have enough power to be considered a dominant class does not imply that lower social classes are totally powerless. *Domination* means the power to set the terms under which other groups and classes must operate, not total control. Highly trained professionals with an interest in environmental and consumer issues have been able to couple their technical information and their understanding of the legislative and judicial processes with well-timed publicity, lobbying, and lawsuits to win governmental restrictions on some corporate practices. Wage and salary employees, when they are organized into unions and have the right to strike, have been able to gain pay increases, shorter hours, better working conditions, and social benefits such as health insurance. Even the most powerless of people—the very poor and those discriminated against—sometimes develop the capacity to influence the power structure through sit-ins, demonstrations, social movements, and other forms of social disruption, and there is evidence that such activities do bring about some redress of grievances, at least for a short time.

More generally, the various challengers to the power elite sometimes work together on policy issues as a *liberal-labor coalition* that is based in unions, local environmental organizations, some minority group communities, university and arts communities, liberal churches, and small newspapers and magazines. Despite a decline in membership over the past twenty years, unions are the largest and best-financed part of the coalition, and the largest organized social force in the country (aside from churches). They also cut across racial and ethnic lines more than any other institutionalized sector of American society....

The policy conflicts between the corporate-conservative and liberal-labor coalitions are best described as *class conflicts* because they primarily concern the distribution of profits and wages, the rate and progressivity of taxation, the usefulness of labor unions, and the degree to which business should be regulated by government. The liberal-labor coalition wants corporations to pay higher wages to employees and higher taxes to government. It wants government to regulate a wide range of business practices, including many that are related to the environment, and help employees to organize unions. The corporate-conservative coalition resists all these policy objectives to a greater or lesser degree, claiming they endanger the freedom of individuals and the efficient workings of the economic marketplace. The conflicts these disagreements generate can manifest themselves in many different ways: workplace protests, industrywide boycotts, massive demonstrations in cities, pressure on Congress, and the outcome of elections.

Neither the corporate-conservative nor the liberal-labor coalition includes a very large percentage of the American population, although each has the regular support of about 25–30 percent of the voters. Both coalitions are made up primarily of financial donors, policy experts, political consultants, and party activists. . . .

Pluralism

The main alternative theory [I] address . . . claims that power is more widely dispersed among groups and classes than a class-dominance theory allows. This general perspective is usually called *pluralism,* meaning there is no one dominant power group. It is the theory most favored by social scientists. In its strongest version, pluralism holds that power is held by the general public through the pressure that public opinion and voting put on elected officials. According to this version, citizens form voluntary groups and pressure groups that shape public opinion, lobby elected officials, and back sympathetic political candidates in the electoral process. . . .

The second version of pluralism sees power as rooted in a wide range of well-organized "interest groups" that are often based in economic interests (e.g., industrialists, bankers, labor unions), but also in other interests as well (e.g., environmental, consumer, and civil rights groups). These interest groups join together in different coalitions depending on the specific issues. Proponents of this version of pluralism sometimes concede that public opinion and voting have only a minimal or indirect influence, but they see business groups as too fragmented and antagonistic to form a cohesive dominant class. They also claim that some business interest groups occasionally join coalitions with liberal or labor groups on specific issues, and that business-dominated coalitions sometimes lose. Furthermore, some proponents of this version of pluralism believe that the Democratic Party is responsive to the wishes of liberal and labor interest groups.

In contrast, I argue that the business interest groups are part of a tightly knit corporate community that is able to develop classwide cohesion on the issues of greatest concern to it: opposition to unions, high taxes, and government regulation. When a business group loses on a specific issue, it is often because other business groups have been opposed; in other words, there are arguments within the corporate community, and these arguments are usually settled within the governmental arena. I also claim that liberal and labor groups are rarely part of coalitions with business groups and that for most of its history the Democratic Party has been dominated by corporate and agribusiness interests in the Southern states, in partnership with the growth coalitions in large urban areas outside the South. Finally, I show that business interests rarely lose on labor and regulatory issues except in times of extreme social disruption like the 1930s and 1960s, when differences of opinion between Northern and Southern corporate leaders made victories for the liberal-labor coalition possible. . . .

How the Power Elite Dominates Government

This [section] shows how the power elite builds on the ideas developed in the policy-formation process and its success in the electoral arena to dominate the federal government. Lobbyists from corporations, law firms, and trade associations play a key role in shaping government on narrow issues of concern to specific corporations or business sectors, but their importance should not be overestimated because a majority of those elected to Congress are predisposed to agree with them. The corporate community and the policy-formation network supply top-level governmental appointees and new policy directions on major issues.

Once again, as seen in the battles for public opinion and electoral success, the power elite faces opposition from a minority of elected officials and their supporters in labor unions and liberal advocacy groups. These opponents are sometimes successful in blocking ultra-conservative initiatives, but most of the victories for the liberal-labor coalition are the result of support from moderate conservatives. . . .

Appointees to Government

The first way to test a class-dominance view of the federal government is to study the social and occupational backgrounds of the people who are appointed to manage the major departments of the executive branch, such as state, treasury, defense, and justice. If pluralists are correct, these appointees should come from a wide range of interest groups. If the state autonomy theorists are correct, they should be disproportionately former elected officials or longtime government employees. If the class-dominance view is correct, they should come disproportionately from the upper class, the corporate community, and the policy-formation network.

There have been numerous studies over the years of major governmental appointees under both Republican and Democratic administrations, usually focusing on the top appointees in the departments that are represented in the president's cabinet. These studies are unanimous in their conclusion that most top appointees in both Republican and Democratic administrations are corporate executives and corporate lawyers—and hence members of the power elite. . . .

Conclusion

This [section] has demonstrated the power elite's wide-ranging access to government through the interest-group and policy-formation processes, as well as through its ability to influence appointments to major government positions. When coupled with the several different kinds of power discussed in earlier [sections] this access and involvement add up to power elite domination of the federal government.

By *domination*, as stated in the first [section], social scientists mean the ability of a class or group to set the terms under which other classes or groups within a social system must operate. By this definition, domination does not mean control on each and every issue, and it does not rest solely on involvement in government. Influence over government is only the final and most visible aspect of power elite domination, which has its roots in the class structure, the corporate control of the investment function, and the operation of the policy-formation network. If government officials did not have to wait for corporate leaders to decide where and when they will invest, and if government officials were not further limited by the general public's acceptance of policy recommendations from the policy-formation network, then power elite involvement in elections and government would count for a lot less than they do under present conditions.

Domination by the power elite does not negate the reality of continuing conflict over government policies, but few conflicts, it has been shown, involve challenges to the rules that create privileges for the upper class and domination by the power elite. Most of the numerous battles within the interest-group process, for example, are only over specific spoils and favors; they often involve disagreements among competing business interests.

Similarly, conflicts within the policy-making process of government often involve differences between the moderate conservative and ultraconservative segments of the dominant class. At other times they involve issues in which the needs of the corporate community as a whole come into conflict with the needs of specific industries, which is what happens to some extent on tariff policies and also on some environmental legislation. In neither case does the nature of the conflict call into question the domination of government by the power elite.

... Contrary to what pluralists claim, there is not a single case study on any issue of any significance that shows a liberal-labor victory over a united corporate-conservative coalition, which is strong evidence for a class-domination theory on the "Who wins?" power indicator. The classic case studies frequently cited by pluralists have been shown to be gravely deficient as evidence for their views. Most of these studies reveal either conflicts among rival groups within the power elite or situations in which the moderate conservatives have decided for their own reasons to side with the liberal-labor coalition....

More generally, it now can be concluded that all four indicators of power introduced in [the first section] point to the corporate rich and their power elite as the dominant organizational structure in American society. First, the wealth and income distributions are skewed in their favor more than in any other industrialized democracy. They are clearly the most powerful group in American society in terms of "Who benefits?" Second, the appointees to government come overwhelmingly from the corporate community and its associated policy-formation network. Thus, the power elite is clearly the most powerful in terms of "Who sits?"

Third, the power elite wins far more often than it loses on policy issues resolved in the federal government. Thus, it is the most powerful in terms of "Who wins?" Finally, as shown in reputational studies in the 1950s and 1970s,... corporate leaders are the most powerful group in terms of "Who shines?" By the usual rules of evidence in a social science investigation using multiple indicators, the owners and managers of large income-producing properties are the dominant class in the United States.

Still, as noted at the end of the first [section], power structures are not immutable. Societies change and power structures evolve or crumble from time to unpredictable time, especially in the face of challenge. When it is added that the liberal-labor coalition persists in the face of its numerous defeats, and that free speech and free elections are not at risk, there remains the possibility that class domination could be replaced by a greater sharing of power in the future.

NO

Jeffrey M. Berry

Citizen Groups and the Changing Nature of Interest Group Politics in America

ABSTRACT: The rise of liberal citizen groups that began in the 1960s has had a strong impact on the evolution of interest group advocacy. The success of these liberal organizations was critical in catalyzing the broader explosion in the numbers of interest groups and in causing the collapse of many subgovernments. New means of resolving policy conflicts had to be established to allow for the participation of broader, more diverse policy communities. Citizen groups have been particularly important in pushing policymakers to create new means of structuring negotiations between large numbers of interest group actors. The greater participation of citizen groups, the increased numbers of all kinds of interest groups, and change in the way policy is made may be making the policymaking process more democratic.

Many protest movements have arisen in the course of American history, each affecting the political system in its own way. The social movements that took hold in the 1960s had their own unique set of roots but seemed to follow a conventional life span. The civil rights and antiwar groups that arose to protest the injustices they saw were classic social movements. Their views were eventually absorbed by one of the political parties, and, after achieving their immediate goals, their vitality was sapped. The antiwar movement disappeared, and black civil rights organizations declined in power. The most enduring and vital citizen groups born in this era of protest were never protest oriented. Consumer groups, environmental groups, and many other kinds of citizen lobbies have enjoyed unprecedented prosperity in the last 25 years. Never before have citizen groups been so prevalent in American politics, and never before have they been so firmly institutionalized into the policymaking process.

The rise of citizen groups has not only empowered many important constituencies, but it has altered the policymaking process as well. This article focuses on how citizen groups have affected interest group politics in general and how these organizations have contributed to the changing nature of public policymaking. A first step is to examine the initial success of liberal advocacy organizations as well as the conservative response to this challenge. Next, I

From Jeffrey M. Berry, "Citizen Groups and the Changing Nature of Interest Group Politics in America," *The Annals of the American Academy of Political and Social Science*, vol. 528 (July 1993). Copyright © 1993 by The American Academy of Political and Social Science. Reprinted by permission of Sage Publications, Inc. Notes omitted.

will look at the impact of this growth of citizen group politics on the policymaking process. Then I will turn to how Congress and the executive branch have tried to cope with a dense population of citizen groups and the complex policymaking environment that now envelops government.

Finally, I will speculate as to how all of this has affected policymaking in terms of how democratic it is. The popular perception is that the rise of interest groups along with the decline of political parties has had a very negative impact on American politics. Analysis of the decline of parties will be left to others, but a central point here is that the growth in the numbers of citizen groups and of other lobbying organizations has not endangered the political system. There are some unfortunate developments, such as the increasing role of political action committees in campaign financing, but the rise of citizen groups in particular has had a beneficial impact on the way policy is formulated. The overall argument may be stated succinctly: the rise of liberal citizen groups was largely responsible for catalyzing an explosion in the growth of all types of interest groups. Efforts to limit the impact of liberal citizen groups failed, and the policymaking process became more open and more participatory. Expanded access and the growth in the numbers of competing interest groups created the potential for gridlock, if not chaos. The government responded, in turn, with institutional changes that have helped to rationalize policymaking in environments with a large number of independent actors.

The Rise of Citizen Groups

The lobbying organizations that emerged out of the era of protest in the 1960s are tied to the civil rights and antiwar movements in two basic ways. First, activism was stimulated by the same broad ideological dissatisfaction with government and the two-party system. There was the same feeling that government was unresponsive, that it was unconcerned about important issues, and that business was far too dominant a force in policymaking. Second, the rise of liberal citizen groups was facilitated by success of the civil rights and antiwar movements. More specifically, future organizers learned from these social movements. They learned that aggressive behavior could get results, and they saw that government could be influenced by liberal advocacy organizations. Some activists who later led Washington-based citizen lobbies cut their teeth as volunteers in these earlier movements.

For liberal consumer and environmental groups, an important lesson of this era was that they should not follow the protest-oriented behavior of the civil rights and antiwar movements. There was a collective realization that lasting influence would come from more conventional lobbying inside the political system. For consumer and environmental organizers, "power to the people" was rejected in favor of staff-run organizations that placed little emphasis on participatory democracy. This is not to say that these new organizations were simply copies of business lobbies; leaders of these groups like Ralph Nader and John Gardner placed themselves above politics-as-usual with their moralistic rhetoric and their attacks against the established political order.

While there was significant support for these groups from middle-class liberals, a major impetus behind their success was financial backing from large philanthropic foundations. The foundations wanted to support social change during a time of political upheaval, but at the same time they wanted responsible activism. This early support, most notably from the Ford Foundation's program in public interest law, was largely directed at supporting groups relying on litigation and administrative lobbying. The seed money for these organizations enabled them to flourish and provided them with time to establish a track record so that they could appeal to individual donors when the foundation money ran out. Other groups emerged without the help of foundations, drawing on a combination of large donors, dues-paying memberships, and government grants. Citizen lobbies proved remarkably effective at raising money and at shifting funding strategies as the times warranted.

Citizen groups emerged in a variety of areas. In addition to consumer and environmental groups, there were organizations interested in hunger and poverty, governmental reform, corporate responsibility, and many other issues. A number of new women's organizations soon followed in the wake of the success of the first wave of citizen groups, and new civil rights groups arose to defend other groups such as Hispanics and gays. As has been well documented, the rise of citizen groups was the beginning of an era of explosive growth in interest groups in national politics. No precise baseline exists, so exact measurement of this growth is impossible. Yet the mobilization of interests is unmistakable. One analysis of organizations represented in Washington in 1980 found that 40 percent of the groups had been started since 1960, and 25 percent had begun after 1970.

The liberal citizen groups that were established in the 1960s and 1970s were not simply the first ripples of a new wave of interest groups; rather, they played a primary role in catalyzing the formation of many of the groups that followed. New business groups, which were by far the most numerous of all the groups started since 1960, were directly stimulated to organize by the success of consumer and environmental groups. There were other reasons why business mobilized, but much of their hostility toward the expanded regulatory state was directed at agencies strongly supported by liberal citizen groups. These organizations had seemingly seized control of the political agenda, and the new social regulation demanded increased business mobilization. New conservative citizen lobbies, many focusing on family issues such as abortion and the Equal Rights Amendment, were also begun to counter the perceived success of the liberal groups.

The swing of the ideological pendulum that led to a conservative takeover of the White House in 1980 led subsequently to efforts to limit the impact of liberal citizen groups. The Reagan administration believed that the election of 1980 was a mandate to eliminate impediments to economic growth. Environmental and consumer groups were seen as organizations that cared little about the faltering American economy; President Reagan referred to liberal public interest lawyers as "a bunch of ideological ambulance chasers." Wherever possible, liberal citizen groups were to be removed from the governmental process. . . .

The Reagan administration certainly succeeded in reducing the liberal groups' access to the executive branch. On a broader level, however, the conservative counterattack against the liberal groups was a failure. The reasons go far beyond the more accommodating stance of the Bush administration or the attitude of any conservative administrations that may follow. These organizations have proved to be remarkably resilient, and they are a strong and stable force in American politics. Most fundamentally, though, the Reagan attempt failed because the transformation of interest group politics led to large-scale structural changes in the public policymaking process.

Consequences

The rise of citizen groups and the rapid expansion of interest group advocacy in general have had many important long-term consequences for the way policy is formulated by the national government. Most important, policymaking moved away from closed subgovernments, each involving a relatively stable and restricted group of lobbyists and key government officials, to much broader policymaking communities. Policymaking in earlier years is typically described as the product of consensual negotiations between a small number of backscratching participants.

Policymaking is now best described as taking place within issue networks rather than in subgovernments. An issue network is a set of organizations that share expertise in a policy area and interact with each other over time as relevant issues are debated. As sociologist Barry Wellman states, "The world is composed of networks, not groups." This is certainly descriptive of Washington policymaking. Policy formulation cannot be portrayed in terms of what a particular group wanted and how officials responded to those demands. The coalitions within networks, often involving scores of groups, define the divisions over issues and drive the policymaking process forward. Alliances are composed of both old friends and strange bedfellows; relationships are built on immediate need as well as on familiarity and trust. Organizations that do not normally work in a particular issue network can easily move into a policymaking community to work on a single issue. The only thing constant in issue networks is the changing nature of the coalitions.

The result of issue network politics is that policymaking has become more open, more conflictual, and more broadly participatory. What is crucial about the role of citizen groups is that they were instrumental in breaking down the barriers to participation in subgovernments. Building upon their own constituency support and working with allies in Congress, citizen groups made themselves players. They have not been outsiders, left to protest policies and a system that excluded them. Rather, they built opposition right into the policymaking communities that had previously operated with some commonality of interest. Even conservative administrators who would prefer to exclude these liberal advocacy groups have recognized that they have to deal with their opponents in one arena or another. The Nuclear Regulatory Commission, the epitome of an agency hostile to liberal advocacy groups, cannot get away with ignoring groups like the Union of Concerned Scientists. The consensus over nuclear power has long been broken. Critics and advocacy groups like the Union of Concerned Scientists have the technical expertise to involve themselves in agency proceedings, and they have the political know-how to get themselves heard on Capitol Hill and in the news media.

Issue networks are not simply divided between citizen groups on one side and business groups on another. Organizations representing business usually encompass a variety of interests, many of which are opposed to each other. As various business markets have undergone rapid change and become increasingly competitive, issue networks have found themselves divided by efforts of one sector of groups to use the policymaking process to try to gain market share from another sector of the network. Citizen groups, rather than simply being the enemy of business, are potential coalition partners for different business sectors. A characteristic of the culture of interest group politics in Washington is that there are no permanent allies and no permanent enemies.

Citizen groups are especially attractive as coalition partners because they have such a high level of credibility with the public and the news media. All groups claim to represent the public interest because they sincerely believe that the course of action they are advocating would be the most beneficial to the country. Since they do not represent any vocational or business interest, citizen groups may be perceived by some to be less biased—though certainly not unbiased—in their approach to public policy problems. This credibility is also built around the high-quality research that many citizen groups produce and distribute to journalists and policymakers in Washington. Reports from advocacy organizations such as Citizens for Tax Justice or the Center for Budget and Policy Priorities are quickly picked up by the media and disseminated across the country. Most business groups would love to have the respect that these citizen groups command in the press. For all the financial strength at the disposal of oil lobbyists, no representative of the oil industry has as much credibility with the public as a lobbyist for the Natural Resources Defense Council.

Despite the growth and stability of citizen groups in national politics, their reach does not extend into every significant policymaking domain. In the broad area of financial services, for example, citizen groups have played a minor role at best. There are some consumer groups that have been marginally active when specific issues involving banks, insurance companies, and securities firms arise, but they have demonstrated little influence or staying power. There is, however, a vital consumer interest at stake as public policymakers grapple with the crumbling walls that have traditionally divided different segments of the financial services market. Defense policy is another area where citizen groups have been relatively minor actors. But if citizen groups are conspicuous by their absence in some important areas, their overall reach is surprisingly broad. They have become major actors in policy areas where they previously had no presence at all. In negotiations over a free trade agreement with Mexico, for example, environmental groups became central players in the bargaining. These groups were concerned that increased U.S. investment in Mexico would result in increased pollution there from unregulated manufacturing, depleted groundwater supplies, and other forms of environmental degradation. To its dismay, the Bush White House found that the only practical course was to negotiate with the groups.

The increasing prominence of citizen groups and the expanding size of issue networks change our conception of the policymaking process. The basic structural attribute of a subgovernment was that it was relatively bounded with a stable set of participants. Even if there was some conflict in that subgovernment, there were predictable divisions and relatively clear expectations of what kind of conciliation between interest groups was possible. In contrast, issue networks seem like free-for-alls. In the health care field alone, 741 organizations have offices in Washington or employ a representative there. Where subgovernments suggested control over public policy by a limited number of participants, issue networks suggest no control whatsoever. Citizen groups make policymaking all the more difficult because they frequently sharpen the ideological debate; they have different organizational incentive systems from those of the corporations and trade groups with which they are often in conflict; and they place little emphasis on the need for economic growth, an assumption shared by most other actors.

This picture of contemporary interest group politics may make it seem impossible to accomplish anything in Washington. Indeed, it is a popular perception that Congress has become unproductive and that we are subject to some sort of national gridlock. Yet the policymaking system is adaptable, and the relationship between citizen groups and other actors in issue networks suggests that there are a number of productive paths for resolving complicated policy issues.

Complex Policymaking

The growth of issue networks is not, of course, the only reason why the policymaking process has become more complex. The increasingly technical nature of policy problems has obviously put an ever higher premium on expertise. Structural changes are critical, too. The decentralization of the House of Representatives that took place in the mid-1970s dispersed power and reduced the autonomy of leaders. Today, in the House, jurisdictions between committees frequently overlap and multiple referrals of bills are common. When an omnibus trade bill passed by both houses in 1987 was sent to conference, the House and the Senate appointed 200 conferees, who broke up into 17 subconferences. The growth of the executive branch has produced a similar problem of overlapping jurisdictions. In recent deliberations on proposed changes in wetlands policy, executive branch participants included the Soil Conservation Service in the Agriculture Department, the Fish and Wildlife Service in Interior, the Army Corps of Engineers, the Environmental Protection Agency (EPA), the Office of Management and Budget, the Council on Competitiveness, and the President's Domestic Policy Council.

Nevertheless, even though the roots of complex policymaking are multifaceted, the rise of citizen groups has been a critical factor in forcing the

Congress and the executive branch to focus more closely on developing procedures to negotiate settlements of policy disputes. The quiet bargaining of traditional subgovernment politics was not an adequate mechanism for handling
negotiations between scores of interest groups, congressional committees, and
executive branch agencies.

Citizen groups have been particularly important in prompting more
structured negotiations for a number of reasons. First, in many policy areas, citizen groups upset long-standing working arrangements between policymakers
and other interest groups. Citizen groups were often the reason subgovernments crumbled; under pressure from congressional allies and public opinion,
they were included in the bargaining and negotiating at some stage in the
policymaking process.

Second, citizen groups could not be easily accommodated in basic negotiating patterns. It was not a matter of simply placing a few more chairs at the
table. These groups' entrance into a policymaking community usually created
a new dividing line between participants. The basic ideological cleavage that
exists between consumer and environmental interests and business is not easy
to bridge, and, consequently, considerable effort has been expended to devise
ways of getting mutual antagonists to negotiate over an extended period. As
argued above, once accepted at the bargaining table, citizen groups could be
attractive coalition partners for business organizations.

Third, ... citizen groups typically have a great deal of credibility with
the press. Thus, in negotiating, they often have had more to gain by going
public to gain leverage with other bargainers. This adds increased uncertainty
and instability to the structure of negotiations.

Fourth, citizen groups are often more unified than their business adver-
saries. The business interests in an issue network may consist of large producers,
small producers, foreign producers, and companies from other industries trying to expand into new markets. All these business interests may be fiercely
divided as each tries to defend or encroach upon established market patterns.
The environmentalists in the same network, while each may have its own niche
in terms of issue specialization, are likely to present a united front on major
policy disputes. In a perverse way, then, the position of citizen groups has been
aided by the proliferation of business groups. (Even without the intrusion of
citizen lobbies, this sharp rise in the number of business groups would have
irretrievably changed the nature of subgovernments.) ...

Conclusion

Citizen groups have changed the policymaking process in valuable and enduring ways. Most important, they have broadened representation in our political system. Many previously unrepresented or underrepresented constituencies
now have a powerful voice in Washington politics. The expanding numbers of
liberal citizen groups and their apparent success helped to stimulate a broad
mobilization on the part of business. The skyrocketing increase in the numbers
of interest groups worked to break down subgovernments and led to the rise of
issue networks.

Issue networks are more fragmented, less predictable policymaking environments. Both Congress and the executive branch have taken steps to bring about greater centralized control and coherence to policymaking. Some of these institutional changes seem aimed directly at citizen groups. Negotiated regulations, for example, are seen as a way of getting around the impasse that often develops between liberal citizen groups and business organizations. Centralized regulatory review has been used by Republican administrations as a means of ensuring that business interests are given primacy; regulators are seen as too sympathetic to the citizen groups that are clients of their agencies.

Although government has established these and other institutional mechanisms for coping with complex policymaking environments, the American public does not seem to feel that the government copes very well at all. Congress has been portrayed as unproductive and spineless, unwilling to tackle the tough problems that require discipline or sacrifice. At the core of this criticism is that interest groups are the culprit. Washington lobbies, representing every conceivable interest and showering legislators with the political action committee donations they crave, are said to be responsible for this country's inability to solve its problems.

Although it is counterintuitive, it may be that the increasing number of interest groups coupled with the rise of citizen groups has actually improved the policymaking system in some important ways. More specifically, our policymaking process may be more democratic today because of these developments. Expanded interest group participation has helped to make the policymaking process more open and visible. The closed nature of subgovernment politics meant not only that participation was restricted but that public scrutiny was minimal. The proliferation of interest groups, Washington media that are more aggressive, and the willingness and ability of citizen groups in particular to go public as part of their advocacy strategy have worked to open up policymaking to the public eye.

The end result of expanded citizen group advocacy is policy communities that are highly participatory and more broadly representative of the public. One can argue that this more democratic policymaking process is also one that is less capable of concerted action; yet there is no reliable evidence that American government is any more or less responsive to pressing policy problems than it has ever been. There are, of course, difficult problems that remain unresolved, but that is surely true of every era. Democracy requires adequate representation of interests as well as institutions capable of addressing difficult policy problems. For policymakers who must balance the demand for representation with the need for results, the key is thinking creatively about how to build coalitions and structure negotiations between large groups of actors.

POSTSCRIPT

Is Government Dominated
by Big Business?

O ne of the problems for any pluralist is the danger that many people may not be properly represented. Suppose, for example, that business and environmental groups in Washington compromise their differences by supporting environmental legislation but passing the costs along to consumers. The legislation may be good, even necessary, but have the consumer's interests been taken into account? There are, of course, self-styled consumer groups, but it is hard to determine whether or not they really speak for the average consumer. The challenge for pluralists is to make their system as inclusive as possible.

Social science literature contains a number of works on the issues of pluralism and corporate power. Political scientist Charles E. Lindblom supported pluralism in the 1950s, but he later changed his mind and concluded that big business dominates American policy making. Lindblom takes the pluralist perspective in his early book *Politics, Economics, and Welfare* (Harper, 1953), written with Robert A. Dahl. His repudiation of pluralism was complete by the time he published *Politics and Markets: The World's Political-Economic Systems* (Basic Books, 1977). Ever since the obvious demonstration of corporate influence in the elections of 1980, Lindblom's view has been dominant. More recent works arguing that corporate elites possess inordinate power in American society are G. William Domhoff, *The Power Elite and the State* (Aldine de Gruyter, 1990) and *State Autonomy or Class Dominance?* (Aldine de Gruyter, 1996); Michael Parenti, *America Besieged* (City Lights Books, 1998); Dan Clawson et al., *Money Talks: Corporate PACs and Political Influence* (Basic Books, 1992); and Mark S. Mizruchi, *The Structure of Corporate Political Action: Interfirm Relations and Their Consequences* (Harvard University Press, 1992). For an analysis of the changes taking place in the organization of corporate power, see Michael Useem, *Investor Capitalism: How Money Managers Are Changing the Face of Corporate America* (Basic Books, 1996).

For some pluralist arguments, see Andrew M. Greeley, *Building Coalitions* (Franklin Watts, 1974); David Vogel, *Fluctuating Fortunes: The Political Power of Business in America* (Basic Books, 1989) and *Kindred Strangers: The Uneasy Relationship Between Politics and Business in America* (Princeton University Press, 1996); John P. Heinz, Edward O. Laumann, Robert L. Nelson, and Robert H. Salisbury, *The Hollow Core: Private Interests in National Policy Making* (Harvard University Press, 1993); Lawrence S. Rothenberg, *Linking Citizens to Government: Interest Group Politics at Common Cause* (Cambridge University Press, 1992); and Susan Herbst, *Numbered Voices: How Opinion Polls Shape American Politics* (University of Chicago Press, 1993).

ISSUE 12

Should Government Intervene in a Capitalist Economy?

YES: Ernest Erber, from "Virtues and Vices of the Market: Balanced Correctives to a Current Craze," *Dissent* (Summer 1990)

NO: Milton Friedman and Rose Friedman, from *Free to Choose: A Personal Statement* (Harcourt Brace Jovanovich, 1980)

ISSUE SUMMARY

YES: Author Ernest Erber argues that capitalism creates serious social problems that need to be redressed by an activist government.

NO: Economists Milton Friedman and Rose Friedman maintain that market competition, when permitted to work unimpeded, protects citizens better than government regulations intended to correct for failures of the market.

The expression "That government is best which governs least" sums up a deeply rooted attitude of many Americans. From early presidents Thomas Jefferson and Andrew Jackson to America's most recent leaders, George Bush, Bill Clinton, and George W. Bush, American politicians have often echoed the popular view that there are certain areas of life best left to the private actions of citizens.

One such area is the economic sphere, where people make their living by buying, selling, and producing goods and services. The tendency of most Americans is to regard direct government involvement in the economic sphere as both unnecessary and dangerous. The purest expression of this view is the economic theory of *laissez-faire*, a French term meaning "let be" or "let alone." The seminal formulation of *laissez-faire* theory was the work of eighteenth-century Scottish philosopher Adam Smith, whose treatise *The Wealth of Nations* appeared in 1776. Smith's thesis was that each individual, pursuing his or her own selfish interests in a competitive market, will be "led by an invisible hand to promote an end which was no part of his intention." In other words, when people singlemindedly seek profit, they actually serve the community because sellers must keep prices down and quality up if they are to meet the competition of other sellers.

Laissez-faire economics was much honored (in theory, if not always in practice) during the nineteenth and early twentieth centuries. But as the nineteenth century drew to a close, the Populist Party sprang up. The Populists denounced eastern bankers, Wall Street stock manipulators, and rich "moneyed interests," and they called for government ownership of railroads, a progressive income tax, and other forms of state intervention. The Populist Party died out early in the twentieth century, but the Populist message was not forgotten. In fact, it was given new life after 1929, when the stock market collapsed and the United States was plunged into the worst economic depression in its history.

By 1932 a quarter of the nation's workforce was unemployed, and most Americans were finding it hard to believe that the "invisible hand" would set things right. Some Americans totally repudiated the idea of a free market and embraced socialism, the belief that the state (or "the community") should run all major industries. Most stopped short of supporting socialism, but they were now prepared to welcome some forms of state intervention in the economy. President Franklin D. Roosevelt, elected in 1932, spoke to this mood when he pledged a "New Deal" to the American people. "New Deal" has come to stand for a variety of programs that were enacted during the first eight years of Roosevelt's presidency, including business and banking regulations, government pension programs, federal aid to the disabled, unemployment compensation, and government-sponsored work programs. Side by side with the "invisible hand" of the marketplace was now the very visible hand of an activist government.

Government intervention in the economic sphere increased during World War II as the government fixed prices, rationed goods, and put millions to work in government-subsidized war industries. Activist government continued during the 1950s, but the biggest leap forward occurred during the late 1960s and early 1970s, when the federal government launched a variety of new welfare and regulatory programs: the multibillion-dollar War on Poverty, new civil rights and affirmative action mandates, and new laws protecting consumers, workers, disabled people, and the environment. These, in turn, led to a proliferation of new government agencies and bureaus, as well as shelves and shelves of published regulations. Proponents of the new activism conceded that it was expensive, but they insisted that activist government was necessary to protect Americans against pollution, discrimination, dangerous products, and other effects of the modern marketplace. Critics of government involvement called attention not only to its direct costs but also to its effect on business activity and individual freedom.

In the following selections, Ernest Erber argues that although competitive markets are very productive, they bring about a variety of negative consequences, and he concludes that business regulation and other forms of government intervention are necessary to counter some of the harmful effects of the marketplace. Milton Friedman and Rose Friedman argue that the "invisible hand" of the market will work effectively if it is allowed to do so without government interference. Although decades old, this debate may well be one of the major debates of the new decade.

Ernest Erber

↱ **YES**

Virtues and Vices of the Market:
Balanced Correctives to a Current Craze

N ot since they encountered it in nursery rhymes have references to the market so intruded into the consciousness of Americans as in recent months. There is now a virtual consensus that the market is the natural state of economic affairs, and its creation in nations not yet blessed with it is the prescription for every economic ailment. This makes vague good sense to most Americans, for whom the market has pleasant associations. Not surprisingly, for the market has long since come to determine their tastes and values, their very lives....

This worldwide consensus would not exist if it did not reflect a body of evidence that links the market with economic growth, increased productivity, and improved living standards. That this historical progress has been facilitated by the market's competitive and entrepreneurial incentives cannot be contested. Neither can the beliefs that the market's function as a pricing mechanism has historically contributed to economic stability conducive to growth, even if plagued by a persistent tendency toward inflation in recent years, nor that the market's negative, even self-destructive, side effects have been largely diminished by state intervention through regulation, credit-budget-tax policies, price supports, and social welfare programs....

Nature of the Market

... The market as we know it today is the historically specific product of industrial capitalism and can only be understood if perceived as such....

The Market is, essentially, an economic decision-making process that determines the allocation of society's resources by deciding what and how much is produced and how and to whom it is distributed. Those who participate in this process are buyers and sellers who "meet" in the "marketplace," though they are not only individuals, since buyers and sellers also include businesses of all sizes, farmers and professionals as groups, governments at all levels.

As an alternative to the Market, society's resources can also be directly allocated by political decisions of government (that is, by "command"). Government can also act deliberately to influence indirectly how the Market functions indirectly. Those who determine a government's economic role

From Ernest Erber, "Virtues and Vices of the Market: Balanced Correctives to a Current Craze," *Dissent* (Summer 1990). Copyright © 1990 by The Foundation for the Study of Independent Social Ideas, Inc. Reprinted by permission.

are citizens, governing officials, and administrators (including, sometimes, planners, though every governmental impact upon the economy should not be called "planning" and, in the United States, it almost never is that). Within capitalist economies, the purpose of governmental intervention in the Market is twofold: (1) to facilitate the functioning of the Market by protecting it from its shortcomings, including tendencies toward self-destructiveness; (2) to supplement the Market by providing those goods and services that the Market has no incentive to supply because they do not entail a profit (public schools, social welfare, low-cost housing, infrastructure, and so on).

The extent to which government should influence the economy is an issue that has been fought over for a very long time. Charles E. Lindblom begins his definitive *Politics and Markets* by observing that "the greatest distinction between one government and another is in the degree to which market replaces government or government replaces market. Both Adam Smith and Karl Marx knew this."

꙳

The word "degree" is used by Lindblom deliberately, for neither the Market nor government replaces the other completely. Thus all economies are a mix of the Market and political decision making. Even the totally mad Stalinist effort to eliminate the Market in Soviet-type societies fell short of complete success, for these societies had to tolerate market operations in corners of the economy, either by compromise, as in permitted sales from garden plots of collective farmers and *kolkhoz* "surplus" production, or through black market sales of scarce commodities, tolerated because they were considered helpful to the economy.

Another variant of madness, though largely rhetorical, is the Thatcherite and Reaganite pronouncements about getting government out of the economy and "letting the market decide." After a decade of such huffing and puffing, the role of government vis-à-vis the economy, both in Great Britain and in the United States, remains essentially unchanged, some privatizations notwithstanding. . . .

꙳

A final aspect of the Market's historical context is the largely forgotten role played by the state in getting market-based economies off the ground in various parts of the world. Japan, Prussia, and Czarist Russia are outstanding examples of the state's role in "jump starting" both capitalist production and market relations through generous credit, subsidies, enactment of special rights, licenses, and so on. Government construction of infrastructure often played a key role.

What we can conclude is that the prevailing view that attributes the material progress of human societies during the last century or two *solely* to the Market is fallacious, because the Market's contribution cannot be sufficiently separated from that of the Industrial Revolution, the capitalist mode of production, or the nourishing role of the state. To the extent that references to the

Market are euphemistic in order to advocate capitalism under another name, there is an implied admission that the Market cannot be separated from capitalism, that is, private property in the means of production, labor as a commodity, unearned income, accumulation, and so forth. But insofar as there now exists an effort to utilize the Market's virtues, while straining out its vices, in order to serve the common welfare, an assessment of its feasibility cannot be made until we have clearer insights into how it would resolve a number of contradictions that seem to make this objective unworkable.

The Market's Side Effects and Political Remedies

The following descriptions of the Market's side effects are valid, on the whole, though in some cases not entirely separable from other causes. The rationale of the Market is competition—for survival and gain. It pits each against all in social Darwinian "survival of the fittest": worker against worker and entrepreneur against entrepreneur, capital against labor and producer against consumer. The weak are eliminated and the strong survive, resulting in the trend toward concentration and monopolies. Businesses live by the "bottom line," with an incentive toward price gouging, adulteration, misrepresentation, environmental degradation. Product or service promotion caters to every human weakness. Advertising seduces consumers to develop endless wants. The central effect is to subvert human solidarity and civic responsibility.

The multitudinous buy/sell decisions that drive the market process are made in total ignorance of their collective impact, as expressed in Adam Smith's now hoary "unseen hand." Its social impact causes society to "fly blind," as when millions of individually bought automobiles collectively spell traffic gridlock and death-dealing air pollution. Government seeks to overcome these destructive results by regulating the manufacture of automobiles and gasoline. If this fails, as is likely, government will have to turn to long-range planning of alternate transportation, replacing private automobile trips with public conveyances. This will be a political decision to allocate resources from the private sector's automobile solution to the public sector's rail and bus solution. This is only one example of the choices between decisions by the Market and by the political process (made with or without planning).

The nineteenth-century laissez-faire market process, almost total economic determination by consumer demand, eventually proved unworkable. This was capitalism as Karl Marx knew it, and unworkable as he had predicted. During the course of the twentieth century, laissez-faire gave way to large-scale political intervention, resulting in state-guided and, increasingly, state-managed capitalism, with the state's control of money flow through central banks (Federal Reserve in the United States), credit control, tariffs and quotas, subsidies, tax policy, industrial and agricultural loans, price supports, wages policy, loan guarantees, savings incentives, marketing assistance, stockpiling, and various regulatory controls. This continuing transformation of market-based economies, which has come to be known as the Keynesian Revolution, is likely to be viewed by historians as of greater significance than the Soviet Revolution.

The proportions of market vs. political decision making in economic affairs does not necessarily reflect the proportions of private vs. state ownership of the economy. State-owned industries in countries such as Austria, Italy, and France, where they form a high proportion of the economy, are largely indistinguishable from the private sector in operating by the rules of the Market to produce in response to consumer demand. On the other hand, despite a relatively small nationalized sector, the state in Sweden is omnipresent in managing economic affairs. *The current widespread tilt toward privatization does not, therefore, diminish the trend toward an increased role of the state in economic affairs.*

The Market process demands that those who wish to participate pay admission. Those who cannot afford to get in—or who drop out—fall through the cracks; if lucky, into a social safety net. As the burden increased beyond private charities' resources, government was forced to assume it and the twentieth century's "welfare state" emerged. Its "transfer" programs of public goods and services exist outside the Market for those who cannot make it within.

The insecurity of various categories of entrepreneurs (such as farmers, oil drillers, ship owners, owners of small businesses, bank depositors), caused by the instability and unpredictability of the market process, led these entrepreneurs to use their political power to seek public assistance through subsidies, loans, insurance, "bailouts," and so forth, eventually becoming entitlements. The latter, together with welfare state transfer payments, proliferated and grew enormously, in part because they reflected the universal transition within affluent societies from satisfying needs to meeting wants. Adding these to the cost of traditional categories of public goods and services (such as national defense, public schools, parks, libraries, streets and roads) resulted in ballooning governmental budgets and the diversion through taxation of increasing proportions of the GNPs of industrial nations to their public sectors.

This had the effect of cutting into the availability of accumulated capital for investment in direct wealth-producing enterprise. Government response differed sharply, depending upon whether it followed a national economic policy or relied upon the Market. Sweden, an example of the former, tapped its Supplementary Pension Program to create the so-called fourth fund for targeted industrial investment, creating and sustaining employment that yielded a flow of payroll deductions back into the fund. The United States, on the other hand, permitted Market forces to drive up interest rates, bringing an inflow of foreign capital and an outflow of dividends and interest.

But, regardless of how the problem is managed, there are political limits to the diversion of funds from the private sector to the public sector via taxation. This can be seen in the "tax revolts" in Europe and the United States in the last two decades, which also had repercussions in the Scandinavian countries, including Sweden. This diversion also triggered the resurgence of laissez-faire ideology and right-wing politics.

Even for those countries in which the Market successfully accumulates the "wealth of nations," there results a lopsided inequality of distribution within the population, resulting in recurring economic instability and social confrontation. (Brazil, a country with the eighth largest Market-based economy in the world, leads all others in polarization between rich and poor.) The Market process generates cyclical and chronic unemployment, bankruptcies, mass layoffs, over- and underproduction, strikes and lockouts, and many other kinds of economic warfare and social tension. There is good reason to believe that the sharp shift in income from earned to unearned during the 1980s will be reflected in rising class conflict in the 1990s.

The Market is not a surefire prescription for the "wealth of nations" because its acclaimed incentives, acting as a spur to economic development, are also historically specific. Just because eighteenth-century England used the Market process to turn itself into a "nation of shopkeepers" and nineteenth-century England used it to lead the way in the Industrial Revolution to become the "world's workshop," is no assurance that, at any other time in history, people of any other culture and level of development can similarly use the Market to the same end—notwithstanding the examples of Western Europe, the United States, Canada, and Japan. (South Korea and Taiwan, judged by their per capita incomes, have not yet made it.)

Internationally, the Market has resulted in hierarchical ranking of nations by wealth, grouping a fortunate few as the rich nations and the rest as relatively or absolutely poor. Market-process relations between the industrially developed nations and the rest take the form of the developed responding to the consumer-driven demands of the underdeveloped for investments, loans, goods, and services, thereby aggravating their dependency, and frustrating their ability to accumulate enough capital to significantly improve their productivity (Argentina, Brazil, Mexico, Egypt, India, to name some).

⋅◈⋅

In summarizing the Market's negative side effects we have noted that it flies blindly; that its growth becomes destructive of communitarian values and institutions and of the natural environment; that its "work ethic" becomes exploitation, even of children (child labor is again on the rise in the United States according to the Department of Labor); that it reduces the cost of production but also triggers inflation; that it produces a cornucopia of goods but also mountains of waste; that its pharmaceutical research lengthens lifespans, but its chemicals (pesticides and herbicides) shorten them; that it makes feverish use of humankind's growing power over nature, born of scientific and technological progress, but puts profits above ecology and market share above the need to conserve natural resources; that it provides conveniences, comforts, and luxuries for an increasing number but shows no ability to close the widening gap between haves and have nots, neither within nor between nations. But, above all, the Market, despite Keynesianism, operates in cycles of boom and bust, victimizing businesses, large and small, farmers, professionals, and wage workers. Left to its own devices, the Market is inherently self-destructive.

Though the Market's negative side effects can be countered through government intervention and largely have been, such countering tends to be ameliorative rather than curative, and often raises new problems requiring additional intervention, thus reinforcing the overall tendency for the state to backstop the Market. But, despite this, Market economies still move blindly, though increasingly within broad channels marked out by government. The Market economy still overheats and runs out of fuel, but government now acts to cool it and then to fuel it (and even attempts to "fine tune" it). Will it prove a viable arrangement in the long term for government to treat the Market as if it were an elemental force of nature?

The people seem to want the benefits of the Market, but look to government to minimize the dreadful side effects that come with it. But one person's "dreadful side effects" are another person's sweet accumulation of capital. Translated into social relations, this conflict of interests expresses itself as interest-group confrontations and social-class struggles. And as decision making in economic affairs continues to shift from the Market to the political process, an ever fiercer political resistance is mounted by the interest groups and classes whose power is far greater and more direct in the Market than in the political arena—for instance, the resurgence of the new right in waging ideological and political warfare on behalf of laissez-faire policies.

The Market's Thrust vs. Societal Guidance

Understanding the direction in which the Market is likely to move in the next few decades is critically important to an assessment of its capacity to accommodate solutions for outstanding problems. In the past, especially since World War II, the Market's contribution to easing the great problems of civilization has been in the form of economic growth. The nature of the problems that now loom, however, makes them less subject to solution through economic growth. The rising tide that once raised all boats now leaves many stuck on muddy bottoms.

Market-based growth has not demonstrated an ability to reduce the glaring inequality in living standards and in educational/cultural levels within and between nations. In the United States during the last decade the gap between the bottom and the top of the income quintiles has widened. And growth solutions now generate new problems: the degradation of the natural environment on earth and in space; the exhaustion of natural resources; the emergence of *social* limits to growth, caused by the level at which acquisition of goods, services, and facilities by enough people spoils the advantages of possessing them; the puzzle of insatiable wants after basic needs have been satisfied (when is enough enough?). There are also the growth of private affluence and public squalor; an individualistic society's reluctance to resort to collective solutions (national health care) before first going through the agony of postponing the inevitable, and other looming problems sensed but seemingly too elusively complex to articulate. These problems join a long list of old problems that go unsolved to become a leaden weight on progress.

◦◦◦

Is there reason to believe that the Market's failure to cope with these problems will (or can) be remedied in the future? Is there anything in the nature and function of the Market that is likely to redirect its performance to be able to solve these problems? Are any of its negative side effects going to be eliminated, except insofar as governmentally applied correctives can curb them without altering the overall thrust of the Market? Left to its own devices, the Market's current trends are likely to expand and exacerbate problems. Are any countervailing forces in view? Yes.

One is the sharpening competition in the world market. The latter is being badly misread. True, a coded message on a computer or fax machine can transfer billions of dollars overseas at the end of the business day and retrieve it first thing in the morning—with earnings added. True, multinationals no longer fly a single flag. But national interests are as sharply defined as ever. And waging war with economic weapons has not reduced competitiveness and aggressiveness. The competitors are dividing into several major blocs: North America (the United States plus Canada and Mexico), Japan (plus the Asian rim countries) and a united Europe. The goal: market share. As Japan has shown (and also Europe to a lesser extent), this warfare requires maximum mobilization of economic resources: capital, management, knowledge-industry, and labor. Japan has shown that the way to bring these together is by making them all part of the corporate state. The power of Japan, Inc. is recognized in all American boardrooms, though a much smaller nation, Sweden, has also used the corporate strategy brilliantly. The striking similarity of Japanese and Swedish economic strategies, though for different social ends, is largely overlooked because the former is dominated by corporations and the latter by organized labor acting through the Social Democratic party.

The corporate state strategy has antimarket overtones. Rather than letting the market decide, it operates through strategic planning and a national industrial (investment) policy. If global market share is the goal, the nation's consumers had better not be permitted to decide on the allocation of resources. Laissez-faire America illustrates why not. The consumers opt for second homes, third cars, snowmobiles, Jacuzzis, and Torneau watches, thereby short-changing education at all levels, skill retraining of the labor force, housing, and health care—all essential ingredients in mobilizing resources to fight for market share.

The last thing any nation needs or will ever want after the debacle of the Stalinist model is an administrative-command economy (misnamed "planning"). Let the Market process determine the number, style, size, and color of shoes. And similarly for other basic needs and reasonable wants. But the nation also has collective needs, and the polity should determine the allocation of resources to supply them. Because this cannot be determined by the blind outcomes of the Market, the latter must be subordinated to strategically planned priorities designed to serve an overriding common purpose.

If coping with the major problems facing humankind in both its social and natural environments requires societal guidance, it necessitates setting goals and choosing strategies to achieve them; in short, strategic planning.

This calls for conscious, deliberate, and coordinated measures to mobilize a nation's resources. The American people with its Market-instilled value system is decidedly averse to this (except in time of war, when by political decision a goal-oriented government controlled wages, employment, prices, profits, manufacturing, and construction).

The twenty-first is not likely to be an American Century. Clinging to the Market, the negation of societal guidance, we might not even come in second. More likely we will be third, after a united Europe and an Asian-rim dominant Japan operating with strategic planning. Americans are more likely to be content with nursery reveries of

> *To market, to market, to buy a fat pig,*
> *Home again, home again, to dance a fast jig.*

Free to Choose

The Power of the Market

The Role of Prices

The key insight of Adam Smith's *Wealth of Nations* is misleadingly simple: if an exchange between two parties is voluntary, it will not take place unless both believe they will benefit from it. Most economic fallacies derive from the neglect of this simple insight, from the tendency to assume that there is a fixed pie, that one party can gain only at the expense of another.

This key insight is obvious for a simple exchange between two individuals. It is far more difficult to understand how it can enable people living all over the world to cooperate to promote their separate interests.

The price system is the mechanism that performs this task without central direction, without requiring people to speak to one another or to like one another. When you buy your pencil or your daily bread, you don't know whether the pencil was made or the wheat was grown by a white man or a black man, by a Chinese or an Indian. As a result, the price system enables people to cooperate peacefully in one phase of their life while each one goes about his own business in respect of everything else.

Adam Smith's flash of genius was his recognition that the prices that emerged from voluntary transactions between buyers and sellers—for short, in a free market—could coordinate the activity of millions of people, each seeking his own interest, in such a way as to make everyone better off. It was a startling idea then, and it remains one today, that economic order can emerge as the unintended consequence of the actions of many people, each seeking his own interest.

The price system works so well, so efficiently, that we are not aware of it most of the time. We never realize how well it functions until it is prevented from functioning, and even then we seldom recognize the source of the trouble.

The long gasoline lines that suddenly emerged in 1974 after the OPEC oil embargo, and again in the spring and summer of 1979 after the revolution in Iran, are a striking recent example. On both occasions there was a sharp disturbance in the supply of crude oil from abroad. But that did not lead to gasoline lines in Germany or Japan, which are wholly dependent on imported oil. It led to long gasoline lines in the United States, even though we produce much of our own oil, for one reason and one reason only: because legislation, administered by a government agency, did not permit the price system to function. Prices in some areas were kept by command below the level that would have equated the amount of gasoline available at the gas stations to the amount consumers wanted to buy at that price. Supplies were allocated to different areas of the country by command, rather than in response to the pressures of demand as reflected in price. The result was surpluses in some areas and shortages plus long gasoline lines in others. The smooth operation of the price system—which for many decades had assured every consumer that he could buy gasoline at any of a large number of service stations at his convenience and with a minimal wait —was replaced by bureaucratic improvisation....

The Role of Government

Where does government enter into the picture?...

[W]hat role should be assigned to government?

It is not easy to improve on the answer that Adam Smith gave to this question two hundred years ago:

> ... According to the system of natural liberty, the sovereign has only three duties to attend to; three duties of great importance, indeed, but plain and intelligible to common understandings: first, the duty of protecting the society from the violence and invasion of other independent societies; secondly, the duty of protecting, as far as possible, every member of the society from the injustice or oppression of every other member of it, or the duty of establishing an exact administration of justice; and thirdly, the duty of erecting and maintaining certain public works and certain public institutions, which it can never be for the interest of any individual, or small number of individuals, to erect and maintain; because the profit could never repay the expence to any individual or small number of individuals, though it may frequently do much more than repay it to a great society.

... A fourth duty of government that Adam Smith did not explicitly mention is the duty to protect members of the community who cannot be regarded as "responsible" individuals. Like Adam Smith's third duty, this one, too, is susceptible of great abuse. Yet it cannot be avoided....

Adam Smith's three duties, or our four duties of government, are indeed "of great importance," but they are far less "plain and intelligible to common understandings" than he supposed. Though we cannot decide the desirability or undesirability of any actual or proposed government intervention by mechanical reference to one or another of them, they provide a set of principles that we can use in casting up a balance sheet of pros and cons. Even on the loosest interpretation, they rule out much existing government intervention—all those "systems either of preference or of restraint" that Adam Smith fought against, that were subsequently destroyed, but have since reappeared in the form of today's tariffs, governmentally fixed prices and wages, restrictions on entry into various occupations, and numerous other departures from his "simple system of natural liberty."...

Cradle to Grave

... At the end of the war [World War II] it looked as if central economic planning was the wave of the future. That outcome was passionately welcomed by some who saw it as the dawn of a world of plenty shared equally. It was just as passionately feared by others, including us, who saw it as a turn to tyranny and misery. So far, neither the hopes of the one nor the fears of the other have been realized.

Government has expanded greatly. However, that expansion has not taken the form of detailed central economic planning accompanied by ever widening nationalization of industry, finance, and commerce, as so many of us feared it would. Experience put an end to detailed economic planning, partly because it was not successful in achieving the announced objectives, but also because it conflicted with freedom....

The failure of planning and nationalization has not eliminated pressure for an ever bigger government. It has simply altered its direction. The expansion of government now takes the form of welfare programs and of regulatory activities. As W. Allen Wallis put it in a somewhat different context, socialism, "intellectually bankrupt after more than a century of seeing one after another of its arguments for socializing the *means* of production demolished—now seeks to socialize the *results* of production."

In the welfare area the change of direction has led to an explosion in recent decades, especially after President Lyndon Johnson declared a "War on Poverty" in 1964. New Deal programs of Social Security, unemployment insurance, and direct relief were all expanded to cover new groups; payments were increased; and Medicare, Medicaid, food stamps, and numerous other programs were added. Public housing and urban renewal programs were enlarged. By now there are literally hundreds of government welfare and income transfer programs. The Department of Health, Education and Welfare, established in 1953 to consolidate the scattered welfare programs, began with a budget of $2 billion, less than 5 percent of expenditures on national defense. Twenty-five years later, in 1978, its budget was $160 billion, one and a half times as much as total spending on the army, the navy, and the air force. It had the third largest budget in the world, exceeded only by the entire budget of the U.S. government and of the Soviet Union....

No one can dispute two superficially contradictory phenomena: widespread dissatisfaction with the results of this explosion in welfare activities; continued pressure for further expansion.

The objectives have all been noble; the results, disappointing. Social Security expenditures have skyrocketed, and the system is in deep financial trouble. Public housing and urban renewal programs have subtracted from rather than added to the housing available to the poor. Public assistance rolls mount despite growing employment. By general agreement, the welfare program is a "mess" saturated with fraud and corruption. As government has paid a larger share of the nation's medical bills, both patients and physicians complain of rocketing costs and of the increasing impersonality of medicine. In education, student performance has dropped as federal intervention has expanded....

The repeated failure of well-intentioned programs is not an accident. It is not simply the result of mistakes of execution. The failure is deeply rooted in the use of bad means to achieve good objectives.

Despite the failure of these programs, the pressure to expand them grows. Failures are attributed to the miserliness of Congress in appropriating funds, and so are met with a cry for still bigger programs. Special interests that benefit from specific programs press for their expansion—foremost among them the massive bureaucracy spawned by the programs....

Created Equal

Capitalism and Equality

Everywhere in the world there are gross inequities of income and wealth. They offend most of us. Few can fail to be moved by the contrast between the luxury enjoyed by some and the grinding poverty suffered by others.

In the past century a myth has grown up that free market capitalism—equality of opportunity as we have interpreted that term—increases such inequalities, that it is a system under which the rich exploit the poor.

Nothing could be further from the truth. Wherever the free market has been permitted to operate, wherever anything approaching equality of opportunity has existed, the ordinary man has been able to attain levels of living never dreamed of before. Nowhere is the gap between rich and poor wider, nowhere are the rich richer and the poor poorer, than in those societies that do not permit the free market to operate. That is true of feudal societies like medieval Europe, India before independence, and much of modern South America, where inherited status determines position. It is equally true of centrally planned societies, like Russia or China or India since independence, where access to government determines position. It is true even where central planning was introduced, as in all three of these countries, in the name of equality....

Who Protects the Consumer?

... The pace of intervention quickened greatly after the New Deal—half of the thirty-two agencies in existence in 1966 were created after FDR's election in 1932. Yet intervention remained fairly moderate and continued in the single-industry mold. The *Federal Register*, established in 1936 to record all the regulations, hearings, and other matters connected with the regulatory agencies, grew, at first rather slowly, then more rapidly. Three volumes, containing 2,599 pages and taking six inches of shelf space, sufficed for 1936; twelve volumes, containing 10,528 pages and taking twenty-six inches of shelf space, for 1956; and thirteen volumes, containing 16,850 pages and taking thirty-six inches of shelf space, for 1966.

Then a veritable explosion in government regulatory activity occurred. No fewer than twenty-one new agencies were established in the next decade. Instead of being concerned with specific industries, they covered the waterfront: the environment, the production and distribution of energy, product safety, occupational safety, and so on. In addition to concern with the consumer's pocketbook, with protecting him from exploitation by sellers, recent agencies are primarily concerned with things like the consumer's safety and well-being, with protecting him not only from sellers but also from himself.

Government expenditures on both older and newer agencies skyrocketed— from less than \$1 billion in 1970 to roughly \$5 billion estimated for 1979. Prices in general roughly doubled, but these expenditures more than quintupled. The number of government bureaucrats employed in regulatory activities tripled, going from 28,000 in 1970 to 81,000 in 1979; the number of pages in the *Federal Register,* from 17,660 in 1970 to 36,487 in 1978, taking 127 inches of shelf space —a veritable ten-foot shelf....

This revolution in the role of government has been accompanied, and largely produced, by an achievement in public persuasion that must have few rivals. Ask yourself what products are currently least satisfactory and have shown the least improvement over time. Postal service, elementary and secondary schooling, railroad passenger transport would surely be high on the list. Ask yourself which products are most satisfactory and have improved the most. Household appliances, television and radio sets, hi-fi equipment, computers, and, we would add, supermarkets and shopping centers would surely come high on that list.

The shoddy products are all produced by government or government-regulated industries. The outstanding products are all produced by private enterprise with little or no government involvement. Yet the public—or a large part of it—has been persuaded that private enterprises produce shoddy products, that we need ever vigilant government employees to keep business from foisting off unsafe, meretricious products at outrageous prices on ignorant, unsuspecting, vulnerable customers. That public relations campaign has succeeded so well that we are in the process of turning over to the kind of people who bring us our postal service the far more critical task of producing and distributing energy....

Government intervention in the marketplace is subject to laws of its own, not legislated laws, but scientific laws. It obeys forces and goes in directions that may have little relationship to the intentions or desires of its initiators or supporters. We have already examined this process in connection with welfare activity. It is present equally when government intervenes in the marketplace, whether to protect consumers against high prices or shoddy goods, to promote their safety, or to preserve the environment. Every act of intervention establishes positions of power. How that power will be used and for what purposes depends far more on the people who are in the best position to get control of that power and what their purposes are than on the aims and objectives of the initial sponsors of the intervention....

Environment

The environmental movement is responsible for one of the most rapidly growing areas of federal intervention. The Environmental Protection Agency, established in 1970 "to protect and enhance the physical environment," has been granted increasing power and authority. Its budget has multiplied sevenfold from 1970 to 1978 and is now more than half a billion dollars. It has a staff of about 7,000. It has imposed costs on industry and local and state governments to meet its standards that total in the tens of billions of dollars a year. Something between a tenth and a quarter of total net investment in new capital equipment by business now goes for antipollution purposes. And this does not count the costs of requirements imposed by other agencies, such as those designed to control emissions of motor vehicles, or the costs of land-use planning or wilderness preservation or a host of other federal, state, and local government activities undertaken in the name of protecting the environment.

The preservation of the environment and the avoidance of undue pollution are real problems and they are problems concerning which the government has an important role to play. When all the costs and benefits of any action, and the people hurt or benefited, are readily identifiable, the market provides an excellent means for assuring that only those actions are undertaken for which the benefits exceed the costs for all participants. But when the costs and benefits or the people affected cannot be identified, there is a market failure....

Government is one means through which we can try to compensate for "market failure," try to use our resources more effectively to produce the amount of clean air, water, and land that we are willing to pay for. Unfortunately, the very factors that produce the market failure also make it difficult for government to achieve a satisfactory solution. Generally, it is no easier for government to identify the specific persons who are hurt and benefited than for market participants, no easier for government to assess the amount of harm or benefit to each. Attempts to use government to correct market failure have often simply substituted government failure for market failure.

Public discussion of the environmental issue is frequently characterized more by emotion than reason. Much of it proceeds as if the issue is pollution versus no pollution, as if it were desirable and possible to have a world without pollution. That is clearly nonsense. No one who contemplates the problem seriously will regard zero pollution as either a desirable or a possible state of affairs. We could have zero pollution from automobiles, for example, by simply abolishing all automobiles. That would also make the kind of agricultural and industrial productivity we now enjoy impossible, and so condemn most of us to a drastically lower standard of living, perhaps many even to death. One source of atmospheric pollution is the carbon dioxide that we all exhale. We could stop that very simply. But the cost would clearly exceed the gain.

It costs something to have clean air, just as it costs something to have other good things we want. Our resources are limited and we must weigh the gains from reducing pollution against the costs. Moreover, "pollution" is not an objective phenomenon. One person's pollution may be another's pleasure. To some of us rock music is noise pollution; to others of us it is pleasure.

The real problem is not "eliminating pollution," but trying to establish arrangements that will yield the "right" amount of pollution: an amount such that the gain from reducing pollution a bit more just balances the sacrifice of the other good things—houses, shoes, coats, and so on—that would have to be given up in order to reduce the pollution. If we go farther than that, we sacrifice more than we gain. . . .

The Market

Perfection is not of this world. There will always be shoddy products, quacks, con artists. But on the whole, market competition, when it is permitted to work, protects the consumer better than do the alternative government mechanisms that have been increasingly superimposed on the market.

As Adam Smith said . . . , competition does not protect the consumer because businessmen are more soft-hearted than the bureaucrats or because they are more altruistic or generous, or even because they are more competent, but only because it is in the self-interest of the businessman to serve the consumer.

If one storekeeper offers you goods of lower quality or of higher price than another, you're not going to continue to patronize his store. If he buys goods to sell that don't serve your needs, you're not going to buy them. The merchants therefore search out all over the world the products that might meet your needs and might appeal to you. And they stand back of them because if they don't, they're going to go out of business. When you enter a store, no one forces you to buy. You are free to do so or go elsewhere. That is the basic difference between the market and a political agency. You are free to choose. There is no policeman to take the money out of your pocket to pay for something you do not want or to make you do something you do not want to do.

But, the advocate of government regulation will say, suppose the FDA weren't there, what would prevent business from distributing adulterated or dangerous products? It would be a very expensive thing to do. . . . It is very poor business practice—not a way to develop a loyal and faithful clientele. Of course, mistakes and accidents occur—but . . . government regulation doesn't prevent them. The difference is that a private firm that makes a serious blunder may go out of business. A government agency is likely to get a bigger budget.

Cases will arise where adverse effects develop that could not have been foreseen—but government has no better means of predicting such developments than private enterprise. The only way to prevent all such developments would be to stop progress, which would also eliminate the possibility of unforeseen favorable developments. . . .

What about the danger of monopoly that led to the antitrust laws? That is a real danger. The most effective way to counter it is not through a bigger antitrust division at the Department of Justice or a larger budget for the Federal Trade Commission, but through removing existing barriers to international trade. That would permit competition from all over the world to be even more effective than it is now in undermining monopoly at home. Freddie Laker of Britain needed no help from the Department of Justice to crack the airline cartel. Japanese and German automobile manufacturers forced American manufacturers to introduce smaller cars.

The great danger to the consumer is monopoly—whether private or governmental. His most effective protection is free competition at home and free trade throughout the world. The consumer is protected from being exploited by one seller by the existence of another seller from whom he can buy and who is eager to sell to him. Alternative sources of supply protect the consumer far more effectively than all the Ralph Naders of the world.

Conclusion

... [T]he reaction of the public to the more extreme attempts to control our behavior—to the requirement of an interlock system on automobiles or the proposed ban of saccharin—is ample evidence that we want no part of it. Insofar as the government has information not generally available about the merits or demerits of the items we ingest or the activities we engage in, let it give us the information. But let it leave us free to choose what chances we want to take with our own lives.

POSTSCRIPT

Should Government Intervene in a Capitalist Economy?

Erber concedes that the market should not be abolished. He writes that a "body of evidence... links the market with economic growth, increased productivity, and improved living standards," and that this linkage "cannot be contested." Nevertheless, he calls for an activist government to subordinate the market to "planned priorities designed to serve an overriding common purpose." The Friedmans believe that such subordination can only destroy the market. The question, then, is whether or not we can successfully graft the market's "invisible hand" to the arm of the state. Would the graft take? Has the experiment perhaps already proven successful in post–New Deal America? Or is the American government in the process of destroying what gave the nation its growth, prosperity, and living standards?

Erber calls the market a "blind" force. The Friedmans seem to agree that the market in itself is amoral, though they feel that it produces good results. But philosopher Michael Novak goes further, contending that the ethic of capitalism transcends mere moneymaking and is (or can be made) compatible with Judeo-Christian morality. See *The Spirit of Democratic Capitalism* (Madison Books, 1991) and *The Catholic Ethic and the Spirit of Capitalism* (Free Press, 1993). Another broad-based defense of capitalism is Peter L. Berger's *The Capitalist Revolution: Fifty Propositions About Prosperity, Equality and Liberty* (Basic Books, 1988). For an attack on capitalism, see Victor Perlo, *Superprofits and Crisis: Modern U.S. Capitalism* (International Publishers, 1988); Samir Amin, *Spectres of Capitalism* (Monthly Review Press, 1998); Jack Barnes, *Capitalism's World Disorder* (Pathfinders, 1999); and John Gray, *False Dawn: The Delusions of Global Capitalism* (Granta Books, 1998). Two captivating analyses of global capitalism are William Greider's *One World, Ready or Not: The Manic Logic of Global Capitalism* (Simon & Schuster, 1997) and Thomas Friedman's *The Lexus and the Olive Tree* (HarperCollins, 1999). For a feminist critique of capitalism, see J. K. Gibson-Graham, *The End of Capitalism (As We Know It): A Feminist Critique of Political Economy* (Blackwell, 1996). For a mixed view of capitalism, see Charles Wolf, Jr., *Markets or Governments: Choosing Between Imperfect Alternatives* (MIT Press, 1993). A strong attack on government interventions in the market is Jonathan Rauch, *Demosclerosis: The Silent Killer of American Government* (Times Books, 1994).

ISSUE 13

Has Welfare Reform Benefited the Poor?

YES: Editors of *The Economist*, from "Welfare Reform: America's Great Achievement," *The Economist* (August 25, 2001)

NO: Randy Albelda, from "What's Wrong With Welfare-to-Work?" *Dollars and Sense* (September/October 2000)

ISSUE SUMMARY

YES: The editors of the *Economist* present the facts on the declining welfare rolls and the dramatic increase in employment for welfare mothers, and they argue that many of these changes are due to the changes in the welfare laws and not simply a strong economy.

NO: Randy Albelda, professor of economics at the University of Massachusetts at Boston, argues that even though the statistics look good, the reality behind them is grim. The old welfare system helped many single mothers get decent jobs through education and training while the new welfare system in most states forces welfare mothers to take terrible jobs at minimal pay.

In his 1984 book *Losing Ground: American Social Policy, 1950–1980* (Basic Books), policy analyst Charles Murray recommends abolishing Aid to Families with Dependent Children (AFDC), the program at the heart of the welfare debate. At the time of the book's publication this suggestion struck many as simply a dramatic way for Murray to make some of his points. However, 14 years later this idea became the dominant idea in Congress. In 1996 President Bill Clinton signed into law the Work Opportunity Reconciliation Act and fulfilled his 1992 campaign pledge to "end welfare as we know it." Murray's thesis that welfare hurt the poor had become widely accepted. In "What to Do About Welfare," *Commentary* (December 1994), Murray argues that welfare contributes to dependency, illegitimacy, and the number of absent fathers, which in turn can have terrible effects on the children involved. He states that workfare, enforced child support, and the abolition of welfare would greatly reduce these problems.

One reason why Congress ended AFDC was the emergence of a widespread backlash against welfare recipients. Much of the backlash, however, was misguided. It often rested on the assumptions that welfare is generous and that most people on welfare are professional loafers. In fact, over the previous two decades payments to families with dependent children eroded considerably relative to the cost of living. Furthermore, most women with dependent children on welfare had intermittent periods of work, were elderly, or were disabled. Petty fraud may be common since welfare payments are insufficient to live on in many cities, but "welfare queens" who cheat the system for spectacular sums are so rare that they should not be part of any serious debate on welfare issues. The majority of people on welfare are those whose condition would become desperate if payments were cut off. Although many believe that women on welfare commonly bear children in order to increase their benefits, there is no conclusive evidence to support this conclusion.

Not all objections to AFDC can be easily dismissed, however. There does seem to be evidence that in some cases AFDC reduces work incentives and increases the likelihood of family breakups. But there is also a positive side to AFDC—it helped many needy people get back on their feet. When all things are considered together, therefore, it is not clear that welfare, meaning AFDC, was bad enough to be abolished. But it was abolished on July 1, 1997, when the Work Opportunity Reconciliation Act went into effect. Now the question is whether the new policy is better than the old policy.

It is too soon to obtain an accurate assessment of the impacts of the act. Nevertheless, AFDC rolls have declined since the act was passed, so many conclude that it is a success rather than a failure. Of course, the early leavers are the ones with the best prospects of succeeding in the work world; the welfare-to-work transition gets harder as the program works with the more difficult cases. The crucial question is whether or not the reform will benefit those it affects. Already many working former welfare recipients are better off. But what about the average or more vulnerable recipient?

In the readings that follow, the editors of the *Economist* call welfare reform "America's great achievement" because employment statistics went up dramatically for welfare mothers and welfare rolls went down dramatically. In the second selection, Randy Albelda calls this welfare-to-work solution "a match made in hell" because it forces women on welfare to make desperate and oppressive choices. According to Albelda, the jobs that these women are forced to take poorly match their needs and make their lives a hell.

Editors of *The Economist*  **YES**

Welfare Reform:
America's Great Achievement

August 22nd marked a milestone in American social policy. On that day, five years ago, Bill Clinton, having promised to "end welfare as we know it", signed into law the Personal Responsibility and Work Opportunity Reconciliation Act, otherwise known as welfare reform. This ended welfare as an entitlement, available to all the parents who qualified, and required recipients—mostly single mothers—to look for work. Rather than simply paying up on demand, the federal government switched to a "block grant" programme, handing over a fixed sum to states ($16.5 billion a year), to disburse as they wished, within limits. There are now, in effect, 51 different plans—one in each state plus a central set of guidelines.

One of those guidelines stipulated that poor people with dependent children would get federal payments for only five years over a lifetime. Their time is up, so payments to parents who have been on the rolls since then should stop. In fact, things should not change much. No one is sure how many of today's 2m welfare families have been on the rolls for the maximum period. Not many probably, because the states have already pushed some recipients off the lists; and the 1996 law also allowed them to exempt up to a fifth of welfare recipients from the five-year time limit. More generally, federal payments now make up a smaller portion of the welfare system than payments from states and local governments.

Still, the beginning of the end of federal welfare funding marks a natural point of reflection for "the most sweeping social change in America in more than half a century" (as Tommy Thompson, one of the reform's pioneers and now its overseer as secretary for health and human services, has put it). Congress must also reauthorise the law next year. What has welfare reform achieved? And can it be improved?

When the reform became law, welfare rolls were near their all-time high. The "revolutionary" Republican Congress of Newt Gingrich tried to turn several social programmes—including Medicaid, the part-state, part-federal health-care system for the poor—into block grants. Welfare was the only Republican plan Bill Clinton did not veto. And he signed it in the teeth of vociferous Democratic opposition.

Welfare is only part of the country's poverty-reduction system, which includes public housing, food stamps, day-care subsidies, Medicaid and the Child Health Insurance Programme. But it has long been the most notorious part, not just because of its scale (in the mid-1990s, one in seven children was on welfare) but because it supposedly bred a culture of dependency.

The first aim of the 1996 law was to break that culture by moving people off welfare and into jobs. Before the reform, states gave out about 80% of the federal money that they dispensed in cash benefits. Now only half goes in cash. The rest goes on job searches, education, training and day-care for children of working mothers. Welfare offices have turned from cash-dispensing machines into job-centres, all using different sticks and carrots to push welfare recipients into work.

Critics on the left predicted disaster: unskilled welfare recipients would be unprepared for the discipline of work. In fact, welfare rolls have fallen more than even supporters predicted: from 5.1m families at the peak in 1994 to just over 2m now (see chart 1). In Wisconsin, where Mr Thompson was governor, Florida and Mississippi the rolls fell by more than 75%. Around two-thirds of those who left welfare are still working. Of the large minority, some returned to welfare, some subsist on other forms of government support and a few—an unknown number—have fallen through the cracks.

The unemployment rate for single mothers had been stuck at around 43% for most of the 1980s and early 1990s. After reform, the rate fell to 28% by 1999. The unemployment rate of never-married mothers fell even faster, from just over half in 1996 to one-third three years later. In the early 1990s, the average stay on welfare had been more than eight years: dependency, indeed. Now, the stay is probably less than half that. In the narrowest sense of the law's aim, it has been a triumph.

This has not been achieved merely by skimming the cream: the worry was that the employable minority would find jobs quickly, leaving behind an unemployable residue who would not find work, even if their benefits were cut off. At some point, presumably, the law of diminishing returns must set in. But that point has not been reached yet.

Studies by the Urban Institute, a Washington think-tank, show that the most recent batch of welfare leavers (those who left in 1997–99) have similar levels of employment and wages as the first batch (who left in 1995–97). And they suffer less hardship than the earlier group, with "only" 41% living below the poverty line, compared with 48% in 1997. There has been no build-up of the worst cases on the rolls. Welfare recipients seem far more employable than critics feared.

It's Not the Economy, Stupid

The reforms took place at a time of unprecedented economic growth. Some wonder whether their success has been enhanced by transient economic factors that have begun to change. Just before the economic slowdown became apparent there was a rise in the caseload between July and September 2000—a mere

Figure 1

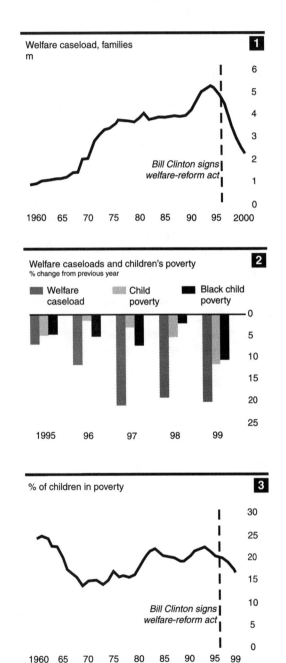

A New Deal

1. Welfare caseload, families (m), 1960–2000, with marker "Bill Clinton signs welfare-reform act"
2. Welfare caseloads and children's poverty, % change from previous year, 1995–99 — Welfare caseload, Child poverty, Black child poverty
3. % of children in poverty, 1960–99, with marker "Bill Clinton signs welfare-reform act"

Source: Congressional Research Service; Department of Health and Human Services; Census Bureau

8,000 families, but the first time that more than a handful of states had seen the numbers rise.

Yet the connection between welfare rolls and the economy is less firm than you would expect. During the 1980s, when America added 20m new jobs, welfare rolls grew by over 500,000 families. Rolls also rose quickly at the beginning of the economic recovery of the early 1990s. The good news did not begin until 1994—when welfare reform began experimentally in some states. It was strongest in those, such as Wisconsin, that went furthest with their own reform measures.

A review by the Urban Institute shows that six studies before 1996 all gave more weight to the economy than policy. Two even found the economy accounted for three-quarters of the change in caseloads. But the two more recent studies of effects after 1996 placed policy above the economy by a ratio of at least four to one.

This hardly settles the argument conclusively. The success so far must owe something to the economy—and a downturn will, at the very least, affect the pace of improvement. On the other hand, worries about the economy should not be allowed to denigrate the achievement. Reform has left recipients better off than they would otherwise have been.

"Better off", however, does not mean much. The first aim of reform was to get people into jobs; the second was to improve the income of the poor. Here reform has been less successful. Reductions in poverty have occurred, but at a slower rate than reductions in welfare rolls (chart 2).

In terms of wages, poor parents improved their lot (albeit at miserable levels). Annual wages for the bottom fifth of single-mother households rose from $1,350 in 1993 to $2,400 in 1999—a nominal rise of more than 80%. Earnings for the next 20% of wage earners increased even more, from $4,800 to $9,600.

Employed, but Not Richer

The trouble is that for every dollar gained in extra earnings, people lost around 40 cents in benefits. The poorest 40% of single-mother households increased earnings by about $3,000 between 1993 and 1999. But their disposable incomes rose by only about $1,850. The poorest of all have been hit hardest. According to Wendell Primus, a former Clinton administration official, and Ron Haskins of the Brookings Institution, 700,000 families are worse off under reform than they were before; and the child-poverty gap—the total amount that would be needed to bring all children up to the poverty line—fell only slightly in 1993-99, from $59.8 billion to $56.3 billion.

That still marks an improvement in the number of children escaping poverty. Until the mid-1990s, the proportion of children living in poverty had been rising erratically (see chart 3). Since then, the trend reversed sharply. In 1999, the child-poverty rate was back to its lowest since 1979 and poverty among black children was at its lowest level ever. Using a broader measure of poverty, the decline in poverty has been comparable to the big gains of the 1960s and was more than twice as great as during the 1980s.

Yet the fact remains: poor parents have seen less improvement in incomes than in their chance of a job. This gets more troubling when you look at wider benefits to children (such as higher school grades and keeping out of trouble with the law.) Such things, according to a study of 11 different welfare schemes by the Manpower Development Research Corporation, improve significantly only when the reforms boost both jobs and income.

But breaking the culture of dependency had wider goals than these. If you read the early pages of the welfare-reform bill, it is startling to find how often the word "marriage" appears. Welfare reform, for many of its proponents, was not to be judged by economic statistics. Rather, as one commentator, Mickey Kaus, says, it was about taking a "culture characterised by welfare dependence, a high rate of births out of wedlock, high male unemployment, and crime and replac[ing] it with a new, more virtuous social dynamic". Marriage is the best indicator of this complex change—and it is here that the most surprising good news is to be found.

For decades before welfare reform there had been a relentless rise in the number of out-of-wedlock births (from 18% in 1980 to 33% in 1999). The number of children living with single mothers was especially marked among the poor and among blacks. Yet in about 1996, these apparently unstoppable trends stopped. According to a study by the Centre for Budget and Policy Priorities (CBPP), the share of children living with single mothers on less than twice the poverty rate fell from 34.2% in 1995 to 32.8% in 2000. This group includes most welfare recipients.

The revival of the nuclear family in the past few years has been driven by many things (from education to a new long-lasting injectible contraceptive). But it has been particularly notable amongst welfare beneficiaries. The proportion of black children living with their married parents rose from 35% in 1995 to 39% in 2000—a rise almost three times bigger than that in the whole population. And a welfare programme in Minnesota which rewarded married couples has yielded startling results. After three years, married couples on the scheme were considerably more likely to stay together than comparable couples on other programmes. Single parents joining the programme were also slightly more likely to get hitched.

One of the authors of the CBPP study, Mr Primus, resigned from the Clinton administration in protest at the decision to sign welfare reform. He now credits that change for creating this most unexpected good news on the family. "Whatever we have been doing over the last five years," he says, "we ought to keep going". That depends on Congress, which has to reauthorise the welfare laws by October 2002.

There is no constituency for a radical overhaul. Welfare hardly merited a mention in the presidential election last year—a remarkable testament to the way in which success in the field has produced political consensus out of controversy in five years. However, there is still room for Congress both to mess things up and improve them.

The big danger, inevitably, involves money. Some congressmen cite the plummeting welfare rolls as a reason to chop the block grant. Yet part of the success of the block-grant system is that, as those falling rolls have left behind the harder cases, it has increased the amount of money available to find jobs for each of those people. That virtuous circle would turn vicious if the money were reduced. Indeed, the possibility of recession suggests that the $2 billion contingency fund—which provides extra money for hard-hit states—should be both increased and made easier to tap. At the moment, states virtually have to declare bankruptcy to get the cash.

The problems to do with "ancillary benefits" (like food stamps) fortunately do not require Congress to authorise more money, just to simplify the rules. Fewer than half the working mothers who leave welfare continue to get food stamps, even though they are entitled to them. Cutting red tape—both at state and federal levels—would do more than any single thing to boost the disposable incomes of welfare-leavers and to reduce child poverty.

The third tricky area is how much welfare reform can be used to promote marriage. This is mostly a matter for the states, and at least two—Oklahoma and Arizona—have set up ambitious programmes that are supposed to boost marriage rates among the poor (including marriage-training classes). Congress could set up additional matching funds to encourage such programmes. Perhaps more important, it could end the marriage penalties in its own tax code, especially in the earned-income tax credit. A study by the Urban Institute found that if a single working mother on the minimum wage marries a man earning $8 an hour, she loses a staggering $8,060 in annual benefits.

These problems are mere sun spots. It is rare enough that any government policy, let alone one dealing with poverty, is so near an unambiguous success as welfare reform has been. For decades, the underclass has loomed as America's deepest social problem. In just five years, reform has halved the size of the problem and made it possible to move on to the next stage. Pray that Congress doesn't blow it.

Randy Albelda   ← **NO**

What's Wrong With Welfare-to-Work?

Ending welfare as we know it" has rapidly become ending welfare. Time limits virtually assure that the majority of families who receive welfare will be cut off at least from federal funding. The current trend is to replace welfare with earnings and is best summed up by the ever-present term "welfare-to-work."

The welfare-to-work "solution" can be thought of as a match made in hell. It puts poor mothers who need the most support and flexibility into jobs in the low-wage labor market which often are the most inflexible, have the least family-necessary benefits (vacation time, health care, sick days), and provide levels of pay that often are insufficient to support a single person, let alone a family. This mismatch is not going to be resolved by providing short-term job training, work vans, poor-quality child care, or even refundable earned income tax credits. It is a political, social, and economic problem that must be addressed in our policies but also in our national psyche. It starts with valuing the work that families do. Raising children—in any and all family configurations—is absolutely vital work to our individual and collective well-being. And it is deserving. Recognizing this will not only transform how we think about welfare, it can and must change how we think about the structure of paid work. We must have access to paid work that allows us to take care of our families and have a family life without relegating all women to the home.

Been There, Done That

Ending welfare poses some historically familiar alternatives for women. Getting married and staying married—thus being dependent on a man—was of course the fond hope and major inspiration for conservatives who sponsored the 1996 Personal Responsibility and Work Opportunity Reconciliation Act (PRWORA). The Act leads with these two "findings": 1) Marriage is the foundation of a successful society; and 2) Marriage is an essential institution of a successful society which promotes the interests of children.

The path most proponents of welfare reform promote publicly, however, is "welfare-to-work." There is a wide range of methods for promoting paid work instead of welfare, from the punitive "work-first" strategies pursued by over half the states to the more liberal strategies (which include a generous package of training and education options, day care, transportation, and health care) put forth by Mary Jo Bane and David Ellwood when they were welfare reform policymakers in the Clinton Administration. Despite its current popularity, the notion of putting welfare mothers to "work" is hardly new. Work requirements have long been part of AFDC, and were seen as an important way to get women, particularly black women, off the welfare rolls. It was only in the early 1990s, however, that paid work became the main alternative in light of benefit time limits.

Most states, as well as the ancillary not-for-profit agencies and for-profit companies that get lucrative welfare-related contracts, are putting significant energies into getting adult welfare recipients to "work." Work in this case means paid employment or unpaid community or public-service placements (workfare). But there are problems with welfare-to-work, some of which states readily recognize and are working to cope with (however inadequately), and others which states do not even recognize.

Inadequate Supports for Welfare-to-Work Moms

One aspect of states' welfare-to-work policy has always been their concern with the "job readiness" of welfare mothers. From vast amounts of published research we know many welfare mothers have low educational attainment and many lack recent job experience (although the vast majority have been employed at some point). Both of these characteristics impede entry into the labor market and, once there, all but assure low wages. This is too bad since welfare-to-work ideology rests on short-term training, which is reinforced by precluding most education from qualifying as "work-related activities" in the work quotas established in PRWORA. This of course means that many state programs will be ineffectual in improving women's skills.

More and more research is uncovering another set of barriers to work, including learning disabilities, severe bouts of depression, and experiences with domestic violence. The prediction is that the easy-to-place recipients will soon be thrown out of the welfare system and those who remain will require much more training and support to get paid employment. Ironically, or perhaps cynically, welfare will become exactly how it was portrayed for years—a system that serves very low-functioning women with children who need long-term assistance. Recent studies show that over 41% of current recipients have less than a high school diploma, and between 10% and 31% of welfare recipients are currently victims of domestic violence. Helping women overcome barriers to employment will take time, quality counseling, and long-term training, something welfare reform is discouraging or prohibiting.

What distinguishes welfare recipients from other poor people is that two thirds of them are children being raised, most often, by a mother on her own. Welfare has always been a program for families with young children. Therefore, welfare-to-work requires a substantial set of ancillary supports that *mothers* with small children *need* to get to work, such as health insurance, transportation, and childcare. Since many jobs available to welfare-to-work mothers do not provide health insurance, states allow women to stay on Medicaid, but typically only for one year after leaving welfare. Then they're on their own. Some states have recognized the transportation challenge mothers face—efficiently getting children to and from day care and school, and getting themselves to and from work in a timely fashion—and some are trying to solve this problem with loaner cars, work vans, and public transportation vouchers. In rural and suburban areas, however, the problems are much more difficult since adequate transportation is just not there. Regarding childcare, policy makers recognize the need for it, but their solutions should make us shiver. Very few states pay any attention to the quality of care. Any care seems to do for poor mothers. In Massachusetts, for example, the state encourages mothers to find low-cost caretakers with reimbursements of $15 a day. Assuming you get what you pay for, such childcare is a disaster for mothers and children. Moreover, it impoverishes and exploits the caregivers.

And What About the Problems With No Name?

Will welfare-to-work actually ensure economic "independence"? Many are avoiding this question because the economic expansion, which has both accompanied and accommodated welfare-to-work, has at least fulfilled one premise of welfare reform—moving women from the rolls to a job. However, come the downturn, many who did get jobs will lose them and caseloads will creep back up. Further, the expansion has allowed states to be slack, if not entirely unimaginative, in their training and education efforts, relying on the economic expansion to reduce rolls and thereby claim victory in the welfare reform battle.

Will finding a job mean earning a living wage? Not likely. What is almost always ignored or conveniently forgotten in the blind faith that all too often accompanies the welfare-to-work mentality is that the U.S. labor market has always failed women who have little formal education and sporadic job experiences. Women have a very hard time supporting themselves, let alone families, on wages from waitressing, sales clerking, cleaning hotel rooms, or even assisting administrators. Yet these are exactly the kinds of jobs welfare-to-work mothers are likely to get.

In addition to the problems of a fickle labor market and chronically low wages, women in the welfare-to-work pipeline must cope with the fact that most jobs are not "mother ready." That is, they do not accommodate mothers' needs, even when training, work, and childcare arrangements are in place. These are not unknown or new needs. They include the remarkably mundane events such as children getting sick, school and medical appointments, school vacations, and early-release school days. Employers, especially those who employ low-wage workers, do not want workers who come in late because a school bus didn't show up, miss days because there was no child care, or worry about their children at 3:00 PM—instead of doing their tedious low-wage-earning tasks. Unfortunately, low-wage employers of current and former welfare recipients are least likely to grant sick leave and vacation time. According to a report in last year's *American Journal of Public Health,* 46% of women who had never been on welfare got sick leave and vacation pay at their jobs, as compared to 24% of women who had been on welfare less than two years, and 19% of women who had been on welfare more than two years.

Most state administrators, politicians, journalists, and researchers see the work of taking care of children as a cost of welfare-to-work, but not as an important and valuable family activity. Devaluing women's unpaid work in the home is clearly evident in studies of welfare reform. Typically, researchers compare welfare families' and employed families' material well-being without imputing any value to women's time. In short, the value of women's unpaid labor in the home when she is receiving welfare is zero. As a policy, welfare-to-work fails to grapple with the fact that adults responsible for children cannot (and probably should not) put their jobs—especially low-wage ones—before the needs of their children.

Family Values/Valuing Families

The ideologues who concern themselves with poor mothers exhibit split personalities when it comes to getting women to work. The conservative architects of welfare reform who want to force poor mothers to do lousy jobs are now busy enacting tax cuts to encourage middle-class moms to stay at home and trying hard to eliminate the "marriage penalty" in the tax code. Liberals, on the other hand, seem preoccupied with providing inadequate supports for full-time employment for poor mothers. What's going on?

One way to make sense of the obsession with employment for poor mothers is to see the emphasis on paid work in welfare reform as a major change in thinking about women and public assistance. Indeed, it is a major value shift. The Social Security Act of 1935 made all poor single mothers entitled to receive Aid to Families with Dependent Children (AFDC), although the levels received were far lower than the other two major programs (Social Security and Unemployment Insurance) in that historic legislation. At that time, the notion of having to "work" for one's benefits was not an expectation of most single mothers. Women who were not attached to male breadwinners received income, but not much.

Another old value set guiding single mothers' receipt of cash assistance pivoted on how women became single mothers. Widows were seen as deserving, while divorced, separated, and never-married mothers were not. Benefit levels reinforced these "values."

What makes a single mother "deserving" today has changed. The salient factor is no longer how she happened to become a single parent, but rather if she is engaged in paid labor. This sentiment is only possible in an age when most women are in the paid labor market and when the moral repugnance of women without men has dissipated. Ironically, both of these accomplishments can be attributed in part to the successes of the women's movement, coupled with modern industrialization. As more and more women are drawn into the labor force, they tend to have fewer children and are not as likely to get or stay married. Interestingly, both conservatives and liberals have lent weight to the idea that working single mothers are more deserving.

The positive value of employment was accompanied by the negative value placed on receiving welfare. Led by Ronald Reagan and conservative thinker Charles Murray in the 1980s, welfare opponents referred to AFDC recipients as "welfare queens." They were presumed to have loads of children, leech resources from the state, and then pass their dysfunctional behavior on to their children. In the mid-1980s through the 1990s, many "liberal" poverty researchers carried this banner as well. "Underclass" authors, notably William Julius Wilson and Christopher Jencks, as well as their left detractors, such as William Darity and Samuel Myers, discussed welfare receipt as a pathology—one of the many "bad" behaviors that helps reproduce poverty. Jencks even referred to women receiving welfare as the "reproductive underclass." Further, when adult recipients have earnings, even if they receive hefty supplements, they are not perceived as receiving "hand-outs" and hence are deserving. It would seem, then, putting welfare mothers to work solves the problem of growing welfare rolls and plays into American values that will help restore safety nets for the poor. On both the Right and the Left, putting poor mothers to work is the prescribed cure to their "dysfunctional" tendencies.

A Progressive Agenda

I do not want to argue here that paid work is bad. Indeed, earnings can and do buy economic security and some independence from men, especially from abusive relationships. In a society that values paid work, doing it can build your self-esteem as well. However, welfare-to-work is a set up. The types of jobs poor mothers get and can keep provide neither much dignity nor sufficient wages. Working enough hours at low wages to support a family is often untenable. Women fail too often. This is not only demoralizing, but economically debilitating. If we don't think both about valuing women's work at home as well as when they do paid work, welfare-to-work is a cruel hoax that makes legislators feel better about themselves, but leaves poor families in the lurch.

Instead of trying to reform poor mothers to become working poor mothers, we need to take a closer look at job structures and what it will take to make work possible for mothers who support families. This might include a shorter work week or at least income supplements to those who take a part-time job so that families can still pay for basic needs like housing, health insurance, childcare, food, and clothing. Paid family and medical leave and expanded unemployment insurance to cover less continuous and low-paying part time work must also be in place. A mother shouldn't lose her job or her weekly pay because her child gets chicken pox. Herein lies the true opportunity of welfare-to-work welfare reform.

A national discussion about the value of women's work in the home is much needed for all women, not just those who turn to public assistance. It would raise several important sets of policy issues, including:

- seriously considering the provision of publicly funded family care such as child care centers, extended day programs, and child allowances;

- working to make sure that welfare is not punitive, and is at least comparable to social security and unemployment insurance; and
- focusing not just on making mothers "job ready," but promoting policies that make paid work "mother-ready"—in other words, conducive to mothers' needs, paying a living wage, and offering opportunities for advancement.

If we as a nation recognized the value of women's work, we wouldn't have welfare reform that merely replaces public assistance with forcing mothers into working jobs at low wages and a shallow set of supports that vanishes quickly. Seeing the work of raising children as a benefit to society, not merely a cost of going to work, would mean developing a welfare-to-work regime that truly supports part-time waged work. Further, it might make us more cognizant that for some families at some points in their lives, having the sole adult in the labor force is not possible or desirable. Public income supports for poor single mothers will always need to exist precisely because we value the work of mothers taking care of their children.

References

Gwendolyn Mink, *Welfare's End,* Cornell University Press, 1998.

P. Loprest and S. R. Zedlewski, November 1999, "Current and Former Welfare Recipients: How Do They Differ?" *Discussion Paper 17* (Washington: The Urban Institute).

Sandra Danziger, et al., *Barriers to the Employment of Welfare Recipients,* revised ed. 9/99, University of Michigan Press.

S. Jody Heymann and Alison Earle, "The Impact of Welfare Reform on Parents' Ability to Care for Their Children's Health," *American Journal of Public Health,* April 1999.

POSTSCRIPT

Has Welfare Reform Benefited the Poor?

There was considerable national agreement that the old welfare system had to be changed so that it would assist people in finding jobs and achieving self-sufficiency. Much success has been gained regarding this goal so far, but some state that numerous problems still remain. Abelda focuses on these problems, especially the inadequate supports for welfare-to-work mothers. The main problem, however, is the large number of poor-paying jobs for the bottom quarter of the labor force. If that problem were solved, the welfare-to-work program would be a great success. In fact, few would need welfare in the first place.

Michael B. Katz, in *The Undeserving Poor: From the War on Poverty to the War on Welfare* (Pantheon Books, 1989), traces the evolution of welfare policies in the United States from the 1960s through the 1980s. Charles Noble traces the evolution of welfare policies into the late 1990s and argues that the structure of the political economy has greatly limited the welfare state in *Welfare as We Knew It: A Political History of the American Welfare State* (Oxford University Press, 1997). Bruce S. Johnson criticizes welfare policies in the United States since the 1930s in *The Sixteen-Trillion-Dollar Mistake: How the U.S. Bungled Its National Priorities From the New Deal to the Present* (Columbia University Press, 2001). Mary Jo Bane and David T. Ellwood are critical of the organization and administration of welfare. See *Welfare Realities: From Rhetoric to Reform* (Harvard University Press, 1994). Marvin Olasky is critical of big government welfare programs and advocates a return to welfare by faith-based groups or local organizations in *Tough Love: Renewing American Compassion* (Free Press, 1996). Studies of the success of welfare-to-work programs include Daniel Friedlander and Gary Burtless, *Five Years After: The Long-Term Effects of Welfare-to-Work Programs* (Russell Sage Foundation, 1995) and Richard L. Koon, *Welfare Reform: Helping the Least Fortunate Become Less Dependent* (Garland Publishing, 1997). For discussions of welfare reform see Charles P. Cozic ed., *Welfare Reform* (Greenhaven Press, 1997); Greg J. Duncan and P. Lindsay Chase-Lansdale, eds., *For Better and for Worse: Welfare Reform and the Well-Being of Children and Families* (Russell Sage Foundation, 2001); Sanford F. Schram and Samuel H. Beer, eds., *Welfare Reform: A Race to the Bottom?* (Woodrow Wilson Center Press, 1999); and David E. Card and Rebecca M. Blank, eds., *Finding Jobs: Work and Welfare Reform* (Russell Sage Foundation, 2000). Two magazines with quality analyses of the welfare reform are the January/February 2001 issue of *Society* and the Summer 2001 issue of the *Brookings Review*. Two books that offer explanations as to why welfare provision is so minimal in the United States are Linda Gordon, *Pitied but Not Entitled: Single Mothers and the History of Welfare* (Free Press, 1994) and Joel F. Handler and Yeheskel Hasenfeld, *The Moral Construction of Poverty: Welfare Reform in America* (Sage Publications, 1991).

ISSUE 14

Is Competition the Solution to the Ills of Public Education?

YES: Chester E. Finn, Jr., Bruno V. Manno, and Gregg Vanourek, from "The Radicalization of School Reform," *Society* (May/June 2001)

NO: James P. Comer, from "Schools That Develop Children," *The American Prospect* (April 23, 2001)

ISSUE SUMMARY

YES: Chester E. Finn, Jr., president of the Thomas B. Fordham Foundation; Bruno V. Manno, senior program associate with the Annie E. Casey Foundation; and Gregg Vanourek, vice president of Charter School Division at K12 Educational Program, propose that relatively autonomous charter schools that are free from most state and local regulations and compete with other public schools will radically reform the education system and greatly improve public education.

NO: James P. Comer, professor of child psychology, contends that all organizational or curricular reforms will have very limited impacts on public education. The only reform that will substantially improve public education, he maintains, is to base all teaching on the principles of developmental psychology.

The quality of American public schooling has been criticized for several decades. Secretary of Education Richard Riley said in 1994 that some American schools are so bad that they "should never be called schools at all." The average school year in the United States is 180 days, while Japanese children attend school 240 days of the year. American schoolchildren score lower than the children of many other Western countries on certain standardized achievement tests. In 1983 the National Commission on Excellence in Education published *A Nation at Risk,* which argued that American education was a failure. Critics of *A Nation at Risk* maintain that the report produced very little evidence to support its thesis, but the public accepted it anyway. Currently, much of the public still thinks that the American school system is failing and needs to be fixed. The solution most frequently proposed today is some form of competition from charter schools to a voucher system.

Today 99 percent of children ages 6 to 13 are in school. In 1900 only about 7 percent of the appropriate age group graduated from high school, but in 1990, 86 percent did. Another success is the extraordinary improvement in the graduation rates for blacks since 1964, when it was 45 percent, to 1987, when it was 83 percent. Now this rate is almost at parity with white graduation rates. And over two-thirds of the present American population has a high school degree. No other nation comes close to these accomplishments. Nevertheless, most voices are very critical of American education.

American education reforms of the past 40 years have focused on quality and on what is taught. In the late 1950s the Soviet Union's launch of the first space satellite convinced the public of the need for more math and science in the curriculum. In the late 1960s and 1970s schools were criticized for rigid authoritarian teaching styles, and schools were made less structured. They became more open, participatory, and individualized in order to stimulate student involvement, creativity, and emotional growth. In the 1980s a crusade for the return to basics was triggered by the announcement that SAT scores had declined since the early 1960s. In the 1990s the continued problems of public schools led many to call for their restructuring by means of school choice, that is, competition.

The debate today is whether or not competition will finally make American schools succeed. The answer depends on whether or not the current structure of schools is the main reason why schools seem to be failing. Many other trends have also affected school performance, so the structure of the school system may not be the key to the problem. For example, many argue that curricula changes away from basics, new unstructured teaching techniques, and the decline of discipline in the classroom have contributed to perceived problems. Perhaps the quality of teachers needs to be raised. There is evidence that those who go into teaching score far lower on SATs than the average college student. In addition, societal trends outside the school may significantly impact school performance. Increasing breakdown of the family, more permissive child-rearing, the substantial decline in the amount of time that parents spend with children, and the increased exposure of children to television are trends that many believe are adversely affecting school performance.

In the selections that follow, two very different proposals for improving public education are advanced. Chester E. Finn, Jr., Bruno V. Manno, and Gregg Vanourek argue that school systems must be restructured to create competition. The specific form of restructuring that they propose is the creation of charter schools to compete with public schools. James P. Comer counters that all reforms to date—including charter schools—have and will fail. He contends that the only avenue to success is to utilize the scientific discipline of child development.

Chester E. Finn, Jr., Bruno V. Manno, and Gregg Vanourek

 **YES**

The Radicalization of School Reform

Much has changed in the education world since the United States was declared a "nation at risk" in 1983 by the National Commission on Excellence in Education. We've been reforming and reforming and reforming some more. In fact, "education reform" has itself become a growth industry, as we have devised a thousand innovations and spent billions to implement them. We have tinkered with class size, fiddled with graduation requirements, sought to end "social promotion," pushed technology into the schools, crafted new academic standards, revamped teacher training, bought different textbooks, and on and on.

Most of these alterations were launched with good will and the honest expectation that they would turn the situation around. But the problem with much of this reform churning is that the people who courageously addressed this issue in 1983 basically took for granted that the public school system as we knew it was the proper vehicle for making those changes and that its familiar machinery could produce better products if it were tuned up, adequately fueled and properly directed. In short, requisite changes would be made by school boards and superintendents, principals and teachers, federal and state education departments, and would be implemented either in time-honored system-wide fashion or through equally familiar "pilot" and "demonstration" programs.

Yet despite bushels of effort, barrels of decent intentions, and billions of dollars, most reform efforts have yielded meager dividends, with little changing for the better. Test scores are generally flat, and U.S. twelfth graders lag far behind their international counterparts in math and science, although our school expenditures are among the planet's highest. On the reports of the National Education Goals Panel which monitors progress toward the ambitious objectives set by President Bush and the governors in 1989, most years we see the number of arrows that point upward just about equaled by the number pointing down. Combining large budgets and weak performance, American schools can fairly be termed the least productive in the industrial world....

Our sense ... is that the chief explanation for their failure is the essential incrementalism of many of these "reforms"—i.e., the conventional reforms of the past two decades don't fundamentally alter our approach to public education in America. They do not replace the basic institutional arrangements, shift power, or rewrite the ground rules. That is acceptable if one believes the old structures remain sound. But that is not how we read the evidence. We judge that the traditional delivery system of U.S. public education is obsolete.

...In other words, the present school enterprise is not just doing poorly; it's incapable of doing much better because it is intellectually misguided, ideologically wrong-headed, and organizationally dysfunctional. The spread of this awareness we term the radicalization of school reform.

At day's end, this radicalization defends the principle and function of public education while arguing for a top-to-bottom makeover of its ground rules and institutional practices. It rejects the Hobson's choice that has long paralyzed serious education reform: the choice between a moribund government-run system and the chimera of privatization. We are, in fact, seeing signs of a new view of education change, one that welcomes decentralized control, entrepreneurial management, and grassroots initiatives within a framework of publicly defined standards and accountability.

Charter schools are the most prominent manifestation of the radicalization of school reform (though publicly financed vouchers are the most controversial). In fact, charters are the liveliest reform in American education today....

What, Exactly, Is a Charter School?

Few outside the charter movement are clear about the definition of a charter school. A workable starting point is that a charter school is an "independent public school of choice, freed from rules but accountable for results." A charter school is a new species, a hybrid, with important similarities to traditional public schools, some of the prized attributes of private schools—and crucial differences from both familiar forms.

As a public school, a charter school is open to all who wish to attend it (i.e., without regard to race, religion, or academic ability); paid for with tax dollars (no tuition charges); and accountable for its results—indeed, for its very existence—to an authoritative public body (such as a state or local school board) as well as to those who enroll (and teach) in it.

Charter schools are also different from standard-issue public schools. Most can be distinguished by four key features: they can be created by almost anyone; they are exempt from most state and local regulations, essentially autonomous in their operations; they are attended by youngsters whose families choose them and staffed by educators who are also there by choice; and they are liable to be closed for not producing satisfactory results.

Charter schools resemble private schools in two important particulars. First, their independence. Although answerable to outside authorities for their results (far more than most private schools), they are free to produce those results as they think best. They are self-governing institutions. They, like private schools, have wide ranging control over their own curriculum, instruction, staffing, budget, internal organization, calendar, schedule, and much more. The second similarity is that they are schools of choice. Nobody is assigned to attend (or teach in) a charter school. Parents select them for their children, much as they would a private school, albeit with greater risk because the new charter school typically has no track record.

The "charter" itself is a formal, legal document, best viewed as a contract between those who propose to launch and run a school and the public body empowered to authorize and monitor such schools. In charter-speak, the former are "operators" and the latter are "sponsors."

A charter operator may be a group of parents, a team of teachers, an existing community organization such as a hospital, boys and Girls Club, university or day care center, even (in several states) a private firm. School systems themselves can and occasionally do start charter schools. Sometimes an existing school seeks to secede from its local public system or, in a few jurisdictions, to convert from a tuition-charging non-sectarian private school to a tax-supported charter school. They apply for a charter and, if successful, are responsible for fulfilling its terms. The application spells out why the charter school is needed, how it will function, what results (academic and otherwise) are expected, and how these will be demonstrated. The operator may contract with someone else— including private companies or "education management organizations" (EMOs) —to manage the school, but the operator remains legally responsible to the sponsor.

The sponsor is ordinarily a state or local school board. In some states, public universities also have authority to issue charters, as do county school boards and city councils. If the sponsor deems an application solid, it will negotiate a more detailed charter (or contract) for a specified period of time, typically five years but sometimes as short as one or as long as fifteen.

During that period, the charter school has wide latitude to function as it sees fit. At least it does if its state enacted a strong charter law and did not hobble charter schools with too many of the constraints under which conventional public schools toil. Key features of the charter idea include waivers from most state and local regulations; fiscal and curricular autonomy; the ability to make its own personnel decisions; and responsibility for delivering the results that it pledged.

If a charter school succeeds, it can reasonably expect to get its charter renewed when the time comes. If it fails, it may be forced to shut down. And if it violates any of the unwaived laws, regulations, or community norms during the term of its charter, it may be shut down sooner.

Where Are We Today?

As of early 2001, there are about 2,100 charter schools, located in 34 states and the District of Columbia. Nearly 518,000 youngsters are enrolled in these schools, slightly more than 1 percent of U.S. public school students. Thirty-six states and the District of Columbia have enabling legislation for the charter schools and several more are considering it. Fifty-nine charter schools have, for various reasons, ceased operation.

Future growth in the number of charter schools depends in considerable part on state legislation, especially whether limits on the number of charters that can be granted by charter sponsors remain in effect. There is a heated debate now underway in several states (e.g., Kansas, Michigan) over raising these caps, while other states (e.g., Alaska, California, Massachusetts, Texas) have already loosened them due to demand-side pressures. Clearly, the fuel for charter growth will have to come either from amending state laws to lift those caps or from states without real limits (such as Arizona and Texas) or with high limits (like California and New Jersey).

Largely due to these statutory constraints (not lack of interest or demand since 70 percent of all charter schools have waiting lists) charter schools are distributed unevenly. Eleven states account for over 80 percent of them. Arizona alone had 352 in 1999–00; there were 239 in California, 173 in Michigan, 167 in Texas, and 111 in Florida. A large proportion of charters is concentrated in the three states of Arizona, California, and Michigan, but that percentage decreased from 79 percent in 1995–96 to 45 percent in 1999–00. . . .

Where Did Charter Schools Come From?

Most charter experts agree that the phrase "charter schools" was first used by the late Albert Shanker, longtime president of the American Federation of Teachers, in a 1988 speech to the National Press Club and a subsequent article. This is ironic, in view of the teacher unions' initial hostility and continuing skepticism to the charter movement. But it was not unusual for the brilliant and venturesome Shanker to suggest education reform concepts well in advance of their time.

Basing his vision on a school he had visited in Cologne, Germany, Shanker urged America to develop "a fundamentally different model of schooling that emerges when we rethink age-old assumptions—the kind of rethinking that is necessary to develop schools to reach the up to 80 percent of our youngsters who are failing in one way or another in the current system."

He contemplated an arrangement that would "enable any school or any group of teachers . . . within a school to develop a proposal for how they could better educate youngsters and then give them a 'charter' to implement that proposal." "All this," Shanker wrote, "would be voluntary."

> No teacher would have to participate and parents would choose whether or not to send their children to a charter school. . . . The school . . . would have to accept students who are representative of other students in the district or building in terms of ability and background. Charter schools also would have to conform to other civil rights guarantees. For its part, the school district would have to agree that so long as teachers continued to want to teach in the charter school and parents continued to send their children there and there was no precipitous decline in student achievement indicators, it would maintain the school for at least 5–10 years. Perhaps at the end of that period, the school could be evaluated to see the extent to which it met its goals, and the charter could be extended or revoked.

Shanker was echoed in a 1989 article by Ray Budde called "Education by Charter." Then a Minnesota legislator named Ember Reichgott Junge resolved to launch this idea in her state, the first to pass charter school legislation in 1991.

Yet that scrap of history doesn't do justice to the many tributaries that fed into the charter idea, both in the education environment and the wider culture. Within the world of education, these ideas include the hunger for higher standards for students and teachers; the realization that education quality would be judged by its results rather than its inputs (e.g., per pupil spending or class size) and its compliance with rules; the impulse to create new and different school designs that meet the needs of today's families; and the movement to give families more choices of schools.

In addition to changes in the education realm, developments in other domains of U.S. society helped clear the path for charter schools. In the corporate sector, traditional bureaucratic arrangements were being restructured, dispensing with middle management and top-down control. In the public sector, the effort to reinvent government was spawned. Both these sectors moved in the direction of a "tight-loose" management strategy: tightly controlled with respect to their goals and standards—the results they must achieve, and the information by which performance is tracked—but loose as to the *means* by which those results get produced.

Besides transformations in education, business, and government, other societal changes helped create a hospitable climate for charter schools. Beginning in the 1960s, there was the broad liberalization of American culture, what political scientist Hugh Heclo grandly terms an "awakening ... to a plurality of authenticities." Its elements have included for better or worse, the decline of traditional authority, the exaltation of personal freedom, the rise of tolerance as a supreme value, and the spread of pluralism, multiculturalism, and diversity....

Reinventing America's Schools

...Charter schools are the farthest-flung example today of a reinvented—a radicalized—public education. But it is important to bear in mind that they are part of a bigger idea: public education in which elected and appointed officials play a strategic rather than a functional role. Public support of schooling without governmental provision of schools....

Viewed from a few inches away, charter schools *do* represent sharp changes in the customary patterns and practices of today's public school systems, especially the large ones. But with more perspective, we readily observe that charter schools embody three familiar and time-tested features of American education.

First, they are rooted in their communities, the true essence of local control of education, not unlike the village schools of the early 19th century and the one-room schoolhouses that could be found across the land through most of the 20th century. They are much like America's original public schools in their local autonomy, their rootedness in communities, their accountability to parents, and their need to generate revenues by attracting and retaining families. Creatures of civil society as much as agencies of government, charter schools would have raised no eyebrows on Alexis de Tocqueville.

Second, charter schools have cousins in the K-12 family. Their DNA looks much the same under the education microscope as that of lab schools, magnet schools, site-managed schools, and special focus schools (e.g., art, drama, science), not to mention private and home schools. Much the same, but not identical. The Bronx High School of Science is selective, while charter schools are not. Hillel Academy and the Santa Maria Middle-School teach religion, while charter schools cannot. The Urban Magnet School of the Arts was probably designed by a downtown bureaucracy and most likely has carefully managed ethnic ratios in its student body, whereas most charter schools do not. Yet the similarities outweigh the differences.

Third, these new schools reveal a classic American response to a problem, challenge, or opportunity: institutional innovation and adaptation. In that respect, they resemble community colleges, which came into being (and spread rapidly and fruitfully) to meet education needs that conventional universities could not accommodate. As an organizational form, then, charter schools are not revolutionary. They are part of what we are and always have been as a nation.

James P. Comer

 **NO**

Schools That Develop Children

American schools are said to be failing. Like nineteenth-century medicine men, everybody is promoting everything, whether there is any evidence that it works or not. Over here we have vouchers, charters, privatization, longer school days, summer school, and merit pay. Over there we have the frequent testing of students, the testing of teachers, smaller class size, report cards on schools, and high-stakes accountability. And over here, a very special offer: student uniforms, flag-raising ceremonies every morning, the posting of the Ten Commandments on schoolhouse walls, and sophisticated diagnostic instruments to identify children at risk for acting violently—when many administrators and teachers can't even identify children who need glasses.

Most of these "cures"—traditional and reform—can't work or, at best, will have limited effectiveness. They all are based on flawed models. We will be able to create a successful system of education nationwide only when we base everything we do on what is known about how children and youths develop and learn. And this knowledge must be applied throughout the enterprise of education—in child rearing before school age, in schools and school districts, in schools of education, in state education departments, in legislatures, and everywhere else that personnel preparation takes place and school policy is made.

Given the purpose of education—to prepare students to become successful workers, family members, and citizens in a democratic society—even many "good" traditional schools, as measured by high test scores, are not doing their job adequately. But test scores alone are too narrow a measure. A good education should help students to solve problems encountered at work and in personal relationships, to take on the responsibility of caring for themselves and their families, to get along well in a variety of life settings, and to be motivated, contributing members of a democratic society. Such learning requires conditions that promote positive child-and-youth development.

Children begin to develop and learn through their first interactions with their consistent caretakers. And the eventual learning of basic academic skills—

From James P. Comer, "Schools That Develop Children," *The American Prospect*, vol. 12, no. 7 (April 23, 2001). Copyright © 2001 by *The American Prospect*. Reprinted by permission of *The American Prospect*, 5 Broad Street, Boston, MA 02109.

reading, writing, mathematics—and development are inextricably linked. Indeed, learning is an aspect of development and simultaneously facilitates it. Basic academic skills grow out of the fertile soil of overall development; they provide the platform for higher-order learning.

Through the early interactions, a bond is established that enables the child to imitate, identify with, and internalize the attitudes, values, and ways of their caretakers, and then those of other people around them. These people become important because they mediate (help make sense of and manage) a child's experiences and protect the child and help him or her to grow along the important developmental pathways—physical, social-interactive, psycho-emotional, ethical, linguistic, intellectual-cognitive, and eventually academic. The more mature thus help the less mature to channel potentially harmful aggressive energy into the energy of constructive learning, work, and play. But good early development is not a kind of inoculation that will protect a child for life. Future good development builds on the past and is mediated continuously by more mature people, step by step.

Understanding this process is no longer a matter of conjecture or the whining of "fuzzy-headed" social scientists or, as in my case, psychiatrists. Hard science—brain research—has confirmed the nature and critical importance of this interactive process. Without it children can lose the "sense"—the intelligence potential—they were born with. Children who have had positive developmental experiences before starting school acquire a set of beliefs, attitudes, and values—as well as social, verbal, and problem-solving skills, connections, and power—that they can use to succeed in school. They are the ones best able to elicit a positive response from people at school and to bond with them.

People at school can then influence children's development in ways similar to competent parents. To be successful, schools must create the conditions that make good development and learning possible: positive and powerful social and academic interactions between students and staff. When this happens, students gain social and academic competence, confidence, and comfort. Also, when parents and their social networks value school success and school experiences are positive and powerful, students are likely to acquire an internal desire to be successful in school and in life, and to gain and express the skills and behavior necessary to do so.

In order to realize the full potential of schools and students, we must create—and adequately support—a wide and deep pool of teachers and administrators who, in addition to having thorough knowledge of their disciplines, know how children develop generally and academically and how to support that development. They must be able to engage the families of students and the institutions and people in communities in a way that benefits student growth in school and society.

Vouchers and similar reforms currently being touted do not address these standards. They are simply changes in infrastructure, curriculum, and service delivery. They do not offer the potential for a nationwide transformation that a developmental focus does. And vouchers can reduce funds needed to improve the schools that must educate the majority of American children.

The Challenge of Change

The function of promoting good child-and-youth development and achievement was once served in our society through families and their social networks and through community life in small towns and rural areas. If students did not do well in school, they could leave, earn a living, still take care of themselves and their families, and become positive, contributing members of their communities. Despite massive and rapid scientific, technological, and social change, children have the same needs they always did: They must be protected and their development must be guided and supported by the people around them. They cannot rear themselves.

High mobility and modern communication created by technological change have undermined supports for child-and-youth development. Children experience many stimulating models of potentially troublesome behaviors—often in the absence of emotionally meaningful, influential adults. As a result, too many young people receive too little help in learning to manage feelings and act appropriately on the increased and more stimulating information they receive. This makes adequate social, psychological, and ethical development difficult.

Meanwhile, the new economy has made a high level of development and education a necessity for 90 percent of the population instead of the 20 percent we got by with half a century ago. Yet the rise of technology has led to an overvaluation of measured intelligence rather than an appreciation of overall development and the kind of intellectual growth that promotes strong problem-solving capacities.

Many successful people are inclined to attribute their situations to their own ability and effort—making them, in their minds, more deserving than less successful people. They ignore the support they received from families, networks of friends and kin, schools, and powerful others. They see no need for improved support of youth development. These misperceptions influence many education policies and practices.

Adequate support for development must be restored. And school is the first place this can happen. It is the common pathway for all children—the only place where a significant number of adults are working with young people in a way that enables them to call on family and community resources to support growth systematically and continually. And school is one of the few places where students, staff, and community can create environments in which to help young people achieve the necessary levels of maturity.

⁂

In the early 1980s, James Coleman, the late and respected University of Chicago sociologist, called what children gain from their parents and their networks "social capital." I do not like this term in discussing humans, but it is much used. Many poor children grow up in primary social networks that are marginal to mainstream institutions and transmit social capital that is different from that needed for school success. School requires mainstream social capital. In a

January 2000 *New York Times Magazine* article, James Traub said that "Coleman consistently pointed out that we now expect the school to provide all the child's human and social capital—an impossibility."

I agree that the school can't do it alone. But schools can do much more than what they now do. Most students, even those from very difficult social conditions, enter school with the potential needed to gain mainstream social capital. But traditional schools—and most reforms—fail such students.

Not long ago I asked approximately 300 experienced teachers and administrators from across the country if they'd taken a child development course; about half had. But when I asked how many had taken a school-based, supervised course in applied child development, only seven hands remained up. This lack of training is why many educators can't discuss the underlying factors involved in a playground fight or how to create social and academic experiences that motivate learning by tapping into the developmental needs and information level of today's students. Even fewer could construct environments conducive to overcoming racial, ethnic, income, and gender barriers.

But schools can succeed if they are prepared to embrace poor or marginalized families and to provide their children with conditions that promote mainstream skills. And when these conditions are continued throughout the school years, children from low-income backgrounds can do well in school; they will have better life chances. I was first convinced that this was the case for very personal reasons.

My mother was born into the family of a sharecropper in rural Mississippi in 1904. Her father was a good man, but he was killed by lightning when she was six years old. There were no family assistance programs, and a cruel, abusive stepfather came into their lives. He would not allow the children to go to school, and they lived under conditions of extreme poverty. At about eight years of age, as a barefoot child in the cotton fields, my mother realized that education was the way to a better life. When she was 16, she ran away to live with a sister in East Chicago, Indiana, with the hope of getting an education. But that was not possible.

When she had to leave school, my mother declared that if she ever had children, she would make certain they all got a good education. And then she set out—very, very, very carefully—to find my father, a person of like mind and purpose. Her caution paid off. My father, with six or seven years of education, worked as a steel mill laborer; and my mother, with no education, worked as a domestic. The two of them eventually sent the five of us to college, where we earned a total of 13 degrees.

Our family was enmeshed in an African-American church culture that provided the necessary social, ethical, and emotional context. My parents took us to everything educational they could afford; they talked and interacted with us in a way that encouraged learning and promoted overall development. Working for and respected by some of the most powerful people in our community, my mother observed and acquired mainstream success skills and made useful social contacts. Most of the summer jobs that helped us pay our way through college came from those contacts. And I enjoyed caviar brought home after parties before my working-class friends knew that it existed. Indeed, many European, black, and brown immigrants "made it" through similar experiences.

My three best friends were as intelligent as anybody in our family and in the predominantly white working- and middle-class school we attended. On the playground and the street corner, they could think as fast and as well as students who were more successful in school. But all three went on a downhill course: one died early from alcoholism, one spent time in jail, and one was in and out of mental institutions until he died recently. My parents had the same kind of jobs as their parents did, and we all attended the same school. Why the difference? It was the more useful developmental experience we were provided.

This notion was confirmed a few years ago when I visited my mother in the hospital. My spry, 80-plus-year-old first-grade teacher, Ms. Walsh, was a hospital volunteer. When she saw me, she threw her arms around me and said, "Oh, my little James." I was 55 years old going on six. She stepped back and said, "We just loved the Comer children. You came to school with those bright, eager eyes, and you got along so well with the other children, and you all were so smart," and more. She was describing the outcome of a home and community experience that provided adequate development and school readiness—social capital, if I must use the term.

I acknowledge that my parents, perhaps even my community and school, were not and are not typical. And again, the community conditions that supported family functioning, child rearing, and development to a much greater degree in the past are weaker today. The positive connections that the poor previously had with the more privileged in American society have decreased.

A few scattered programs make good education and life opportunities possible for poor and working-class children. Prep for Prep lays the groundwork for students to attend elite private schools; A Better Chance places students in good suburban schools; the Summer Study Skills Program prepares students for challenging academic courses. These "pull-out" programs provide the social capital, knowledge, and skills needed for mainstream participation. But they do not serve that large body of able young people, like my childhood friends, who are lost in elementary schools. Prepared and supported differently, such children could succeed.

Models of Development

The Yale Child Study Center's School Development Program has been working with schools for the past 32 years. The outcomes suggest that by basing what we do in schools (and in the education enterprise beyond schools) on what we know about how children develop and learn, we can provide most children with what they need to succeed in school and in life.

I recently visited the Samuel Gompers Elementary School in one of the poorest neighborhoods in Detroit, a school with 97 percent student poverty. The Yale program has been used in this school for the past six years. The neighborhood was a disaster; the school was a pearl. The students were lively, spontaneous, and engaged in their work at appropriate times, yet quiet and attentive when they were supposed to be. They got along well with one another and were eager to demonstrate their skills to their parents and teachers. Eighty percent of the students passed the 1999 fourth-grade Michigan Educational Assessment Program (MEAP) test in reading and science, and 100 percent passed in mathematics. In 2000 they achieved the highest MEAP test scores among elementary schools in their size category in the state. Why here? It is not a mystery.

❧

The Gompers school's success is related as much to the conditions that promote development and learning as it is to curriculum and instruction. How did it create these conditions and achieve good academic outcomes? The Yale program provided the conceptual and operational framework, child development-centered training for staff and parents, and very limited field support. The Skillman Foundation in Detroit, the Detroit Public Schools, Eastern Michigan University College of Education staff members, and parents (key members of the education enterprise) all came together to help the Gompers school and others provide the social capital the students need. The philosophy of the principal, Marilee Bylsma, is an important underpinning: "The school should be a safe haven for children, someplace that inspires learning." The staff, parents, and students did the work.

Committees, operations, and guidelines help schools create a culture of mutual respect and collaboration as well as social and academic programs that enable them to support students' development and learning. The transformation is gradual but frequent in schools that work to form good adult relationships. Good student relationships can follow.

At Gompers there is a 15-minute assembly every morning in which the students say the Pledge of Allegiance and make a school pledge. They sing a patriotic song and the school song. The custodian recognizes the "birthday boys and girls." (Message: It's everybody's school; we all play important roles.) The class with the best previous-day behavior gets "Gator points." Other recognitions take place. During the announcements, the students often discuss what's going on in their lives—the unexpected death of a teacher, problems in the neighborhood, and so on—and the adults help them learn to manage related feelings.

When the school basketball team lost a tournament they had expected to win, the principal gave much thought to how to help the players manage their disappointment and grow from the experience. The next morning, she talked about how important it is to try to be number one in all you do. But the team members should celebrate their effort, she explained—they came in third in a large field—and look forward to the next opportunity. The students can tell you that they participate in extracurricular activities to create a good community, a condition that they value.

Activities and interactions like those at Gompers can't be carried out very long, if at all, in a school where the staff members don't like, trust, or respect one another or the parents. And you can't just mandate these conditions.

Child development-oriented structures and processes must operate in a way that brings about these conditions.

❧

Initially, the Yale program's work was just in elementary schools, but it is now being carried out in many middle schools and high schools. Admittedly, middle school is difficult, and high school is even more so. That's when teens are "placing" themselves in the world and establishing their identity. Young people who place themselves and their futures in family and social networks that are dysfunctional are likely to perform in school in ways that lead to similar poor or marginal outcomes for themselves. Additionally, they are physically able to engage in adult behaviors. Only a half-century ago, many teens were married, working, and raising families; but in these more complex times, they often lack the experiences and resultant judgment, personal control, discipline, and problem solving skills needed to manage adult living.

In traditional high schools, teachers are often much more anchored in subject matter than in student development. Peer groups provide belonging and therefore become very powerful. They are sometimes positive, but too often are troublesome—it's the inexperienced and immature leading the inexperienced and immature. Aside from athletic coaches and teachers in the arts and other special areas, too few mature adults can interact with students in sustained and meaningful ways. These are powder keg conditions. And in communities where there are too few constructive supports for good development both inside and outside school, bad things happen—among staff, students, and parents.

In all schools—but particularly in low-income and nonmainstream communities—it is important for the staff to expose students to mainstream work as well as civic activities so that the connection between learning and later expectations is clear. School should help young people to learn what is needed for life success. Social and academic skills, attitudes, management of feelings, and other attributes needed to participate successfully in the mainstream can then be developed.

West Mecklenburg High School in Charlotte, North Carolina, received an additional 222 students in 1992 from a competing high school; its enrollment went from 1,144 to 1,366, precipitating a crisis. The school was almost evenly divided between whites and African Americans. Most of the students were children of blue-collar workers. Fourteen guns and many knives were confiscated during the first year, and parents, teachers, and students were concerned about their safety. Dennis Williams was assigned to the school as principal; Haywood Homsley, then the guidance counselor and coach, became the Yale program facilitator. Williams and Homsley began to focus on reducing intergroup tensions and creating a climate that enabled staff members to consider and respond to the developmental needs of the students.

The transformation was dramatic. On April 28, 1995, *The Leader,* Charlotte's major newspaper, highlighted the gains seen at West Mecklenburg since the Yale program was introduced: Scholastic Assessment Test (SAT) scores rose by an average of 16 points; the number of students who made the honor roll jumped 75 percent; the number of students enrolled in advanced courses increased 25 percent; and the average daily attendance rate for the year went from 89 percent to almost 94 percent. The process of change at West Mecklenberg was essentially the same as in elementary schools like Gompers except that the students themselves were more involved in the thinking and planning of the programs.

In the 1994–1995 academic year, West Mecklenberg was designated a "school of excellence" by the state of North Carolina for the high level at which it reached its benchmark goals, and it was the only high school of 11 in its district to attain this status. Despite the fact that there have been three principals since 1992, the school has held the "excellence" rating for three of the past five years.

Sustaining Gains

...Before a school can experience large, widespread, sustained achievement-test gains and adequately prepare students for adult life, it must be able to promote student development and manage its way to success, as Gompers, West Mecklenberg, and others have done. For this to be possible, we must produce large numbers of adequately prepared and supported staff. The policies and practices of the major players in the education enterprise nationwide—schools of education, legislators at all levels, state and federal departments of education, school districts, businesses—must be coherent by virtue of being based in child-and-youth development....

Few schools of education or university programs are presently prepared to work in this way. We should not rush into such programs without sound pilot and infrastructure work. But knowledge, organization, and support can be acquired. The states—who are legally responsible for educating America's children—should support such efforts. Most, largely through their departments of education, have been involved in standard-setting as well as in regulatory and oversight activities. They are involved in takeovers of failing districts. Yet they have little experience in—and no mechanisms for—correcting the complex problems involved in school improvement.

The decisions we make in the next few years will involve significant amounts of money and will lock us into helpful or harmful directions. A miracle quick fix is not possible. But if we today begin to mount programs that connect to practice and to policy what we know about how children develop and learn, we could soon be well on our way to having better-functioning systems of education in five years and good ones in a decade. If we continue to be guided by tradition, ideology, and power, however, we will reach a point of no return—one where too many young people are undereducated, acting out, and gradually undermining our economy and our democracy.

POSTSCRIPT

Is Competition the Solution to the Ills of Public Education?

Since school reformers have focused on school choice, the literature on it has mushroomed. The choice proposal first gained public attention in 1955 when Milton Friedman wrote about vouchers in "The Role of Government in Education," in Robert Solo, ed., *Economics and the Public Interest* (Rutgers University Press). More recent school choice advocates include David Harmer, *School Choice: Why We Need It, How We Get It* (Cato Institute, 1994); Daniel McGroarty, *Break These Chains: The Battle for School Choice* (Forum, 1996); Harry Brighouse, *School Choice and Social Justice* (Oxford University Press, 2000); Mark Schneider, *Choosing Schools: Consumer Choice and the Quality of American Schools* (Princeton University Press, 2000); Rosemary C. Salomone, *Visions of Schooling* (Yale University Press, 2000); and Philip A. Woods, *School Choice and Competition: Markets in the Public Interest* (Routledge, 1998). For a less partisan view see Joseph P. Viteritti, *Choosing Equality: School Choice, the Constitution, and Civil Society* (Brookings Institute Press, 1999). For comparisons of school choice with other reforms, see Margaret C. Wang and Herbert J. Walberg, eds., *School Choice or Best Systems: What Improves Education?* (L. Erlbaum Associates, 2001). Some advocates of choice would limit the choices in major ways. Timothy W. Young and Evans Clinchy, in *Choice in Public Education* (Teachers College Press, 1992), contend that there is already considerable choice in public education in that there are alternative and magnet schools, intradistrict choice plans, "second chance" options, postsecondary options, and interdistrict choice plans. Research shows that these options work well, so the authors recommend that they be expanded. They argue against a voucher system, which they feel will divert badly needed financial resources from the public schools to give further support to parents who can already afford private schools. In the end they promote a limited choice plan rather than a fully free market plan. For another proposal of a limited choice plan, see Peter W. Cookson, Jr., *School Choice: The Struggle for the Soul of American Education* (Yale University Press, 1994).

Important critiques of school choice include Albert Shanker and Bella Rosenberg, *Politics, Markets, and America's Schools: The Fallacies of Private School Choice* (American Federation of Teachers, 1991); Jeffrey R. Henig, *Rethinking School Choice: Limits of the Market Metaphor* (Princeton University Press, 1994); Kevin B. Smith and Kenneth J. Meier, *The Case Against School Choice: Politics, Markets, and Fools* (M. E. Sharpe, 1995); and Judith Pearson, *Myths of Educational Choice* (Praeger, 1993). Jerome J. Hanus and Peter W. Cookson, Jr., debate the issue of vouchers in *Choosing Schools: Vouchers and American Education* (American University Press, 1996).

ISSUE 15

Should Doctor-Assisted Suicide Be Legalized for the Terminally Ill?

YES: Marcia Angell, from "The Supreme Court and Physician-Assisted Suicide: The Ultimate Right," *The New England Journal of Medicine* (January 2, 1997)

NO: Paul R. McHugh, from "The Kevorkian Epidemic," *The American Scholar* (Winter 1997)

ISSUE SUMMARY

YES: Marcia Angell, executive editor of *The New England Journal of Medicine*, presents medical and ethical reasons justifying doctor-assisted suicide, including that it honors the autonomy of the patient and is merciful in cases when pain cannot be adequately relieved.

NO: Paul R. McHugh, director of the Department of Psychiatry and Behavioral Sciences at the Johns Hopkins University School of Medicine, argues that sick people who wish to kill themselves suffer from verifiable mental illness and that, since they can be treated for their pain and depressed state, physicians cannot be allowed to kill them.

According to a recent anonymous survey of almost 2,000 doctors who regularly care for dying patients, 6 percent of physicians say they have assisted patient suicides. Only 18 percent had received such requests, and one-third of these had given the requested help. Most physicians who admitted assisting in patients' deaths said they did it only once or twice, so the practice seems to be fairly uncommon. One-third of all doctors surveyed said that they would write prescriptions for deadly doses of drugs in certain cases if the law allowed, and one-quarter would give lethal injections if it were legal. *Officially* the medical community is adamantly opposed to doctor-assisted suicide.

The issue of doctor-assisted suicide is quite complex and confusing. Part of the confusion relates to definitions. Doctor-assisted suicide does not refer to a doctor injecting a patient with a lethal drug nor assisting the suicide of someone who is not terminally ill. The most common method of doctor-assisted suicide is for the doctor to prescribe a drug and then telling the patient how much of it would be lethal. The patient then administers the drug himself or herself. Doctor-assisted suicide lies between letting patients die by removing life-support systems at their request and euthanasia. The first is legal according to the Supreme Court's 1990 decision in *Cruzan v. Director, Missouri Department of Health,* and the latter is considered murder. So the question arises whether doctor-assisted suicide is more like the legal removal of life-support systems or the illegal euthanasia.

The legal, social, and moral issues involved add to the complexity and confusion. First, doctor-assisted suicide is a hotly contested legal issue governed by laws and court decisions. The legal issue was somewhat clarified by the Supreme Court on June 26, 1997, when it unanimously decided that terminally ill people have no constitutional right to die and, therefore, no right to doctor-assisted suicide. Thus, the Supreme Court will not declare invalid state laws that prohibit this practice.

Second, doctor-assisted suicide is a complex social issue with very active groups championing both sides of the debate. Medical technologies have advanced to the point that death can be postponed for a long time after the mind has ceased to function or after the quality of life has declined deeply into the negative. This produces countless situations in which people should not go on living in the judgment of most people. But what should be done for them? The situation for some may suggest that they should be helped to die. How should such a decision be made and how should it be carried out? The patient, of course, should make such decisions, if such decisions are even allowed. Painful ambiguity still remains for those who cannot make intelligent decisions and for those who have chosen to die but may not be competent to make that decision. Furthermore, what are loved ones to do when consulted by the patient or when the patient is no longer capable of making these decisions? The high medical costs for prolonging the lives of some of these very ill people may affect loved ones' decisions regarding the care or life extension of the patient and make the purity of their motives questionable. But costs cannot be totally ignored either.

Third, doctor-assisted suicide is a divisive moral issue. There is no consensus on the norms that should apply to these situations. A strong norm against euthanasia is the belief that stopping someone's life is murder even if that person wants to die. Some people apply the same norm to assisted suicide because they see little difference between injecting a patient with a lethal drug and supplying the patient with the drug to ingest. On the other side, many believe that love and mercy demand assisted suicide or even euthanasia for the terminally ill when great suffering accompanies all other options.

The following selections provide strong arguments for and against doctor-assisted suicide. Marcia Angell contends that the relieving of suffering and honoring the patient's wishes are the overriding concerns, which fully justify the practice in light of the absence of compelling arguments to the contrary. Paul R. McHugh, citing the case of Dr. Jack Kevorkian, maintains that the patients that Kevorkian helped to die were all suffering from depression and that Kevorkian should have advised them to get competent psychological help, which would have restored their desire to live.

Marcia Angell  **YES**

The Supreme Court and Physician-Assisted Suicide— The Ultimate Right

T he U.S. Supreme Court will decide later this year whether to let stand decisions by two appeals courts permitting doctors to help terminally ill patients commit suicide.[1] The Ninth and Second Circuit Courts of Appeals last spring held that state laws in Washington and New York that ban assistance in suicide were unconstitutional as applied to doctors and their dying patients.[2,3] If the Supreme Court lets the decisions stand, physicians in 12 states, which include about half the population of the United States, would be allowed to provide the means for terminally ill patients to take their own lives, and the remaining states would rapidly follow suit. Not since *Roe* v. *Wade* has a Supreme Court decision been so fateful.

The decision will culminate several years of intense national debate, fueled by a number of highly publicized events. Perhaps most important among them is Dr. Jack Kevorkian's defiant assistance in some 44 suicides since 1990, to the dismay of many in the medical and legal establishments, but with substantial public support, as evidenced by the fact that three juries refused to convict him even in the face of a Michigan statute enacted for that purpose. Also since 1990, voters in three states have considered ballot initiatives that would legalize some form of physician-assisted dying, and in 1994 Oregon became the first state to approve such a measure.[4] (The Oregon law was stayed pending a court challenge.) Several surveys indicate that roughly two thirds of the American public now support physician-assisted suicide,[5,6] as do more than half the doctors in the United States,[6,7] despite the fact that influential physicians' organizations are opposed. It seems clear that many Americans are now so concerned about the possibility of a lingering, high-technology death that they are receptive to the idea of doctors' being allowed to help them die.

In this editorial I will explain why I believe the appeals courts were right and why I hope the Supreme Court will uphold their decisions. I am aware that this is a highly contentious issue, with good people and strong arguments on both sides. The American Medical Association (AMA) filed an amicus brief opposing the legalization of physician-assisted suicide,[8] and the Massachusetts

Medical Society, which owns the *Journal,* was a signatory to it. But here I speak for myself not the *Journal* or the Massachusetts Medical Society. The legal aspects of the case have been well discussed elsewhere, to me most compellingly in Ronald Dworkin's essay in the *New York Review of Books.*[9] I will focus primarily on the medical and ethical aspects.

I begin with the generally accepted premise that one of the most important ethical principles in medicine is respect for each patient's autonomy, and that when this principle conflicts with others, it should almost always take precedence. This premise is incorporated into our laws governing medical practice and research, including the requirement of informed consent to any treatment. In medicine, patients exercise their self-determination most dramatically when they ask that life-sustaining treatment be withdrawn. Although others may sometimes consider the request ill-founded, we are bound to honor it if the patient is mentally competent—that is, if the patient can understand the nature of the decision and its consequences.

A second starting point is the recognition that death is not fair and is often cruel. Some people die quickly, and others die slowly but peacefully. Some find personal or religious meaning in the process, as well as an opportunity for a final reconciliation with loved ones. But others, especially those with cancer, AIDS, or progressive neurologic disorders, may die by inches and in great anguish, despite every effort of their doctors and nurses. Although nearly all pain can be relieved, some cannot, and other symptoms, such as dyspnea, nausea, and weakness, are even more difficult to control. In addition, dying sometimes holds great indignities and existential suffering. Patients who happen to require some treatment to sustain their lives, such as assisted ventilation or dialysis, can hasten death by having the life-sustaining treatment withdrawn, but those who are not receiving life-sustaining treatment may desperately need help they cannot now get.

If the decisions of the appeals courts are upheld, states will not be able to prohibit doctors from helping such patients to die by prescribing a lethal dose of a drug and advising them on its use for suicide. State laws barring euthanasia (the administration of a lethal drug by a doctor) and assisted suicide for patients who are not terminally ill would not be affected. Furthermore, doctors would not be *required* to assist in suicide; they would simply have that option. Both appeals courts based their decisions on constitutional questions. This is important, because it shifted the focus of the debate from what the majority would approve through the political process, as exemplified by the Oregon initiative, to a matter of fundamental rights, which are largely immune from the political process. Indeed, the Ninth Circuit Court drew an explicit analogy between suicide and abortion, saying that both were personal choices protected by the Constitution and that forbidding doctors to assist would in effect nullify these rights. Although states could regulate assisted suicide, as they do abortion, they would not be permitted to regulate it out of existence.

It is hard to quarrel with the desire of a greatly suffering, dying patient for a quicker, more humane death or to disagree that it may be merciful to help bring that about. In those circumstances, loved ones are often relieved when death finally comes, as are the attending doctors and nurses. As the Second

Circuit Court said, the state has no interest in prolonging such a life. Why, then, do so many people oppose legalizing physician-assisted suicide in these cases? There are a number of arguments against it, some stronger than others, but I believe none of them can offset the overriding duties of doctors to relieve suffering and to respect their patients' autonomy. Below I list several of the more important arguments against physician-assisted suicide and discuss why I believe they are in the last analysis unpersuasive.

Assisted suicide is a form of killing, which is always wrong. In contrast, withdrawing life-sustaining treatment simply allows the disease to take its course. There are three methods of hastening the death of a dying patient: withdrawing life-sustaining treatment, assisting suicide, and euthanasia. The right to stop treatment has been recognized repeatedly since the 1976 case of Karen Ann Quinlan[10] and was affirmed by the U.S. Supreme Court in the 1990 *Cruzan* decision[11] and the U.S. Congress in its 1990 Patient Self-Determination Act.[12] Although the legal underpinning is the right to be free of unwanted bodily invasion, the purpose of hastening death was explicitly acknowledged. In contrast, assisted suicide and euthanasia have not been accepted; euthanasia is illegal in all states, and assisted suicide is illegal in most of them.

Why the distinctions? Most would say they turn on the doctor's role: whether it is passive or active. When life-sustaining treatment is withdrawn, the doctor's role is considered passive and the cause of death is the underlying disease, despite the fact that switching off the ventilator of a patient dependent on it looks anything but passive and would be considered homicide if done without the consent of the patient or a proxy. In contrast, euthanasia by the injection of a lethal drug is active and directly causes the patient's death. Assisting suicide by supplying the necessary drugs is considered somewhere in between, more active than switching off a ventilator but less active than injecting drugs, hence morally and legally more ambiguous.

I believe, however, that these distinctions are too doctor-centered and not sufficiently patient-centered. We should ask ourselves not so much whether the doctor's role is passive or active but whether the *patient's* role is passive or active. From that perspective, the three methods of hastening death line up quite differently. When life-sustaining treatment is withdrawn from an incompetent patient at the request of a proxy or when euthanasia is performed, the patient may be utterly passive. Indeed, either act can be performed even if the patient is unaware of the decision. In sharp contrast, assisted suicide, by definition, cannot occur without the patient's knowledge and participation. Therefore, it must be active—that is to say, voluntary. That is a crucial distinction, because it provides an inherent safeguard against abuse that is not present with the other two methods of hastening death. If the loaded term "kill" is to be used, it is not the doctor who kills, but the patient. Primarily because euthanasia can be performed without the patient's participation, I oppose its legalization in this country.

Assisted suicide is not necessary. All suffering can be relieved if care givers are sufficiently skillful and compassionate, as illustrated by the hospice movement. I have no doubt that if expert palliative care were available to everyone who needed it, there would be few requests for assisted suicide. Even under the best of circumstances, however, there will always be a few patients whose suffering simply cannot be adequately alleviated. And there will be some who would prefer suicide to any other measures available, including the withdrawal of life-sustaining treatment or the use of heavy sedation. Surely, every effort should be made to improve palliative care, as I argued 15 years ago,[13] but when those efforts are unavailing and suffering patients desperately long to end their lives, physician-assisted suicide should be allowed. The argument that permitting it would divert us from redoubling our commitment to comfort care asks these patients to pay the penalty for our failings. It is also illogical. Good comfort care and the availability of physician-assisted suicide are no more mutually exclusive than good cardiologic care and the availability of heart transplantation.

Permitting assisted suicide would put us on a moral "slippery slope." Although in itself assisted suicide might be acceptable, it would lead inexorably to involuntary euthanasia. It is impossible to avoid slippery slopes in medicine (or in any aspect of life). The issue is how and where to find a purchase. For example, we accept the right of proxies to terminate life-sustaining treatment, despite the obvious potential for abuse, because the reasons for doing so outweigh the risks. We hope our procedures will safeguard patients. In the case of assisted suicide, its voluntary nature is the best protection against sliding down a slippery slope, but we also need to ensure that the request is thoughtful and freely made. Although it is possible that we may someday decide to legalize voluntary euthanasia under certain circumstances or assisted suicide for patients who are not terminally ill, legalizing assisted suicide for the dying does not in itself make these other decisions inevitable. Interestingly, recent reports from the Netherlands, where both euthanasia and physician-assisted suicide are permitted, indicate that fears about a slippery slope there have not been borne out.[14–16]

Assisted suicide would be a threat to the economically and socially vulnerable. The poor disabled, and elderly might be coerced to request it. Admittedly, overburdened families or cost-conscious doctors might pressure vulnerable patients to request suicide, but similar wrongdoing is at least as likely in the case of withdrawing life-sustaining treatment, since that decision can be made by proxy. Yet, there is no evidence of widespread abuse. The Ninth Circuit Court recalled that it was feared *Roe* v. *Wade* would lead to coercion of poor and uneducated women to request abortions, but that did not happen. The concern that coercion is more likely in this era of managed care, although understandable, would hold suffering patients hostage to the deficiencies of our health care system. Unfortunately, no human endeavor is immune to abuses. The question is not whether a perfect system can be devised, but whether abuses are likely to be sufficiently rare to be offset by the benefits to patients who otherwise would be condemned to face the end of their lives in protracted agony.

Depressed patients would seek physician-assisted suicide rather than help for their depression. Even in the terminally ill, a request for assisted suicide might signify treatable depression, not irreversible suffering. Patients suffering greatly at the end of life may also be depressed, but the depression does not necessarily explain their decision to commit suicide or make it irrational. Nor is it simple to diagnose depression in terminally ill patients. Sadness is to be expected, and some of the vegetative symptoms of depression are similar to the symptoms of terminal illness. The success of antidepressant treatment in these circumstances is also not ensured. Although there are anecdotes about patients who changed their minds about suicide after treatment,[17] we do not have good studies of how often that happens or the relation to antidepressant treatment. Dying patients who request assisted suicide and seem depressed should certainly be strongly encouraged to accept psychiatric treatment, but I do not believe that competent patients should be *required* to accept it as a condition of receiving assistance with suicide. On the other hand, doctors would not be required to comply with all requests; they would be expected to use their judgment, just as they do in so many other types of life-and-death decisions in medical practice.

Doctors should never participate in taking life. If there is to be assisted suicide, doctor must not be involved. Although most doctors favor permitting assisted suicide under certain circumstances, many who favor it believe that doctors should not provide the assistance.[6,7] To them, doctors should be unambiguously committed to life (although most doctors who hold this view would readily honor a patient's decision to have life-sustaining treatment withdrawn). The AMA, too, seems to object to physician-assisted suicide primarily because it violates the profession's mission. Like others, I find that position too abstract.[18] The highest ethical imperative of doctors should be to provide care in whatever way best serves patients' interests, in accord with each patient's wishes, not with a theoretical commitment to preserve life no matter what the cost in suffering.[19] If a patient requests help with suicide and the doctor believes the request is appropriate, requiring someone else to provide the assistance would be a form of abandonment. Doctors who are opposed in principle need not assist, but they should make their patients aware of their position early in the relationship so that a patient who chooses to select another doctor can do so. The greatest harm we can do is to consign a desperate patient to unbearable suffering—or force the patient to seek out a stranger like Dr. Kevorkian. Contrary to the frequent assertion that permitting physician-assisted suicide would lead patients to distrust their doctors, I believe distrust is more likely to arise from uncertainty about whether a doctor will honor a patient's wishes.

Physician-assisted suicide may occasionally be warranted, but it should remain illegal. If doctors risk prosecution, they will think twice before assisting with suicide. This argument wrongly shifts the focus from the patient to the doctor. Instead of reflecting the condition and wishes of patients, assisted suicide would reflect the courage and compassion of their doctors. Thus, patients with doctors like Timothy Quill, who described in a 1991 *Journal* article how he helped a patient take her life,[20] would get the help they need and want, but similar patients with less steadfast doctors would not. That makes no sense.

People do not need assistance to commit suicide. With enough determination, they can do it themselves. This is perhaps the cruelest of the arguments against physician-assisted suicide. Many patients at the end of life are, in fact, physically unable to commit suicide on their own. Others lack the resources to do so. It has sometimes been suggested that they can simply stop eating and drinking and kill themselves that way. Although this method has been described as peaceful under certain conditions,[21] no one should count on that. The fact is that this argument leaves most patients to their suffering. Some, usually men, manage to commit suicide using violent methods. Percy Bridgman, a Nobel laureate in physics who in 1961 shot himself rather than die of metastatic cancer, said in his suicide note, "It is not decent for Society to make a man do this to himself."[22]

My father, who knew nothing of Percy Bridgman, committed suicide under similar circumstances. He was 81 and had metastatic prostate cancer. The night before he was scheduled to be admitted to the hospital, he shot himself. Like Bridgman, he thought it might be his last chance. At the time, he was not in extreme pain, nor was he close to death (his life expectancy was probably longer than six months). But he was suffering nonetheless—from nausea and the side effects of antiemetic agents, weakness, incontinence, and hopelessness. Was he depressed? He would probably have freely admitted that he was, but he would have thought it beside the point. In any case, he was an intensely private man who would have refused psychiatric care. Was he overly concerned with maintaining control of the circumstances of his life and death? Many people would say so, but that was the way he was. It is the job of medicine to deal with patients as they are, not as we would like them to be.

I tell my father's story here because it makes an abstract issue very concrete. If physician-assisted suicide had been available, I have no doubt my father would have chosen it. He was protective of his family, and if he had felt he had the choice, he would have spared my mother the shock of finding his body. He did not tell her what he planned to do, because he knew she would stop him. I also believe my father would have waited if physician-assisted suicide had been available. If patients have access to drugs they can take when they choose, they will not feel they must commit suicide early, while they are still able to do it on their own. They would probably live longer and certainly more peacefully, and they might not even use the drugs.

Long before my father's death, I believed that physician-assisted suicide ought to be permissible under some circumstances, but his death strengthened my conviction that it is simply a part of good medical care—something to be done reluctantly and sadly, as a last resort, but done nonetheless. There should be safeguards to ensure that the decision is well considered and consistent, but they should not be so daunting or violative of privacy that they become obstacles instead of protections. In particular, they should be directed not toward reviewing the reasons for an autonomous decision, but only toward ensuring that the decision is indeed autonomous. If the Supreme Court upholds the decisions of the appeals courts, assisted suicide will not be forced on either patients or doctors, but it will be a choice for those patients who need it and those doctors willing to help. If, on the other hand, the Supreme Court overturns the lower courts' decisions, the issue will continue to be grappled with state by state, through the political process. But sooner or later, given the need and the widespread public support, physician-assisted suicide will be demanded of a compassionate profession.

References

1. Greenhouse L. High court to say if the dying have a right to suicide help. New York Times. October 2, 1996:A1.
2. Compassion in Dying v. Washington, 79 F.3d 790 (9th Cir. 1996).
3. Quill v. Vacco, 80 F.3d 716 (2d Cir. 1996).
4. Annas GJ. Death by prescription—the Oregon initiative. N Engl J Med 1994;331:1240-3.
5. Blendon RJ, Szalay US, Knox RA. Should physicians aid their patients in dying? The public perspective. JAMA 1992;267:2658-62.
6. Bachman JG, Alcser KH, Doukas DJ, Lichtenstein RL, Corning AD, Brody H. Attitudes of Michigan physicians and the public toward legalizing physician-assisted suicide and voluntary euthanasia. N Engl J Med 1996;334:303-9.
7. Lee MA, Nelson HD, Tilden VP, Ganzini L, Schmidt TA, Tolle SW. Legalizing assisted suicide—views of physicians in Oregon. N Engl J Med 1996;334:310-5.
8. Gianelli DM. AMA to court: no suicide aid. American Medical News. November 25, 1996:1, 27, 28.
9. Dworkin R. Sex, death, and the courts. New York Review of Books. August 8, 1996.
10. In re: Quinlan, 70 N.J. 10, 355 A.2d 647 (1976).
11. Cruzan v. Director, Missouri Department of Health, 497 U.S. 261, 110 S.Ct. 2841 (1990).
12. Omnibus Budget Reconciliation Act of 1990, P.L. 101-508, sec. 4206 and 4751, 104 Stat. 1388, 1388-115, and 1388-204 (classified respectively at 42 U.S.C. 1395cc(f) (Medicare) and 1396a(w) (Medicaid) (1994).
13. Angell M. The quality of mercy. N Engl J Med 1982;306:98-9.
14. van der Maas PJ, van der Wal G, Haverkate I, et al. Euthanasia, physician-assisted suicide, and other medical practices involving the end of life in the Netherlands, 1990–1995. N Engl J Med 1996;335:1699-705.
15. van der Wal G, van der Maas PJ, Bosma JM, et al. Evaluation of the notification procedure for physician-assisted death in the Netherlands. N Engl J Med 1996;335:1706-11.
16. Angell M. Euthanasia in the Netherlands—good news or bad? N Engl J Med 1996;335:1676-8.
17. Chochinov HM, Wilson KG, Enns M, et al.Desire for death in the terminally ill. Am J Psychiatry 1995;152:1185-91.
18. Cassel CK, Meier DE. Morals and moralism in the debate over euthanasia and assisted suicide. N Engl J Med 1990;323:750-2.
19. Angell M. Doctors and assisted suicide. Ann R Coll Physicians Surg Can 1991;24:493-4.
20. Quill TE. Death and dignity—a case of individualized decision making. N Engl J Med 1991;324:691-4.
21. Lynn J, Childress JF. Must patients always be given food and water? Hastings Cent Rep 1983;13(5):17-21.
22. Nuland SB. How we die. New York: Alfred A. Knopf, 1994:152.

NO ↵

Paul R. McHugh

The Kevorkian Epidemic

Dr. Jack Kevorkian of Detroit has been in the papers most days this past summer and autumn [1997] helping sick people kill themselves. He is said to receive hundreds of calls a week. Although his acts are illegal by statute and common law in Michigan, no one stops him. Many citizens, including members of three juries, believe he means well, perhaps thinking: Who knows? Just maybe, we ourselves shall need his services some day.

To me it looks like madness from every quarter. The patients are mad by definition in that they are suicidally depressed and demoralized; Dr. Kevorkian is "certifiable" in that his passions render him, as the state code specifies, "dangerous to others"; and the usually reliable people of Michigan are confused and anxious to the point of incoherence by terrors of choice that are everyday issues for doctors. These three disordered parties have converged as a triad of host-agent-environment to interact synergistically in provoking a local epidemic of premature death.

Let me begin with the injured hosts of this epidemic, the patients mad by definition. At this writing, more than forty, as best we know, have submitted to Dr. Kevorkian's deadly charms. They came to him with a variety of medical conditions: Alzheimer's disease, multiple sclerosis, chronic pain, amyotrophic lateral sclerosis, cancer, drug addiction, and more. These are certainly disorders from which anyone might seek relief. But what kind of relief do patients with these conditions usually seek when they do not have a Dr. Kevorkian to extinguish their pain?

Both clinical experience and research on this question are extensive—and telling. A search for death does not accompany most terminal or progressive diseases. Pain-ridden patients customarily call doctors for remedies, not for termination of life. Physical incapacity, as with advanced arthritis, does not generate suicide. Even amyotrophic lateral sclerosis, or Lou Gehrig's disease, a harrowing condition I shall describe presently, is not associated with increased suicide amongst its sufferers. Most doctors learn these facts as they help patients and their families burdened by these conditions.

But we don't have to rely solely upon the testimonies of experienced physicians. Recently cancer patients in New England were asked about their attitudes toward death. The investigators—apparently surprised to discover a will to live when they expected to find an urge to die—reported in the *Lancet* (vol. 347, pp. 1805–1810, 1996) two striking findings. First, that cancer patients enduring pain were not inclined to want euthanasia or physician-assisted suicide. In fact, "patients actually experiencing pain were more likely to find euthanasia or physician-assisted suicide unacceptable." Second, those patients inclined toward suicide—whether in pain or not—were suffering from depression. As the investigators noted: "These data indicate a conflict between attitudes and possible practices related to euthanasia and physician-assisted suicide. These *interventions* were approved of for terminally ill patients with unremitting pain, but these are not the patients most likely to request such *interventions*.... There is *some* concern that with legislation of euthanasia or physician-assisted suicide non-psychiatric physicians, who generally have a poor ability to detect and treat depression, may allow life-ending *interventions* when treatment of depression may be more appropriate." (Italics added to identify mealymouthed expressions: *interventions* means homicides, and *some* means that we investigators should stay cool in our concerns—after all, it's not we who are dying.)

None of this is news to psychiatrists who have studied suicides associated with medical illnesses. Depression, the driving force in most cases, comes in two varieties: symptomatic depression found as a feature of particular diseases —that is, as one of the several symptoms of that disease; and demoralization, the common state of mind of people in need of guidance for facing discouraging circumstances alone. Both forms of depression render patients vulnerable to feelings of hopelessness that, if not adequately confronted, may lead to suicide.

Let me first concentrate on the symptomatic depressions because an understanding of them illuminates much of the problem. By the term *symptomatic,* psychiatrists mean that with some physical diseases suicidal depression is one of the condition's characteristic features. Careful students of these diseases come to appreciate that this variety of depression is not to be accepted as a natural feeling of discouragement provoked by bad circumstances—that is, similar to the down-hearted state of, say, a bankrupt man or a grief-stricken widow. Instead the depression we are talking about here, with its beclouding of judgment, sense of misery, and suicidal inclinations, is a symptom identical in nature to the fevers, pains, or loss of energy that are signs of the disease itself....

The problematic nature of symptomatic depression goes beyond the painful state of mind of the patient. Other observers—such as family members and physicians—may well take the depressive's disturbed, indeed insane, point of view as a proper assessment of his or her situation. It was this point that Huntington, long before the time of modern anti-depressant treatment, wished to emphasize by identifying it as an insanity. He knew that failure to diagnose this feature will lead to the neglect of efforts to treat the patient properly and to protect him or her from suicide until the symptom remits.

Such neglect is a crucial blunder, because, whether the underlying condition is Huntington's disease, Alzheimer's disease, MS, or something else, modern anti-depressant treatment is usually effective at relieving the mood disorder and restoring the patient's emotional equilibrium. In Michigan and in Holland, where physician-assisted suicide also takes place, these actions to hasten death are the ultimate neglect of patients with symptomatic depression; they are, really, a form of collusion with insanity.

The diagnosis of symptomatic depression is not overly difficult if its existence is remembered and its features systematically sought. But many of its characteristics—such as its capacity to provoke bodily pains—are not known to all physicians. The fact that such depression occurs in dire conditions, such as Huntington's disease, may weigh against its prompt diagnosis and treatment. Again and again, kindly intended physicians presume that a depression "makes sense"—given the patient's situation—and overlook the stereotypic signs of the insanity. They presume justifiable demoralization and forget the pharmacologically treatable depressions.

Over the last decade, at least among psychiatrists, the reality of symptomatic depressions has become familiar and treatment readiness has become the rule. Yet not all sick patients with life-threatening depression have symptomatic depressions. Many physically ill patients are depressed for perfectly understandable reasons, given the grueling circumstances of their progressive and intractable disease. Just as any misfortune can provoke grief and anxiety, so can awareness of loss of health and of a closed future.

Well-titled *demoralization,* this depression, too, has a number of attributes. It waxes and wanes with experiences and events, comes in waves, and is worse at certain times—such as during the night, when contemplating future discomforts and burdens, and when the patient is alone or uninstructed about the benefits that modern treatments can bring him.

In contrast to the symptomatic depressions that run their own course almost independent of events, demoralization is sensitive to circumstances and especially to the conduct of doctors toward the patient. Companionship, especially that which provides understanding and clear explanations of the actions to be taken in opposing disease and disability, can be immensely helpful in overcoming this state and sustaining the patient in a hopeful frame of mind....

This is the point: Depression, both in the form of a symptomatic mental state and in the form of demoralization, is the result of illness and circumstances combined and is treatable just as are other effects of illness. These treatments are the everyday skills of many physicians, but particularly of those physicians who are specialists in these disorders and can advance the treatments most confidently.

Most suicidally depressed patients are not rational individuals who have weighed the balance sheet of their lives and discovered more red than black ink. They are victims of altered attitudes about themselves and their situation, which cause powerful feelings of hopelessness to abound. Doctors can protect them from these attitudes by providing information, guidance, and support all along the way. Dr. Kevorkian, however, trades upon the vulnerabilities and mental disorders of these patients and in so doing makes a mockery of medicine as a discipline of informed concern for patients.

Let us turn to Dr. Kevorkian, the agent of this epidemic in Michigan, and consider why I think that he is "certifiably" insane, by which I mean that he suffers from a mental condition rendering him dangerous to others.

Without question, Dr. Kevorkian has proven himself dangerous, having participated in killing more than forty people already, with no end in sight....

The question is whether his behavior is a product of a mental disorder. Not everyone agrees on an answer. Indeed the *British Medical Journal (BMJ)* described Dr. Kevorkian as a "hero."

His champions see no discernible motive for Dr. Kevorkian other than that he believes his work is fitting. The *BMJ* notes that greed for money or fame or some sadistic urge does not motivate Dr. Kevorkian. They make much of the fact that he does not charge a fee for killing.

Because of the absence of such motives, the editors presume that he is a hero among doctors since it is only a "personal code of honor that admits of no qualification" that leads him into action.

But let us look rather more closely at "personal codes that admit no qualification." We have seen a few of them before and not all were admirable. As Dr. Kevorkian motors around Michigan carrying cylinders of carbon monoxide or bottles of potassium chloride to dispatch the sick, his is the motivation of a person with an "overvalued idea," a diagnostic formulation first spelled out by the psychiatrist Carl Wernicke in 1906. Wernicke differentiated overvalued ideas from obsessions and delusions. Overvalued ideas are often at the motivational heart of "personal codes that admit no qualification" and certainly provide a drive as powerful as that of hunger for money, fame, or sexual gratification.

An individual with an overvalued idea is someone who has taken up an idea shared by others in his milieu or culture and transformed it into a ruling passion or "monomania" for himself. It becomes the goal of all his efforts and he is prepared to sacrifice everything—family, reputation, health, even life itself —for it. He presumes that what he does in its service is right regardless of any losses that he or others suffer for it. He sees all opposition as at best misguided and at worst malevolent.

For Dr. Kevorkian, people may die before their time and the fabric of their families may be torn apart, but it's all for the good if he can presume they were "suffering pain unnecessarily" and he has eliminated it. He scorns all opposition—in particular constitutional democratic opposition—as resting on bad faith or ignorance. Empowered by his idea, he feels free to disregard the law and any of its officers.

An overvalued idea has three characteristics: (1) it is a self-dominating but not idiosyncratic opinion, given great importance by (2) intense emotional feelings over its significance, and evoking (3) persistent behavior in its service. For Dr. Kevorkian, thinking about how to terminate the sick has become his exclusive concern. His belief in the justice of his ideas is intense enough for him to starve himself if thwarted by law.

Dr. Kevorkian thinks that all opposition to him is "bad faith" and thus worthy of contempt—a contempt he expresses with no reservation. He is fond of saying that the judicial system of our country is "corrupt," the religious members of our society are "irrational," the medical profession is "insane," the press is "meretricious."

He considers his own behavior "humanitarian." Dr. Kevorkian holds himself beyond reproach, even after killing one patient he believed had multiple sclerosis but whose autopsy revealed no evidence of that disease and another patient with the vague condition of "chronic fatigue syndrome" in whom no pathological process could be found at autopsy—only Kevorkian's poison. He acts without taking a careful medical history, trying alternative treatments, or reflecting on how his actions affect such people as surviving family members.

Dr. Kevorkian's is a confident business. As the news reports flow out of Michigan, it appears that his threshold for medicide is getting lower. Physician-assisted suicide that had previously demanded an incurable disease such as Alzheimer's is now practiced upon patients with such chronic complaints as pelvic pain and emphysema, whose life expectancy cannot be specified. He can justify the active termination of anyone with an ailment—which is just what might be expected once the boundary against active killing by doctors has been breached. What's to stop him now that juries have found his actions to be de facto legal in Michigan?

A crucial aspect of overvalued ideas is that, in contrast to delusions, they are not idiosyncratic. They are ideas that can be found in a proportion of the public—often an influential proportion. It is from such reservoirs of opinion that the particular individual harnesses and amplifies an idea with the disproportionate zeal characteristic of a ruling passion. That Dr. Kevorkian can find people in the highest places—even within the medical profession—to support his ideas and say that they see heroism in his actions is not surprising, given the passion of the contemporary debate over euthanasia. In this way the person with the overvalued idea may be seen, by those who share his opinion but not his self-sacrificing zeal, as giving expression to their hopes—disregarding the slower processes of democracy, filled with prejudice against all who resist, and pumped up with a sense of a higher purpose and justice.

People such as Dr. Kevorkian have found a place in history. With some, with the passage of time, we come to agree with the idea if not the method by which the idea was first expressed. Such was John Brown, the abolitionist, ready to hack five anonymous farmers to death in the Pottowatomi massacre to advance his cause. With others we may come to tolerate some aspect of the idea but see its expression in actual behavior as ludicrous. Such was Carry Nation, the scourge of Kansas barkeeps and boozers, who went to jail hundreds of times for chopping up saloons with a small hatchet in the cause of temperance. Finally, for some, we come to recognize the potential for horror in an overvalued idea held by a person in high authority. Such was Adolf Hitler.

But how is it that anxieties and confusions about medical practice and death can so afflict the judicious people of Michigan as to paralyze them before the outrageous behavior of Dr. Kevorkian and thus generate an environment for this epidemic? In Michigan these states of mind derive from conflicting concerns over medical decisions. The citizens—like any inexpert group—are relatively uninformed about what doctors can do for patients, even in extreme situations. Conflicting goals and unfamiliar practices—common enough around medical decisions—produce anxiety and confusion every time.

No one thinks happily about dying, especially dying in pain. Death is bad; dying can be worse. Anyone who says he does not fear dying—and all the pain and suffering tied to it—has probably not experienced much in life.

This concern, though, certainly has been exaggerated in our times, even though now much can be done to relieve the heaviest burdens of terminally ill patients. Yet through a variety of sources—such as movies, newspapers, and essays—all the negative aspects of dying have been emphasized, the agonies embellished, and the loss of control represented by disease accentuated. Horror stories feed upon one another, and rumors of medical lack of interest grow into opinions that doctors both neglect the dying and hold back relief. Doctors are regularly accused of surrendering to professional taboos or to legal advice to avoid risk of malpractice or prosecution—and in this way are presumed ready to sacrifice their patients out of selfish fear for themselves.

On the contrary, most doctors try to collaborate with patients and do listen to their wishes, especially when treatments that carry painful burdens are contemplated. As Dr. Kevorkian can demonstrate—with videotapes, no less—the patients he killed asked him repeatedly for help in dying rather than for help in living. Do not they have some right to die at their own hands steadied by Dr. Kevorkian? Is not the matter of assisted suicide simply a matter of rights and wants to which any citizen of Michigan is entitled?

The idea of a right to suicide provokes most psychiatrists. Psychiatry has worked to teach everyone that suicide is not an uncomplicated, voluntary act to which rights attach. It has shown that suicide is an act provoked, indeed compelled, by mental disorder—such as a disorienting depression or a set of misdirected, even delusionary, ideas. In that sense psychiatry taught that suicidal people were not "responsible" for this behavior—no matter what they said or wrote in final letters or testaments—any more than they would be for epileptic seizures.

This idea—generated from the careful study of the clinical circumstances and past histories of suicidal patients—gradually prevailed in civil law and even in the canon law of churches. As a result, laws against suicide were repealed— not to make suicide a "right" but to remove it from the status of a crime.

We psychiatrists thought we had done a worthy thing for our society, for families of patients, and even for patients themselves. We were not saying, not for a moment, that we approved of suicide. Far from it. We knew such deaths to be ugly and misguided—misguided in particular because the disposition to die, the wish for suicide, was, on inspection, often a symptom of the very mental disorders that psychiatry treats. Suicide in almost all cases is as far from a rational choice based on a weighing of the balance books of life as is responding to hallucinated voices or succumbing to the paranoid ideas of a charismatic madman such as Jim Jones, who at Jonestown directed a gruesome exhibition of mass assisted suicide.

Psychiatrists were united in their views about suicide and shook their heads when contemplating past traditions when suicides were considered scandalous. We did not think too deeply into the consequences of our actions. For, after suicide ceased to be a crime, it soon became a right and, conceivably under some circumstances, such as when costs of care grow onerous, an obligation. Psychiatrists, who had worked for decades demonstrating that suicides were insane acts, are now recruited in Holland to assure that requests for suicide made by patients offered "no hope of cure" by their doctors are "rational."

What had begun as an effort at explanation and understanding of the tragic act of suicide has developed into complicity in the seduction of vulnerable people into that very behavior. The patients are seduced just as the victims in Jonestown were—by isolating them, sustaining their despair, revoking alternatives, stressing examples of others choosing to die, and sweetening the deadly poison by speaking of death with dignity. If even psychiatrists succumb to this complicity with death, what can be expected of the lay public in Michigan? ...

One can think of ways to combat the deadly convergence of madnesses in Michigan and to deter the spread of this local epidemic to other regions of our country. The suicidal patients certainly should be treated for their depressive vulnerabilities by doctors able to assist them with their underlying illnesses. Dr. Kevorkian, the agent of their extinction, should be stopped by whatever means the state has at its disposal to stay dangerous men. And the people of Michigan should be taught about the capacities of modern medicine. With this information, the hope is, they will emerge from their anxious confusions, accept mortality for what it is rather than for what they imagine, and, at last, end their support for this insanity.

POSTSCRIPT

Should Doctor-Assisted Suicide Be Legalized for the Terminally Ill?

Angell tells the story of her father's suicide because he seemed to be a perfect candidate for doctor-assisted suicide. Since it was not available to him, he shot himself before being hospitalized for his cancer. Like any case this one allows for various interpretations, but it points up the problem of a blanket rule for all cases. What if we were to come to the conclusion that doctor-assisted suicide is wrong in most cases when patients request it but right in a minority of cases? Maybe both sides are right at times and wrong at other times. The problem is that it is difficult to make laws that apply only sometimes. Most laws provide too little leeway to be adjusted to the peculiarities of individual cases. For example, if a man goes over the speed limit, he breaks the law, even if he is driving his wife to the hospital to deliver a baby. Fortunately, most policemen would not write this man a ticket but rather turn on their siren and escort him to the hospital. For many laws the discretion of judges and juries, like that of the policeman, provides some badly needed flexibility, but problems will always remain.

The literature on doctor-assisted suicide and the larger issue of euthanasia has mushroomed in the last decade. For arguments against these practices, see Robert Laurence Barry, *Breaking the Thread of Life: On Rational Suicide* (Transaction Publishers, 1994); Tom Beauchamp, *Ethical Issues in Death and Dying* (Prentice Hall, 1996); Herbert Hendin, *Seduced by Death: Doctors, Patients and the Dutch Cure* (W. W. Norton, 1996); and Wesley J. Smith, *Forced Exit: The Slippery Slope From Assisted Suicide to Legalized Murder* (Times Books, 1997).

For works that favor doctor-assisted suicide or euthanasia or that contain various viewpoints, see Ira Byock, *Dying Well: The Prospect for Growth at the End of Life* (Thorndike Press, 1997); Timothy E. Quill, *A Midwife Through the Dying Process* (Johns Hopkins University Press, 1996); and Marylin Webb, *The Good Death: The New American Search to Reshape the End of Life* (Bantam Books, 1997). For works that present or analyze the issues as debates, see Michael M. Uhlman, ed., *Last Rights? Assisted Suicide and Euthanasia Debated* (William B. Eerdmans, 1998); Tamara Roleff, ed., *Suicide: Opposing Viewpoints* (Greenhaven Press, 1998); and Carol Wedesser, ed., *Euthanasia: Opposing Viewpoints* (Greenhaven Press, 1995). For multiple views on doctor-assisted suicide and euthanasia, see Melvin I. Urofsky and Philip E. Urofsky, eds., *The Right to Die: A Two-Volume Anthology of Scholarly Articles* (Garland, 1996) and Robert F. Weir et al., *Physician-Assisted Suicide* (Indiana University Press, 1997).

On the Internet ...

DUSHKIN ONLINE

American Society of Criminology

The American Society of Criminology Web site is an excellent starting point for studying all aspects of criminology and criminal justice. This page provides links to sites on criminal justice in general, international criminal justice, juvenile justice, courts, the police, and the government.

http://www.bsos.umd.edu/asc/four.html

Crime Times

This Crime Times site lists research reviews and other information regarding the causes of criminal and violent behavior. It is provided by the nonprofit Wacker Foundation, publishers of Crime Times.

http://www.crime-times.org

Justice Information Center (JIC)

Provided by the National Criminal Justice Reference Service, the Justice Information Center (JIC) site connects to information about corrections, courts, crime prevention, criminal justice, statistics, drugs and crime, law enforcement, and victims, among other topics.

http://www.ncjrs.org

PART 5

Crime and Social Control

*A*ll *societies label certain hurtful actions as crimes and punish those who commit them. Other harmful actions, however, are not defined as crimes, and the perpetrators are not punished. Today the definition of crime and the appropriate treatment of criminals is widely debated. Some of the major questions are: Does street crime pose more of a threat to the public's well-being than white-collar crime? Billions of dollars have been spent on the "war on drugs," but who is winning? Would legalizing some drugs free up money that could be directed to other types of social welfare programs, such as the rehabilitation of addicts? What about the death penalty? Do certain crimes justify its use?*

- Is Street Crime More Harmful Than White-Collar Crime?

- Should Drug Use Be Decriminalized?

- Is Capital Punishment Justified?

ISSUE 16

Is Street Crime More Harmful Than White-Collar Crime?

YES: John J. DiIulio, Jr., from "The Impact of Inner-City Crime," *The Public Interest* (Summer 1989)

NO: Jeffrey Reiman, from *The Rich Get Richer and the Poor Get Prison: Ideology, Class, and Criminal Justice,* 5th ed. (Allyn & Bacon, 1998)

ISSUE SUMMARY

YES: John J. DiIulio, Jr., a professor of politics and public affairs, analyzes the enormous harm done—especially to the urban poor and, by extension, to all of society—by street criminals and their activities.

NO: Professor of philosophy Jeffrey Reiman argues that the dangers posed by negligent corporations and white-collar criminals are a greater menace to society than are the activities of typical street criminals.

T he word *crime* entered the English language (from the Old French) around A.D. 1250, when it was identified with "sinfulness." Later, the meaning of the word was modified: crime became the kind of sinfulness that was rightly punishable by law. Even medieval writers, who did not distinguish very sharply between church and state, recognized that there were some sins for which punishment was best left to God; the laws should punish only those that cause harm to the community. Of course, their concept of harm was a very broad one, embracing such offenses as witchcraft and blasphemy. Modern jurists, even those who deplore such practices, would say that the state has no business punishing the perpetrators of these types of offenses.

What, then, should the laws punish? The answer depends in part on our notion of harm. We usually limit the term to the kind of harm that is tangible and obvious: taking a life, causing bodily injury or psychological trauma, and destroying property. For most Americans today, particularly those who live in cities, the word *crime* is practically synonymous with street crime. Anyone who has ever been robbed or beaten by street criminals will never forget the experience. The harm that these criminals cause is tangible, and the connection between the harm and the perpetrator is very direct.

But suppose the connection is not so direct. Suppose, for example, that A hires B to shoot C. Is that any less a crime? B is the actual shooter, but is A any less guilty? Of course not, we say; he may even be more guilty, since he is the ultimate mover behind the crime. A would be guilty even if the chain of command were much longer, involving A's orders to B, and B's to C, then on to D, E, and F to kill G. Organized crime kingpins go to jail even when they are far removed from the people who carry out their orders. High officials of the Nixon administration, even though they were not directly involved in the burglary attempt at the Democratic National Committee headquarters at the Watergate Hotel complex in 1972, were imprisoned.

This brings us to the topic of white-collar crime. The burglars at the Watergate Hotel were acting on orders that trickled down from the highest reaches of political power in the United States. Other white-collar criminals are as varied as the occupations from which they come. They include stockbrokers who make millions through insider trading, as Ivan Boesky did; members of Congress who take payoffs; and people who cheat on their income taxes, like hotel owner and billionaire Leona Helmsley. Some, like Helmsley, get stiff prison sentences when convicted, though many others (like most of the officials in the Watergate scandal) do little or no time in prison. Do they deserve stiffer punishment, or are their crimes less harmful than the crimes of street criminals?

Although white-collar criminals do not directly cause physical harm or relieve people of their wallets, they can still end up doing considerable harm. The harm done by Nixon's aides threatened the integrity of the U.S. electoral system. Every embezzler, corrupt politician, and tax cheat exacts a toll on our society. Individuals can be hurt in more tangible ways by decisions made in corporate boardrooms: Auto executives, for example, have approved design features that have caused fatalities. Managers of chemical companies have allowed practices that have polluted the environment with cancer-causing agents. And heads of corporations have presided over industries wherein workers have been needlessly killed or maimed.

Whether or not these decisions should be considered crimes is debatable. A crime must always involve "malicious intent," or what the legal system calls *mens rea*. This certainly applies to street crime—the mugger obviously has sinister designs—but does it apply to every decision made in a boardroom that ends up causing harm? And does that harm match or exceed the harm caused by street criminals? In the following selections, John J. DiIulio, Jr., focuses on the enormous harm done—especially to the poor—by street criminals. Not only does street crime cause loss, injury, terror, and death for individuals, he argues, but it also causes neighborhood decline, community disintegration, loss of pride, business decline and failure, hampered schools, and middle-class flight to the suburbs. According to Jeffrey Reiman, white-collar crime also does more harm than is commonly recognized. By his count, white-collar crime causes far more deaths, injuries, illnesses, and financial loss than street crime. In light of this, he argues, we must redefine our ideas about what crime is and who the criminals are.

John J. DiIulio, Jr.

 **YES**

The Impact of Inner-City Crime

My grandmother, an Italian immigrant, lived in the same Philadelphia row house from 1921 till her death in 1986. When she moved there, and for the four decades thereafter, most of her neighbors were Irish and Italian. When she died, virtually all of her neighbors were black. Like the whites who fled, the first blacks who moved in were mostly working-class people living just above the poverty level.

Until around 1970, the neighborhood changed little. The houses were well-maintained. The children played in the streets and were polite. The teenagers hung out on the street corners in the evenings, sometimes doing mischief, but rarely—if ever—doing anything worse. The local grocers and other small businesspeople (both blacks and the few remaining whites) stayed open well past dark. Day or night, my grandmother journeyed the streets just as she had during the days of the Great Depression, taking the bus to visit her friends and relatives, going shopping, attending church, and so on.

She was a conspicuous and popular figure in this black community. She was conspicuous for her race, accent, and advanced age; she was popular for the homespun advice (and home-baked goods) she dispensed freely to the teenagers hanging out on the corners, to the youngsters playing ball in the street in front of her house, and to their parents (many of them mothers living without a husband).

Like the generations of ethnics who had lived there before them, these people were near the bottom of the socioeconomic ladder. I often heard my grandmother say that her new neighbors were "just like us," by which she meant that they were honest, decent, law-abiding people working hard to advance themselves and to make a better life for their children.

But in the early 1970s, the neighborhood began to change. Some, though by no means all, of the black families my grandmother had come to know moved out of the neighborhood. The new neighbors kept to themselves. The exteriors of the houses started to look ratty. The streets grew dirty. The grocery and variety stores closed or did business only during daylight hours. The children played in the schoolyard but not in front of their homes. The teenagers on the corners were replaced by adult drug dealers and their "runners." Vandalism

Excerpted from John J. DiIulio, Jr., "The Impact of Inner-City Crime," *The Public Interest*, no. 96 (Summer 1989), pp. 28–46. Copyright © 1989 by National Affairs, Inc. Reprinted by permission of *The Public Interest* and the author.

and graffiti became commonplace. My grandmother was mugged twice, both times by black teenagers; once she was severely beaten in broad daylight.

In the few years before she died at age eighty-four, and after years of pleading by her children and dozens of grandchildren, she stopped going out and kept her doors and windows locked at all times. On drives to visit her, when I got within four blocks of her home, I instinctively checked to make sure that my car doors were locked. Her house, where I myself had been raised, was in a "bad neighborhood," and it did not make sense to take any chances. I have not returned to the area since the day of her funeral.

My old ethnic and ghetto neighborhood had become an underclass neighborhood. Why is it that most readers of this article avoid, and advise their friends and relatives to avoid, walking or driving through such neighborhoods? Obviously we are not worried about being infected somehow by the extremely high levels of poverty, joblessness, illiteracy, welfare dependency, or drug abuse that characterize these places. Instead we shun these places because we suppose them to contain exceedingly high numbers of predatory street criminals, who hit, rape, rob, deal drugs, burglarize, and murder.

This supposition is absolutely correct. The underclass problem, contrary to the leading academic and journalistic understandings, is mainly a crime problem. It is a crime problem, moreover, that can be reduced dramatically (although not eliminated) with the human and financial resources already at hand.

Only two things are required: common sense and compassion. Once we understand the underclass problem as a crime problem, neither of those two qualities should be scarce. Until we understand the underclass problem as a crime problem, policymakers and others will continue to fiddle while the underclass ghettos of Philadelphia, Newark, Chicago, Los Angeles, Miami, Washington, D.C., and other cities burn. . . .

The Truly Deviant

Liberals . . . have understood the worsening of ghetto conditions mainly as the by-product of a complex process of economic and social change. One of the latest and most influential statements of this view is William Julius Wilson's *The Truly Disadvantaged: The Inner City, the Underclass, and Public Policy* (1987).

Wilson argues that over the last two decades a new and socially destructive class structure has emerged in the ghetto. As he sees it, the main culprit is deindustrialization. As plants have closed, urban areas, especially black urban areas, have lost entry-level jobs. To survive economically, or to enjoy their material success, ghetto residents in a position to do so have moved out, leaving behind them an immobilized "underclass." . . .

Wilson has focused our attention on the socioeconomic straits of the truly disadvantaged with an elegance and rhetorical force that is truly admirable.[1] But despite its many strengths, his often subtle analysis of the underclass problem wrongly deemphasizes one obvious possibility: "The truly disadvantaged" exist mainly because of the activities of "the truly deviant"—the large numbers of chronic and predatory street criminals—in their midst. One in every nine adult black males in this country is under some form of correctional supervision (prison, jail, probation, or parole).[2] Criminals come disproportionately from underclass neighborhoods. They victimize their neighbors directly through crime, and indirectly by creating or worsening the multiple social and economic ills that define the sad lot of today's ghetto dwellers.

Predatory Ghetto Criminals

I propose [another] way of thinking about the underclass problem. The members of the underclass are, overwhelmingly, decent and law-abiding residents of America's most distressed inner cities. Fundamentally, what makes them different from the rest of us is not only their higher than normal levels of welfare dependency and the like, but their far higher than normal levels of victimization by predatory criminals.

This victimization by criminals takes several forms. There is *direct victimization*—being mugged, raped, or murdered; being threatened and extorted; living in fear about whether you can send your children to school or let them go out and play without their being bothered by dope dealers, pressured by gang members, or even struck by a stray bullet. And there is *indirect victimization*—dampened neighborhood economic development, loss of a sizable fraction of the neighborhood's male population to prison or jail, the undue influence on young people exercised by criminal "role models" like the cash-rich drug lords who rule the streets, and so on.

Baldly stated, my hypothesis is that this victimization causes and perpetuates the other ills of our underclass neighborhoods. Schools in these neighborhoods are unable to function effectively because of their disorderly atmosphere and because of the violent behavior of the criminals (especially gang members) who hang around their classrooms. The truly deviant are responsible for a high percentage of teen pregnancies, rapes, and sexual assaults. Similarly, many of the chronically welfare-dependent, female-headed households in these neighborhoods owe their plights to the fact that the men involved are either unable (because they are under some form of correctional supervision) or unwilling (because it does not jibe well with their criminal lifestyles) to seek and secure gainful employment and live with their families. And much of the poverty and joblessness in these neighborhoods can be laid at the door of criminals whose presence deters local business activity, including the development of residential real estate.

Blacks are victims of violent crimes at much higher rates than whites. Most lone-offender crime against blacks is committed by blacks, while most such crimes against whites are committed by whites; in 1986, for instance, 83.5 percent of violent crimes against blacks were committed by blacks, while 80.3 percent of violent crimes against whites were committed by whites. This monochrome picture of victim-offender relationships also holds for multiple-offender crimes. In 1986, for example, 79.6 percent of multiple-offender violent crimes against blacks were committed by blacks; the "white-on-white" figure was 59.4 percent.

Criminals are most likely to commit crimes against people of their own race. The main reason is presumably their physical proximity to potential victims. If so, then it is not hard to understand why underclass neighborhoods, which have more than their share of would-be criminals, have more than their share of crime.

Prison is the most costly form of correctional supervision, and it is normally reserved for the most dangerous felons—violent or repeat offenders. Most of my readers do not personally know anyone in prison; most ghetto dwellers of a decade or two ago probably would not have known anyone in prison either. But most of today's underclass citizens do; the convicted felons were their relatives and neighbors—and often their victimizers.

For example, in 1980 Newark was the street-crime capital of New Jersey. In the Newark area, there were more than 920 violent crimes (murders, nonnegligent manslaughters, forcible rapes, robberies, and aggravated assaults) per 100,000 residents; in the rest of the state the figure was under 500, and in affluent towns like Princeton it was virtually nil. In the same year, New Jersey prisons held 5,866 criminals, 2,697 of them from the Newark area.[3] In virtually all of the most distressed parts of this distressed city, at least one of every two hundred residents was an imprisoned felon.[4] The same basic picture holds for other big cities.[5]

Correlation, however, is not causation, and we could extend and refine this sort of crude, exploratory analysis of the relationship between crime rates, concentrations of correctional supervisees, and the underclass neighborhoods from which they disproportionately come. But except to satisfy curiosity, I see no commanding need for such studies. For much the same picture emerges from the anecdotal accounts of people who have actually spent years wrestling with—as opposed to merely researching—the problem.

For example, in 1988 the nation's capital became its murder capital. Washington, D.C., had 372 killings, 82 percent of them committed on the streets by young black males against other young black males. The city vied with Detroit for the highest juvenile homicide rate in America. Here is part of the eloquent testimony on this development given by Isaac Fulwood, a native Washingtonian and the city's police-chief designate:

> The murder statistics don't capture what these people are doing. We've had in excess of 1,260 drug-related shootings.... People are scared of these kids. Someone can get shot in broad daylight, and nobody saw anything.... Nobody talks. And that's so different from the way it was in my childhood.

The same thing can be said about the underclass neighborhoods of other major cities. In Detroit, for instance, most of the hundreds of ghetto residents murdered over the last six years were killed within blocks of their homes by their truly deviant neighbors.

To devise meaningful law-enforcement and correctional responses to the underclass problem, we need to understand why concentrations of crime and criminals are so high in these neighborhoods, and to change our government's criminal-justice policies and practices accordingly.

Understanding the Problem

We begin with a chicken-and-egg question: Does urban decay cause crime, or does crime cause urban decay?

In conventional criminology, which derives mainly from sociology, ghettos are portrayed as "breeding grounds" for predatory street crime. Poverty, joblessness, broken homes, single-parent families, and similar factors are identified as the "underlying causes" of crime.[6] These conditions cause crime, the argument goes; as they worsen—as the ghetto community becomes the underclass neighborhood—crime worsens. This remains the dominant academic perspective on the subject, one that is shared implicitly by most public officials who are close to the problem.

Beginning in the mid-1970s, however, a number of influential studies appeared that challenged this conventional criminological wisdom.[7] Almost without exception, these studies have cast grave doubts on the classic sociological explanation of crime, suggesting that the actual relationships between such variables as poverty, illiteracy, and unemployment, on the one hand, and criminality, on the other, are far more ambiguous than most analysts freely assumed only a decade or so ago. . . .

Locks, Cops, and Studies

Camden, New Jersey, is directly across the bridge from Philadelphia. Once-decent areas have become just like my grandmother's old neighborhood: isolated, crime-torn urban war zones. In February 1989 a priest doing social work in Camden was ordered off the streets by drug dealers and threatened with death if he did not obey. The police chief of Camden sent some extra men into the area, but the violent drug dealers remained the real rulers of the city's streets.

The month before the incident in Camden, the Rockefeller Foundation announced that it was going to devote some of its annual budget (which exceeds $100 million) to researching the underclass problem. Other foundations, big and small, have already spent (or misspent) much money on the problem. But Rockefeller's president was quoted as follows: "Nobody knows who they are, what they do. . . . The underclass is not a topic to pursue from the library. You get out and look for them."

His statement was heartening, but it revealed a deep misunderstanding of the problem. Rather than intimating that the underclass was somehow hard to locate, he would have done better to declare that his charity would purchase deadbolt locks for the homes of ghetto dwellers in New York City who lacked them, and subsidize policing and private-security services in the easily identifiable neighborhoods where these poor people are concentrated.

More street-level research would be nice, especially for the networks of policy intellectuals (liberal and conservative) who benefit directly from such endeavors. But more locks, cops, and corrections officers would make a more positive, tangible, and lasting difference in the lives of today's ghetto dwellers.

Notes

1. In addition, he has canvassed competing academic perspectives on the underclass; see William Julius Wilson, ed., "The Ghetto Underclass: Social Science Perspectives," *Annals of the American Academy of Political and Social Science* (January 1989). It should also be noted that he is directing a $2.7 million research project on poverty in Chicago that promises to be the most comprehensive study of its kind yet undertaken.

2. According to the Bureau of Justice Statistics, in 1986 there were 234,430 adult black males in prison, 101,000 in jail, an estimated 512,000 on probation, and 133,300 on parole. There were 8,985,000 adult black males in the national residential population. I am grateful to Larry Greenfeld for his assistance in compiling these figures.

3. I am grateful to Hank Pierre, Stan Repko, and Commissioner William H. Fauver of the New Jersey Department of Corrections for granting me access to these figures and to related data on density of prisoner residence; to Andy Ripps for his heroic efforts in organizing them; and to my Princeton colleague Mark Alan Hughes for his expert help in analyzing the data.

4. Ten of the thirteen most distressed Newark census tracts were places where the density of prisoner residence was that high. In other words, 76.9 percent of the worst underclass areas of Newark had such extremely high concentrations of hardcore offenders. In most of the rest of Newark, and throughout the rest of the state, such concentrations were virtually nonexistent.

5. In 1980 in the Chicago area, for example, in 182 of the 1,521 census tracts at least one of every two hundred residents was an imprisoned felon. Fully twenty of the thirty-five worst underclass tracts had such extraordinary concentrations of serious criminals; in several of them, more than one of every hundred residents was behind prison bars. I am grateful to Wayne Carroll and Commissioner Michael Lane of the Illinois Department of Corrections for helping me with these data.

6. For example, see the classic statement by Edwin H. Sutherland and Donald R. Cressey, *Principles of Criminology*, 7th rev. ed. (Philadelphia: J. P. Lippincott, 1966).

7. See, for example, James Q. Wilson, *Thinking About Crime* (New York: Basic Books, 1975), especially the third chapter.

A Crime by Any Other Name . . .

If one individual inflicts a bodily injury upon another which leads to the death of the person attacked we call it manslaughter; on the other hand, if the attacker knows beforehand that the blow will be fatal we call it murder. Murder has also been committed if society places hundreds of workers in such a position that they inevitably come to premature and unnatural ends. Their death is as violent as if they had been stabbed or shot. . . . Murder has been committed if society knows perfectly well that thousands of workers cannot avoid being sacrificed so long as these conditions are allowed to continue. Murder of this sort is just as culpable as the murder committed by an individual.

— Frederick Engels
The Condition of the Working Class in England

What's in a Name?

If it takes you an hour to read this chapter, by the time you reach the last page, three of your fellow citizens will have been murdered. *During that same time, at least four Americans will die as a result of unhealthy or unsafe conditions in the workplace!* Although these work-related deaths could have been prevented, they are not called murders. Why not? Doesn't a crime by any other name still cause misery and suffering? What's in a name?

The fact is that the label "crime" is not used in America to name all or the worst of the actions that cause misery and suffering to Americans. It is primarily reserved for the dangerous actions of the poor.

In the February 21, 1993, edition of the *New York Times,* an article appears with the headline: "Company in Mine Deaths Set to Pay Big Fine." It describes an agreement by the owners of a Kentucky mine to pay a fine for safety misconduct that may have led to "the worst American mining accident in nearly a decade." Ten workers died in a methane explosion, and the company pleaded guilty to "a pattern of safety misconduct" that included falsifying reports of methane levels and requiring miners to work under unsupported roofs. The company was fined $3.75 million. The acting foreman at the mine was the only individual charged by the federal government, and for his cooperation with the investigation, prosecutors were recommending that he receive the minimum sentence: probation to six months in prison. The company's president expressed regret for the tragedy that occurred. And the U.S. attorney said he hoped the case "sent a clear message that violations of Federal safety and health regulations that endanger the lives of our citizens will not be tolerated."

Compare this with the story of Colin Ferguson, who prompted an editorial in the *New York Times* of December 10, 1993, with the headline: "Mass Murder on the 5:33." A few days earlier, Colin had boarded a commuter train in Garden City, Long Island, and methodically shot passengers with a 9-millimeter pistol, killing 5 and wounding 18. Colin Ferguson was surely a murderer, maybe a mass murderer. My question is, Why wasn't the death of the miners also murder? Why weren't those responsible for subjecting ten miners to deadly conditions also "mass murderers"?

Why do ten dead miners amount to an "accident," a "tragedy," and five dead commuters a "mass murder"? "Murder" suggests a murderer, whereas "accident" and "tragedy" suggest the work of impersonal forces. But the charge against the company that owned the mine said that they "repeatedly exposed the mine's work crews to danger and that such conditions were frequently concealed from Federal inspectors responsible for enforcing the mine safety act." And the acting foreman admitted to falsifying records of methane levels only two months before the fatal blast. Someone was responsible for the conditions that led to the death of ten miners. Is that person not a murderer, perhaps even a *mass murderer?*

These questions are at this point rhetorical. My aim is not to discuss this case but rather to point to the blinders we wear when we look at such an "accident." There was an investigation. One person, the acting foreman, was held responsible for falsifying records. He is to be sentenced to six months in prison (at most). The company was fined. But no one will be tried for *murder.* No one will be thought of as a murderer. *Why not?* . . .

Didn't those miners have a right to protection from the violence that took their lives? *And if not, why not?*

Once we are ready to ask this question seriously, we are in a position to see that the reality of crime—that is, the acts we label crime, the acts we think of as crime, the actors and actions we treat as criminal—is *created:* It is an image shaped by decisions as to *what* will be called crime and *who* will be treated as a criminal.

The Carnival Mirror

. . . The American criminal justice system is a mirror that shows a distorted image of the dangers that threaten us—an image created more by the shape of the mirror than by the reality reflected. What do we see when we look in the criminal justice mirror? . . .

He is, first of all, a *he.* Out of 2,012,906 persons arrested for FBI Index crimes [which are criminal homicide, forcible rape, robbery, aggravated assault, burglary, larceny, and motor vehicle theft] in 1991, 1,572,591, or 78 percent, were males. Second, he is a *youth.* . . . Third, he is predominantly *urban.* . . .

Fourth, he is disproportionately *black*—blacks are arrested for Index crimes at a rate three times that of their percentage in the national population.... Finally, he is *poor:* Among state prisoners in 1991, 33 percent were unemployed prior to being arrested—a rate nearly four times that of males in the general population....

This is the Typical Criminal feared by most law-abiding Americans. Poor, young, urban, (disproportionately) black males make up the core of the enemy forces in the war against crime. They are the heart of a vicious, unorganized guerrilla army, threatening the lives, limbs, and possessions of the law-abiding members of society—necessitating recourse to the ultimate weapons of force and detention in our common defense.

... The acts of the Typical Criminal are not the only acts that endanger us, nor are they the acts that endanger us the most. As I shall show..., we have as great or sometimes even a greater chance of being killed or disabled by an occupational injury or disease, by unnecessary surgery, or by shoddy emergency medical services than by aggravated assault or even homicide! Yet even though these threats to our well-being are graver than those posed by our poor young criminals, they do not show up in the FBI's Index of serious crimes. The individuals responsible for them do not turn up in arrest records or prison statistics. *They never become part of the reality reflected in the criminal justice mirror, although the danger they pose is at least as great and often greater than the danger posed by those who do!*

Similarly, the general public loses more money *by far*... from price-fixing and monopolistic practices and from consumer deception and embezzlement than from all the property crimes in the FBI's Index combined. Yet these far more costly acts are either not criminal, or if technically criminal, not prosecuted, or if prosecuted, not punished, or if punished, only mildly.... *Their faces rarely appear in the criminal justice mirror, although the danger they pose is at least as great and often greater than that of those who do....*

The criminal justice system is like a mirror in which society can see the face of the evil in its midst. Because the system deals with some evil and not with others, because it treats some evils as the gravest and treats some of the gravest evils as minor, the image it throws back is distorted like the image in a carnival mirror. Thus, the image cast back is false not because it is invented out of thin air but because the proportions of the real are distorted....

If criminal justice really gives us a carnival-mirror of "crime," we are doubly deceived. First, we are led to believe that the criminal justice system is protecting us against the gravest threats to our well-being when, in fact, the system is protecting us against only some threats and not necessarily the gravest ones. We are deceived about how much protection we are receiving and thus left vulnerable. The second deception is just the other side of this one. If people believe that the carnival mirror is a true mirror—that is, if they believe the criminal justice system simply *reacts* to the gravest threats to their well-being— they come to believe that whatever is the target of the criminal justice system must be the greatest threat to their well-being....

A Crime by Any Other Name...

Think of a crime, any crime. Picture the first "crime" that comes into your mind. What do you see? The odds are you are not imagining a mining company executive sitting at his desk, calculating the costs of proper safety precautions and deciding not to invest in them. Probably what you do see with your mind's eye is one person physically attacking another or robbing something from another via the threat of physical attack. Look more closely. What does the attacker look like? It's a safe bet he (and it is a *he,* of course) is not wearing a suit and tie. In fact, my hunch is that you—like me, like almost anyone else in America —picture a young, tough lower-class male when the thought of crime first pops into your head. You (we) picture someone like the Typical Criminal described above. The crime itself is one in which the Typical Criminal sets out to attack or rob some specific person....

It is important to identify this model of the Typical Crime because it functions like a set of blinders. It keeps us from calling a mine disaster a mass murder even if ten men are killed, even if someone is responsible for the unsafe conditions in which they worked and died. I contend that this particular piece of mental furniture so blocks our view that it keeps us from using the criminal justice system to protect ourselves from the greatest threats to our persons and possessions.

What keeps a mine disaster from being a mass murder in our eyes is that it is not a one-on-one harm. What is important in one-on-one harm is not the numbers but the *desire of someone (or ones) to harm someone (or ones) else.* An attack by a gang on one or more persons or an attack by one individual on several fits the model of one-on-one harm; that is, for each person harmed there is at least one individual who wanted to harm that person. Once he selects his victim, the rapist, the mugger, the murderer all want this person they have selected to suffer. A mine executive, on the other hand, does not want his employees to be harmed. He would truly prefer that there be no accident, no injured or dead miners. What he does want is something legitimate. It is what he has been hired to get: maximum profits at minimum costs. If he cuts corners to save a buck, he is just doing his job. If ten men die because he cut corners on safety, we may think him crude or callous but not a murderer. He is, at most, responsible for an *indirect harm,* not a one-on-one harm. For this, he may even be criminally indictable for violating safety regulations—but not for murder. The ten men are dead as an unwanted consequence of his (perhaps overzealous or undercautious) pursuit of a legitimate goal. So, unlike the Typical Criminal, he has not committed the Typical Crime—or so we generally believe. As a result, ten men are dead who might be alive now if cutting corners of the kind that leads to loss of life, whether suffering is specifically aimed at or not, were treated as murder.

This is my point. Because we accept the belief... that the model for crime is one person specifically trying to harm another, we accept a legal system that leaves us unprotected against much greater dangers to our lives and well-being than those threatened by the Typical Criminal....

According to the FBI's *Uniform Crime Reports,* in 1991, there were 24,703 murders and nonnegligent manslaughters, and 1,092,739 aggravated assaults.

In 1992, there were 23,760 murders and nonnegligent manslaughters, and 1,126,970 aggravated assaults.... Thus, as a measure of the physical harm done by crime in the beginning of the 1990s, we can say that reported crimes lead to roughly 24,000 deaths and 1,000,000 instances of serious bodily injury short of death a year. As a measure of monetary loss due to property crime, we can use $15.1 billion—the total estimated dollar losses due to property crime in 1992 according to the UCR. Whatever the shortcomings of these reported crime statistics, they are the statistics upon which public policy has traditionally been based. Thus, I will consider any actions that lead to loss of life, physical harm, and property loss comparable to the figures in the UCR as actions that pose grave dangers to the community comparable to the threats posed by crimes....

In testimony before the Senate Committee on Labor and Human Resources, Dr. Philip Landrigan, director of the Division of Environmental and Occupational Medicine at the Mount Sinai School of Medicine in New York City, stated that

> ... [I]t may be calculated that occupational disease is responsible each year in the United States for 50,000 to 70,000 deaths, and for approximately 350,000 new cases of illness.

... The BLS estimate of 330,000 job-related illnesses for 1990 roughly matches Dr. Landrigan's estimates. For 1991, BLS estimates 368,000 job-related illnesses. These illnesses are of varying severity.... Because I want to compare these occupational harms with those resulting from aggravated assault, I shall stay on the conservative side here too, as with deaths from occupational diseases, and say that there are annually in the United States approximately 150,000 job-related serious illnesses. Taken together with 25,000 deaths from occupational diseases, how does this compare with the threat posed by crime?

Before jumping to any conclusions, note that the risk of occupational disease and death falls only on members of the labor force, whereas the risk of crime falls on the whole population, from infants to the elderly. Because the labor force is about half the total population (124,810,000 in 1990, out of a total population of 249,900,000), to get a true picture of the *relative* threat posed by occupational diseases compared with that posed by crimes, we should *halve* the crime statistics when comparing them with the figures for industrial disease and death. Using the crime figures for the first years of the 1990s, ... we note that the *comparable* figures would be

	Occupational Disease	Crime (halved)
Death	25,000	12,000
Other physical harm	150,000	500,000

... Note ... that the estimates in the last chart are *only* for occupational *diseases* and deaths from those diseases. They do not include death and disability from work-related injuries. Here, too, the statistics are gruesome. The National Safety Council reported that in 1991, work-related accidents caused 9,600 deaths and 1.7 million disabling work injuries, a total cost to the economy of $63.3 billion. This brings the number of occupation-related deaths to

34,600 a year and other physical harms to 1,850,000. If, on the basis of these additional figures, we recalculated our chart comparing occupational harms from both disease and accident with criminal harms, it would look like this:

	Occupational Hazard	Crime (halved)
Death	34,600	12,000
Other physical harm	1,850,000	500,000

Can there be any doubt that workers are more likely to stay alive and healthy in the face of the danger from the underworld than in the work-world? ...

To say that some of these workers died from accidents due to their own carelessness is about as helpful as saying that some of those who died at the hands of murderers asked for it. It overlooks the fact that where workers are careless, it is not because they love to live dangerously. They have production quotas to meet, quotas that they themselves do not set. If quotas were set with an eye to keeping work at a safe pace rather than to keeping the production-to-wages ratio as high as possible, it might be more reasonable to expect workers to take the time to be careful. Beyond this, we should bear in mind that the vast majority of occupational deaths result from disease, not accident, and disease is generally a function of conditions outside a worker's control. Examples of such conditions are the level of coal dust in the air ("260,000 miners receive benefits for [black lung] disease, and perhaps as many as 4,000 retired miners die from the illness or its complications each year"; about 10,000 currently working miners "have X-ray evidence of the beginnings of the crippling and often fatal disease") or textile dust ... or asbestos fibers ... or coal tars ...; (coke oven workers develop cancer of the scrotum at a rate five times that of the general population). Also, some 800,000 people suffer from occupationally related skin disease each year. ...

To blame the workers for occupational disease and deaths is to ignore the history of governmental attempts to compel industrial firms to meet safety standards that would keep dangers (such as chemicals or fibers or dust particles in the air) that are outside the worker's control down to a safe level. This has been a continual struggle, with firms using everything from their own "independent" research institutes to more direct and often questionable forms of political pressure to influence government in the direction of loose standards and lax enforcement. So far, industry has been winning because OSHA [Occupational Safety and Health Administration] has been given neither the personnel nor the mandate to fulfill its purpose. It is so understaffed that, in 1973, when 1,500 federal sky marshals guarded the nation's airplanes from hijackers, only 500 OSHA inspectors toured the nation's workplaces. By 1980, OSHA employed 1,581 compliance safety and health officers, but this still enabled inspection of only roughly 2 percent of the 2.5 million establishments covered by OSHA. The *New York Times* reports that in 1987 the number of OSHA inspectors was down to 1,044. As might be expected, the agency performs fewer inspections that it did a dozen years ago. ...

According to a report issued by the AFL-CIO [American Federation of Labor and Congress of Industrial Organizations] in 1992, "The median penalty paid by an employer during the years 1972–1990 following an incident resulting in death or serious injury of a worker was just $480." The same report claims that the federal government spends $1.1 billion a year to protect fish and wildlife and only $300 million a year to protect workers from health and safety hazards on the job....

Is a person who kills another in a bar brawl a greater threat to society than a business executive who refuses to cut into his profits to make his plant a safe place to work? By any measure of death and suffering the latter is by far a greater danger than the former. Because he wishes his workers no harm, because he is only indirectly responsible for death and disability while pursuing legitimate economic goals, his acts are not called "crimes." Once we free our imagination from the blinders of the one-on-one model of crime, can there be any doubt that the criminal justice system does *not* protect us from the gravest threats to life and limb? It seeks to protect us when danger comes from a young, lower-class male in the inner city. When a threat comes from an upper-class business executive in an office, the criminal justice system looks the other way. This is in the face of growing evidence that for every three American citizens murdered by thugs, at least four American workers are killed by the recklessness of their bosses and the indifference of their government.

Health Care May Be Dangerous to Your Health

... On July 15, 1975, Dr. Sidney Wolfe of Ralph Nader's Public Interest Health Research Group testified before the House Commerce Oversight and Investigations Subcommittee that there "were 3.2 million cases of unnecessary surgery performed each year in the United States." These unneeded operations, Wolfe added, "cost close to $5 billion a year and kill as many as 16,000 Americans." ...

In an article on an experimental program by Blue Cross and Blue Shield aimed at curbing unnecessary surgery, *Newsweek* reports that

> a Congressional committee earlier this year [1976] estimated that more than
> 2 million of the elective operations performed in 1974 were not only unnec-
> essary—but also killed about 12,000 patients and cost nearly $4 billion.

Because the number of surgical operations performed in the United States rose from 16.7 million in 1975 to 22.4 million in 1991, there is reason to believe that at least somewhere between... 12,000 and... 16,000 people a year still die from unnecessary surgery. In 1991, the FBI reported that 3,405 murders were committed by a "cutting or stabbing instrument." Obviously, the FBI does not include the scalpel as a cutting or stabbing instrument. If they did, they would have had to report that between 15,405 and 19,405 persons were killed by "cutting or stabbing" in 1991.... No matter how you slice it, the scalpel may be more dangerous than the switchblade....

Waging Chemical Warfare Against America

One in 4 Americans can expect to contract cancer during their lifetimes. The American Cancer Society estimated that 420,000 Americans would die of cancer in 1981. The National Cancer Institute's estimate for 1993 is 526,000 deaths from cancer. "A 1978 report issued by the President's Council on Environmental Quality (CEQ) unequivocally states that 'most researchers agree that 70 to 90 percent of cancers are caused by environmental influences and are hence theoretically preventable.' " This means that a concerted national effort could result in saving 350,000 or more lives a year and reducing each individual's chances of getting cancer in his or her lifetime from 1 in 4 to 1 in 12 or fewer. If you think this would require a massive effort in terms of money and personnel, you are right. How much of an effort, though, would the nation make to stop a foreign invader who was killing a thousand people and bent on capturing one-quarter of the present population?

In face of this "invasion" that is already under way, the U.S. government has allocated $1.9 billion to the National Cancer Institute (NCI) for fiscal year 1992, and NCI has allocated $219 million to the study of the physical and chemical (i.e., environmental) causes of cancer. Compare this with the (at least) $45 billion spent to fight the Persian Gulf War. The simple truth is that the government that strove so mightily to protect the borders of a small, undemocratic nation 7,000 miles away is doing next to nothing to protect us against the chemical war in our midst. This war is being waged against us on three fronts:

- Pollution
- Cigarette smoking
- Food additives

... The evidence linking *air pollution* and cancer, as well as other serious and often fatal diseases, has been rapidly accumulating in recent years. In 1993, the *Journal of the American Medical Association* reported on research that found " 'robust' associations between premature mortality and air pollution levels." They estimate that pollutants cause about 2 percent of all cancer deaths (at least 10,000 a year)....

A ... recent study ... concluded that air pollution at 1988 levels was responsible for 60,000 deaths a year. The Natural Resources Defense Council sued the EPA [Environmental Protection Agency] for its foot-dragging in implementation of the Clean Air Act, charging that "One hundred million people live in areas of unhealthy air."

This chemical war is not limited to the air. The National Cancer Institute has identified as carcinogens or suspected carcinogens 23 of the chemicals commonly found in our drinking water. Moreover, according to one observer, we are now facing a "new plague—toxic exposure." ...

The evidence linking *cigarette smoking* and cancer is overwhelming and need not be repeated here. The Centers for Disease Control estimates that cigarettes cause 87 percent of lung cancers—approximately 146,000 in 1992. Tobacco continues to kill an estimated 400,000 Americans a year. Cigarettes are widely estimated to cause 30 percent of all cancer deaths....

This is enough to expose the hypocrisy of running a full-scale war against heroin (which produces no degenerative disease) while allowing cigarette sales and advertising to flourish. It also should be enough to underscore the point that once again there are threats to our lives much greater than criminal homicide. The legal order does not protect us against them. Indeed, not only does our government fail to protect us against this threat, it promotes it! ...

Based on the knowledge we have, there can be no doubt that air pollution, tobacco, and food additives amount to a chemical war that makes the crime wave look like a football scrimmage. Even with the most conservative estimates, it is clear that *the death toll in this war is far higher than the number of people killed by criminal homicide!* ...

Summary

Once again, our investigations lead to the same result. The criminal justice system does not protect us against the gravest threats to life, limb, or possessions. Its definitions of crime are not simply a reflection of the objective dangers that threaten us. The workplace, the medical profession, the air we breathe, and the poverty we refuse to rectify lead to far more human suffering, far more death and disability, and take far more dollars from our pockets than the murders, aggravated assaults, and thefts reported annually by the FBI. What is more, this human suffering is preventable. A government really intent on protecting our well-being could enforce work safety regulations, police the medical profession, require that clean air standards be met, and funnel sufficient money to the poor to alleviate the major disabilities of poverty—but it does not. Instead we hear a lot of cant about law and order and a lot of rant about crime in the streets. It is as if our leaders were not only refusing to protect us from the major threats to our well-being but trying to cover up this refusal by diverting our attention to crime—as if this were the only real threat.

POSTSCRIPT

Is Street Crime More Harmful Than White-Collar Crime?

It is important to consider both the suffering and the wider ramifications caused by crimes. DiIulio captures many of these dimensions and gives a full account of the harms of street crime. Today the public is very concerned about street crime, especially wanton violence. However, it seems relatively unconcerned about white-collar crime. Reiman tries to change that perception. By defining many harmful actions by managers and professionals as crimes, he argues that white-collar crime is worse than street crime. He says that more people are killed and injured by "occupational injury or disease, by unnecessary surgery, and by shoddy emergency medical services than by aggravated assault or even homicide!" But are shoddy medical services a crime? In the end, the questions remain: What is a crime? Who are the criminals?

A set of readings that support Reiman's viewpoint is *Corporate Violence: Injury and Death for Profit* edited by Stuart L. Hills (Rowman & Littlefield, 1987). Further support is provided by Marshall B. Clinard, *Corporate Corruption: The Abuse of Power* (Praeger, 1990). *White-Collar Crime*, edited by Gilbert Geis and Robert F. Meier (Free Press, 1977), is a useful compilation of essays on corporate and political crime, as is Gary Green's *Occupational Crime* (Nelson-Hall, 1990). Four other books that focus on crime in high places are J. Douglas and J. M. Johnson, *Official Deviance* (J. B. Lippincott, 1977); J. Anthony Lukas, *Nightmare: The Underside of the Nixon Years* (Viking Press, 1976); Marshall B. Clinard, *Corporate Elites and Crime* (Sage Publications, 1983); and David R. Simon and Stanley Eitzen, *Elite Deviance* (Allyn & Bacon, 1982). A work that deals with the prevalence and fear of street crime is Elliott Currie, *Confronting Crime: An American Challenge* (Pantheon Books, 1985). Two works on gangs, which are often connected with violent street crime, are Martin Sanchez Jankowski, *Islands in the Street: Gangs and American Urban Society* (University of California Press, 1991) and Felix M. Padilla, *The Gang as an American Enterprise* (Rutgers University Press, 1992). William J. Bennett, John J. DiIulio, and John P. Walters, in *Body Count: Moral Poverty—and How to Win America's War Against Crime and Drugs* (Simon & Schuster, 1996), argue that moral poverty is the root cause of crime (meaning street crime). How applicable is this thesis to white-collar crime? One interesting aspect of many corporate, or white-collar, crimes is that they involve crimes of obedience, as discussed in Herman C. Kelman and V. Lee Hamilton, *Crimes of Obedience: Toward a Social Psychology of Authority and Responsibility* (Yale University Press, 1989).

ISSUE 17

Should Drug Use Be Decriminalized?

YES: Ethan A. Nadelmann, from "Commonsense Drug Policy,"
Foreign Affairs (January/February 1998)

NO: Eric A. Voth, from "America's Longest 'War,'" *The World & I*
(February 2000)

ISSUE SUMMARY

YES: Ethan A. Nadelmann, director of the Lindesmith Center, a drug
policy research institute, argues that history shows that drug prohibition is costly and futile. Examining the drug policies in other
countries, he finds that decriminalization plus sane and humane
drug policies and treatment programs can greatly reduce the harms
from drugs.

NO: Eric A. Voth, chairman of the International Drug Strategy Institute, contends that drugs are very harmful and that our drug policies
have succeeded in substantially reducing drug use.

$\mathbf{A}$century ago, drugs of every kind were freely available to Americans. Lau-
danum, a mixture of opium and alcohol, was popularly used as a painkiller.
One drug company even claimed that it was a very useful substance for calm-
ing hyperactive children, and the company called it Mother's Helper. Morphine
came into common use during the Civil War. Heroin, developed as a supposedly less addictive substitute for morphine, began to be marketed at the end
of the nineteenth century. By that time, drug paraphernalia could be ordered
through Sears and Roebuck catalogues, and Coca-Cola, which contained small
quantities of cocaine, had become a popular drink.

Public concerns about addiction and dangerous patent medicines, and an
active campaign for drug laws waged by Dr. Harvey Wiley, a chemist in the
U.S. Department of Agriculture, led Congress to pass the first national drug
regulation act in 1906. The Pure Food and Drug Act required that medicines
containing certain drugs, such as opium, must say so on their labels. The Harrison Narcotic Act of 1914 went much further and cut off completely the supply
of legal opiates to addicts. Since then, ever-stricter drug laws have been passed
by Congress and by state legislatures.

Drug abuse in America again came to the forefront of public discourse during the 1960s, when heroin addiction started growing rapidly in inner-city neighborhoods. Also, by the end of the decade, drug experimentation had spread to the middle-class, affluent baby boomers who were then attending college. Indeed, certain types of drugs began to be celebrated by some of the leaders of the counterculture. Heroin was still taboo, but other drugs, notably marijuana and LSD (a psychedelic drug), were regarded as harmless and even spiritually transforming. At music festivals like Woodstock in 1969, marijuana and LSD were used openly and associated with love, peace, and heightened sensitivity. Much of this enthusiasm cooled over the next 20 years as baby boomers entered the workforce full-time and began their careers. But even among the careerists, certain types of drugs enjoyed high status. Cocaine, noted for its highly stimulating effects, became the drug of choice for many hard-driving young lawyers, television writers, and Wall Street bond traders.

The high price of cocaine put it out of reach for many people, but in the early 1980s, cheap substitutes began to appear on the streets and to overtake poor urban communities. Crack cocaine, a potent, highly addictive, smokable form of cocaine, came into widespread use. By the end of the 1980s, the drug known as "ice," or as it is called on the West Coast, "L.A. glass," a smokable form of amphetamine, had hit the streets. These stimulants tend to produce very violent, disorderly behavior. Moreover, the street gangs who sell them are frequently at war with one another and are well armed. Not only gang members but also many innocent people have become victims of contract killings, street battles, and drive-by shootings.

This new drug epidemic prompted President George Bush to declare a "war on drugs," and in 1989 he asked Congress to appropriate $10.6 billion for the fight. Although most Americans support such measures against illegal drugs, some say that in the years since Bush made his declaration, the drug situation has not showed any signs of improvement. Some believe that legalization would be the best way to fight the drug problem.

The drug decriminalization issue is especially interesting to sociologists because it raises basic questions about what should be socially sanctioned or approved, what is illegal or legal, and what is immoral or moral. An aspect of the basic value system of America is under review. The process of value change may be taking place in front of our eyes. As part of this debate, Ethan A. Nadelmann argues that the present policy does not work and that it is counterproductive. Legalization, he contends, would stop much of the disease, violence, and crime associated with illegal drugs. Although Nadelmann concedes that it may increase the use of lower-potency drugs, he believes that legalization would reduce the use of the worst drugs. Eric A. Voth maintains that legalization would be madness because he asserts that the current drug policies in effect are working.

Ethan A. Nadelmann  **YES**

Commonsense Drug Policy

First, Reduce Harm

In 1988 Congress passed a resolution proclaiming its goal of "a drug-free America by 1995." U.S. drug policy has failed persistently over the decades because it has preferred such rhetoric to reality, and moralism to pragmatism. Politicians confess their youthful indiscretions, then call for tougher drug laws. Drug control officials make assertions with no basis in fact or science. Police officers, generals, politicians, and guardians of public morals qualify as drug czars—but not, to date, a single doctor or public health figure. Independent commissions are appointed to evaluate drug policies, only to see their recommendations ignored as politically risky. And drug policies are designed, implemented, and enforced with virtually no input from the millions of Americans they affect most: drug users. Drug abuse is a serious problem, both for individual citizens and society at large, but the "war on drugs" has made matters worse, not better.

Drug warriors often point to the 1980s as a time in which the drug war really worked. Illicit drug use by teenagers peaked around 1980, then fell more than 50 percent over the next 12 years. During the 1996 presidential campaign, Republican challenger Bob Dole made much of the recent rise in teenagers' use of illicit drugs, contrasting it with the sharp drop during the Reagan and Bush administrations. President Clinton's response was tepid, in part because he accepted the notion that teen drug use is the principal measure of drug policy's success or failure; at best, he could point out that the level was still barely half what it had been in 1980.

In 1980, however, no one had ever heard of the cheap, smokable form of cocaine called crack, or drug-related HIV infection or AIDS. By the 1990s, both had reached epidemic proportions in American cities, largely driven by prohibitionist economics and morals indifferent to the human consequences of the drug war. In 1980, the federal budget for drug control was about $1 billion, and state and local budgets were perhaps two or three times that. By 1997, the federal drug control budget had ballooned to $16 billion, two-thirds of it for law enforcement agencies, and state and local funding to at least that. On any day in 1980, approximately 50,000 people were behind bars for violating a drug law. By 1997, the number had increased eightfold, to about 400,000. These are

From Ethan A. Nadelmann, "Commonsense Drug Policy," *Foreign Affairs,* vol. 77, no. 1 (January/February 1998). Copyright © 1998 by The Council on Foreign Relations, Inc. Reprinted by permission of *Foreign Affairs.* Notes omitted.

the results of a drug policy overreliant on criminal justice "solutions," ideologically wedded to abstinence-only treatment, and insulated from cost-benefit analysis.

Imagine instead a policy that starts by acknowledging that drugs are here to stay, and that we have no choice but to learn how to live with them so that they cause the least possible harm. Imagine a policy that focuses on reducing not illicit drug use per se but the crime and misery caused by both drug abuse and prohibitionist policies. And imagine a drug policy based not on the fear, prejudice, and ignorance that drive America's current approach but rather on common sense, science, public health concerns, and human rights. Such a policy is possible in the United States, especially if Americans are willing to learn from the experiences of other countries where such policies are emerging.

Attitudes Abroad

Americans are not averse to looking abroad for solutions to the nation's drug problems. Unfortunately, they have been looking in the wrong places: Asia and Latin America, where much of the world's heroin and cocaine originates. Decades of U.S. efforts to keep drugs from being produced abroad and exported to American markets have failed. Illicit drug production is bigger business than ever before. The opium poppy, source of morphine and heroin, and *cannabis sativa*, from which marijuana and hashish are prepared, grow readily around the world; the coca plant, from whose leaves cocaine is extracted, can be cultivated far from its native environment in the Andes. Crop substitution programs designed to persuade Third World peasants to grow legal crops cannot compete with the profits that drug prohibition makes inevitable. Crop eradication campaigns occasionally reduce production in one country, but new suppliers pop up elsewhere. International law enforcement efforts can disrupt drug trafficking organizations and routes, but they rarely have much impact on U.S. drug markets....

While looking to Latin America and Asia for supply-reduction solutions to America's drug problems is futile, the harm-reduction approaches spreading throughout Europe and Australia and even into corners of North America show promise. These approaches start by acknowledging that supply-reduction initiatives are inherently limited, that criminal justice responses can be costly and counterproductive, and that single-minded pursuit of a "drug-free society" is dangerously quixotic. Demand-reduction efforts to prevent drug abuse among children and adults are important, but so are harm-reduction efforts to lessen the damage to those unable or unwilling to stop using drugs immediately, and to those around them.

Most proponents of harm reduction do not favor legalization. They recognize that prohibition has failed to curtail drug abuse, that it is responsible for much of the crime, corruption, disease, and death associated with drugs, and that its costs mount every year. But they also see legalization as politically unwise and as risking increased drug use. The challenge is thus making drug prohibition work better, but with a focus on reducing the negative consequences of both drug use and prohibitionist policies....

Harm-reduction innovations include efforts to stem the spread of HIV by making sterile syringes readily available and collecting used syringes; allowing doctors to prescribe oral methadone for heroin addiction treatment, as well as heroin and other drugs for addicts who would otherwise buy them on the black market; establishing "safe injection rooms" so addicts do not congregate in public places or dangerous "shooting galleries"; employing drug analysis units at the large dance parties called raves to test the quality and potency of MDMA, known as Ecstasy, and other drugs that patrons buy and consume there; decriminalizing (but not legalizing) possession and retail sale of cannabis and, in some cases, possession of small amounts of "hard" drugs; and integrating harm-reduction policies and principles into community policing strategies. Some of these measures are under way or under consideration in parts of the United States, but rarely to the extent found in growing numbers of foreign countries.

Stopping HIV With Sterile Syringes

The spread of HIV, the virus that causes AIDS, among people who inject drugs illegally was what prompted governments in Europe and Australia to experiment with harm-reduction policies. During the early 1980s public health officials realized that infected users were spreading HIV by sharing needles. Having already experienced a hepatitis epidemic attributed to the same mode of transmission, the Dutch were the first to tell drug users about the risks of needle sharing and to make sterile syringes available and collect dirty needles through pharmacies, needle exchange and methadone programs, and public health services. Governments elsewhere in Europe and in Australia soon followed suit. The few countries in which a prescription was necessary to obtain a syringe dropped the requirement. Local authorities in Germany, Switzerland, and other European countries authorized needle exchange machines to ensure 24-hour access. In some European cities, addicts can exchange used syringes for clean ones at local police stations without fear of prosecution or harassment. Prisons are instituting similar policies to help discourage the spread of HIV among inmates, recognizing that illegal drug injecting cannot be eliminated even behind bars.

These initiatives were not adopted without controversy. Conservative politicians argued that needle exchange programs condoned illicit and immoral behavior and that government policies should focus on punishing drug users or making them drug-free. But by the late 1980s, the consensus in most of Western Europe, Oceania, and Canada was that while drug abuse was a serious problem, AIDS was worse. Slowing the spread of a fatal disease for which no cure exists was the greater moral imperative. There was also a fiscal imperative. Needle exchange programs' costs are minuscule compared with those of treating people who would otherwise become infected with HIV.

Only in the United States has this logic not prevailed, even though AIDS was the leading killer of Americans ages 25 to 44 for most of the 1990s and is now No. 2. The Centers for Disease Control (CDC) estimates that half of new HIV infections in the country stem from injection drug use. Yet both the White House and Congress block allocation of AIDS or drug-abuse prevention funds for needle exchange, and virtually all state governments retain drug para-phernalia laws, pharmacy regulations, and other restrictions on access to sterile syringes. During the 1980s, AIDS activists engaging in civil disobedience set up more syringe exchange programs than state and local governments. There are now more than 100 such programs in 28 states, Washington, D.C., and Puerto Rico, but they reach only an estimated 10 percent of injection drug users.

Governments at all levels in the United States refuse to fund needle ex-change for political reasons, even though dozens of scientific studies, domestic and foreign, have found that needle exchange and other distribution programs reduce needle sharing, bring hard-to-reach drug users into contact with health care systems, and inform addicts about treatment programs, yet do not increase illegal drug use. In 1991 the National AIDS Commission appointed by Presi-dent Bush called the lack of federal support for such programs "bewildering and tragic." In 1993 a CDC-sponsored review of research on needle exchange recommended federal funding, but top officials in the Clinton administration suppressed a favorable evaluation of the report within the Department of Health and Human Services. In July 1996 President Clinton's Advisory Council on HIV/AIDS criticized the administration for its failure to heed the National Academy of Sciences' recommendation that it authorize the use of federal money to support needle exchange programs. An independent panel convened by the National In-stitute[s] of Health reached the same conclusion in February 1997. Last summer, the American Medical Association, the American Bar Association, and even the politicized U.S. Conference of Mayors endorsed the concept of needle exchange. In the fall, an endorsement followed from the World Bank.

To date, America's failure in this regard is conservatively estimated to have resulted in the infection of up to 10,000 people with HIV. Mounting scien-tific evidence and the stark reality of the continuing AIDS crisis have convinced the public, if not politicians, that needle exchange saves lives; polls consis-tently find that a majority of Americans support needle exchange, with approval highest among those most familiar with the notion. Prejudice and political cow-ardice are poor excuses for allowing more citizens to suffer from and die of AIDS, especially when effective interventions are cheap, safe, and easy.

Methadone and Other Alternatives

The United States pioneered the use of the synthetic opiate methadone to treat heroin addiction in the 1960s and 1970s, but now lags behind much of Europe and Australia in making methadone accessible and effective. Methadone is the best available treatment in terms of reducing illicit heroin use and associated crime, disease, and death. In the early 1990s the National Academy of Sciences' Institute of Medicine stated that of all forms of drug treatment, "methadone maintenance has been the most rigorously studied modality and has yielded the most incontrovertibly positive results.... Consumption of all illicit drugs, especially heroin, declines. Crime is reduced, fewer individuals become HIV positive, and individual functioning is improved." However, the institute went on to declare, "Current policy ... puts too much emphasis on protecting society from methadone, and not enough on protecting society from the epidemics of addiction, violence, and infectious diseases that methadone can help reduce."

Methadone is to street heroin what nicotine skin patches and chewing gum are to cigarettes—with the added benefit of legality. Taken orally, methadone has little of injected heroin's effect on mood or cognition. It can be consumed for decades with few if any negative health consequences, and its purity and concentration, unlike street heroin's, are assured. Like other opiates, it can create physical dependence if taken regularly, but the "addiction" is more like a diabetic's "addiction" to insulin than a heroin addict's to product brought on the street. Methadone patients can and do drive safely, hold good jobs, and care for their children. When prescribed adequate doses, they can be indistinguishable from people who have never used heroin or methadone.

Popular misconceptions and prejudice, however, have all but prevented any expansion of methadone treatment in the United States. The 115,000 Americans receiving methadone today represent only a small increase over the number 20 years ago. For every ten heroin addicts, there are only one or two methadone treatment slots. Methadone is the most tightly controlled drug in the pharmacopoeia, subject to unique federal and state restrictions. Doctors cannot prescribe it for addiction treatment outside designated programs. Regulations dictate not only security, documentation, and staffing requirements but maximum doses, admission criteria, time spent in the program, and a host of other specifics, none of which has much to do with quality of treatment. Moreover, the regulations do not prevent poor treatment; many clinics provide insufficient doses, prematurely detoxify clients, expel clients for offensive behavior, and engage in other practices that would be regarded as unethical in any other field of medicine. Attempts to open new clinics tend to be blocked by residents who don't want addicts in their neighborhood....

The Swiss government began a nationwide trial in 1994 to determine whether prescribing heroin, morphine, or injectable methadone could reduce crime, disease, and other drug-related ills. Some 1,000 volunteers—only heroin addicts with at least two unsuccessful experiences in methadone or other conventional treatment programs were considered—took part in the experiment. The trial quickly determined that virtually all participants preferred heroin, and doctors subsequently prescribed it for them. Last July the government reported the results so far: criminal offenses and the number of criminal offenders dropped 60 percent, the percentage of income from illegal and semilegal activities fell from 69 to 10 percent, illegal heroin *and* cocaine use declined dramatically (although use of alcohol, cannabis, and tranquilizers like Valium remained fairly constant), stable employment increased from 14 to 32 percent, physical health improved enormously, and most participants greatly reduced their contact with the drug scene. There were no deaths from overdoses, and no prescribed drugs were diverted to the black market. More than half those who dropped out of the study switched to another form of drug treatment, including 83 who began abstinence therapy. A cost-benefit analysis of the program found a net economic benefit of $30 per patient per day, mostly because of reduced criminal justice and health care costs.

The Swiss study has undermined several myths about heroin and its habitual users. The results to date demonstrate that, given relatively unlimited availability, heroin users will voluntarily stabilize or reduce their dosage and some will even choose abstinence; that long-addicted users can lead relatively normal, stable lives if provided legal access to their drug of choice; and that ordinary citizens will support such initiatives. In recent referendums in Zurich, Basel, and Zug, substantial majorities voted to continue funding local arms of the experiment. And last September, a nationwide referendum to end the government's heroin maintenance and other harm-reduction initiatives was rejected by 71 percent of Swiss voters, including majorities in all 26 cantons....

Reefer Sanity

Cannabis, in the form of marijuana and hashish, is by far the most popular illicit drug in the United States. More than a quarter of Americans admit to having tried it. Marijuana's popularity peaked in 1980, dropped steadily until the early 1990s, and is now on the rise again. Although it is not entirely safe, especially when consumed by children, smoked heavily, or used when driving, it is clearly among the least dangerous psychoactive drugs in common use. In 1988 the administrative law judge for the Drug Enforcement Administration, Francis Young, reviewed the evidence and concluded that "marihuana, in its natural form, is one of the safest therapeutically active substances known to man."

As with needle exchange and methadone treatment, American politicians have ignored or spurned the findings of government commissions and scientific organizations concerning marijuana policy. In 1972 the National Commission on Marihuana and Drug Abuse—created by President Nixon and chaired by a former Republican governor, Raymond Shafer—recommended that possession of up to one ounce of marijuana be decriminalized. Nixon rejected the recommendation. In 1982 a panel appointed by the National Academy of Sciences reached the same conclusions as the Shafer Commission.

Between 1973 and 1978, with attitudes changing, 11 states approved decriminalization statutes that reclassified marijuana possession as a misdemeanor, petty offense, or civil violation punishable by no more than a $100 fine. Consumption trends in those states and in states that retained stricter sanctions were indistinguishable. A 1988 scholarly evaluation of the Moscone Act, California's 1976 decriminalization law, estimated that the state had saved half a billion dollars in arrest costs since the law's passage. Nonetheless, public opinion began to shift in 1978. No other states decriminalized marijuana, and some eventually recriminalized it.

Between 1973 and 1989, annual arrests on marijuana charges by state and local police ranged between 360,000 and 460,000. The annual total fell to 283,700 in 1991, but has since more than doubled. In 1996, 641,642 people were arrested for marijuana, 85 percent of them for possession, not sale, of the drug. Prompted by concern over rising marijuana use among adolescents and fears of being labeled soft on drugs, the Clinton administration launched its own anti-marijuana campaign in 1995. But the administration's claims to have identified new risks of marijuana consumption—including a purported link between marijuana and violent behavior—have not withstood scrutiny. Neither Congress nor the White House seems likely to put the issue of marijuana policy before a truly independent advisory commission, given the consistency with which such commissions have reached politically unacceptable conclusions....

Will It Work?

Both at home and abroad, the U.S. government has attempted to block resolutions supporting harm reduction, suppress scientific studies that reached politically inconvenient conclusions, and silence critics of official drug policy. In May 1994, the State Department forced the last-minute cancellation of a World Bank conference on drug trafficking to which critics of U.S. drug policy had been invited. That December the U.S. delegation to an international meeting of the U.N. Drug Control Program refused to sign any statement incorporating the phrase "harm reduction." In early 1995 the State Department successfully pressured the World Health Organization to scuttle the release of a report it had commissioned from a panel that included many of the world's leading experts on cocaine because it included the scientifically incontrovertible observations that traditional use of coca leaf in the Andes causes little harm to users and that most consumers of cocaine use the drug in moderation with few detrimental effects. Hundreds of congressional hearings have addressed multitudinous aspects of the drug problem, but few have inquired into the European harm-reduction policies described above. When former Secretary of State George Shultz, then–Surgeon General M. Joycelyn Elders, and Baltimore Mayor Kurt Schmoke pointed to the failure of current policies and called for new approaches, they were mocked, fired, and ignored, respectively—and thereafter mischaracterized as advocating the outright legalization of drugs.

In Europe, in contrast, informed, public debate about drug policy is increasingly common in government, even at the EU level. In June 1995 the European Parliament issued a report acknowledging that "there will always be a demand for drugs in our societies ... the policies followed so far have not been able to prevent the illegal drug trade from flourishing." The EU called for serious consideration of the Frankfurt Resolution, a statement of harm-reduction principles supported by a transnational coalition of 31 cities and regions. In October 1996 Emma Bonino, the European commissioner for consumer policy, advocated decriminalizing soft drugs and initiating a broad prescription program for hard drugs. Greece's minister for European affairs, George Papandreou, seconded her. Last February the monarch of Liechtenstein, Prince Hans Adam, spoke out in favor of controlled drug legalization. Even Raymond Kendall, secretary general of Interpol, was quoted in the August 20, 1994, *Guardian* as saying, "The prosecution of thousands of otherwise law-abiding citizens every year is both hypocritical and an affront to individual, civil and human rights.... Drug use should no longer be a criminal offense. I am totally against legalization, but in favor of decriminalization for the user."...

The lessons from Europe and Australia are compelling. Drug control policies should focus on reducing drug-related crime, disease, and death, not the number of casual drug users. Stopping the spread of HIV by and among drug users by making sterile syringes and methadone readily available must be the first priority. American politicians need to explore, not ignore or automatically condemn, promising policy options such as cannabis decriminalization, heroin prescription, and the integration of harm-reduction principles into community policing strategies. Central governments must back, or at least not hinder, the efforts of municipal officials and citizens to devise pragmatic approaches to local drug problems. Like citizens in Europe, the American public has supported such innovations when they are adequately explained and allowed to prove themselves. As the evidence comes in, what works is increasingly apparent. All that remains is mustering the political courage.

Eric A. Voth

 **NO**

America's Longest "War"

Bashing our drug policy is a popular activity. The advocates of legalization and decriminalization repeatedly contend that restrictive drug policy is failing, in the hope that this becomes a self-fulfilling prophecy. An objective look at the history of drug policy in the United States, especially in comparison to other countries, demonstrates that, indeed, our policies are working. What we also see is the clear presence of a well-organized and well-financed drug culture lobby that seeks to tear down restrictive drug policy and replace it with permissive policies that could seriously jeopardize our country's viability.

To understand our current situation, we must examine the last 25 years. The 1970s were a time of great social turmoil for the United States, and drug use was finding its way into the fabric of society. Policymakers were uncertain how to deal with drugs. As permissive advisers dominated the discussion, drug use climbed. The National Household Survey and the Monitoring the Future Survey both confirm that drug use peaked in the late 1970s. Twenty-five million Americans were current users of drugs in 1979, 37 percent of high school seniors had used marijuana in the prior 30 days, and 10. 7 percent of them used marijuana daily. During the same time frame, 13 states embraced the permissive social attitude and legalized or decriminalized marijuana.

In the late 1970s, policymakers, parents, and law enforcement began to realize that our drug situation was leading to Armageddon. As never before, a coordinated war on drugs was set in motion that demanded a no-use message. This was largely driven by parents who were sick of their children falling prey to drugs. The "Just Say No" movement was the centerpiece of antidrug activities during the subsequent years. A solid national antidrug message was coupled with rigorous law enforcement. The results were striking. As perception of the harmfulness of drugs increased, their use dropped drastically. By 1992, marijuana use by high school students in the prior 30 days had dropped to 11.9 percent and daily use to 1.9 percent.

Breakdown in the 1990s

Unfortunately, several major events derailed our policy successes in the early 1990s, resulting in an approximate doubling of drug use since that time. From a national vantage point, a sense of complacency set in. Satisfied that the drug war was won, we lost national leadership. Federal funding for antidrug programs became mired in bureaucracy and difficult for small prevention organizations to obtain. A new generation of drug specialists entered the scene. Lacking experience of the ravages of the 1970s, they were willing to accept softening of policy. The Internet exploded as an open forum for the dissemination of inaccurate, deceptive, and manipulative information supporting permissive policy, even discussions of how to obtain and use drugs. The greatest audience has been young people, who are exposed to a plethora of drug-permissive information without filter or validation.

The entertainment media have provided a steady diet of alcohol and drug use for young people to witness. A recent study commissioned by the White House Office of National Drug Control Policy found that alcohol appeared in more than 93 percent of movies and illicit drugs in 22 percent, of which 51 percent depicted marijuana use. Concurrently, the news media have begun to demonstrate bias toward softening of drug policy, having the net effect of changing public opinion.

The single most dramatic influence, however, came in the transformation of the drug culture from a disorganized group of legalization advocates to a well-funded and well-organized machine. With funding from several large donors, drug-culture advocates were able to initiate large-scale attacks on the media and policymakers. The most prominent funder is the billionaire George Soros, who has spent millions toward the initiation of organizations such as the Drug Policy Foundation, Lindesmith Center, medical-marijuana-advocacy and needle-handout groups, to name a few projects.

A slick strategic shift toward compartmentalizing and dissecting restrictive drug policy has resulted in what is termed the "harm reduction" movement. After all, who would oppose the idea of reducing the harm to society caused by drug use? The philosophy of the harm reduction movement is well summarized by Ethan Nadelman of the Lindesmith Center (also funded by Soros), who is considered the godfather of the legalization movement:

> Let's start by dropping the "zero tolerance" rhetoric and policies and the illusory goal of drug-free societies. Accept that drug use is here to stay and that we have no choice but to learn to live with drugs so that they cause the least possible harm. Recognize that many, perhaps most, "drug problems" in the Americas are the results not of drug use per se but of our prohibitionist policies....

The harm reduction movement has attacked the individual components of restrictive drug policy and created strategies to weaken it. Some of these strategies include giving heroin to addicts; handing out needles to addicts; encouraging use of crack cocaine instead of intravenous drugs; reducing drug-related criminal penalties; teaching "responsible" drug use to adolescents instead of working toward prevention of use; the medical marijuana movement; and the expansion of the industrial hemp movement.

Softening Drug Policies

The move toward soft drug policy has created some strange bedfellows. On one hand, supporters of liberal policy such as Gov. Gary Johnson of New Mexico have always taken the misguided view that individuals should have a right to use whatever they want in order to feel good. They often point to their own "survival" of drug use as justification for loosening laws and letting others experiment. Interestingly, the governor's public safety secretary quit as a result of being undermined by Johnson's destructive stand on legalization. Libertarian conservatives such as Milton Friedman and William Buckley have attacked drug policy as an infringement of civil liberties and have incorrectly considered drug use to be a victimless event. Societal problems such as homelessness, domestic abuse, numerous health problems, crimes under the influence, poor job performance, decreased productivity, and declining educational levels have strong connections to drug use and cost our society financially and spiritually.

The notion that decriminalizing or legalizing drugs will drive the criminal element out of the market is flawed and reflects a total lack of understanding of drug use and addiction. Drug use creates its own market, and often the only thing limiting the amount of drugs that an addict uses is the amount of money available. Further, if drugs were legalized, what would the legal scenario be? Would anyone be allowed to sell drugs? Would they be sold by the government? If so, what strengths would be available? If there were any limitations on strength or availability, a black market would immediately develop. Most rational people can easily recognize this slippery slope.

Consistently, drug-culture advocates assert that policy has failed and is extremely costly. This is a calculated strategy to demoralize the population and turn public sentiment against restrictive policy. The real question is, has restrictive policy failed? First we should consider the issues of cost. An effective way to determine cost-effectiveness is to compare the costs to society of legal versus illegal drugs. Estimates from 1990 suggest that the costs of illegal drugs were $70 billion, as compared to that of alcohol alone at $99 billion and tobacco at $72 billion. Estimates from 1992 put the costs of alcohol dependence at $148 billion and all illegal drugs (including the criminal justice system costs) at $98 billion.

Referring to the National Household Survey data from 1998, there were 13.6 million current users of illicit drugs compared to 113 million users of alcohol and 60 million tobacco smokers. There is one difference: legal status of the drugs. The Monitoring the Future Survey of high school seniors suggests that in 1995, some 52.5 percent of seniors had been drunk within the previous year as compared to 34.7 percent who had used marijuana. *Yet,* alcohol is illegal for teenagers. The only difference is, again, the legal status of the two substances.

Results of Legalization

Permissive drug policy has been tried both in the United States and abroad. In 1985, during the period in which Alaska legalized marijuana, the use of marijuana and cocaine among adolescents was more than twice as high as in other parts of the country. Baltimore has long been heralded as a center-piece for harm reduction drug policy. Interestingly, the rate of heroin use found among arrestees in Baltimore was higher than in any other city in the United States. Thirty-seven percent of male and 48 percent of female arrestees were positive, compared with 6–23 percent for Washington, D.C., Philadelphia, and Manhattan.

Since liberalizing its marijuana-enforcement policies, the Netherlands has found that marijuana use among 11- to 18-year-olds has increased 142 percent from 1990 to 1995. Crime has risen steadily to the point that aggravated theft and breaking and entering occur three to four times more than in the United States. Along with the staggering increases in marijuana use, the Netherlands has become one of the major suppliers of the drug Ecstacy. Australia is flirting with substantial softening of drug policy. That is already taking a toll. Drug use there among 16- to 29-year-olds is 52 percent as compared with 9 percent in Sweden, a country with a restrictive drug policy. In Vancouver in 1988, HIV prevalence among IV drug addicts was only 1–2 percent. In 1997 it was 23 percent, after wide adoption of harm reduction policies. Vancouver has the largest needle exchange in North America.

Clearly, the last few years have witnessed some very positive changes in policy and our antidrug efforts. A steady national voice opposing drug use is again being heard. Efforts are being made to increase cooperation between the treatment and law enforcement communities to allow greater access to treatment. The primary prevention movement is strong and gaining greater footholds. The increases in drug use witnessed in the early 1990s have slowed.

On the other hand, the drug culture has been successful at some efforts to soften drug policy. Medical marijuana initiatives have successfully passed in several states. These were gross examples of abuse of the ballot initiative process. Large amounts of money purchased slick media campaigns and seduced the public into supporting medical marijuana under the guise of compassion. Industrial hemp initiatives are popping up all over the country in an attempt to hurt anti-marijuana law enforcement and soften public opinion. Needle hand-outs are being touted as successes, while the evidence is clearly demonstrating failures and increases in HIV, hepatitis B, and hepatitis C. Internationally, our Canadian neighbors are moving down a very destructive road toward drug legalization and harm reduction. The Swiss are experimenting with the lives of addicts by implementing heroin handouts and selective drug legalization. In this international atmosphere, children's attitudes about the harmfulness of drugs teeter in the balance.

Future drug policy must continue to emphasize and fund primary prevention, with the goal of no use of illegal drugs and no illegal use of legal drugs. Treatment availability must be seriously enhanced, but treatment must not be a revolving door. It must be carefully designed and outcomes based. The Rand Drug Policy Research Center concluded that the costs of cocaine use could be reduced by $33.9 billion through the layering of treatment for heavy users on top of our current enforcement efforts.

Drug screening is an extremely effective means for identifying drug use. It should be widely extended into business and industry, other social arenas, and schools. Screening must be coupled with a rehabilitative approach, however, and not simply punishment. The self-serving strategies of the drug culture must be exposed. The public needs to become aware of how drug-culture advocates are manipulating public opinion in the same fashion that the tobacco industry has for so many years.

A compassionate but restrictive drug policy that partners prevention, rehabilitation, and law enforcement will continue to show the greatest chance for success. Drug policy must focus on harm prevention through clear primary prevention messages, and it must focus upon harm elimination through treatment availability and rigorous law enforcement.

POSTSCRIPT

Should Drug Use Be Decriminalized?

The analogy often cited by proponents of drug legalization is the ill-fated attempt to ban the sale of liquor in the United States, which lasted from 1919 to 1933. Prohibition has been called "an experiment noble in purpose," but it was an experiment that greatly contributed to the rise of organized crime. The repeal of Prohibition brought about an increase in liquor consumption and alcoholism, but it also deprived organized crime of an important source of income. Would drug decriminalization similarly strike a blow at the drug dealers? Possibly, and such a prospect is obviously appealing. But would drug decriminalization also exacerbate some of the ills associated with drugs? Would there be more violence, more severe addiction, and more crack babies born to addicted mothers?

There are a variety of publications and theories pertaining to drug use and society. Ronald L. Akers, in *Drugs, Alcohol, and Society* (Wadsworth, 1992), relates drug patterns to social structure. For a comprehensive overview of the history, effects, and prevention of drug use, see Weldon L. Witters, Peter J. Venturelli, and Glen R. Hanson, *Drugs and Society*, 3rd ed. (Jones & Bartlett, 1992) and Mike Gray, *Drug Crazy: How We Got Into This Mess and How We Can Get Out* (Random House, 1998). Terry Williams describes the goings-on in a crackhouse in *Crackhouse: Notes From the End of the Zone* (Addison-Wesley, 1992). James A. Inciardi, Ruth Horowitz, and Anne El Pottieger focus on street kids and drugs in *Street Kids, Street Drugs, Street Crime: An Examination of Drug Use and Serious Delinquency in Miami* (Wadsworth, 1993). For an excellent study of how users of the drug ecstasy perceive the experience, see Jerome Beck and Marsha Rosenbaum, *Pursuit of Ecstasy: The MDMA Experience* (SUNY Press, 1994). For studies of female drug-using groups, see Carl S. Taylor, *Girls, Gangs, Women and Drugs* (Michigan State University Press, 1993) and Avril Taylor, *Women Drug Users: An Ethnography of a Female Injecting Community* (Clarendon Press, 1993). For a relatively balanced yet innovative set of drug policies, see Elliott Carrie, *Reckoning: Drugs, the Cities, and the American Future* (Hill & Wang, 1993). William O. Walker III, ed., *Drug Control Policy* (Pennsylvania State University Press, 1992) critically evaluates drug policies from historical and comparative perspectives. On the legalization debate, see Eric Goode, *Between Politics and Reason: The Drug Legalization Debate* (St. Martin's Press, 1997) and Arnold Trebach and James A. Inciardi, *Legalize It? Debating American Drug Policy* (American University Press, 1993). For criticism of the current drug policies, see Dan Baum, *Smoke and Mirrors: The War on Drugs and the Politics of Failure* (Little, Brown, 1996) and Leif Rosenberger, *America's Drug War Debacle* (Avebury, 1996).

ISSUE 18

Is Capital Punishment Justified?

YES: Robert W. Lee, from "Deserving to Die," *The New American* (August 13, 1990)

NO: Eric M. Freedman, from "The Case Against the Death Penalty," *USA Today Magazine* (March 1997)

ISSUE SUMMARY

YES: Editor and author Robert W. Lee argues that capital punishment is needed to deter people from committing murder and other heinous crimes, but more importantly, it is the punishment that is the most appropriate for these crimes.

NO: Legal scholar Eric M. Freedman counters that the death penalty does not deter crime and has unacceptable negative consequences, including the potential of killing innocent people, reducing public safety, and imposing considerable costs on society.

O n January 13, 2000, Governor George Ryan of Illinois imposed a moratorium on executions in his state because 13 death row inmates had been released when found to have been wrongly convicted. Ryan was a pro-death-penalty Republican but was deeply concerned about the possibility of executing innocent people. Recent use of DNA evidence had proven that the justice system can be deeply flawed. The Supreme Court supported the constitutionality of the death penalty in 1976 and since then 87 people have been freed from death row on the basis of new evidence.

In 1997 The Death Penalty Information Center issued a report by its director Richard C. Dieter entitled, "The Death Penalty: The Increasing Danger of Executing the Innocent." The executive summary of this report states:

> Twenty-one condemned inmates have been released since 1993 . . . Many of these cases were discovered not because of the normal appeals process, but rather as a result of new scientific techniques, investigations by journalists, and the dedicated work of expert attorneys, not available to the typical death row inmate.
>
> This report tells the stories of people like Rolando Cruz, released after 10 years on Illinois's death row, despite the fact that another man had confessed to the crime shortly after his conviction; and Ricardo Aldape Guerra,

who returned to Mexico after 15 years on Texas's death row because of a prosecution that a federal judge called outrageous and designed to simply achieve another notch on the prosecutor's gun. This report particularly looks at the dramatic narrowing of the opportunity to appeal and to raise newly discovered evidence of one's innocence. The federal funding for the death penalty resource centers, which helped discover and vindicate several of the innocent people cited in this report, has been completely withdrawn. Some courts have now taken the position that it is permissible for executions to go forward even in the face of considerable doubt about the defendant's guilt.

How flawed is the criminal justice system? Is there too much potential for error when it comes to capital punishment? Some argue that there is. Too many innocent people die for crimes that they did not commit.

However, some would point out that a murderer, once executed, will never commit murder again. In Utah there have been three executions since 1976. After each execution, the murder rate decreased significantly. It can be argued that the execution acted as a deterrent in those three cases.

Is life imprisonment a suitable alternative to capital punishment? Some state that the rate of escape for "lifers" puts too many innocent people at risk. Does a life sentence provide adequate protection for society? Do the criminals deserve to be killed? Some state that certain crimes warrant the strictest of punishments, thus placing the burden of crime onto the criminal and away from the innocent.

The public currently favors the death penalty according to recent polls. A *Newsweek* poll in 2000 found that 73 percent of Americans support capital punishment, an increase from 42 percent in 1966. Executions have also increased. There were no executions from 1968 to 1976, 117 people were executed in the 1980s, and 478 in the 1990s. Executions rose rapidly in the 1990s from 14 in 1991 to 98 in 1999, which makes America a world leader behind China with 1,077, Iran with 165, Saudi Arabia with 103, and the Congo with 100. The concern is with victims' rights, while defendants' rights are being cut back because some defendants' rights provisions are perceived as too greatly interfering with effective law enforcement.

Can we evaluate how effective a deterrent capital punishment is? Is there enough information available to make an accurate assessment? Is capital punishment administered in a racially biased manner? Is capital punishment the only way to guarantee adequate protection against people who commit heinous crimes? What burden should society at large assume concerning the few who commit heinous crimes? These are important questions to consider when deciding if capital punishment is justified or not.

In the following selections, Robert W. Lee advocates capital punishment as required justice for certain crimes and the only effective deterrent in some situations. Eric M. Freedman disagrees about the deterrent effect of capital punishment and raises concerns about the execution of innocent people.

Robert W. Lee

 **YES**

Deserving to Die

A key issue in the debate over capital punishment is whether or not it is an effective deterrent to violent crime. In at least one important respect, it unquestionably is: It simply cannot be contested that a killer, once executed, is forever deterred from killing again. The deterrent effect on others, however, depends largely on how swiftly and surely the penalty is applied. Since capital punishment has not been used with any consistency over the years, it is virtually impossible to evaluate its deterrent effect accurately. Abolitionists claim that a lack of significant difference between the murder rates for states with and without capital punishment proves that the death penalty does not deter. But the states with the death penalty on their books have used it so little over the years as to preclude any meaningful comparison between states. Through July 18, 1990 there had been 134 executions since 1976. Only 14 states (less than 40 percent of those that authorize the death penalty) were involved. Any punishment, including death, will cease to be an effective deterrent if it is recognized as mostly bluff. Due to costly delays and endless appeals, the death penalty has been largely turned into a paper tiger by the same crowd that calls for its abolition on the grounds that it is not an effective deterrent!

To allege that capital punishment, if imposed consistently and without undue delay, would not be a deterrent to crime is, in essence, to say that people are not afraid of dying. If so, as columnist Jenkin Lloyd Jones once observed, then warning signs reading "Slow Down," "Bridge Out," and "Danger—40,000 Volts" are futile relics of an age gone by when men feared death. To be sure, the death penalty could never become a 100-percent deterrent to heinous crime, because the fear of death varies among individuals. Some race automobiles, climb mountains, parachute jump, walk circus high-wires, ride Brahma bulls in rodeos, and otherwise engage in endeavors that are more than normally hazardous. But, as author Bernard Cohen notes in his book *Law and Order*, "there are even more people who refrain from participating in these activities mainly because risking their lives is not to their taste."

Merit System

On occasion, circumstances *have* led to meaningful statistical evaluations of the death penalty's deterrent effect. In Utah, for instance, there have been three executions since the Supreme Court's 1976 ruling:

- Gary Gilmore faced a firing squad at the Utah State Prison on January 17, 1977. There had been 55 murders in the Beehive State during 1976 (4.5 per 100,000 population). During 1977, in the wake of the Gilmore execution, there were 44 murders (3.5 per 100,000), a 20 percent decrease.

- More than a decade later, on August 28, 1987, Pierre Dale Selby (one of the two infamous "hi-fi killers" who in 1974 forced five persons in an Ogden hi-fi shop to drink liquid drain cleaner, kicked a ballpoint pen into the ear of one, then killed three) was executed. During all of 1987, there were 54 murders (3.2 per 100,000). The count for January through August was 38 (a monthly average of 4.75). For September–December (in the aftermath of the Selby execution) there were 16 (4.0 per month, a nearly 16 percent decrease). For July and August there were six and seven murders, respectively. In September (the first month following Selby's demise) there were three.

- Arthur Gary Bishop, who sodomized and killed a number of young boys, was executed on June 10, 1988. For all of 1988 there were 47 murders (2.7 per 100,000, the fewest since 1977). During January–June, there were 26; for July–December (after the Bishop execution) the tally was 21 (a 19 percent difference).

In the wake of all three Utah executions, there have been notable decreases in both the number and the rate of murders within the state. To be sure, there are other variables that could have influenced the results, but the figures are there and abolitionists to date have tended simply to ignore them.

Deterrence should never be considered the *primary* reason for administering the death penalty. It would be both immoral and unjust to punish one man merely as an example to others. The basic consideration should be: Is the punishment deserved? If not, it should not be administered regardless of what its deterrent impact might be. After all, once deterrence supersedes justice as the basis for a criminal sanction, the guilt or innocence of the accused becomes largely irrelevant. Deterrence can be achieved as effectively by executing an innocent person as a guilty one (something that communists and other totalitarians discovered long ago). If a punishment administered to one person deters someone else from committing a crime, fine. But that result should be viewed as a bonus of justice properly applied, not as a reason for the punishment. The decisive consideration should be: Has the accused *earned* the penalty?

The Cost of Execution

The exorbitant financial expense of death penalty cases is regularly cited by abolitionists as a reason for abolishing capital punishment altogether. They prefer to ignore, however, the extent to which they themselves are responsible for the interminable legal maneuvers that run up the costs....

As presently pursued, death-penalty prosecutions *are* outrageously expensive. But, again, the cost is primarily due to redundant appeals, time-consuming delays, bizarre court rulings, and legal histrionics by defense attorneys:

> Willie Darden, who had already survived three death warrants, was scheduled to die in Florida's electric chair on September 4, 1985 for a murder he had committed in 1973. Darden's lawyer made a last-minute emergency appeal to the Supreme Court, which voted against postponing the execution until a formal appeal could be filed. So the attorney (in what he later described as "last-minute ingenuity") then requested that the emergency appeal be technically transformed into a formal appeal. Four Justices agreed (enough to force the full court to review the appeal) and the execution was stayed. After additional years of delay and expense, Darden was eventually put out of our misery on March 15, 1988.
>
> Ronald Gene Simmons killed 14 members of his family during Christmas week in 1987. He was sentenced to death, said he was willing to die, and refused to appeal. But his scheduled March 16, 1989 execution was delayed when a fellow inmate, also on death row, persuaded the Supreme Court to block it (while Simmons was having what he expected to be his last meal) on the grounds that the execution could have repercussions for other death-row inmates. It took the Court until April 24th of [1990] to reject that challenge. Simmons was executed on June 25th.
>
> Robert Alton Harris was convicted in California of the 1978 murders of two San Diego teenagers whose car he wanted for a bank robbery. Following a seemingly interminable series of appeals, he was at last sentenced to die on April 3rd of [1990]. Four days earlier, a 9th U.S. Circuit Court of Appeals judge stayed the execution, largely on the claim that Harris was brain-damaged and therefore may possibly have been unable to "premeditate" the murders (as required under California law for the death penalty). On April 10th, the *Washington Times* reported that the series of tests used to evaluate Harris's condition had been described by some experts as inaccurate and "a hoax."
>
> The psychiatric game is being played for all it is worth. On May 14th, Harris's attorneys argued before the 9th Circuit Court that he should be spared the death penalty because he received

"inadequate" psychiatric advice during his original trial. In 1985, the Supreme Court had ruled that a defendant has a constitutional right to "a competent psychiatrist who will conduct an appropriate examination." Harris had access to a licensed psychiatrist, but now argues that—since the recent (highly questionable) evaluations indicated brain damage and other alleged disorders that the original psychiatrist failed to detect (and which may have influenced the jury not to impose the death sentence)—a new trial (or at least a re-sentencing) is in order. If the courts buy this argument, hundreds (perhaps thousands) of cases could be reopened for psychiatric challenge.

On April 2, 1974 William Neal Moore shot and killed a man in Georgia. Following his arrest, he pleaded guilty to armed robbery and murder and was convicted and sentenced to death. On July 20, 1975 the Georgia Supreme Court denied his petition for review. On July 16, 1976 the U.S. Supreme Court denied his petition for review. On May 13, 1977 the Jefferson County Superior Court turned down a petition for a new sentencing hearing (the state Supreme Court affirmed the denial, and the U.S. Supreme Court again denied a review). On March 30, 1978 a Tattnall County Superior Court judge held a hearing on a petition alleging sundry grounds for a writ of *habeas corpus,* but declined on July 13, 1978 to issue a writ. On October 17, 1978 the state Supreme Court declined to review that ruling. Moore petitioned the U.S. District Court for Southern Georgia. After a delay of more than two years, a U.S. District Court judge granted the writ on April 29, 1981. After another two-year delay, the 11th U.S. Circuit Court of Appeals upheld the writ on June 23, 1983. On September 30, 1983 the Circuit Court reversed itself and ruled that the writ should be denied. On March 5, 1984 the Supreme Court rejected the case for the third time.

Moore's execution was set for May 24, 1984. On May 11, 1984 his attorneys filed a petition in Butts County Superior Court, but a writ was denied. The same petition was filed in the U.S. District Court for Georgia's Southern District on May 18th, but both a writ and a stay of execution were denied. Then, on May 23rd (the day before the scheduled execution) the 11th Circuit Court of Appeals granted a stay. On June 4, 1984 a three-judge panel of the Circuit Court voted to deny a writ. After another delay of more than three years, the Circuit Court voted 7 to 4 to override its three-judge panel and rule in Moore's favor. On April 18, 1988, the Supreme Court accepted the case. On April 17, 1989 it sent the case back to the 11th Circuit Court for review in light of new restrictions that the High Court had placed on *habeas corpus.* On September 28, 1989 the Circuit Court ruled 6 to 5 that Moore had abused the writ process. On December 18, 1989 Moore's attorneys again appealed to the Supreme Court.

Moore's case was described in detail in *Insight* magazine for February 12, 1990. By the end of [1989] his case had gone through 20 separate court reviews, involving some 118 state and federal judges. It had been to the Supreme Court and back four times. There had been a substantial turnover of his attorneys, creating an excuse for one team of lawyers to file a petition claiming that all of the prior attorneys had given ineffective representation. No wonder capital cases cost so much!

Meanwhile, the American Bar Association proposes to make matters even worse by requiring states (as summarized by *Insight*) "to appoint two lawyers for every stage of the proceeding, require them to have past death penalty experience and pay them at 'reasonable' rates to be set by the court."

During an address to the American Law Institute on May 16, 1990, Chief Justice Rehnquist asserted that the "system at present verges on the chaotic" and "cries out for reform." The time expended between sentencing and execution, he declared, "is consumed not by structured review... but in fits of frantic action followed by periods of inaction." He urged that death row inmates be given one chance to challenge their sentences in state courts, and one challenge in federal courts, period.

Lifetime to Escape

Is life imprisonment an adequate substitute for the death penalty? Presently, according to the polls, approximately three-fourths of the American people favor capital punishment. But abolitionists try to discount that figure by claiming that support for the death penalty weakens when life imprisonment without the possibility of parole is offered as an alternative. (At other times, abolitionists argue that parole is imperative to give "lifers" some hope for the future and deter their violent acts in prison.)

Life imprisonment is a flawed alternative to the death penalty, if for no other reason than that so many "lifers" escape. Many innocent persons have died at the hands of men previously convicted and imprisoned for murder, supposedly for "life." The ways in which flaws in our justice system, combined with criminal ingenuity, have worked to allow "lifers" to escape include these recent examples:

- On June 10, 1977, James Earl Ray, who was serving a 99-year term for killing Dr. Martin Luther King Jr., escaped with six other inmates from the Brushy Mountain State Prison in Tennessee (he was captured three days later).
- Brothers Linwood and James Briley were executed in Virginia on October 12, 1984 and April 18, 1985, respectively. Linwood had murdered a disc jockey in 1979 during a crime spree. During the same spree, James raped and killed a woman (who was eight months pregnant) and killed her five-year-old son. On May 31, 1984, the Briley brothers organized and led an escape of five death-row inmates (the largest death-row breakout in U.S. history). They were at large for 19 days.

- On August 1, 1984 convicted murderers Wesley Allen Tuttle and Walter Wood, along with another inmate, escaped from the Utah State Prison. All were eventually apprehended. Wood subsequently sued the state for $2 million for violating his rights by allowing him to escape. In his complaint, he charged that, by allowing him to escape, prison officials had subjected him to several life-threatening situations: "Because of extreme fear of being shot to death, I was forced to swim several irrigation canals, attempt to swim a 'raging' Jordan River and expose myself to innumerable bites by many insects. At one point I heard a volley of shotgun blasts and this completed my anxiety."

- On April 3, 1988 three murderers serving life sentences without the chance of parole escaped from the maximum-security West Virginia Penitentiary. One, Bobby Stacy, had killed a Huntington police officer in 1981. At the time, he had been free on bail after having been arrested for shooting an Ohio patrolman.

- On November 21, 1988 Gonzalo Marrero, who had been convicted of two murders and sentenced to two life terms, escaped from New Jersey's Trenton state prison by burrowing through a three-foot-thick cell wall, then scaling a 20-foot outer wall with a makeshift ladder.

- In August 1989 Arthur Carroll, a self-proclaimed enforcer for an East Oakland street gang, was convicted of murdering a man. On September 28th, he was sentenced to serve 27-years-to-life in prison. On October 10th he was transferred to San Quentin prison. On October 25th he was set free after a paperwork snafu led officials to believe that he had served enough time. An all-points bulletin was promptly issued.

- On February 11, 1990 six convicts, including three murderers, escaped from their segregation cells in the maximum security Joliet Correctional Center in Illinois by cutting through bars on their cells, breaking a window, and crossing a fence. In what may be the understatement of the year, a prison spokesman told reporters: "Obviously, this is a breach of security."

Clearly, life sentences do not adequately protect society, whereas the death penalty properly applied does so with certainty.

Equal Opportunity Execution

Abolitionists often cite statistics indicating that capital punishment has been administered in a discriminatory manner, so that the poor, the black, the friendless, etc., have suffered a disproportionate share of executions. Even if true, such discrimination would not be a valid reason for abandoning the death penalty unless it could be shown that it was responsible for the execution of *innocent* persons (which it has not been, to date). Most attempts to pin the "discrimination" label on capital convictions are similar to one conducted at Stanford University a few years ago, which found that murderers of white people (whether white or black) are more likely to be punished with death than are killers of black people (whether white or black). But the study also concluded that blacks who murdered whites were somewhat *less* likely to receive death sentences than were whites who killed whites.

Using such data, the ACLU attempted to halt the execution of Chester Lee Wicker in Texas on August 26, 1986. Wicker, who was white, had killed a white person. The ACLU contended that Texas unfairly imposes the death penalty because a white is more likely than a black to be sentenced to death for killing a white. The Supreme Court rejected the argument. On the other hand, the execution of Willie Darden in Florida attracted worldwide pleas for amnesty from sundry abolitionists who, ignoring the Stanford study, claimed that Darden had been "railroaded" because he was black and his victim was white.

All criminal laws—in all countries, throughout all human history—have tended to be administered in an imperfect and uneven manner. As a result, some elements in society have been able to evade justice more consistently than others. But why should the imperfect administration of justice persuade us to abandon any attempt to attain it?

The most flagrant example of discrimination in the administration of the death penalty does not involve race, income, or social status, but gender. Women commit around 13 percent of the murders in America, yet, from 1930 to June 30, 1990, only 33 of the 3991 executions (less than 1 percent) involved women. Only one of the 134 persons executed since 1976 (through July 18th [1990]) has been a woman (Velma Barfield in North Carolina on November 2, 1984). One state governor commuted the death sentence of a woman because "humanity does not apply to women the inexorable law that it does to men."

According to L. Kay Gillespie, professor of sociology at Weber State College in Utah, evidence indicates that women who cried during their trials had a better chance of getting away with murder and avoiding the death penalty. Perhaps the National Organization for Women can do something about this glaring example of sexist "inequality" and "injustice." In the meantime, we shall continue to support the death penalty despite the disproportionate number of men who have been required to pay a just penalty for their heinous crimes.

Forgive and Forget?

Another aspect of the death penalty debate is the extent to which justice should be tempered by mercy in the case of killers. After all, abolitionists argue, is it not the duty of Christians to forgive those who trespass against them? In Biblical terms, the most responsible sources to extend mercy and forgiveness are (1) God and (2) the victim of the injustice. In the case of murder, so far as *this* world is concerned, the victim is no longer here to extend mercy and forgiveness. Does the state or any other earthly party have the right or authority to intervene and tender mercy on behalf of a murder victim? In the anthology *Essays on the Death Penalty,* the Reverend E. L. H. Taylor clarifies the answer this way: "Now it is quite natural and proper for a man to forgive something you do to *him.* Thus if somebody cheats me out of $20.00 it is quite possible and reasonable for me to say, 'Well, I forgive him, we will say no more about it.' But what would you say if somebody had done you out of $20.00 and I said, 'That's all right. I forgive him on your behalf'?"

The point is simply that there is no way, in *this* life, for a murderer to be reconciled to his victim, and secure the victim's forgiveness. This leaves the civil authority with no other responsible alternative but to adopt *justice* as the standard for assigning punishment in such cases.

Author Bernard Cohen raises an interesting point: " . . . if it is allowable to deprive a would-be murderer of his life, in order to forestall his attack, why is it wrong to take away his life after he has successfully carried out his dastardly business?" Does anyone question the right of an individual to kill an assailant should it be necessary to preserve his or her life or that of a loved one?

Happily, however, both scripture and our legal system uphold the morality and legality of taking the life of an assailant, if necessary, *before* he kills us. How, then, can it be deemed immoral for civil authority to take his life *after* he kills us?

Intolerant Victims?

Sometimes those who defend the death penalty are portrayed as being "intolerant." But isn't one of our real problems today that Americans are *too tolerant* of evil? Are we not accepting acts of violence, cruelty, lying, and immorality with all too little righteous indignation? Such indignation is not, as some would have us believe, a form of "hatred." In *Reflections on the Psalms,* C. S. Lewis discussed the supposed spirit of "hatred" that some critics claimed to see in parts of the Psalms: "Such hatreds are the kind of thing that cruelty and injustice, by a sort of natural law, produce. . . . Not to perceive it at all—not even to be tempted to resentment—to accept it as the most ordinary thing in the world—argues a terrifying insensibility. Thus the absence of anger, especially that sort of anger which we call indignation, can, in my opinion, be a most alarming symptom."

When mass murderer Ted Bundy was executed in Florida on January 24, 1989, a crowd of some 2000 spectators gathered across from the prison to cheer and celebrate. Many liberal commentators were appalled. Some contended that it was a spectacle on a par with Bundy's own callous disrespect for human life. One headline read: "Exhibition witnessed outside prison was more revolting than execution." What nonsense! As C. S. Lewis observed in his commentary on the Psalms: "If the Jews cursed more bitterly than the Pagans this was, I think, at least in part because they took right and wrong more seriously." It is long past time for us all to being taking right and wrong more seriously. . . .

Seeds of Anarchy

As we have seen, most discussions of the death penalty tend to focus on whether it should exist for murder or be abolished altogether. The issue should be reframed so that the question instead becomes whether or not it should be imposed for certain terrible crimes in addition to murder (such as habitual law-breaking, clearly proven cases of rape, and monstrous child abuse).

In 1953 the renowned British jurist Lord Denning asserted: "Punishment is the way in which society expresses its denunciation of wrongdoing; and in order to maintain respect for law, it is essential that the punishment for grave crimes shall adequately reflect the revulsion felt by a great majority of citizens for them." Nineteen years later, U.S. Supreme Court Justice Potter Stewart noted (while nevertheless concurring in the Court's 1972 opinion that temporarily banned capital punishment) that the "instinct for retribution is part of the nature of man and channeling that instinct in the administration of criminal justice serves an important purpose in promoting the stability of a society governed by law. When people begin to believe that organized society is unwilling or unable to impose upon criminal offenders the punishment they 'deserve,' then there are sown the seeds of anarchy—of self-help, vigilante justice, and lynch law."

To protect the innocent and transfer the fear and burden of crime to the criminal element where it belongs, we must demand that capital punishment be imposed when justified and expanded to cover terrible crimes in addition to murder.

NO

Eric M. Freedman

The Case Against the Death Penalty

On Sept. 1, 1995, New York rejoined the ranks of states imposing capital punishment. Although the first death sentence has yet to be imposed, an overwhelming factual record from around the country makes the consequence of this action easily predictable: New Yorkers will get less crime control than they had before.

Anyone whose public policy goals are to provide a criminal justice system that delivers swift, accurate, and evenhanded results—and to reduce the number of crimes that actually threaten most people in their daily lives—should be a death penalty opponent. The reason is simple: The death penalty not only is useless in itself, but counterproductive to achieving those goals. It wastes enormous resources—fiscal and moral—on a tiny handful of cases, to the detriment of measures that might have a significant impact in improving public safety.

Those who believe the death penalty somehow is an emotionally satisfying response to horrific crimes should ask themselves whether they wish to adhere to that initial reaction in light of the well-documented facts:

Fact: The death penalty does not reduce crime.

Capital punishment proponents sometimes assert that it simply is logical to think that the death penalty is a deterrent. Whether or not the idea is logical, it is not true, an example of the reality that many intuitively obvious propositions—*e.g.*, that a heavy ball will fall faster if dropped from the Leaning Tower of Pisa than a light one—are factually false.

People who commit capital murders generally do not engage in probability analysis concerning the likelihood of getting the death penalty if they are caught. They may be severely mentally disturbed people like Ted Bundy, who chose Florida for his final crimes *because* it had a death penalty.

Whether one chooses to obtain data from scholarly studies, the evidence of long-term experience, or accounts of knowledgeable individuals, he or she will search in vain for empirical support for the proposition that imposing the death penalty cuts the crime rate. Instead, that person will find:

- The question of the supposed deterrent effect of capital punishment is perhaps the single most studied issue in the social sciences. The results are as unanimous as scholarly studies can be in finding the death penalty not to be a deterrent.
- Eighteen of the 20 states with the highest murder rates have and use the death penalty. Of the nation's 20 big cities with the highest murder rates, 17 are in death penalty jurisdictions. Between 1975 and 1985, almost twice as many law enforcement officers were killed in death penalty states as in non-death penalty states. Over nearly two decades, the neighboring states of Michigan, with no death penalty, and Indiana, which regularly imposes death sentences and carries out executions, have had virtually indistinguishable homicide rates.
- Myron Love, the presiding judge in Harris County, Tex. (which includes Houston), the county responsible for 10% of all executions in the entire country since 1976, admits that "We are not getting what I think we should be wanting and that is to deter crime.... In fact, the result is the opposite. We're having more violence, more crime."

Fact: The death penalty is extraordinarily expensive.

Contrary to popular intuition, a system with a death penalty is vastly more expensive than one where the maximum penalty is keeping murderers in prison for life. A 1982 New York study estimated the death penalty cost conservatively at three times that of life imprisonment, the ratio that Texas (with a system that is on the brink of collapse due to underfunding) has experienced. In Florida, each execution runs the state $3,200,000—six times the expense of life imprisonment. California has succeeded in executing just two defendants (one a volunteer) since 1976, but could save about $90,000,000 *per year* by abolishing the death penalty and re-sentencing all of its Death Row inmates to life.

In response, it often is proposed to reduce the costs by eliminating "all those endless appeals in death penalty cases." This is not a new idea. In recent years, numerous efforts have been made on the state and Federal levels to do precisely that. Their failure reflects some simple truths:

- Most of the extra costs of the death penalty are incurred prior to and at trial, not in postconviction proceedings. Trials are far more likely under a death penalty system (since there is so little incentive to plea-bargain). They have two separate phases (unlike other trials) and typically are preceded by special motions and extra jury selection questioning—steps that, if not taken before trial, most likely will result in the eventual reversal of the conviction.

- Much more investigation usually is done in capital cases, particularly by the prosecution. In New York, for instance, the office of the State Attorney General (which generally does not participate in local criminal prosecutions) is creating a new multi-lawyer unit to provide support to county district attorneys in capital cases.
- These expenses are incurred even though the outcome of most such trials is a sentence other than death and even though up to 50% of the death verdicts that are returned are reversed on the constitutionally required first appeal. Thus, the taxpayers foot the bill for all the extra costs of capital pretrial and trial proceedings and then must pay either for incarcerating the prisoner for life or the expenses of a retrial, which itself often leads to a life sentence. In short, even if all post-conviction proceedings following the first appeal were abolished, the death penalty system still would be more expensive than the alternative.

In fact, the concept of making such an extreme change in the justice system enjoys virtually no support in any political quarter. The writ of *habeas corpus* to protect against illegal imprisonment is available to every defendant in any criminal case, whether he or she is charged with being a petty thief or looting an S&L. It justly is considered a cornerstone of the American system of civil liberties. To eliminate all those "endless appeals" either would require weakening the system for everyone or differentially with respect to death penalty cases.

Giving less due process in capital cases is the opposite of what common sense and elementary justice call for and eventually could lead to innocent people being executed. Since the rate of constitutional violations is far greater in capital cases than in others—capital defendants seeking Federal *habeas corpus* relief succeed some 40% of the time, compared to a success rate of less than five percent for non-capital defendants—the idea of providing less searching review in death penalty cases is perverse.

Considering that the vast majority of post-conviction death penalty appeals arise from the inadequacies of appointed trial counsel, the most cost-effective and just way of decreasing the number of years devoted to capital proceedings, other than the best way—not enacting the death penalty—would be to provide adequate funding to the defense at the beginning of the process. Such a system, although more expensive than one without capital punishment, at least would result in some predictability. The innocent would be acquitted speedily; the less culpable would be sentenced promptly to lesser punishments; and the results of the trials of those defendants convicted and sentenced to death ordinarily would be final.

Instead, as matters now stand, there is roughly a 70% chance that a defendant sentenced to death eventually will succeed in getting the outcome set aside. The fault for this situation—which is unacceptable to the defense and prosecution bars alike—lies squarely with the states. It is they that have created the endless appeals by attempting to avoid the ineluctable monetary costs of death penalty systems and to run them on the cheap by refusing to provide adequate funding for defense counsel.

Fact: The death penalty actually reduces public safety.

The costs of the death penalty go far beyond the tens of millions of dollars wasted in the pursuit of a chimera. The reality is that, in a time of fixed or declining budgets, those dollars are taken away from a range of programs that would be beneficial. For example:

- New York State, due to financial constraints, can not provide bullet-proof vests for every peace officer—a project that, unlike the death penalty, certainly would save law enforcement lives.
- According to FBI statistics, the rate at which murders are solved has dropped to an all-time low. Yet, empirical studies consistently demonstrate that, as with other crimes, the murder rate decreases as the probability of detection increases. Putting money into investigative resources, rather than wasting it on the death penalty, could have a significant effect on crime.
- Despite the large percentage of ordinary street crimes that are narcotics-related, the states lack the funding to permit drug treatment on demand. The result is that people who are motivated to cure their own addictions are relegated to supporting themselves through crime, while the money that could fund treatment programs is poured down the death penalty drain.

Fact: The death penalty is arbitrary in operation.

Any reasonably conscientious supporter of the death penalty surely would agree with the proposition that, before someone is executed by the state, he or she first should receive the benefits of a judicial process that is as fair as humanly possible.

However, the one thing that is clear about the death penalty system that actually exists—as opposed to the idealized one some capital punishment proponents assume to exist—is that it does not provide a level of fairness which comes even close to equaling the gravity of the irreversible sanction being imposed. This failure of the system to function even reasonably well when it should be performing excellently breeds public cynicism as to how satisfactorily the system runs in ordinary, non-capital cases.

That reaction, although destructive, is understandable, because the factors that are significant in determining whether or not a particular defendant receives a death sentence have nothing at all to do with the seriousness of his or her crime. The key variables, rather, are:

- Racial discrimination in death-sentencing, which has been documented repeatedly. For instance, in the five-year period following their re-institution of the death penalty, the sentencing patterns in Georgia and Florida were as follows: when black kills white—Georgia, 20.1% (32 of 159 cases) and Florida, 13.7% (34 of 249); white kills white—Georgia, 5.7% (35 of 614) and Florida, 5.2% (80 of 1,547); white kills black—

Georgia, 2.9% (one of 34) and Florida, 4.3% (three of 69); black kills black—Georgia, 0.8% (11 of 1,310) and Florida, 0.7% (three of 69).

A fair objection may be that these statistics are too stark because they fail to take into account other neutral variables—*e.g.*, the brutality of the crime and the number and age of the victims. Nevertheless, many subsequent studies, whose validity has been confirmed in a major analysis for Congress by the General Accounting Office, have addressed these issues. They uniformly have found that, even when all other factors are held constant, the races of the victim and defendant are critical variables in determining who is sentenced to death.

Thus, black citizens are the victim of double discrimination. From initial charging decisions to plea bargaining to jury sentencing, they are treated more harshly when they are defendants, but their lives are given less value when they are victims. Moreover, all-white or virtually all-white juries still are commonplace in many places.

One common reaction to this evidence is not to deny it, but to attempt to evade the facts by taking refuge in the assertion that any effective system for guarding against racial discrimination would mean the end of the death penalty. Such a statement is a powerful admission that governments are incapable of running racially neutral capital punishment systems. The response of any fair-minded person should be that, if such is the case, governments should not be running capital punishment systems.

- Income discrimination. Most capital defendants can not afford an attorney, so the court must appoint counsel. Every major study of this issue, including those of the Powell Commission appointed by Chief Justice William Rehnquist, the American Bar Association, the Association of the Bar of the City of New York, and innumerable scholarly journals, has found that the quality of defense representation in capital murder trials generally is far lower than in felony cases.

  The field is a highly specialized one, and since the states have failed to pay the amounts necessary to attract competent counsel, there is an overwhelming record of poor people being subjected to convictions and death sentences that equally or more culpable—but more affluent—defendants would not have suffered.

- Mental disability. Jurors are more likely to sentence to death people who seem different from themselves than individuals who seem similar to themselves. That is the reality underlying the stark fact that those with mental disabilities are sentenced to death at a rate far higher than can be justified by any neutral explanation. This reflects prejudice, pure and simple.

Fact: Capital punishment inevitably will be inflicted on the innocent.

It is ironic that, just as New York was reinstating the death penalty, it was in the midst of a convulsive scandal involving the widespread fabrication of evidence by the New York State Police that had led to scores of people—

including some innocent ones—being convicted and sentenced to prison terms. Miscarriages of justice unquestionably will occur in any human system, but the death penalty presents two special problems in this regard:

- The arbitrary factors discussed above have an enormous negative impact on accuracy. In combination with the emotional atmosphere generally surrounding capital cases, they lead to a situation where the truth-finding process in capital cases is *less* reliable than in others. Indeed, a 1993 House of Representatives subcommittee report found 48 instances over the previous two decades in which innocent people had been sentenced to death.
- The stark reality is that death is final. A mistake can not be corrected if the defendant has been executed.

How often innocent people have been executed is difficult to quantify; once a defendant has been executed, few resources generally are devoted to the continued investigation of the case. Nonetheless, within the past few years, independent investigations by major news organizations have uncovered three cases, two in Florida and one in Mississippi, where people were put to death for crimes they did not commit. Over time, others doubtless will come to light (while still others will remain undiscovered), but it will be too late.

The fact that the system sometimes works—for those who are lucky enough to obtain somehow the legal and investigative resources or media attention necessary to vindicate their claims of innocence—does not mean that most innocent people on Death Row are equally fortunate. Moreover, many Death Row inmates who have been exonerated would have been executed if the legal system had moved more quickly, as would occur if, as those now in power in Congress have proposed, Federal *habeas corpus* is eviscerated.

The death penalty is not just useless—it is positively harmful and diverts resources from genuine crime control measures. Arbitrarily selecting out for execution not the worst criminals, but a racially determined handful of the poorest, most badly represented, least mentally healthy, and unluckiest defendants—some of whom are innocent—breeds cynicism about the entire criminal justice system.

Thus, the Criminal Justice Section of the New York State Bar Association—which includes prosecutors, judges, and defense attorneys—opposed reinstitution of the death penalty because of "the enormous cost associated with such a measure, and the serious negative impact on the delivery of prosecution and defense services throughout the state that will result." Meanwhile, Chief Justice Dixon of the Louisiana Supreme Court put it starkly: "Capital punishment is destroying the system."

POSTSCRIPT

Is Capital Punishment Justified?

The death penalty is currently a hotly debated topic with a rapidly growing literature. The two main arguments in favor of capital punishment consider its deterrence effects and the moral argument that an ultimate punishment is needed for certain heinous crimes. The latter argument is the main thesis of Walter Bern's *For Capital Punishment: Crime and the Morality of the Death Penalty* (University Press of America, 1991). The moral argument against capital punishment is presented in most treatments of the topic but particularly in *Executing Justice: The Moral Meaning of the Death Penalty* by Lloyd Steffen (Pilgrim Press, 1998) and in *Punishment and the Death Penalty: The Current Debate,* Robert M. Baird and Stuart E. Rosenbaum, eds. (Prometheus Books, 1995).

Two books that present various religious views are James J. Megivern, *The Death Penalty: An Historical and Theological Survey* (Paulist Press, 1997) and Gardner C. Hanks, *Against the Death Penalty: Christian and Secular Arguments Against the Death Penalty* (Herald Press, 1997). For books that present various viewpoints on this debate see Hugo Adam Bedau, ed., *The Death Penalty in America: Current Controversies* (Oxford University Press, 1997); Mark Costanzo, *Just Revenge: Costs and Consequences of the Death Penalty* (St. Martin's Press, 1997); and Stephen E. Schonebaum, ed., *Does Capital Punishment Deter Crime?* (Greenhaven Press, 1998).

The main argument against capital punishment is that innocent people are executed and some recent works that present evidence of this include Barry Scheck, Peter Neufeld, and Jim Dwyer, *Actual Innocence: Five Days to Execution and Other Dispatches From the Wrongly Convicted* (Doubleday, 2000) and Rob Warden and David L. Protess, *A Promise of Justice: The Eighteen-Year Fight to Save Four Innocent Men* (Hyperion Press, 1998).

For historical treatments of the death penalty see Laura E. Randa, ed., *Society's Final Solution: A History and Discussion of the Death Penalty* (University Press of America, 1997); James R. Acker, et al., eds., *America's Experiment With Capital Punishment* (Carolina Academic Press, 1998); Bryan Vila and Cynthia Morris, eds., *Capital Punishment in the United States: A Documentary History* (Greenwood Press, 1997); and Herbert H. Haines, *Against Capital Punishment: The Anti-Death Penalty Movement in America 1972–1994* (Oxford University Press, 1996). Two works that explore the racial dimension of this issue are David Cole, *No Equal Justice: Race and Class in the American Criminal Justice System* (New Press, 1999) and Jesse Jackson, *Legal Lynching: Racism, Injustice and the Death Penalty* (Marlowe and Company, 1996).

On the Internet ...

United Nations Environment Program (UNEP)

The United Nations Environment Program (UNEP) Web site offers links to environmental topics of critical concern to sociologists. The site will direct you to useful databases and global resource information.

http://www.unep.ch

Worldwatch Institute Home Page

The Worldwatch Institute is dedicated to fostering the evolution of an environmentally sustainable society in which human needs are met without threatening the health of the natural environment. This site provides access to *World Watch Magazine* and *State of the World 2000*.

http://www.worldwatch.org

WWW Virtual Library: Demography and Population Studies

The WWW Virtual Library provides a definitive guide to demography and population studies. A multitude of important links to information about global poverty and hunger can be found at this site.

http://demography.anu.edu.au/VirtualLibrary/

William Davidson Institute

The William Davidson Institute at the University of Michigan Business School is dedicated to the understanding and promotion of economic transition. Consult this site for discussions of topics related to the changing global economy and the effects of globalization on society.

http://www.wdi.bus.umich.edu

World Future Society

The World Future Society is an educational and scientific organization for those interested in how social and technological developments are shaping the future.

http://www.wfs.org

PART 6

The
Future: Population/Environment/ Society

*T*he leading issues for the beginning of the twenty-first century include global warming, environmental decline, and globalization. The
state of the environment and the effects of globalization produce strong
arguments concerning what can be harmful or beneficial. Technology
has increased enormously in the last 100 years, as have worldwide population growth, consumption, and new forms of pollution that threaten
to undermine the world's fragile ecological support system. Although all
nations have a stake in the health of the planet, many believe that none
are doing enough to protect its health. Will technology itself be the key
to controlling or accommodating the increase of population and consumption, along with the resulting increase in waste production? Perhaps
so, but new policies will also be needed. Technology is driving the process of globalization, which can be seen as both good and bad. Those
who support globalization theory state that globalization increases competition, production, wealth, and the peaceful integration of nations.
However, not everyone agrees. This section explores what is occurring in
our environment and in our current global economy.

- Is Mankind Dangerously Harming the Environment?

- Is Globalization Good for Mankind?

ISSUE 19

Is Mankind Dangerously Harming the Environment?

YES: Chris Bright, from "Anticipating Environmental 'Surprise,'" in Lester R. Brown et al., *State of the World 2000: A Worldwatch Institute Report on Progress Toward a Sustainable Society* (W. W. Norton, 2000)

NO: Bjorn Lomborg, from "The Truth About the Environment," *The Economist* (August 4, 2001)

ISSUE SUMMARY

YES: Research associate Chris Bright demonstrates how human actions are inadvertently altering and degrading the environment in ways that are harmful to humans.

NO: Bjorn Lomborg, a statistician at the University of Aarhus, Denmark, presents evidence that population growth is slowing down, natural resources are not running out, species are disappearing very slowly, the environment is improving in some ways, and assertions about environmental decline are exaggerated.

M uch of the literature on socioeconomic development in the 1960s was premised on the assumption of inevitable material progress for all. It largely ignored the impacts of development on the environment and presumed that the availability of raw materials would not be a problem. The belief was that all societies would get richer because all societies were investing in new equipment and technologies that would increase productivity and wealth. Theorists recognized that some poor countries were having trouble developing, but they blamed those problems on the deficiencies of the values and attitudes of those countries and on inefficient organizations.

In the late 1960s and early 1970s an intellectual revolution occurred. Environmentalists had criticized the growth paradigm throughout the 1960s, but they were not taken very seriously at first. By the end of the 1960s, however, marine scientist Rachel Carson's book *Silent Spring* (Alfred A. Knopf, 1962) had worked its way into the public's consciousness. Carson's book traces the noticeable loss of birds to the use of pesticides. Her book made the middle and upper classes in the United States realize that pollution affects complex ecological systems in ways that put even the wealthy at risk.

In 1968 Paul Ehrlich, a professor of population studies, published *The Population Bomb* (Ballantine Books), which states that overpopulation is the major problem facing mankind. This means that population has to be controlled or the human race might cause the collapse of the global ecosystems and the deaths of many humans. Ehrlich explained why he thought the devastation of the world was imminent:

> Because the human population of the planet is about five times too large, and we're managing to support all these people—at today's level of misery— only by spending our capital, burning our fossil fuels, dispersing our mineral resources and turning our fresh water into salt water. We have not only overpopulated but overstretched our environment. We are poisoning the ecological systems of the earth—systems upon which we are ultimately dependent for all of our food, for all of our oxygen and for all of our waste disposal.

In 1973 *The Limits to Growth* (Universe) by Donella H. Meadows et al. was published. It presents a dynamic systems computer model for world economic, demographic, and environmental trends. When the computer model projected trends into the future, it predicted that the world would experience ecological collapse and population die-off unless population growth and economic activity were greatly reduced. This study was both attacked and defended, and the debate about the health of the world has been heated ever since.

Let us examine the population growth rates for the past, present, and future. At about A.D. 1, the world had about one-quarter billion people. It took about 1,650 years to double this number to one-half billion and 200 years to double the world population again to 1 billion by 1850. The next doubling took only about 80 years, and the last doubling took about 45 years (from 2 billion in 1930 to about 4 billion in 1975). The world population may double again to 8 billion sometime between 2010 and 2020. At the same time that population is growing people are trying to get richer, which means consuming more, polluting more, and using more resources. Are all these trends threatening the carrying capacity of the planet and jeopardizing the prospects for future generations?

In the following selections, Chris Bright explains how human activities can disturb ecological systems, including their balancing mechanisms, in ways that can have devastating ramifications for humans. He is not predicting eco-collapse and the end of the world, but he asserts that humans are endangering their future unless they radically change the way they use and manage the environment. Bjorn Lomborg counters that the evidence supports optimism— not environmental pessimism. He maintains that resources are becoming more abundant, food per capita is increasing, the extinction of species is at a very slow rate, and environmental problems are transient and will get better.

Chris Bright

 **YES**

Anticipating Environmental "Surprise"

If there is any comfort to be found in the prospect of environmental decline, it lies in the idea that the process is gradual and predictable. All sorts of soothing cliches follow from this notion: Even if we have not turned the trends around, our children will rise to the challenge. There's time. We're constantly learning; you can see plenty of progress already.

But this way of thinking is sleepwalking. To understand why, you have to look at decline close up. Here, for instance, is how it has happened in one small country, with big implications. Honduras, in the early 1970s, was caught up in a drive to build agricultural exports. Landowners in the south increased their production of cattle, sugarcane, and cotton. This more intensive farming reduced the soil's water absorbency, so more and more rain ran off the fields and less remained to evaporate back into the air. The drier air reduced cloud cover and rainfall. The region grew warmer—a lot warmer. The local weather station recorded an increase in the median annual temperature of 7.5 degrees Celsius between 1972 and 1990, by which time it had exceeded 30 degrees.

The hotter, drier landscape was poor habitat for the kind of mosquitoes that carry malaria, so the mosquitoes largely dried off and malaria infection declined. But of course the land was also becoming less productive, so people began to leave. Many found work on big plantations that were being carved out of the rainforests to the north. The plantations were growing export crops too, primarily bananas, melons, and pineapples. But it is difficult to mass-produce big, succulent fruits in a rainforest—even a badly fragmented rainforest—because there are no many insects and fungi around to eat them. So the plantations came to rely heavily on pesticides. From 1989 to 1991, Honduran pesticide imports increased more than fivefold, to about 8,000 tons.

This steaming, ragged forest was perfect habitat for malaria mosquitoes. Around the plantations, the insecticide drizzle suppressed them for a time, but they eventually acquired resistance to a whole spectrum of chemicals, and that basically released them from human control. When their populations bounced back, they encountered a landscape stocked with their favorite prey: people. And since these people were from an area where malaria infection had become rare, their immunity to the disease was low. Malaria rapidly reasserted itself: from 1987 to 1993, the number of cases in Honduras jumped from 20,000 to 90,000.

The situation was brought to light in 1993 by a group of researchers concerned about the public health implications of environmental decline. But their primary interest was not in what had already happened—it was in what might happen next. Some very nasty surprises might be tangled up somewhere in this web of pressures. They argued, for example, that deforestation and changing patterns of disease had made the country "especially vulnerable to climatic change and climate instability."

They were right. In October 1998, Hurricane Mitch slammed into the Gulf coast of Central America and stalled there for four days. Nightmarish mudslides obliterated entire villages; half the population of Honduras was displaced and the country lost 95 percent of its agricultural production. Mitch was the fourth strongest hurricane to enter the Caribbean this century, but much of the damage was caused by deforestation: had forests been gripping the soil on those hills, fewer villages would have been buried in mudslides. And in the chaos and filth of Mitch's wake there followed tens of thousands of additional cases of malaria, cholera, and dengue fever.

It is hard to shake the feeling that "normal change"—even change for the worse—should not happen this way. In the first place, too many trends in this scenario are spiking. Instead of gradual change, the picture is full of discontinuities—very rapid shifts that are much harder to anticipate. There is a rapid warming in the south, then an abrupt expansion in deforestation in the north, as plantations are developed. Then malaria infections jump. Then those mudslides, in addition to killing thousands of people, cause a huge increase in the rate of topsoil loss.

There also seem to be too many overlapping pressures—too many synergisms. The mudslides were not the work of Mitch alone; they were caused by Mitch plus the social conditions that encouraged the farming of upland forests. The malaria emerged not just from the mosquitoes, but from the movement of a low-immunity population into a mosquito-infested area, and from heavy pesticide use....

"When one problem combines with another problem, the outcome may be not a double problem, but a super-problem." That is the assessment of Norman Myers, an Oxford-based ecologist who is one of the most active pioneers in the field of environmental surprise. We have hardly begun to identify those potential super-problems, but in the plant's increasingly stressed natural systems, the possibility of rapid, unexpected change is pervasive and growing.

You can find this potential nearly anywhere, but this chapter will consider three of the most important theaters of surprise—tropical rainforests, coral reefs, and the atmosphere.

Tropical Rainforests: The Inferno Beneath the Canopy

Eight thousand years ago, before people began to clear land on a broad scale, more than 6 billion hectares, or around 40 percent of the planet's land surface, were covered with forest. Today, Earth's tattered cloak of natural forests (as opposed to tree plantations) amounts to 3.6 billion hectares at most. Every year, at least another 14 million hectares are lost—and maybe considerably more than that. This is an enormous evolutionary tragedy. Among the many thousands of species that are believed to go extinct every year, the overwhelming majority are forest creatures, primarily tropical insects, who have been denied their habitat. That, anyway, is the best estimate, but the forests are vanishing far more rapidly than they can be studied. We really don't even know what we are losing.

Currently, well over 90 percent of forest loss is occurring in the tropics—on a scale so vast that it might appear to have exceeded its capacity to surprise us. In 1997 and 1998, fire set to clear land in Amazonia claimed more than 5.2 million hectares of Brazilian forest, brush, and savanna—an area nearly 1.5 times the size of Taiwan. In Indonesia, some 2 million hectares of forest were torched during 1997 and 1998. All this is certainly news, but if you are interested in conservation, it is the kind of dreadful news you have come to expect.

And yet our expectations may not be an adequate guide to the sequel, assuming the destruction continues at its current pace. A substantial portion of the damage is "hidden"—it does not show up in the conventional analysis. But once you take the full extent of the damage into account, you can begin to make out some of the surprises it is likely to trigger.

Consider, for example, the destruction of Amazonia. Over half the world's remaining tropical rainforest lies within the Amazon basin, where more forest is being lost than anywhere else on Earth. Deforestation statistics for the area are intended primarily to track the conversion of forest into farms and ranches. Typically, the process begins with the construction of a road, which opens up a new tract of forest to settlement. In June 1997, for instance, some 6 million hectares of forest were officially released for settlement along a major new highway, BR-174, which runs from Manaus, in central Amazonia, over 1,000 kilometers north to Venezuela. Ranchers and subsistence farmers clearcut patches of forest along the road and burn the slash during the July–November dry season. (The farmers generally have few other options: Brazil has large numbers of poor, land-hungry people, and the plots they cut from the forest usually lose their fertility rapidly, so there is a constant demand for fresh soil.)

But the damage to the forest generally extends much farther than the areas that are "deforested" in this conventional sense, because of the way fire works in Amazonia. In the past, major fires have not been a frequent enough occurrence to promote any kind of adaptive "fire proofing" in the region's dominant tree species. Some temperate-zone and northern trees, by contrast, are "fire-adapted" in one way or another—they may have especially thick bark, for example, or the ability to resprout after burning. The lack of such adaptations in Amazonian trees means that even a small fire can begin to unravel the forest.

During the burning season, the flames often escape the cuts and sneak into neighboring forest. Even in intact forest, there will be patches of forest floor that are dry enough at that time of year to allow a small "surface fire" to feed on the dead leaves. Surface fires do not climb trees and become crown fires. They just crackle along the forest floor, here and there, as little patches of flame, going out at night, when the temperature drops, and rekindling the next day. They will not kill the really big trees, and they do not cover every bit of ground in a burned patch. But they are fatal to most of the smaller trees they touch. Overall, an initial surface fire may kill perhaps 10 percent of the living forest biomass.

The damage may not look all that dramatic, but another tract of forest may already be doomed by an incipient positive feedback loop of fire and drying. After a surface fire, the amount of shade is reduced from about 90 percent to around 60 percent, and the dead and injured trees rain debris down on the floor. So a year or two later, the next fire in that spot finds more tinder, and a warmer, drier floor. Some 40 percent of forest biomass may die in the second fire. At this point, the forest's integrity is seriously damaged; grasses and vines invade and contribute to the accumulation of combustible material. The next dry season may eliminate the forest entirely. Once the original forest is gone, the scrubby second growth or pasture that replaces it will almost certainly burn too frequently to allow the forest to restore itself.

New roads admit not just settlers and ranches but loggers as well. Commercial logging involves a form of damage that is in some ways similar to the surface fires. Unlike its temperate-zone counterparts, the Amazonian timber industry does not generally clearcut. Most of its operations are what foresters call "high grading"—the best specimens of the most desirable species are cut and hauled out. The result is not outright deforestation, but the forest loses its largest trees and suffers extensive collateral damage from the felling and hauling. An intricate network of logging roads undermines the canopy—a human termite's nest through the wood. An Amazonian timber operation typically kills 10–40 percent of the forest biomass, thereby reducing canopy coverage by up to 50 percent. The forest floor grows warmer and drier; the forest becomes increasingly flammable.

As the main mechanisms of deforestation, the logging and burning are hardly surprising per se, but a great deal of the resulting damage is still obscure. Deforestation estimates are derived primarily from satellite photos, and while the photos show a great deal of detail, the mapping process is generally designed to give a picture of gross canopy destruction. Damage that leaves most of the canopy intact, or that has been masked by second growth, is usually not factored in to the estimates....

As the Amazonian forest dwindles, a more surprising second-order effect may emerge as the hydrological cycle changes. Because trees exhale so much water vapor, a forest to some degree creates its own climate. Much of this water vapor condenses out below the canopy and drips back into the soil. Some of it rises higher before falling back in as rain—researchers estimate that most of the Amazon's rainfall comes from water vapor exhaled by the forest. Widespread deforestation will therefore tend to make the region substantially drier, and that will accelerate the feedback loop created by the fires.

Some degree of deforestation-induced drought already appears to have affected other parts of the humid tropics—parts of Central America, for instance, Côte d'Ivoire, and peninsular Malaysia, where the drying has been severe enough to force the abandonment of some 20,000 hectares of rice paddy. It may not be possible to define the point at which such a drought takes hold in Amazonia, but about 13 percent of the Brazilian Amazon has now been deforested outright. If you add to that the tracts of forest that have been seriously degraded—by logging, surface fires, and fragmentation—that fraction could rise to more than a third.

The fire feedback loop is also likely to gain momentum from forces outside the region. Over the past two decades, Amazonia has seen several unusually intense dry seasons, during which the burning was far worse than normal. These periods corresponded with recent El Niño weather events (in 1982–83, 1992–93, and 1997–98). El Niño events appear to be growing longer, more intense, and more frequent. Many climatologists regard this trend as a likely effect of climate change—the change in the behavior of Earth's climate system caused by increasing atmospheric concentrations of carbon dioxide (CO_2) and other greenhouse gases. Climate change, in other words, may be accelerating the Amazonian fire cycle. By burning large amounts of coal and oil, the United States, China, and other major carbon-emitting countries may in effect be burning the Amazon....

The Atmosphere: An Invisible Confluence of Poisons

The delicate membrane of gases that makes up our atmosphere is as thin, comparatively speaking, as the skin of an onion. The atmosphere's outer border is very diffuse—a faint scattering of gas molecules extends into space for hundreds of kilometers—but 90 percent of those molecules like within 16 kilometers of sea level. Every ecosystem on Earth is linked to the chemistry of the membrane that separates us from outer space, and that chemistry is changing in many ways. Levels of some "trace gases," such as sulfur dioxide, nitrogen oxides, and carbon dioxide, are increasing. Many novel compounds have entered the brew as well—for instance, chlorofluorocarbons, the ozone-destroying chemicals used as refrigerants. From this immense potential for change, look at just three basic phenomena: acid rain, nitrogen pollution, and increasing levels of CO_2.

Fossil fuel combustion is the source of acid rain (which falls not just as rain but also as dry particles). Acid rain is composed in large measure of sulfuric acid, which derives from the sulfur dioxide released by coal-burning power plants and metal smelters. (Sulfur is a common contaminant of coal and metal ores.) Smoke stack "scrubbers" and a growing preference for low-sulfur coal and natural gas have helped reduce sulfur dioxide emissions in North America and Western Europe, although high sulfur emissions are still common elsewhere. The other primary constituent of acid rain is nitric acid, which is generated from the nitrogen oxides in fossil fuel emissions. Unfortunately, nitric acid is likely to be more difficult to control than sulfuric acid, since a substantial share of the nitrogen oxides comes from gasoline burned in the world's expanding fleets of cars.

Acid rain can travel downwind for hundreds of kilometers—then fall on forests and farmland, where the idea of air pollution may seem quite incongruous. The acid can damage plant tissues directly, but its worst effects come as a series of discontinuities that are much harder to see. As the acid drips into the soil, decade after decade, it tends to leach out the stock of calcium and magnesium, both essential plant nutrients. Depending upon how nutrient-rich a soil is to begin with, this process may or may not be an immediate concern, but if it persists, the nutrient decline will eventually cross a threshold of scarcity: it will begin to cripple plant growth.

A second discontinuity will occur once soil calcium has grown scarce. Without calcium to neutralize it, the incoming acid will just build up in the soil —soil acidification will increase abruptly, even if the amount of incoming acid remains constant. The growing acidity will work another change, by releasing aluminum from its mineral matrix. Aluminum is a common soil constituent; when bonded to other minerals, it is biologically inert, but free aluminum in acid conditions is toxic to both plants and animals. In plants, acidity plus aluminum damages the fine roots. That could affect water uptake, and thereby increase susceptibility to drought. Root damage will also cripple a plant's ability to absorb whatever nutrients remain in the soil.

Acid lowers the calcium level, which allows the acid to build up, which releases aluminum, which interferes with calcium uptake. There is a cascade of chemical effects here, reinforcing the nutrient starvation. Other kinds of second-order effects may emerge as well. In the United States, for example, recent research over a swath of the Midwest from southern Illinois to southern Ohio has uncovered a correlation between increasing acidity in forest soils and a decline of soil organisms—earthworms, beetles, and so on. As biological activity in these soils has dropped off, decay of woody debris appears to have slowed radically, so the calcium "locked up" in the dead wood is not being released back into the soil. The nutrient cycle has apparently been constricted to some degree.

Because they are chronic, these changes in soil chemistry also create many opportunities for synergisms. Aluminum, for example, is not the only metal that acid tends to "mobilize." Toxic heavy metals such as cadmium, lead, and mercury may also be present in the soil, or they may arrive in trace amounts, on the same winds that brought in the acid. (Like sulfur, heavy metals are common contaminants of coal and ores, although usually in much smaller amounts.) Increasing acidity will tend to make these metals more soluble and toxic as well.

Even though it involves discontinuities, acid-induced decline may still unfold for decades as a hidden process that largely escapes casual notice. Does a tract of forest have fewer large trees than it once did, or fewer species that need more alkaline soil? Even if it does, it may still be perfectly green. It may still show vigorous growth, but the growth may be concentrated in younger plants, and in acid-tolerant species. It may be on its way to becoming a kind of "acid thicket." . . .

Acid rain overlaps with another, broader form of global change: the alteration of the planet's "nitrogen cycle." Nitrogen is an essential plant nutrient and the main constituent of the atmosphere: 78 percent of the air is nitrogen gas. But plants cannot metabolize this pure, elemental nitrogen directly. The nitrogen must be "fixed" into compounds with hydrogen or oxygen before it can become part of the biological cycle. In nature this process is accomplished by certain types of algae and bacteria, as well as by lightning strikes, which fuse atmospheric oxygen and nitrogen into nitrogen oxides.

Humans have radically amplified this process. Farmers boost the nitro-gen level of their land through fertilizers and the planting of nitrogen-fixing crops (actually, symbiotic microbes do the fixing). The burning of forests and the draining of wetlands releases additional quantities of fixed nitrogen that had been stored in vegetation and organic debris. And fossil fuel combustion produces still more fixed nitrogen, in the form of nitrogen oxides. Natural processes probably incorporate around 140 million tons of nitrogen into the terrestrial nitrogen cycle every year. (The ocean cycle is largely a mystery.) Thus far, human activity has at least doubled that amount.

Fixed nitrogen is often a "limiting nutrient" in terrestrial ecosystems: it is in high demand and relatively short supply, so its availability determines the amount of plant growth. If you add more, you get more growth—at least in some species. That is why fertilizer is mostly nitrogen. But if you keep adding more, you run into trouble. The excess nitrogen becomes a kind of poison that may interact synergistically with acid rain and other pressures. (Of course, since ni-trogen compounds often contribute to the acidity, the processes are not entirely distinct.)

In forests, for example, excess nitrogen tends to inhibit fine root growth, just as the acid-aluminum combination does. Acidity plus nitrogen pollution could therefore deal a double blow to trees' ability to withstand drought and to take in calcium and magnesium. Above ground, excess nitrogen may stim-ulate extra growth, but it is likely to be produced faster than the tree can absorb those mineral nutrients. The new growth will therefore tend to be weak —essentially, malnourished. This effect also can be exacerbated by acid rain, since acid leaches out those minerals in the first place.

The weakness of the new growth is not just physical—there can be chem-ical weaknesses too. Since nitrogen may also be a limiting nutrient for insects and other small organisms that feed on trees, nitrogen-rich foliage is likely to be very attractive to pests. And the low mineral concentrations within the tree's tissues can interfere with its ability to produce the chemicals that make up its "immune system"—compounds that, for example, inhibit infection or make fo-liage less palatable to insects. Other physiological effects are probably at work as well; excess nitrogen, for instance, appears to lower a tree's ability to cope with cold weather.

Combinations of various effects like these may eventually produce sub-stantial discontinuities. In one monitoring experiment in the U.S. Northeast, researchers found that by increasing the nitrogen in pine and spruce-fir stands, they induced declines in growth and increases in tree mortality over a period of just six years....

An Agenda for the Unexpected

Human pressures on Earth's natural systems have reached a point at which they are more and more likely to engender problems that we are less and less likely to anticipate. Dealing with this predicament is obviously going to require more than simply reacting to problems as they appear. We need to forge a new ethic for managing our relationship with nature—one that emphasizes minimal interference in the lives of wild beings and in the broad natural processes that sustain all living things. Such an ethic might begin with three basic principles.

First, nature is a system of unfathomable complexity. Our predominant response to that complexity has been specialization, in both the sciences and public policy. Learning a lot about a little is a form of progress, but it comes at a cost. Expertise is seductive: it is easy for specialists to get into the habit of thinking that they understand all the consequences of a plan. But in a complex, highly stressed system, the biggest consequences may not emerge where the experts are in the habit of looking. This inherent unpredictability condemns us to some degree of error, so it is important to err on the side of minimal disruption whenever possible.

Second, nature gives away nothing for free. You cannot get an appreciable quantity of anything out of nature without sacrificing something in the process. Even sustainable resource management is a trade-off—it's simply one we regard as acceptable. In our dealings with nature, as with any other sort of transaction, we need to know the full cost of the goods before deciding whether they are worth the price, or whether there is a better way to pay for them.

Third, nature has no reset button. Environmental corrosion is not just killing off individual species—it is setting off system-level changes that are, for all practical purposes, irreversible. Even if, for example, all the world's coral reef species were miraculously to survive the impending bout of rapid climate change, that does not mean that our descendants will be able to reconstruct reef communities. The near impossibility of restoring complex systems to some previous state is another strong argument for minimal disruption.

These are basic features of the natural world: we will never understand it completely, it will not do our bidding for free, and we cannot put it back the way it was.

 **NO**

The Truth About the Environment

$\mathbf{E}$cology and economics should push in the same direction. After all, the "eco" part of each word derives from the greek word for "home", and the protagonists of both claim to have humanity's welfare as their goal. Yet enviornmentalists and economists are often at loggerheads. For economists, the world seems to be getting better. For many environmentalists, it seems to be getting worse.

These environmentalists, led by such veterans as Paul Ehrlich of Stanford University, and Lester Brown of the Worldwatch Institute, have developed a sort of "litany" of four big environmental fears:

- Natural resources are running out.
- The population is ever growing, leaving less and less to eat.
- Species are becoming extinct in vast numbers: forests are disappearing and fish stocks are collapsing.
- The planet's air and water are becoming ever more polluted.

Human activity is thus defiling the earth, and humanity may end up killing itself in the process.

The trouble is, the evidence does not back up this litany. First, energy and other natural resources have become more abundant, not less so since the Club of Rome published "The Limits to Growth" in 1972. Second, more food is now produced per head of the world's population than at any time in history. Fewer people are starving. Third, although species are indeed becoming extinct, only about 0.7% of them are expected to disappear in the next 50 years, not 25–50%, as has so often been predicted. And finally, most forms of environmental pollution either appear to have been exaggerated, or are transient—associated with the early phrases of industrialisation and therefore best cured not by restricting economic growth, but by accelerating it. One form of pollution—the release of greenhouse gases that causes global warming—does appear to be a long-term phenomenon, but its total impact is unlikely to pose a devastating problem for the future of humanity. A bigger problem may well turn out to be an inappropriate response to it.

Can Things Only Get Better?

Take these four points one by one. First, the exhaustion of natural resources. The early environmental movement worried that the mineral resources on which modern industry depends would run out. Clearly, there must be some limit to the amount of fossil fuels and metal ores that can be extracted from the earth: the planet, after all, has a finite mass. But that limit is far greater than many environmentalists would have people believe.

Reserves of natural resources have to be located, a process that costs money. That, not natural scarcity, is the main limit on their availability. However, known reserves of all fossil fuels, and of most commercially important metals, are now larger than they were when "the Limits to Growth" was published. In the case of oil, for example, reserves that could be extracted at reasonably competitive prices would keep the world economy running for about 150 years at present consumption rates. Add to that the fact that the price of solar energy has fallen by half in every decade for the past 30 years, and appears likely to continue to do so into the future, and energy shortages do not look like a serious threat either to the economy or to the environment.

The development for non-fuel resources has been similar. Cement, aluminum, iron, copper, gold, nitrogen and zinc account for more than 75% of global expenditure on raw materials. Despite an increase in consumption of these materials of between two- and ten-fold over the past 50 years, the number of years of available reserves has actually grown. Moreover, the increasing abundance is reflected in an ever-decreasing price: *The Economist's* index of prices of industrial raw materials has dropped some 80% in inflation-adjusted terms since 1845.

Next, the population explosion is also turning out to be a bugaboo. In 1968, Dr Ehrlich predicted in his best selling book, "The Population Bomb", that "the battle to feed humanity is over. In the course of the 1970s the world will experience starvation of tragic proportions—hundreds of millions of people will starve to death."

That did not happen. Instead, according to the United Nations, agricultural production in the developing world has increased by 52% per person since 1961. The daily food intake in poor countries has increased from 1,932 calories, barely enough for survival, in 1961 to 2,650 calories in 1998, and is expected to rise to 3,020 by 2030. Likewise, the proportion of people in developing countries who are starving has dropped from 45% in 1949 to 18% today, and is expected to decline even further to 12% in 2010 and just 6% in 2030. Food, in other words, is becoming not scarcer but ever more abundant. This is reflected in its price. Since 1800 food prices have decreased by more than 90%, and in 2000, according to the World Bank, prices were lower than ever before.

Modern Malthus

Dr Ehrlich's prediction echoes that made 170 years earlier by Thomas Malthus. Malthus claimed that, if unchecked, human population would expand exponentially, while food production could increase only linearly, by bringing new

Figure 1

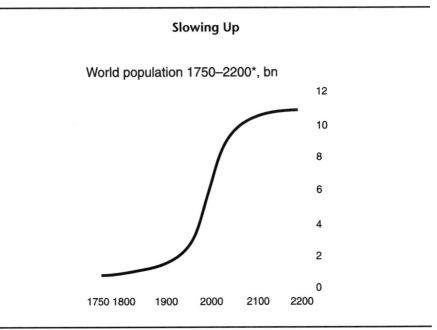

Slowing Up

World population 1750–2200*, bn

*UN medium-variant forecast from 2000
Source: UNPD

land into cultivation. He was wrong. Population growth has turned out to have an internal check: as people grow richer and healthier, they have smaller families. Indeed, the growth rate of the human population reached its peak, of more than 2% a year, in the early 1960s. The rate of increase has been declining ever since. It is now 1.26%, and is expected to fall to 0.46% in 2050. The United Nations estimates that most of the world's population growth will be over by 2100, with the population stabilising at just below 11 billion (see Figure 1).

Malthus also failed to take account of developments in agricultural technology. These have squeezed more and more food out of each hectare of land. It is this application of human ingenuity that has boosted food production, not merely in line with, but ahead of, population growth. It has also, incidentally, reduced the need to take new land into cultivation, thus reducing the pressure on biodiversity.

Third, that threat of biodiversity loss is real, but exaggerated. Most early estimates used simple island models that linked a loss in habitat with a loss of biodiversity. A rule-of-thumb indicated that loss of 90% of forest meant a 50% loss of species. As rainforests seemed to be cut at alarming rates, estimates of annual species loss of 20,000–100,000 abounded. Many people expected the number of species to fall by half globally within a generation or two.

However, the data simply does not bear out these predictions. In the eastern United States, forests were reduced over two centuries to fragments totalling just 1–2% of their original area, yet this resulted in the extinction of only one forest bird. In Puerto Rico, the primary forest area has been reduced over the past 400 years by 99%, yet "only" seven of 60 species of bird has become extinct. All but 12% of the Brazilian Atlantic rainforest was cleared in the 19th century, leaving only scattered fragments. According to the rule-of-thumb, half of all its species should have become extinct. Yet, when the World Conservation Union and the Brazilian Society of Zoology analysed all 291 known Atlantic forest animals, none could be declared extinct. Species, therefore, seem more resilient than expected. And tropical forests are not lost at annual rates of 2.4%, as many enviornmentalists have claimed: the latest UN figures indicate a loss of less than 0.5%.

Fourth, pollution is also exaggerated. Many analyses show that air pollution diminishes when a society becomes rich enough to be able to afford to be concerned about the environment. For London, the city for which the best data are available, air pollution peaked around 1890 (see Figure 2). Today, the air is cleaner than it has been since 1585. There is good reason to believe that this general picture holds true for all developed countries. And, although air pollution is increasing in many developing countries, they are merely replicating the development of the industrialised countries. When they grow sufficiently rich they, too, will start to reduce their air pollution.

All this contradicts the litany. Yet opinion polls suggest that many people, in the rich world, at least, nurture the belief that environmental standards are declining. Four factors cause this disjunction between perception and reality.

Figure 2

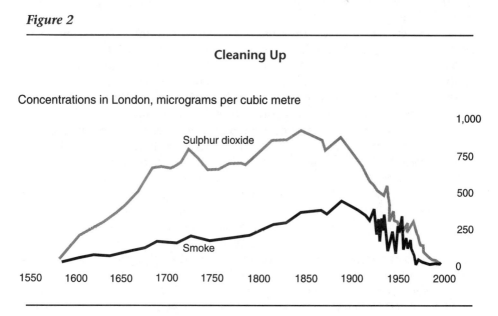

Cleaning Up

Concentrations in London, micrograms per cubic metre

Source: B. Lomborg

Always Look on the Dark Side of Life

One is the lopsidedness built into scientific research. Scientific funding goes mainly to areas with many problems. That may be wise policy, but it will also create an impression that many more potential problems exist than is the case.

Secondly, environmental groups need to be noticed by the mass media. They also need to keep the money rolling in. Understandably, perhaps, they sometimes exaggerate. In 1997, for example, the Worldwide Fund for Nature issued a press release entitled, "Two-thirds of the world's forests lost forever". The truth turns out to be nearer 20%.

Though these groups are run overwhelmingly by selfless folk, they nevertheless share many of the characteristics of other lobby groups. That would matter less if people applied the same degree of scepticism to environmental lobbying as they do to lobby groups in other fields. A trade organisation arguing for, say, weaker pollution controls is instantly seen as self-interested. Yet a green organisation opposing such a weakening is seen as altruistic, even if a dispassionate view of the controls in question might suggest they are doing more harm than good.

A third source of confusion is the attitude of the media. People are clearly more curious about bad news than good. Newspapers and broadcasters are there to provide what the public wants. That, however, can lead to significant distortions of perception. An example was America's encounter with El Niño in 1997 and 1998. This climatic phenomenon was accused of wrecking tourism, causing allergies, melting the ski-slopes and causing 22 deaths by dumping snow in Ohio.

A more balanced view comes from a recent article in the *Bulletin of the American Meteorological Society*. This tries to count up both the problems and the benefits of the 1997–98 Niño. The damage it did was estimated at $4 billion. However, the benefits amounted to some $19 billion. These came from higher winter temperatures (which saved an estimated 850 lives, reduced heating costs and diminished spring floods caused by meltwaters, and from the well-documented connection between past Niños and fewer Atlantic hurricanes. In 1998, America experienced no big Atlantic hurricanes and thus avoided huge losses. These benefits were not reported as widely as the losses.

The fourth factor is poor individual perception. People worry that the endless rise in the amount of stuff everyone throws away will cause the world to run out of places to dispose of waste. Yet, even if America's trash output continues to rise as it has done in the past, and even if the American population doubles by 2100, all the rubbish America produces through the entire 21st century will still take up only the area of a square, each of whose sides measures 28km (18 miles). That is just one-12,000th of the area of the entire United States.

Ignorance matters only when it leads to faulty judgments. But fear of largely imaginary environmental problems can divert political energy from dealing with real ones. The table, showing the cost in the United States of various measures to save a year of a person's life, illustrates the danger. Some environmental policies, such as reducing lead in petrol and sulphur-dioxide emissions from fuel oil, are very cost-effective. But many of these are already

Table 1

The Price of a Life

Cost of saving one year of one person's life -1993$

Passing laws to make seat-belt use mandatory	69
Sickle-cell anaemia screening for black new-borns	240
Mammography for women aged 50	810
Pneumonia vaccination for people aged over 65	2,000
Giving advice on stopping smoking to people who smoke more than one packet a day	9,800
Putting men aged 30 on a low-cholesterol diet	19,000
Regular leisure-time physical activity, such as jogging for men aged 35	38,000
Making pedestrians and cyclists more visible	73,000
Installing air-bags (rather than manual lap belts) in cars	120,000
Installing arsenic emission-control at glass-manufacturing plants	51,000,000
Setting radiation emission standards for nuclear-power plants	180,000,000
Installing benzene emission control at rubber-tyre manufacturing plants	20,000,000,000

Source: T. Tengs et al, *Risk Analysis*, June 1995

in place. Most environmental measures are less cost-effective than interventions aimed at improving safety (such as installing air-bags in cars) and those involving medical screening and vaccination. Some are absurdly expensive.

Yet a false perception of risk may be about to lead to errors more expensive even than controlling the emission of benzene at tyre plants. Carbon-dioxide emissions are causing the planet to warm. The best estimates are that the temperature will rise by some 2°–3°C in this century, causing considerable problems, almost exclusively in the developing world, at a total cost of $5,000 billion. Getting rid of global warming would thus seem to be a good idea. The question is whether the cure will actually be more costly than ailment.

Despite the intuition that something drastic needs to be done about such a costly problem, economic analyses clearly show that it will be far more expensive to cut carbon-dioxide emissions radically than to pay the costs of adaptation to the increased temperatures. The effect of the Kyoto Protocol on the climate would be minuscule, even if it were implemented in full. A model by Tom Wigley, one of the main authors of the reports of the UN Climate Change

Panel, shows how an expected temperature increase of 2.1°C in 2100 would be diminished by the treaty to an increase of 1.9°C instead. Or, to put it another way, the temperature increase that the planet would have experienced in 2094 would be postponed to 2100.

So the Kyoto agreement does not prevent global warming, but merely buys the world six years. Yet, the cost of Kyoto, for the United States alone, will be higher than the cost of solving the world's single most pressing health problems: providing universal access to clean drinking water and sanitation. Such measures would avoid 2m deaths every year, and prevent half a billion people from becoming seriously ill.

And that is the best case. If the treaty were implemented inefficiently, the cost of Kyoto could approach $1 trillion, or more than five times the cost of worldwide water and sanitation coverage. For comparison, the total global-aid budget today is about $50 billion a year.

To replace the litany with facts is crucial if people want to make the best possible decisions for the future. Of course, rational environmental management and environmental investment are good ideas—but the costs and benefits of such investments should be compared to those of similar investments in all the other important areas of human endeavour. It may be costly to be overly optimistic—but more costly still to be too pessimistic.

POSTSCRIPT

Is Mankind Dangerously Harming the Environment?

Though a number of works (see below) support Lomborg's argument, his evidence has come under heavy attack (see Richard C. Bell, "How Did *The Skeptical Environmentalist* Pull the Wool Over the Eyes of So Many Editors?" *WorldWatch* [March–April 2002] and *Scientific American* [January 2002]). The issue of the state of the environment and prospects for the future have been hotly debated for 30 years with little chance of ending soon. Two key issues are the potential impacts of global warming and the net effects of future agricultural technologies, which will be used to feed growing populations with richer diets. On the former, see the reports on global warming in *Time* (April 9, 2001); *U.S. News & World Report* (February 5, 2001); and *The Ecologist* (March 2002). On the latter, see Vaclav Smil, *Feeding the World: A Challenge for the Twenty-First Century* (MIT Press, 2000).

Paul R. Ehrlich and Anne H. Ehrlich wrote *Betrayal of Science and Reason: How Anti-Environmental Rhetoric Threatens Our Future* (Island Press, 1996) to refute statements by those who do not agree with the messages of the concerned environmentalists. Julian Lincoln Simon counters with *Hoodwinking the Nation* (Transaction, 1999). For a debate on this issue see Norman Myers and Julian L. Simon, *Scarcity or Abundance? A Debate on the Environment* (W. W. Norton, 1994).

Publications that are optimistic about the availability of resources and the health of the environment include Ronald Bailey, ed., *The True State of the Planet* (Free Press, 1995) and Gregg Easterbrook, *A Moment on the Earth: The Coming Age of Environmental Optimism* (Viking, 1995). Publications by some who believe that population growth and human interventions in the environment have dangerous consequences for the future of mankind include Joseph Wayne Smith, Graham Lyons, and Gary Sauer-Thompson, *Healing a Wounded World* (Praeger, 1997); Douglas E. Booth, *The Environmental Consequences of Growth* (Routledge, 1998); and Bill McKibben, *Hope, Human and Wild: True Stories of Living Lightly on the Earth* (Little, Brown, 1995).

Several works relate environmental problems to very severe political, social, and economic problems, including Michael Renner, *Fighting for Survival* (W. W. Norton, 1996); Michael N. Dobkowski and Isidor Wallimann, eds., *The Coming Age of Scarcity: Preventing Mass Death and Genocide in the Twenty-First Century* (Syracuse University Press, 1998); and one with a long timeframe, Sing C. Chew, *World Ecological Degradation: Accumulation, Urbanization, and Deforestation, 3000BC–AD2000* (Roman and Littlefield, 2001). An important series of publications on environmental problems is by the Worldwatch Institute, including two annuals: *State of the World* and *Vital Signs*.

ISSUE 20

Is Globalization Good for Mankind?

YES: Murray Weidenbaum, from "Globalization Is Not a Dirty Word: Dispelling the Myth About the Global Economy," *Vital Speeches of the Day* (March 1, 2001)

NO: Herman E. Daly, from "Globalization and Its Discontents," *Philosophy & Public Policy Quarterly* (Spring/Summer 2001)

ISSUE SUMMARY

YES: Murray Weidenbaum, chairman of the Weidenbaum Center at Washington University in St. Louis, argues that economic globalization benefits all countries that participate in world markets. Globalization produces more jobs than it eliminates, he contends, both for the world and for the United States.

NO: Herman E. Daly, professor at the School of Public Affairs at the University of Maryland, does not object to international trade and relations, but he does object to globalization that erases national boundaries and hurts workers and the environment.

Areally big issue of today is globalization, which stands for worldwide processes, activities, and institutions. It involves world markets, world finance, world communications, world media, world religions, world popular culture, world rights movements, world drug trade, etc. The focus of most commentators is on the world economy, which many believe promises strong growth in world wealth. Critics focus on the world economy's negative impacts on workers' wages, environmental protections and regulations, and national and local cultures. Many say that it is easy for Americans to feel positive toward globalization because America and its businesses, media, and culture are at the center of the globalized world, which ensures that America gains more than its proportional share of the benefits. But the real debate is whether or not globalization benefits all mankind. When the whole world is considered, there may be far more minuses to be weighed against the pluses. It is hard to settle this debate because so many different dimensions that are incomparable must be included in the calculation of the cost-benefit ratio.

The concept of globalization forces us to think about many complicated issues at the same time. There are technological, economic, political, cultural, and ethical aspects of globalization. Technological developments make possible the communication, transportation, coordination, and organization that make economic globalization possible. Political factors have made this a relatively free global economy. Restrictions on trade and production have been greatly reduced, and competition has greatly increased. The results have been increased production and wealth and celebration in financial circles. But competition creates losers as well as winners, so peoples throughout the world are protesting and resisting economic globalization. Many are also resisting cultural globalization because their own cultures are threatened. They feel that the global culture is materialistic, sexualized, secular, and egocentric—and they may be right. But many also consider the strengths of the global culture, such as championing human rights, democracy, and justice.

In the selections that follow, Murray Weidenbaum reports on the benefits of the global economy by arguing against what he calls "dangerous myths" that are used to critique economic globalization. He asserts that globalization produces more jobs than it replaces. Herman E. Daly opposes globalization and favors the alternative of internationalization. Both involve the increasing importance of relations among nations, but globalization erases national boundaries while internationalization does not. The negative effects of globalization, he states, are standards-lowering competition, an increased tolerance of mergers and monopoly power, intense national specialization, and the excessive monopolization of knowledge as "intellectual property."

Murray Weidenbaum

 **YES**

Globalization Is Not a Dirty Word

Delivered to the Economic Club of Detroit, Detroit, Michigan, January 22, 2001

Today I want to deal with a perplexing conundrum facing the United Sates: this is a time when the American business system is producing unparalleled levels of prosperity, yet private enterprise is under increasing attack. The critics are an unusual alliance of unions, environmentalists, and human rights groups and they are focusing on the overseas activities of business. In many circles, globalization has become a dirty word.

How can we respond in a constructive way? In my interaction with these interest groups, I find that very often their views arise from basic misunderstandings of the real world of competitive enterprise. I have identified ten myths about the global economy—dangerous myths—which need to be dispelled. Here they are:

1. Globalization costs jobs.
2. The United States is an island of free trade in a world of protectionism.
3. Americans are hurt by imports.
4. U.S. companies are running away, especially to low-cost areas overseas.
5. American companies doing business overseas take advantage of local people, especially in poor countries. They also pollute their environments.
6. The trade deficit is hurting our economy and we should eliminate it.
7. It's not fair to run such large trade deficits with China or Japan.
8. Sanctions work. So do export controls.
9. Trade agreements should be used to raise environmental and labor standards around the world.
10. America's manufacturing base is eroding in the face of unfair global competition.

That's an impressive array of frequently heard charges and they are polluting our political environment. Worse yet, these widely held myths fly in the face of the facts. I'd like to take up each of them and knock them down.

1. Globalization Costs Jobs

This is a time when the American job miracle is the envy of the rest of the world, so it is hard to take that charge seriously. Yet some people do fall for it. The facts are clear: U.S. employment is at a record high and unemployment is at a 30 year low. Moreover, the United States created more than 20 million new jobs between 1993 and 2000, far more than Western Europe and Japan combined. Contrary to a widely held view, most of those new jobs pay well, often better than the average for existing jobs.

Of course, in the best of times, some people lose their jobs or their businesses fail, and that happens today. However, most researchers who have studied this question conclude that, in the typical case, technological progress, not international trade, is the main reason for making old jobs obsolete. Of course, at the same time far more new jobs are created to take their place.

2. The United States Is an Island of Free Trade in a World of Protectionism

Do other nations erect trade barriers? Of course they do—although the trend has been to cut back these obstacles to commerce. But our hands are not as clean as we like to think. There is no shortage of restrictions on importers trying to ship their products into this country. These exceptions to free trade come in all shapes, sizes, and varieties. They are imposed by federal, state, and local governments. U.S. import barriers include the following and more:

Buy-American laws give preference in government procurement to domestic producers. Many states and localities show similar favoritism. Here in Michigan, preference is given to in-state printing firms; the Jones Act prohibits foreign ships from engaging in waterborne commerce between U.S. ports;

many statutes limit the import of specific agricultural and manufactured products, ranging from sugar to pillowcases;

we impose selective high tariffs on specific items, notably textiles; and many state and local regulatory barriers, such as building codes, are aimed at protecting domestic producers.

It's strange that consumer groups and consumer activists are mute on this subject. After all, it is the American consumer who has to pay higher prices as a result of all of this special interest legislation. But these barriers to trade ultimately are disappointing. Nations open to trade grow faster than those that are closed.

3. Americans Are Hurt by Imports

The myth that imports are bad will be quickly recognized by students of economics as the mercantilist approach discredited by Adam Smith over two centuries ago. The fact is that we benefit from imports in many ways. Consumers get access to a wider array of goods and services. Domestic companies obtain lower cost components and thus are more competitive. We get access to vital metals and minerals that are just not found in the United States. Also, imports prod our own producers to improve productivity and invest in developing new technology.

I'll present a painful example. By the way, I have never bought a foreign car. But we all know how the quality of our domestic autos has improved because of foreign competition. More recently, we had a striking example of the broader benefits to imports. In 1997–98 the expanded flow of lower-cost products from Asia kept inflation low here at a time when otherwise the Fed could have been raising interest rates to fight inflation. The result would have been a weaker economy. Moreover, in a full employment economy, imports enable the American people to enjoy a higher living standard than would be possible if sales were limited to domestic production.

In our interconnected economy, the fact is that the jobs "lost" from imports are quickly replaced by jobs elsewhere in the economy—either in export industries or in companies selling domestically. The facts are fascinating: the sharp run-up in U.S. imports in recent years paralleled the rapid growth in total U.S. employment. Both trends, of course, reflected the underlying health of our business economy.

The special importance of imports was recently highlighted by the director of the Washington State Council on International Trade: "The people who benefit most critically are families at the lower end of the wage scale who have school-age children and those elderly who must live frugally." She goes on to conclude: "It is a cruel deception that an open system of the free trade is not good for working people."

4. U.S. Companies Are Running Away Especially to Low Cost Areas Overseas

Right off the bat, the critics have the direction wrong. The flow of money to buy and operate factories and other businesses is overwhelmingly into the United States. We haven't had a net outflow of investment since the 1960s. That's the flip side of our trade deficit. Financing large trade deficits means that far more investment capital comes into this country than is leaving.

But let us examine the overseas investments by American companies. The largest proportion goes not to poor countries, but to the most developed nations, those with high labor costs and also high environmental standards. The primary motive is to gain access to markets. That's not too surprising when we consider that the people in the most industrially advanced nations are the best customers for sophisticated American products. By the way, only one-third of the exports by the foreign branches of U.S. companies goes to the United States. About 70 percent goes to other markets, primarily to the industrialized nations.

Turning to American investments in Mexico, China, and other developing countries, the result often is to enhance U.S. domestic competitiveness and job opportunities. This is so because many of these overseas factories provide low-cost components and material to U.S.-based producers who are thus able to improve their international competitiveness.

In some cases, notably the pharmaceutical industry, the overseas investments are made in countries with more enlightened regulatory regimes, such as the Netherlands. "More enlightened" is not a euphemism for lower standards. The Dutch maintain a strong but more modern regulatory system than we do.

5. American Companies Doing Business Overseas Take Advantage of Local People and Pollute Their Environments

There are always exceptions. But by and large, American-owned and managed factories in foreign countries are top-of-the-line in terms of both better working conditions and higher environmental standards than locally-owned firms. This is why so many developing countries compete enthusiastically for the overseas location of U.S. business activities—and why so many local workers seek jobs at the American factories. After all, American companies manufacturing overseas frequently follow the same high operating standards that they do here at home.

I serve on a panel of Americans who investigate the conditions in some factories in China. I wish the critics could see for themselves the differences between the factories that produce for an American company under its worldwide standards and those that are not subject to our truly enlightened sense of social responsibility.

I'll give you a very personal example of the second category of facilities. While making an inspection tour, I tore my pants on an unguarded piece of equipment in one of those poorly-lit factories. An inch closer and that protruding part would have dug into my thigh. I also had to leave the factory floor every hour or so to breathe some fresh air. When I said that, in contrast, the American-owned factories were top-of-the-line, that wasn't poetry.

Yes, foreign investment is essential to the economic development of poor countries. By definition, they lack the capability to finance growth. The critics do those poor countries no favor when they try to discourage American firms from investing there. The critics forget that, during much of the nineteenth century, European investors financed many of our canals, railroads, steel mills, and other essentials for becoming an industrialized nation. It is sad to think where the United States would be today if Europe in the nineteenth century had had an array of powerful interest groups that were so suspicious of economic progress.

6. The Trade Deficit Is Hurting Our Economy and We Should Eliminate It

Yes, the U.S. trade deficit is at a record high. But it is part of a "virtuous circle" in our economy. The trade deficit mainly reflects the widespread prosperity in the United States, which is substantially greater than in most of the countries we trade with. After all, a strong economy, such as ours operating so close to full employment and full capacity, depends on a substantial amount of imports to satisfy our demands for goods and services. Our exports are lower primarily because the demand for imports by other nations is much weaker.

The acid test is that our trade deficit quickly declines in the years when our economy slows down and that deficit rises again when the economy perks up. Serious studies show that, if the United States had deliberately tried to curb the trade deficit in the 1990s, the result would have been a weak economy with high inflation and fewer jobs. The trade deficit is a byproduct of economic performance. It should not become a goal of economic policy.

There is a constructive way of reducing the trade deficit. To most economists, the persistence of our trade imbalance (and especially of the related and more comprehensive current account deficit) is due to the fact that we do not generate enough domestic saving to finance domestic investment. The gap between such saving and investment is equal to the current account deficit.

Nobel laureate Milton Friedman summed up this point very clearly: "The remarkable performance of the United States economy in the past few years would have been impossible without the inflow of foreign capital, which is a mirror image of large balance of payments deficits."

The positive solution is clear: increase the amount that Americans save. Easier said than done, of course. The shift from budget deficits (dissaving) to budget surpluses (government saving) helps. A further shift to a tax system that does not hit saving as hard as ours does would also help. The United States taxes saving more heavily than any other advanced industrialized nation. Replacing the income tax with a consumption tax, even a progressive one, would surely be in order—but that deserves to be the subject of another talk.

7. It's Not Fair to Run Such Large Trade Deficits With China or Japan

Putting the scary rhetoric aside, there really is no good reason for any two countries to have balanced trade between them. We don't have to search for sinister causes for our trade deficits with China or Japan. Bilateral trade imbalances exist for many benign reasons, such as differences in per capita incomes and in the relative size of the two economies. One of the best kept secrets of international trade is that the average Japanese buys more U.S. goods than the average American buys Japanese goods. Yes, Japan's per capita imports from the United States are larger than our per capita imports from Japan ($539 versus $432 in 1996). We have a large trade deficit with them because we have more "capita" (population).

8. Sanctions Work, So Do Export Controls

It is ironic that so many people who worry about the trade deficit simultaneously support sanctions and export controls. There is practically no evidence that unilateral sanctions are effective in getting other nations to change their policies or actions. Those restrictions on trade do, however, have an impact: they backfire. U.S. business, labor, and agriculture are harmed. We lost an overseas market for what is merely a symbolic gesture. Sanctions often are evaded. Shipping goods through third countries can disguise the ultimate recipient in the nation on which the sanctions are imposed. On balance, these sanctions reduced American exports in 1995 by an estimated $15–20 billion.

As for export controls, where American producers do not have a monopoly on a particular technology—which is frequent—producers in other nations can deliver the same technology or product without the handicap imposed on U.S companies. A recent report at the Center for the Study of American Business showed that many business executives believe that sanctions and export controls are major obstacles to the expansion of U.S. foreign trade.

9. Trade Agreements Should Be Used to Raise Environmental and Labor Standards Around the World

At first blush, this sounds like such a nice and high-minded way of doing good. But, as a practical matter, it is counterproductive to try to impose such costly social regulations on developing countries as a requirement for doing business with them. The acid test is that most developing nations oppose these trade restrictions. They see them for what they really are—a disguised form of protectionism designed to keep their relatively low-priced goods out of the markets of the more advanced, developed nations. All that feeds the developing nations' sense of cynicism toward us.

In the case of labor standards, there is an existing organization, the International Labor Organization [ILO], which has been set up to deal specifically with these matters. Of all the international organizations, the ILO is unique in having equal representation from business, labor, and government. The United States and most other nations *are* members. The ILO is where issues of labor standards should be handled. To be taken more seriously, the United States should support the ILO more vigorously than it has.

As for environmental matters, we saw at the unsuccessful meetings on climate change at the Hague [recently] how difficult it is to get broad international agreement on environmental issues even in sympathetic meetings of an international environmental agency. To attempt to tie such controversial environmental matters to trade agreements arouses my suspicions about the intent of the sponsors. It is hard to avoid jumping to the conclusion that the basic motivation is to prevent progress on the trade front.

I still recall the signs carried by one of the protesters in Seattle, "Food is for people, not for export." Frankly, it's hard to deal with such an irrational position. After all, if the United States did not export a major part of its abundant farm output, millions of people overseas would be starving or malnourished. Also, thousands of our farmers would go broke.

The most effective way to help developing countries improve their working conditions and environmental protection is to trade with and invest in them. As for the charge that companies invest in poor, developing nations in order to minimize their environmental costs, studies of the issue show that environmental factors are not important influences in business location decisions. As I pointed out earlier, most U.S. overseas direct investment goes to developed nations with high labor costs and also high environmental standards.

10. America's Manufacturing Base Is Eroding in the Face of Unfair Global Competition

Unfortunately, some of our fellow citizens seem to feel that the only fair form of foreign competition is the kind that does not succeed in landing any of their goods on our shores. But to get to the heart of the issue, there is no factual basis for the charge that our manufacturing base is eroding—or even stagnant. The official statistics are reporting record highs in output year after year. Total industrial production in the United States today is 45 percent higher than in 1992—that's not in dollars, but in terms of real output.

Of course, not all industries or companies go up—or down—in unison. Some specific industries, especially low-tech, have had to cut back. But simultaneously, other industries, mainly high-tech, have been expanding rapidly. Such changes are natural and to be expected in an open, dynamic economy. By the way, the United States regularly runs a trade surplus in high-tech products.

It's important to understand the process at work here. Technological progress generates improved industrial productivity. In the United States, that means to some degree fewer blue-collar jobs and more while-collar jobs. That is hardly a recent development. The shift from physical labor to knowledge workers has been the trend since the beginning of the 20th century. On balance, as I noted earlier, total U.S. employment is at an all-time high.

If you have any doubt about the importance of rising productivity to our society, just consider where we would be if over the past century agriculture had not enjoyed rising productivity (that is, more output per worker/hour). Most of us would still be farmers.

It is vital that we correct the erroneous views of the anti-globalists. Contrary to their claims, our open economy has raised living standards and helped to contain inflation. International commerce is more important to our economy today than at any time in the past. By dollar value and volume, the United States is the world's largest trading nation. We are the largest importer, exporter, foreign investor, and host to foreign investment. Trying to stop the global economy is futile and contrary to America's self-interest.

Nevertheless, we must recognize that globalization, like any other major change, generates costs as well as benefits. It is essential to address these consequences. Otherwise, we will not be able to maintain a national consensus that responds to the challenges of the world marketplace by focusing on opening markets instead of closing them. The challenge to all of us is to urge courses of action that help those who are hurt without doing far more harm to the much larger number who benefit from the international marketplace.

We need to focus more attention on those who don't share the benefits of the rapid pace of economic change. Both private and public efforts should be increased to provide more effective adjustment assistance to those who lose their jobs. The focus of adjustment policy should not be on providing relief from economic change, but on positive approaches that help more of our people participate in economic prosperity.

As you may know, I recently chaired a bipartisan commission established by Congress to deal with the trade deficit. Our commission included leaders of business and labor, former senior government officials, and academics. We could not agree on all the issues that we dealt with. But we were unanimous in concluding that the most fundamental part of an effective long-run trade adjustment policy is to do a much better job of educating and training. More Americans should be given the opportunity to become productive and high-wage members of the nation's workforce.

No, I'm not building up to a plea to donate to the college of your choice, although that's a pretty good idea.

Even though I teach at major research universities—and strongly believe in their vital mission—let me make a plea for greater attention to our junior colleges. They are an overlooked part of the educational system. Junior colleges have a key role to play. Many of these community oriented institutions of learning are now organized to specially meet the needs of displaced workers, including those who need to brush up on their basic language and math skills. In some cases, these community colleges help people launch new businesses, especially in areas where traditional manufacturing is declining. A better trained and more productive workforce is the key to our long-term international competitiveness. That is the most effective way of resisting the calls for economic isolationism.

Let me leave you with a final thought. The most powerful benefit of the global economy is not economic at all, even though it involves important economic and business activities. By enabling more people to use modern technology to communicate across traditional national boundaries, the international marketplace makes possible more than an accelerated flow of data. The worldwide marketplace encourages a far greater exchange of the most powerful of all factors of production—new ideas. That process enriches and empowers the individual in ways never before possible.

As an educator, I take this as a challenge to educate the anti-globalists to the great harm that would result from a turn to economic isolationism. For the twenty-first century, the global flow of information is the endless frontier.

Herman E. Daly

 NO

Globalization and Its Discontents

Every day, newspaper articles and television reports insist that those who oppose globalization must be isolationists or—even worse—xenophobes. This judgment is nonsense. The relevant alternative to globalization is internationalization, which is neither isolationist nor xenophobic. Yet it is impossible to recognize the cogency of this alternative if one does not properly distinguish these two terms.

"Internalization" refers to the increasing importance of relations among nations. Although the basic unit of community and policy remains the nation, increasingly trade, treaties, alliances, protocols, and other formal agreements and communications are necessary elements for nations to thrive. "Globalization" refers to global economic integration of many formerly national economies into one global economy. Economic integration is made possible by free trade—especially by free capital mobility—and by easy or uncontrolled migration. In contrast to internationalization, which simply recognizes that nations increasingly rely on understandings among one another, globalization is the effective erasure of national boundaries for economic purposes. National boundaries become totally porous with respect to goods and capital, and ever more porous with respect to people, who are simply viewed as cheap labor—or in some cases as cheap human capital.

In short, globalization is the economic integration of the globe. But exactly what is "integration"? The word derives from *integer,* meaning one, complete, or whole. Integration means much more than "interdependence"—it is the act of combining separate although related units into a single whole. Since there can be only one whole, only one unity with reference to which parts are integrated, it follows that global economic integration logically implies national economic *dis*integration—parts are torn out of their national context (dis-integrated), in order to be re-integrated into the new whole, the globalized economy.

As the saying goes, to make an omelet you have to break some eggs. The disintegration of the national egg is necessary to integrate the global omelet. But this obvious logic, as well as the cost of disintegration, is frequently met with denial. This article argues that globalization is neither inevitable nor to be embraced, much less celebrated. Acceptance of globalization entails several

From Herman E. Daly, "Globalization and Its Discontents," *Philosophy & Public Policy Quarterly*, vol. 21, no. 2/3 (Spring/Summer 2001). Copyright © 2001 by The Institute for Philosophy & Public Policy. Reprinted by permission.

serious consequences, namely, standards-lowering competition, an increased tolerance of mergers and monopoly power, intense national specialization, and the excessive monopolization of knowledge as "intellectual property." This article discusses these likely consequences, and concludes by advocating the adoption of internationalization, and not globalization.

The Inevitability of Globalization?

Some accept the inevitability of globalization and encourage others in the faith. With admirable clarity, honesty, and brevity, Renato Ruggiero, former director-general of the World Trade Organization, insists that "We are no longer writing the rules of interaction among separate national economies. We are writing the constitution of a single global economy." His sentiments clearly affirm globalization and reject internationalization as above defined. Further, those who hold Ruggiero's view also subvert the charter of the Bretton Woods institutions. Named after a New Hampshire resort where representatives of forty-four nations met in 1944 to design the world's post–World War II economic order, the institutions conceived at the Bretton Woods International Monetary Conference include the World Bank and the International Monetary Fund. The World Trade Organization evolved later, but functions as a third sister to the World Bank and the International Monetary Fund. The nations at the conference considered proposals by the U.S., U.K., and Canadian governments, and developed the "Bretton Woods system," which established a stable international environment through such policies as fixed exchange rates, currency convertibility, and provision for orderly exchange rate adjustments. The Bretton Woods Institutions were designed to facilitate *internationalization, not globalization,* a point ignored by director-general Ruggiero.

The World Bank, along with its sister institutions, seems to have lost sight of its mission. After the disruption of its meetings in Washington, D.C. in April 2000, the World Bank sponsored an Internet discussion on globalization. The closest the World Bank came to offering a definition of the subject under discussion was the following: "The most common core sense of economic globalization... surely refers to the observation that in recent years a quickly rising share of economic activity in the world seems to be taking place between people who live in different countries (rather than in the same country)." This ambiguous description was not improved upon by Mr. Wolfensohn, president of the World Bank, who told the audience at a subsequent Aspen Institute Conference that "Globalization is a practical methodology for empowering the poor to improve their lives." That is neither a definition nor a description—it is a wish. Further, this wish also flies in the face of the real consequences of global economic integration. One could only sympathize with demonstrators protesting Mr. Wolfensohn's speech some fifty yards from the Aspen conference facility. The reaction of the Aspen elite was to accept as truth the title of Mr. Wolfensohn's speech, "Making Globalization Work for the Poor," and then ask in grieved tones, "How could anyone demonstrate against *that?*"

Serious consequences flow from the World Banks' lack of precision in defining globalization but lauding it nonetheless. For one thing, the so-called definition of globalization conflates the concept with that of internalization. As a result, one cannot reasonably address a crucial question: Should these increasing transactions between people living in different countries take place *across national boundaries* that are economically significant, or *within an integrated world* in which national boundaries are economically meaningless?

The ambiguous understanding of globalization deprives citizens of the opportunity to decide whether they are willing to abandon national monetary and fiscal policy, as well as the minimum wage. One also fails to carefully consider whether economic integration entails political and cultural integration. In short, will political communities and cultural traditions wither away, subsumed under some monolithic economic imperative? Although one might suspect economic integration would lead to political integration, it is hard to decide which would be worse—an economically integrated world *with,* or *without,* political integration. Everyone recognizes the desirability of community for the world as a whole—but one can conceive of two very different models of world community: (1) a federated community of real national communities (internationalization), versus (2) a cosmopolitan direct membership in a single abstract global community (globalization). However, at present our confused conversations about globalization deprive us of the opportunity to reflect deeply on these very different possibilities.

This article has suggested that at present organizations such as the International Monetary Fund and the World Bank (and, by extension, the World Trade Organization) no longer serve the interests of their member nations as defined in their charters. Yet if one asks whose interests are served, we are told they service the interests of the integrated "global economy." If one tries to glimpse a concrete reality behind that grand abstraction, however, one can find no individual workers, peasants, or small businessmen represented, but only giant fictitious individuals, the transnational corporations. In globalization, power is drained away from national communities and local enterprises, and aggregates in transnational corporations.

The Consequences of Globalization

Globalization—the erasure of national boundaries for economic purposes—risks serious consequences. Briefly, they include, first of all, standards-lowering competition to externalize social and environmental costs with the goal of achievement of a competitive advantage. This results, in effect, in a race to the bottom so far as efficiency in cost accounting and equity in income distribution are concerned. Globalization also risks increased tolerance of mergers and monopoly power in domestic markets in order that corporations become big enough to compete internationally. Third, globalization risks more intense national specialization according to the dictates of competitive advantage. Such specialization reduces the range of choice of ways to earn a livelihood, and increases dependence on other countries. Finally, worldwide enforcement of a muddled and self-serving doctrine of "trade-related intellectual property rights" is a direct contradiction of the Jeffersonian dictum that "knowledge is the common property of mankind."

Each of these risks of globalization deserves closer scrutiny.

1. Standards-lowering competition Globalization undercuts the ability of nations to internalize environmental and social costs into prices. Instead, economic integration under free market conditions promotes standards-lowering competition—a race to the bottom, in short. The country that does the poorest job of internalizing all social and environmental costs of production into its prices gets a competitive advantage in international trade. The external social and environmental costs are left to be borne by the population at large. Further, more of world production shifts to countries that do the poorest job of counting costs—a sure recipe for reducing the efficiency of global production. As uncounted, externalized costs increase, the positive correlation between gross domestic product (GDP) growth and welfare disappears, or even becomes negative. We enter a world foreseen by the nineteenth-century social critic John Ruskin, who observed that "that which seems to be wealth is in verity but a gilded index of far-reaching ruin."

Another dimension of the race to the bottom is that globalization fosters increasing inequality in the distribution of income in high-wage countries, such as the U.S. Historically, in the U.S. there has been an implicit social contract established to ameliorate industrial strife between labor and capital. As a consequence, the distribution of income between labor and capital has been considered more equal and just in the U.S. compared to the world as a whole. However, global integration of markets necessarily abrogates that social contract. U.S. wages would fall drastically because labor is relatively more abundant globally than nationally. Further, returns to capital in the U.S. would increase because capital is relatively more scarce globally than nationally. Although one could make the theoretical argument that wages would be *bid up* in the rest of the world, the increase would be so small as to be insignificant. Making such an argument from the relative numbers would be analogous to insisting that, theoretically, when I jump off a ladder gravity not only pulls me to the earth, but also moves the earth towards me. This technical point offers cold comfort to anyone seeking a softer landing.

2. Increased tolerance of mergers and monopoly power Fostering global competitive advantage is used as an excuse for tolerance of corporate mergers and monopoly in national markets. Chicago School economist and Nobel laureate Ronald Coase, in his classic article on the theory of the firm, suggests that corporate entities are "islands of central planning in a sea of market relationships." The islands of central planning become larger and larger relative to the remaining sea of market relationships as a result of merger. More and more resources are allocated by within-firm central planning, and less by between-firm market relationships. Corporations are the victor, and the market principle is the loser, as governments lose the strength to regulate corporate capital and maintain competitive markets in the public interest. Of the hundred largest economic organizations, fifty-two are corporations and forty-eight are nations. The distribution of income within these centrally-planned corporations has become much more concentrated. The ratio of the salary of the Chief Executive

Officer to the average employee has passed 400 (as one would expect, since chief central planners set their own salaries).

3. Intense national specialization   Free trade and free capital mobility increase pressures for specialization in order to gain or maintain a competitive advantage. As a consequence, globalization demands that workers accept an ever-narrowing range of ways to earn a livelihood. In Uruguay, for example, everyone would have to be either a shepherd or a cowboy to conform to the dictates of competitive advantage in the global market. Everything else should be imported in exchange for beef, mutton, wool, and leather. Any Uruguayan who wants to play in a symphony orchestra or be an airline pilot should emigrate.

Of course, most people derive as much satisfaction from how they earn their income as from how they spend it. Narrowing that range of choice is a welfare loss uncounted by trade theorists. Globalization assumes either that emigration and immigration are costless, or that narrowing the range of occupational choice within a nation is costless. Both assumptions are false.

While trade theorists ignore the range of choice in *earning* one's income, they at the same time exaggerate the welfare effects of range of choice in *spending* that income. For example, the U.S. imports Danish butter cookies and Denmark imports U.S. butter cookies. Although the gains from trading such similar commodities cannot be great, trade theorists insist that the welfare of cookie connoisseurs is increased by expanding the range of consumer choice to the limit.

Perhaps, but one wonders whether those gains might be realized more cheaply by simply trading recipes? Although one would think so, *recipes*—trade-related intellectual property rights—are the one thing that free traders really want to protect.

4. Intellectual property rights   Of all things, knowledge is that which should be most freely shared, since in sharing, knowledge is multiplied rather than divided. Yet trade theorists have rejected Thomas Jefferson's dictum that "Knowledge is the common property of mankind" and instead have accepted a muddled doctrine of "trade-related intellectual property rights." This notion of rights grants private corporations monopoly ownership of the very basis of life itself—patents to seeds (including the patent-protecting, life-denying terminator gene) and to knowledge of basic genetic structures.

The argument offered to support this grab is that, without the economic incentive of monopoly ownership, little new knowledge and innovation will be forthcoming. Yet, so far as I know, James Watson and Francis Crick, co-discoverers of the structure of DNA, do not share in the patent royalties reaped by their successors. Nor of course did Gregor Mendel get any royalties—but then he was a monk motivated by mere curiosity about how Creation works!

Once knowledge exists, its proper price is the marginal opportunity cost of sharing it, which is close to zero, since nothing is lost by sharing knowledge. Of course, one does lose the *monopoly* on that knowledge, but then economists have traditionally argued that monopoly is inefficient as well as unjust because it creates an artificial scarcity of the monopolized item.

Certainly, the cost of production of new knowledge is not zero, even though the cost of sharing it is. This allows biotech corporations to claim that they deserve a fifteen- or twenty-year monopoly for the expenses incurred in research and development. Although corporations deserve to profit from their efforts, they are not entitled to monopolize on Watson and Crick's contribution—without which they could do nothing—or on the contributions of Gregor Mendel and all the great scientists of the past who made fundamental discoveries. As early twentieth-century economist Joseph Schumpeter emphasized, being the first with an innovation already gives one the advantage of novelty, a natural temporary monopoly, which in his view was the major source of profit in a competitive economy.

As the great Swiss economist, Jean Sismondi, argued over two centuries ago, not all new knowledge is of benefit to humankind. We need a sieve to select beneficial knowledge. Perhaps the worse selective principle is hope for private monetary gain. A much better selective motive for knowledge is a search in hopes of benefit to our fellows. This is not to say that we should abolish all intellectual property rights—that would create more problems than it would solve. But we should certainly begin restricting the domain and length of patent monopolies rather than increasing them so rapidly and recklessly. We should also become much more willing to share knowledge. Shared knowledge increases the productivity of all labor, capital, and resources. Further, international development aid should consist far more of freely-shared knowledge, and far less of foreign investment and interest-bearing loans.

Let me close with my favorite quote from John Maynard Keynes, one of the founders of the recently subverted Bretton Woods Institutions:

> I sympathize therefore, with those who would minimize, rather than those who would maximize, economic entanglement between nations. Ideas, knowledge, art, hospitality, travel—these are the things which should of their nature be international. But let goods be homespun whenever it is reasonably and conveniently possible; and, above all, let finance be primarily national.

POSTSCRIPT

Is Globalization Good for Mankind?

Weidenbaum's argument in favor of economic globalization emphasizes the economic benefits it produces. He maintains that even groups that expect to be economically hurt by globalization will benefit from it. Daly, however, believes that the economy is inexorably connected to culture and politics. He therefore asks, "Will political communities and cultural traditions wither away, subsumed under some monolithic economic imperative?" Economic integration will spawn greater political integration and cultural integration, he concludes, theorizing that in globalization, power is drained away from national communities and local enterprises and aggregates in transnational corporations.

There has been an explosion of books on globalization recently. A bestseller is Thomas Friedman's *The Lexus and the Olive Tree* (Farrar, Straus, Giroux, 2000), which tells the story of the new global economy and many of its ramifications. Friedman sees the United States as the nation that is best able to capitalize on that global economy, so it has the brightest future. Other works that applaud globalization include Barry Asmas, *The Best Is Yet to Come* (AmeriPress, 2001); Diane Coyle, *Paradoxes of Prosperity: Why the New Capitalism Benefits All* (Texere, 2001); Anthony Giddens, *Runaway World: How Globalization Is Reshaping Our Lives* (Routledge, 2000); John Micklethwait and Adrian Wooldridge, *Future Perfect: The Challenge and Hidden Promise of Globalization* (Crown Business, 2000); Robert and Jean M. Gilpin, *The Challenge of Global Capitalism* (Princeton University Press, 2000), which acknowledges that appropriate political institutions are essential to its benefits; and Jacques Bandot, ed., *Building a World Community: Globalization and the Common Good* (University of Washington Press, 2001).

Attacks on globalization are prolific and include Robert Went, *Globalization: Neoliberal Challenge, Radical Responses* (Pluto Press, 2000); James H. Mittelman, *The Globalization Syndrome* (Princeton University Press, 2000); William K. Tabb, *The Amoral Elephant: Globalization and the Struggle for Social Justice in the Twenty-First Century* (Monthly Review Press, 2001); Frank Bealey, *Power in Business and the State: An Historical Analysis of Its Concentration* (Routledge, 2001); Walden Bello, *Future in Balance: Essays on Globalization and Resistance* (Food First Books, 2001); Jeremy Brecher, Tim Costello, and Brenden Smith, *Globalization From Below: The Power of Solidarity* (South End Press, 2000); Vic George and Paul Wilding, *Globalization and Human Welfare* (Palgrave, 2002); Gary Teeple, *Globalization and the Decline of Social Reform* (Humanity Books, 2000); Noreena Hertz, *The Silent Takeover: Global Capitalism and the Death of Democracy* (Free Press, 2002); and Alan Tomelson, *Race to the Bottom: Why a*

Worldwide Worker Surplus and Uncontrolled Free Trade Are Sinking American Living Standards (Westview, 2000).

For relatively balanced discussions of globalization see Mohammed A. Bamyeh, *The Ends of Globalization* (University of Minnesota Press, 2000); Arthur P. J. Mol, *Globalization and Environmental Reform: The Ecological Modernization of the Global Economy* (MIT Press, 2001), which points to the environmental degradation that results from globalization but also actions that retard degradation and improve environmental quality; Richard Langhome, *The Coming of Globalization: Its Evolution and Contemporary Consequences* (St. Martin's Press, 2001); Barbara Harris-White, ed., *Globalization and Insecurity: Political, Economic, and Physical Challenges* (Palgrave, 2002); and Dani Rodnik, *Has Globalization Gone Too Far?* (Institute for International Economics, 1997). For interesting discussions of the cultural aspects of globalization see Paul Kennedy and Catherine J. Danks, eds., *Globalization and National Identities: Crisis or Opportunity* (Palgrave, 2001); Tyler Cowen, *Creative Destruction: How Globalization Is Changing the World's Cultures* (Princeton University Press, 2002); Alison Brysk, ed., *Globalization and Human Rights* (University of California Press, 2002); and Elisabeth Madimbee-Boyi, ed., *Beyond Dichotomies: Histories, Identities, Cultures, and the Challenge of Globalization* (SUNY, 2002).

Contributors to This Volume

EDITOR

KURT FINSTERBUSCH is a professor of sociology at the University of Maryland at College Park. He received a B.A. in history from Princeton University in 1957, a B.D. from Grace Theological Seminary in 1960, and a Ph.D. in sociology from Columbia University in 1969. He is the author of *Understanding Social Impacts* (Sage Publications, 1980), and he is the coauthor, with Annabelle Bender Motz, of *Social Research for Policy Decisions* (Wadsworth, 1980) and, with Jerald Hage, of *Organizational Change as a Development Strategy* (Lynne Rienner, 1987). He is the editor of *Annual Editions: Sociology* (McGraw-Hill/Dushkin); *Annual Editions: Social Problems* (McGraw-Hill/Dushkin); and *Sources: Notable Selections in Sociology,* 3rd ed. (McGraw-Hill/Dushkin, 1999).

STAFF

Theodore Knight   List Manager
David Brackley   Senior Developmental Editor
Juliana Gribbins   Developmental Editor
Rose Gleich   Administrative Assistant
Brenda S. Filley   Director of Production/Design
Juliana Arbo   Typesetting Supervisor
Diane Barker   Proofreader
Richard Tietjen   Publishing Systems Manager
Larry Killian   Copier Coordinator

AUTHORS

RANDY ALBELDA, professor of economics at the University of Massachusetts in Boston and researcher at the Center for Popular Economics, works on poverty issues. He is the author, with Nancy Folbre, of *The War on the Poor: A Defense Manual* (W. W. Norton, 1996) and, with Charles Tilly, *Glass Ceilings and Bottomless Pits: Women's Work, Women's Poverty* (South End Press, 1997).

MARCIA ANGELL is a senior lecturer in social medicine at the Harvard Medical School and former editor-in-chief of *The New England Journal of Medicine*. She is the author of *Science on Trial: The Clash of Medical Evidence and the Law in the Breast Implant Case* (W. W. Norton, 1996).

JEFFREY M. BERRY is John Richard Skuse Professor of Political Science at Tufts University. He is the author of *The New Liberalism: The Rising Power of Citizen Groups* (Brookings Institution Press, 2000) and *The Interest Group Society*, 3rd ed. (Addison-Wesley, 2001).

CHRIS BRIGHT is a senior researcher of the Worldwatch Institute and senior editor of the institute's magazine, *World Watch*.

PATRICK BUCHANAN was a presidential candidate in 2000. Currently, he is a political analyst, television commentator, and the author of *The Death of the West* (Thomas Dunne Books, 2000), which focuses on the issue of immigration.

JAMES P. COMER is the Maurice Falk Professor of Child Psychiatry at the Yale University Child Study Center. He founded the center's school development program in 1968.

STEPHANIE COONTZ teaches history and family studies at the Evergreen State College in Olympia, Washington. She is the author of *The Way We Never Were: American Families and the Nostalgia Trap* (Basic Books, 1992) and *The Way We Really Are: Coming to Terms With America's Changing Families* (Basic Books, 1997). She is coeditor of *American Families: A Multicultural Reader* (Routledge, 1998).

MARY CRAWFORD is a professor of psychology at the University of Connecticut. She is the author, with Rhoda Unger, of *Talking Difference: On Gender and Language* (Sage Publications, 1995) and *Women and Gender: A Feminist Psychology*, 3rd ed. (McGraw-Hill, 2000).

HERMAN E. DALY is a professor in the School of Public Affairs at the University of Maryland and the author of a classic on the subject of environmental economics, *Steady-State Economics: The Economics of Biophysical Equilibrium and Moral Growth* (W. H. Freeman, 1977). Recently he authored *Beyond Growth: The Economics of Sustainable Development* (Beacon Press, 1996) and *Ecological Economics and the Ecology of Economics: Essays in Criticism* (Edward Elgar, 1999).

CHRISTOPHER C. DeMUTH is president of the American Enterprise Institute for Public Policy. He is also editor, with William Kristol, of *The Neoconservative Imagination: Essays in Honor of Irving Kristol* (American Enterprise

Institute for Public Policy Research, 1995) and coauthor of *The Reagan Doctrine and Beyond* (American Enterprise Institute for Public Policy Research, 1988).

JOHN J. DiIULIO, JR., is a professor of politics and public affairs at Princeton University. His publications include *No Escape: The Future of American Corrections* (Basic Books, 1991) and *American Government: The Essentials,* 8th ed. (Houghton Mifflin, 2001).

G. WILLIAM DOMHOFF has been teaching psychology and sociology at the University of California, Santa Cruz, since 1965. His books on political sociology include *Who Rules America?* (Prentice-Hall, 1967); *The Power Elite and the State: How Policy Is Made in America* (Aldine de Gruyter, 1990); and *Diversity in the Power Elite* (Yale University Press, 1998).

ERNEST ERBER is affiliated with the American Planning Association in Washington, D.C., which is involved in urban and rural development.

SUSAN FALUDI is a Pulitzer Prize–winning journalist who writes for magazines such as *The Nation* and the *New Yorker.* She is the author of *Backlash: The Undeclared War Against American Women* (Random House, 1995) and *Stiffed: The Betrayal of the American Man* (William Morrow & Company, 1999).

CHESTER E. FINN, JR., is a former U.S. assistant secretary of education and currently is president of the Thomas B. Fordham Foundation and senior fellow with the Manhattan Institute. He is the author, with Bruno V. Manno and Gregg Vanourek, *Charter Schools in Action: Renewing Public Education* (Princeton University Press, 2000).

JIB FOWLES is a professor of communication at the University of Houston at Clear Lake and the author of *The Case for Television Violence* (Sage Publications, 1999).

ERIC M. FREEDMAN is a professor of law in the School of Law at Hofstra University. He chairs the Committee on Civil Rights of the Association of the Bar of the City of New York. He is coauthor, with Monroe H. Freedman, of *Group Defamation and Freedom of Speech: The Relationship Between Language and Violence* (Greenwood, 1995) and *Understanding Lawyers' Ethics* (Matthew Bender & Company, 1990). He is the sole author of *Habeas Corpus: Rethinking the Great Writ of Liberty* (New York University Press, 2001).

MILTON FRIEDMAN is a senior research fellow at the Stanford University Hoover Institution on War, Revolution, and Peace. He was the recipient of the 1976 Nobel Prize in economic science. He has authored *Monetarist Economics* (Blackwell, 1991) and *Why Government Is the Problem* (Hoover Institution Press, 1993). He and his wife, **ROSE FRIEDMAN,** who also writes on economic topics, have coauthored several publications, including *Tyranny of the Status Quo* (Harcourt Brace Jovanovich, 1984); *Free to Choose: A Personal Statement* (Harcourt Brace Jovanovich, 1980); and *Capitalism and Freedom* (University of Chicago Press, 1982).

JEFF GRABMEIER is managing editor of research news at Ohio State University in Columbus, Ohio.

GERTRUDE HIMMELFARB is a professor emeritus of history at the Graduate School of the City University of New York. She is the author of *One Nation, Two Cultures* (Alfred A. Knopf, 1999) and *On Looking Into the Abyss: Untimely Thoughts on Culture and Society* (Alfred A. Knopf, 1994).

CHRISTOPHER JENCKS is a professor of social policy at the Kennedy School at Harvard University and the author of many books on poverty and inequality, including *Rethinking Social Policy: Race, Poverty, and the Underclass* (Harvard University Press, 1992).

WILBERT JENKINS is associate professor of history at Temple University and the author of *Climbing Up to Glory: A Short History of African Americans During the Civil War and Reconstruction* (Scholarly Resources, 2002).

ROBERT W. LEE is a contributing editor at *The New American* and the author of *The United Nations Conspiracy* (Western Islands, 1981).

BJORN LOMBORG is a statistician at the University of Aarhus and the author of the controversial book *The Skeptical Environmentalist: Measuring the Real State of the World* (Cambridge University Press, 2001).

BRUNO V. MANNO is a former assistant secretary of education and currently is senior program associate with the Annie E. Casey Foundation. He is the author, with Chester E. Finn, Jr. and Gregg Vanourek, of *Charter Schools in Action: Renewing Public Education* (Princeton University Press, 2000).

PAUL R. McHUGH is Henry Phipps Professor and director of the Department of Psychiatry and Behavioral Sciences at the Johns Hopkins University School of Medicine. He is the author, with Phillip R. Slavney, of *The Perspectives of Psychiatry*, 2d ed. (Johns Hopkins University Press, 1998).

CHARLES MURRAY is Bradley Fellow at the American Enterprise Institute. He is the author of *Losing Ground: American Social Policy, 1950–1980*, 10th ed. (Basic Books, 1994) and *The Underclass Revisited* (AEI Press, 1999). He is coauthor, with Richard J. Herrnstein, of *The Bell Curve* (Free Press, 1994).

ETHAN A. NADELMANN is director of the Lindesmith Center of the Drug Policy Foundation, a New York drug policy research institute, and professor of politics and public affairs in the Woodrow Wilson School of Public and International Affairs at Princeton University. He is the author of *Cops Across Borders: The Internationalization of U.S. Criminal Law Enforcement* (Pennsylvania State University Press, 1993).

DAVID POPENOE is a professor of sociology at Rutgers–The State University in New Brunswick, New Jersey. He is the author of *Disturbing the Nest* (Aldine de Gruyter, 1988) and *Life Without Father: Compelling New Evidence That Fatherhood and Marriage are Indispensable for the Good of Children and Society* (Martin Kessler Books, 1996). He is editor, with Jean Bethke Elshtain and David Blankenhorn, of *Promises to Keep: Decline and Renewal of Marriage in America* (Rowman & Littlefield Publishers, 1996).

W. JAMES POTTER is a professor of sociology at Florida State University and the author of *On Media Violence* (Sage Publications, 1999).

JEFFREY REIMAN is the William Fraser McDowell Professor of Philosophy at American University in Washington, D.C. He is the author of *Justice and Modern Moral Philosophy* (Yale University Press, 1992) and *The Rich Get Richer and the Poor Get Prison: Ideology, Class, and Criminal Justice,* 6th ed. (Allyn and Bacon, 2001). He is also editor, with Paul Leighton, of *Criminal Justice Ethics* (Prentice Hall, 2001).

BARRY SCHWARTZ is the Dorwin Cartwright Professor of Social Theory and Social Action and professor of psychology at Swarthmore College. He is the author of *The Costs of Living: How Market Freedom Erodes the Best Things in Life* (W. W. Norton, 1994).

ANDREW SULLIVAN is a former editor of *The New Republic.* His articles have been published in the *New York Times,* the *Wall Street Journal, Esquire, The Public Interest,* and the *Times* of London. He is the author of *The Distant Intimacy* (Random House, 1999) and *Virtually Normal: An Argument About Homosexuality* (Alfred A. Knopf, 1995). He is also editor of *Same-Sex Marriage, Pro and Con: A Reader* (Vintage Books, 1997).

GREGG VANOUREK is vice president of KIZ, heads its Charter School Division, and is the author, with Chester E. Finn, Jr. and Gregg Vanourek, of *Charter Schools in Action: Renewing Public Education* (Princeton University Press, 2000).

ERIC A. VOTH is a physician and chairman of the International Drug Strategy Institute.

BEN WATTENBERG is a senior fellow at the American Enterprise Institute and is the author of *The First Universal Nation: Leading Indicators and Ideas About the Surge of America in the 1990s* (Free Press, 1991). He is coauthor, with Theodore Caplow and Louis Hicks, of *The First Measured Century: An Illustrated Guide to Trends in America, 1900-2000* (AEI Press, 2001).

MURRAY WEIDENBAUM is the chairman of the Weidenbaum Center at Washington University in St. Louis. He is also the author of *Business and Government in the Global Marketplace,* 6th ed. (Prentice Hall, 1999) and *Looking for Common Ground on U.S. Trade Policy* (Center for Strategic and International Studies, 2001).

DAVID WHITMAN is a senior writer for *U.S. News & World Report* and the author of *The Optimism Gap: The I'm Ok–They're Not Syndrome and the Myth of American Decline* (Walker & Company, 1998).

WALTER E. WILLIAMS is the John M. Olin Distinguished Professor of Economics at George Mason University.

JAMES Q. WILSON, a criminologist and sociologist, is the James Collins Professor of Management and Public Policy at the University of California at Los Angeles. He has authored, coauthored, or edited numerous books on crime, government, and politics, including *Bureaucracy: What Government Agencies Do and Why They Do It* (Basic Books, 1989); *American Government* (Houghton Mifflin, 1996); *The Moral Sense* (Simon & Schuster, 1997); *Moral*

Judgment: Does the Abuse Excuse Threaten Our Legal System? (Basic Books, 1997); and *The Decline of Marriage* (HarperCollins, 2002).

PHILIP YANCEY serves as editor-at-large for *Christianity Today* magazine. He has authored numerous books, including *The Jesus I Never Knew* (Zondervan Publishing House, 1995) and *What's so Amazing About Grace?* (Zondervan Publishing House, 1997).

Index

Comer, James P., on competition as the solution to the ills of public education, 250–257

communication, the controversy over gender differences in conversation style and, 82–96

"communitarian" individualism, decline of the traditional family and, 116

consequences, the effects of television violence and portrayals of, for violent actions, 30

conservatism, 157

consumer protection, in a capitalist economy, 219–220, 222

consumption, income inequality and, 145

conversation styles, the controversy over gender differences in, 82–96

Coontz, Stephanie, on the decline of the traditional family, 122–127

corporate-conservative coalition, the controversy over government as dominated by big business and, 190–196

"counter-counterculture," 9–10

Crawford, Mary, on gender differences in conversation styles, 88–96

crime: the controversy over street crime as more harmful than white-collar, 282–296; the controversy over whether television violence makes children more violent and, 24–25; moral decline and, 4–5, 15; underclass and, 150–151

crop eradication campaigns, drugs and, 301

crop substitution programs, drugs and, 301

cultivation effects, the controversy over whether television violence makes children more violent and, 35

Daly, Herman E., on globalization, 362–367

Darden, Willie, 318, 322

death penalty. *See* capital punishment

decriminalization of drugs, the controversy over, 300–312

"Defining Deviancy Down" (Moynihan), 6

"Defining Deviancy Up," 6

deforestation, 337–340

DeMuth, Christopher C., on economic inequality, 142–146

depression, the controversy over doctor-assisted suicide and, 265–266, 270–272

desensitization, the controversy over whether television violence makes children more violent and, 25, 32–33, 35, 38–39

deterrence, capital punishment as, 316–317, 325–327

Dickens, Charles, 20

DiIulio, John J., Jr., on whether street crime is more harmful than white-collar crime, 282–287

disinhibition, the controversy over whether television violence makes children more violent and, 26–27, 34

divorce: decline of the traditional family and, 115; moral decline and, 5, 6

doctor-assisted suicide, the controversy over, 262–275

domestic partnerships, the controversy over legal recognition of same-sex marriage and, 103

domestic violence, the controversy over the burden of new sex roles and, 71–72

Domhoff, G. William, on government as dominated by big business, 190–196

drought, deforestation and, 339

drug abuse, gender differences in coping with stress and, 69

drug use, moral decline and, 15–16

drugs, the controversy over the decriminalization of, 300–312

duty, 161

economic conservatism, 157

economic inequality: capitalism and, 158–159; the controversy over, as serious problem, 134–146; globalization and, 365

Economist, The, editors of, on welfare reform, 228–233

economy. *See* capitalist economy

education: controversy over competition as key for reform in, 244–257; lack of decline in scholastic achievement and, 16

educational opportunity, income inequality and, 138–139

Ehrlich, Paul, 345

El Niño, 340, 348

Engels, Frederick, 288

entertainment media, drug use in, 309

entrepreneurs, 190–191

environment: the controversy over danger of human harms to, 336–350; the controversy over globalization and, 357, 359, 365; the controversy over the intervention of government in a capitalist economy and, 221–222

Environmental Protection Agency (EPA), 221

Equal Protection clause, affirmative action and, 172

equality, capitalist economy and, 219

Erber, Ernest, on the intervention of government in a capitalist economy, 208–215

Ernst, Morris, 10

escapes, lifetime imprisonment and, 320–321

Essays on the Death Penalty, 322–323

euthanasia, the controversy over legalization of doctor-assisted suicide and, 262–275

Evangelicalism, morality in Victorian England and, 8

export controls, globalization and, 358–359

"expressive" individualism, decline of the traditional family and, 117